July 19, 201

To you my dear one,
beautiful Sienna
With love light,
many blessings and grace

Vivi
(Vivian and Noah)

Realize Your True Enlightened Nature

BECOMING

THE

Light

Vivianne Nantel

GREENLEAF
BOOK GROUP PRESS

Except for most public figures, names of persons are fictitious to protect their privacy. Most women characters are named after flowers. Also, most of the place-names of towns and areas in which the author has lived are fictitious.

Published by Greenleaf Book Group Press
Austin, Texas
www.gbgpress.com

Distributed by Greenleaf Book Group

For ordering information or special discounts for bulk purchases, please contact Greenleaf Book Group at PO Box 91869, Austin, TX 78709, 512.891.6100.

Design and composition by Greenleaf Book Group
Cover design by Greenleaf Book Group

Cataloging-in-Publication data is available.

Print ISBN: 978-1-62634-501-0

eBook ISBN: 978-1-62634-502-7

Part of the Tree Neutral® program, which offsets the number of trees consumed in the production and printing of this book by taking proactive steps, such as planting trees in direct proportion to the number of trees used: www.treeneutral.com

Printed in the United States of America on acid-free paper

18 19 20 21 22 23   10 9 8 7 6 5 4 3 2 1

First Edition

To all who can hear, see, touch, and feel the longing of their hearts . . . to the sleeper, the procrastinator, the wanderer, the player, the lost one, and the sincere seeker. May this book open an unimaginable gateway and guide you to the boundless treasures of your true magnificence and Divine nature.

ACKNOWLEDGMENTS

To all the maha avatars, ascended masters of the beyond, and to Gurunath, His Holiness the Dalai Lama and Thích Nhat Hanh (Thay), His Holiness Sri Sri Ravi Shankar (Gurudev), and Sadhguru (Vasudev Sadhguru Jaggi) who have indirectly assisted and supported my being through the miracle of life and manifestation of *Becoming the Light*, I eternally bow down.

To all my precious editors: Herta Feely, Lois Winsen, Krissa Lagos, Elizabeth Brown, Elizabeth Chenette, and especially to April Murphy at Greenleaf Book Group who have helped me grow my wings as an author, my deepest heart-felt gratitude for all that you are and do. Without you, *Becoming the Light: Realize Your True Enlightened Nature* could not have been the same. You have pushed my literary boundaries!

To my beautiful friends Blanca Hall, Kiah Bosy, and Amber Elandt— thank you for the valuable input you have shared for my book. Thank you to my dear Michael who has always provided devotional loving support while I was writing this book. I am forever grateful to all of you.

Finally, to my dear Prashant, I am deeply grateful for your devotional loving support in the last stages of manifesting *Becoming the Light*.

PROLOGUE

BY THE TIME I TURNED thirty-three years old, the same age as Jesus when he was crucified, I was bearing my own cross—a major clinical depression and an excruciating heartbreak I could not see my way out of. I concluded that I did not belong in this world. No one knew how depressed I had become, not even my psychotherapist. Like Alice in Wonderland, I had fallen down the rabbit hole into the most profound and dreadful darkness.

But I am not Alice, and this is not a fairy tale.

From untruth to truth, darkness to light, ignorance to enlightenment, this has been my journey. *Becoming the Light: Realize Your True Enlightened Nature* can be a gateway to unleashing your true and blissful nature. Filled with timeless wisdom, spiritual knowledge, inner knowing, and insights, it is a narrative of duality and transcendence expressed in all its nuances, an exploration of the colorful spectrum of the human condition, from the deepest suffering to the most blissful and ecstatic samadhi state. *Becoming the Light* is the true story of my voyage, the profound cry of one who desperately longed to go beyond the physical dimension and find existential truth, and her path to liberation.

Becoming the Light is more than just a compelling spiritual memoir; it is a moving odyssey into the beyond. It intimately chronicles my life's quest to overcome a battered childhood; to survive severe depression, advanced breast cancer, a near-death experience, and more; and tells of my journey as a seeker in the mystical land of India, and walking the spiritual path with several enlightened masters, such as Yogiraj Gurunath Siddhanath, His Holiness Sri Sri Ravi Shankar, His Holiness the Dalai Lama, and Vasudev Jaggi Sadhguru, over several decades.

As I share my story, I will delve into the science of yoga and the ancient yogic art of consecration, mysticism, and transcendence in the pursuit of self-realization. I will discuss phenomena such as divine feminine energy, inner power, mindfulness, the body as a temple, the power of belonging, creative flow and intuition, the many natures of love, walking the spiritual path, and transcendence.

I explore these subjects through the awakening experiences I had—both painful and joyful—to show what is possible when one finds the path of awakening, union, and liberation. The journey, however personal, is still a universal one. I have spent over eight years working on this book in the hope of helping other suffering living beings—those who long for inner well-being or to go beyond the physical and find existential truth.

It is my deepest hope that *Becoming the Light* will provide a window into a world of transformation, happiness, insights, inner discovery, ecstasy, and bliss, whatever your chosen path. Also anyone who seeks well-being, happiness, love, serenity, blissfulness, ecstasy, inclusive consciousness, a sense of belonging, and truth can find a portal to explore and embark on their own inner voyage. Whether you are already on a journey to well-being and enlightenment or just at its threshold, may this book provide the insights, inspiration, and courage you need to find your way.

Any major life event may trigger the beginning of an awakening journey. Mine began the day I was born.

We must always start a journey with the first baby step; often we fall many times before rising and flying . . .

One

WAKE UP, BABY!

I KEPT HEARING A DISTANT, hostile sound in my ears. Was it a nightmare?

"Miss Nantel, wake up! . . . WAKE UP!"

I could not open my eyes. My eyelids were as heavy as my heart and the fluorescent light burned. There was no nurse in the room, except for this stranger yelling. Half conscious, I opened an eye partway, raised my arm, and pulled long tubes from my nose. Blood spurted out. No one paid attention. The blood kept rolling over my mouth, my chin, and toward my neck.

"Wake up, dear! I am Miss Clark, a social worker. I am here to ask you a few questions. Can you hear me?"

She must have been there for a long time. Everything was a foggy blur. My head spun. Like a zombie, I could not think, could not even see. I began to weep.

"You were brought unconscious to this hospital last night. The doctors have pumped out your stomach. You have survived. Did anyone force you to do this? Did you try to take your life?"

"I want to go back home!" I cried out and fell unconscious once again.

Later that night, I was transported by an ambulance to a special recovery center.

The following late afternoon, a different nurse entered my room and roused me. "Vivianne, please wake up!" she said. "You have been sleeping for over twenty hours. Dr. Larose will see you soon. Try to wake up."

As she touched my shoulder I looked around, disoriented and lost.

I wandered to the bathroom and took a shower. The room felt dead cold. Chills traveled along my spine like hundreds of ants crawling up a bamboo tree. My hands shook; my mouth quivered. Agony tormented my soul; I felt there was no way to escape it, as if I was trapped in a deep black hole. I kept thinking, *Please, Divine Mother, let me come back to you. I don't belong here. The pain is unbearable. I beg you.*

Since I was a child I have always viewed God or the Source, whatever thousands of names we attribute to our Creator, as "the Divine Mother." I longed to go back home to her, beyond the blue sky. I longed for that now, in the grip of my severe depression and my bleeding heart.

Silently I dried my hair with the towel, got in bed, and pulled the covers over my head until the nurse returned. She held my hand and took me to the cafeteria for some warm oatmeal before my appointment with the clinical psychiatrist.

I had been living like a zombie for over a year, walking in a constant daze, stupefied by dizziness, intense sorrow, and lethargy. I was lost and trapped in the abyss of a major depression and an agonizing heartbreak. As I sat in Dr. Larose's office, I was devoid of personality. It felt as if God had robbed me of my ego.

"*Bonjour,* Vivianne," the doctor said. He was gentle and kind. "*Je suis* Dr. Larose. How are you feeling today? I looked at your reports. Why did you attempt to take your life?"

I remained mute.

Dr. Larose gazed into my eyes with a piercing regard. "Do you realize how blessed you are, Vivianne? Not everyone who overdoses and falls into a coma for almost four days—turning blue—comes back to life without serious brain damage or major handicaps. Most never do. Severe hypoventilation is fatal."

I sat there drained of all energy, as cold as the winter. I looked through the tall window and felt myself empty from any thoughts. It was an existential Zen moment—eternal instant. The dead branches swaying against the puffy dark clouds mesmerized my being. I was lost, lonely among six billion souls.

Watching the snowflakes float down from heaven like messengers of love, I realized my suicide attempt was a distressed emergency call—an expression of my longing to be liberated from my mortal jail.

"Vivianne, can you hear me? Do you realize you are a miracle, *ma belle?*" Dr. Larose uttered with his sweet French Haitian accent. He looked deeply into my eyes.

I snapped out of this existential eternal moment and began to wonder how I got here in my life. *Who am I? Why am I here? Where do I come from? Where I am going? What is the meaning of my life? Why do I long so to go back home? I want to go back to you, dear God, and never return to this earth.*

Two

BEGINNINGS

MY BEAUTIFUL MAMA, WHOM MY siblings and I often called *Mou-mou,* was in her early forties when she had me. Mama said I was an accident and was her last child. With her delicate yet chiseled cheekbones; deep brownish-hazel eyes; long, graceful neck; and dark auburn hair, Mama had the features of a movie star.

Both of my parents grew up in Canada in the French part of Quebec during the Great Depression. My ancestors had emigrated from France generations earlier. Papa grew up in a middle-class family of eight kids. Mama had a harsher life. She grew up in a large, poor Catholic family with nine other kids and an abusive, alcoholic father. In her late teens when she met my father, Mama played both Hawaiian and classical guitar. Papa played the violin and guitar and loved to sing, draw, and paint. Papa was a handsome Casanova with sleek, dark ash-blond hair and magnetic, large green eyes, and exuberant laughter. He was a charming rascal with an insatiable appetite for love, music, beauty, and elegance.

In 1938 my parents formed a string quartet with a few close friends. Over the following years, the group performed at many venues and recorded several records. They gained a reputation as talented artists. Eventually, my parents' hearts bonded in love and they married.

Not long after my parents wed, Canada was involved in the Second World War. With little demand for musicians during the war, Papa and Mama's income fell at the same time they were starting to deal with the new responsibilities of a growing family.

With music no longer able to provide a living, Papa was forced to work in a manufacturing plant for a few years, painting refrigerators. He was a fine artist—a figure painter, not a refrigerator painter. For a while he did all kinds of odd jobs to survive.

My parents put their artistic dreams aside, not realizing this would be the end of their musical careers, even though they continued to create music as a hobby.

Many women were entering the workplace, so Mama did too, becoming a hairstylist and opening her own salon. It proved to be a lucrative and enjoyable business, and soon she became the main breadwinner.

Mama's reputation grew. Most of the ladies in the area had their hair coiffed by her. Her salon was adjacent to our home, separated only by a wood door. It became a social entertainment center where ladies, and even men, would come to praise, commiserate, dance, sing, eat, laugh, and of course have their hair done. Mama's clients all adored her.

Over the years, married life became a burden for Mama; she had the task of caring for a difficult husband and seven children. When she smiled, though, our hearts melted with hers and the whole world smiled. One day she proposed to teach Papa how to do hair. He agreed and learned quickly. Yet to his frustration over the years, Mama would not let Papa become an accomplished hairstylist on his own.

"*Ma chérie,* it is your salon, your clients. I do so much, but you never let me do the final touches," Papa complained. Competition set in, the beginning of the slow decline in their loving relationship. A decade and a half later, Papa left the hairstyling business, vowing never to return. Instead he spent more time helping around the house and drinking beer, trying to determine what to do with the rest of his life. He was becoming a miserable old man. He gained weight and lost hair. Only when he played music at home, a bit drunk, did his jovial, exuberant self reappear.

When I was five years old, my parents bought a hundred-year-old cottage, a quaint but modest country house set amid golden, rolling fields in the prairie of St-Marie a few hours away from our home in the suburbs. Grandmama on my mother's side had grown up in this house. Coco—my older brother by one year, a striking boy with big green eyes, thick black eyelashes, and a sweet, delicate soul—and I started to spend every summer there with

Madame Fleurette, our silver-haired nanny. Our parents and many of our siblings came to visit on weekends, but mostly it was just the three of us.

For Coco and me, St-Marie became a sanctuary from the insanity of our dysfunctional parents—especially Papa, who was becoming increasingly abusive with every year that passed. Often his temper would explode, and he would yell at us with a frightening glare in his eyes. He would grab us by the collar, pull our pajamas down, turn us on his lap with our bottoms exposed, and hit us with his leather belt until red welts rose on our skin.

But not at the cottage. There, we were free to run wild in nature and play with the animals. The cottage was a quarter of a mile from a small farm and offered every possible dream for our creative imaginations. Sometimes Coco and I pretended to be farmers, piling stacks of hay for the animals to eat. Other days, I became Coco's Pegasus, pulling the miniature cart over the endless field of blond wheat.

Coco and I had the blessing of discovering the great joy of connecting with other species. By the end of each summer, we had made many new, dear animal friends. My most profound bonds were with the furry creatures, especially cats.

This was my first exposure to farm animals. In those days, animals ran free and happy on farms, expressing their natural behaviors—not like today where they live in inhumane farm factories, piled on top of each other and abused. When we were back in town, Papa often sent me to buy meat at the butcher a block away from home. Each time I approached the counter, I shuddered. When Monsieur Butcher stepped into the cold room behind him to get a dead animal, I noticed all the large red carcasses hanging upside down from huge iron hooks. It gave me chills, and I could not wait to leave. Buying meat repulsed me. Yet I had not made the conscious connection that meat, hot dogs, and burgers were the slaughtered farm animals I loved and cherished as my dear friends.

Still, in my child's mind, I equated adults with pain and suffering, but cats and other animals understood me and always gave me unconditional love. I loved having conversations with my cats. "Minet, why are we here? If I don't exist, where would I be? What is behind the blue sky?" I spent countless nights wondering about the mysteries of life and why I was here. Even at this young age, I was realizing that any living creature could become a gateway to our Creator if we allow them to be.

This reminded my being that when I was seventeen, my five-year-old gray-and-white Angora cat, Thisbe, came home very ill. Thisbe was priceless, my best friend. He had not touched food or drink for several days when I took him to the vet. The vet believed Thisbe had been poisoned and said there was nothing he could do to help. He put Thisbe back in my arms and suggested my cat might survive if I kept him well hydrated with water.

Back home I filled a syringe many times with water and dripped it into Thisbe's mouth, making sure he swallowed. Finally, I dozed off in bed, sad at heart. I woke with a start as Coco cried, "Vivi, Thisbe is calling for you. Hurry up!"

I ran to the kitchen. Thisbe lay there flat on the floor, yowling. I had never heard such distressing cries or experienced the sight of deep suffering like this before. His pain tore my heart. I did not know what to do except invoke the Divine. Blood poured from his mouth and rectum, but even in all his pain, Thisbe raised his head for the last time and gazed into my eyes. Looks of love and gratitude passed between us, though agony lingered in our hearts as I flashed back to my first weeks with him, remembering the tiny, mischievous two-week-old kitten I had bottle-fed dozens of times each day. I had nursed the whole litter for several months while I was in high school, caring for Coquette, their regal white Turkish Angora mother. Coquette had a three-inch open sore on her belly and could not nurse her litter. I decided to help her out. This was my joy during my adolescence, losing myself in this process. Connecting with another species produces a feeling beyond words. There on the kitchen floor, Thisbe's last breath mixed with mine. I wept on my knees and held him in my arms. I could not let go of my only true love.

I decided I would never love again. Love brought too much pain, misery, and suffering.

The following day, Coco picked up Thisbe's lifeless body, wrapped it in newspaper, and put it in the garbage container outside. In my bedroom, I had a greeting card with the likeness of an Angora cat that looked like Thisbe. I took the card and wrote:

Dearest Thisbe,

The love of my life, I am so very grateful for all the love and joy you brought me in my life. No one has ever held my heart like you. You have taught me how to play, never grow old, to love and have compassion by giving to all living beings. We will always be together in spirit. I love you so very dearly, my beloved Thisbe.

I went outside and put the card on top of Thisbe's corpse in the garbage bin. I closed my eyes and sent out invocations for his spirit's well-being. I never found the courage to bury him.

Years later, Mama surprised me with the card. She had seen me on that day, outside over the garbage, and after I left for work she retrieved my love letter. When she handed it to me all that time later, she said, "Ma belle, Vivi, when I read your card for Thisbe, it made me cry. I could not stop. I want you to keep it. Now I know why you are in my life."

Thisbe's death left me emptied, drained, and confused for a long time. It took me more than seven years before I could open my heart again to adopt another cat. But he was also my first true teacher. From him I learned that all creatures suffer pain and misery and that, like us, animals have emotions, feelings, and experience love, fear, and anguish. And I realized that compassion is the most beautiful and treasured human quality.

⁓

AS CHILDREN, ON ONE PARTICULAR dazzling humid day in St-Marie, Madame Fleurette took us on a long nature walk for a picnic. We picked raspberries in the fields near where the tall golden wheat heads danced to the movement of the warm breeze, and Coco and I pirouetted up and down, leaping into the air.

"Coco, Vivi, look at the blue sky," Madame Fleurette said, smiling. "Can you see the Mother Virgin Mary is there looking at us? She is everywhere, protecting us. When we need help, we pray to the Mother. If you love her with all your heart, she comes. Can you feel her presence in the wind?"

"I don't see her, Madame Fleurette," Coco said.

"I feel the Mother!" I yelled, still jumping, feeling so light that I could have soared like a white swan. My tiny body vibrated with a tickling and ecstatic love that is hard to describe. It was a euphoric and expanded sensation, as if my spirit was moving beyond the confinement of my body. I had never experienced such a sensation before, but it was not scary. Instead, I felt intense happiness and love.

We sat down and ate our peanut butter and banana sandwiches. I kept staring at the sky. That night, the three of us sat in our pajamas on the porch, admiring the luminous moon and eating bowls of raspberries bathed in fresh cream and sugar. At bedtime, I buried myself under my blanket with my baby dolls and our kitten, feeling a little spooked, wondering when I would feel and see the Virgin Mother again.

I was still five years old when Mama convinced herself that ballet classes would help focus me and subdue my exuberant and ecstatic nature. After my first year, I told Mama I loved dancing so much that one day I would become a prima ballerina. That became my treasured dream, and I went on to pursue ballet for decades.

~

THE FIRST TIME MY SISTERS, Rose and Jasmine, took me shopping on the most famous main avenue back home in the city several years later, I must have been eight years old. Jasmine was as delicate and frail as the jasmine flower. Like me, she was a blonde with big blue eyes. Rose was the oldest, and we three were each seven years apart. It was a hot summer day. We rode in the sleek, modern metro underneath the earth like rodents in tunnels until we reached downtown.

When we arrived at the avenue, an exotic bazaar was the first to catch my attention. Through the windows I noticed several Buddha statues, parasols, sandals, and colorful shawls, among other cultural objects from faraway lands. I tugged my sisters inside.

Inside the store, sandalwood incense pervaded my nostrils, transporting my spirit to past lifetimes. This kind of mystical sensation was different from my mysterious Virgin Mary experience. An inner knowing of a past life in Asia, somewhere in India, and of having already been on a spiritual path vibrated within my being as an energetic phenomenon. The subtle reminiscences flirted with my unconscious and conscious mind all at once. Yet I could not recall what it was that haunted my being, or what it was I sought so deeply.

I stopped near the Buddhas, admiring their peaceful expressions, hoping one day to be like them. I bought my first incense box and patchouli bottle and my first pair of flip-flop Indian sandals with the ten-dollar bill Mama had given me for helping in her hair salon. I splashed a few drops of patchouli over my neck and put the sandals on before walking back outside.

On the ride home, I stared at my sandaled feet, wondering about life after death and reincarnation. The smell at the bazaar had propelled me into a mystified inward journey I did not yet understand but wanted to continue.

In 1971, Papa started going out by himself. Most Friday and Saturday nights, while Mama worked in her salon, he took off and returned late. She would wait for him.

"I was worried about you," Mama would say, holding him. She could smell the alcohol on his breath and perfume on his shirt. Papa would turn off the light in silence and go to his twin bed by himself, drunk. After a time, Mama started to follow him like a detective. Once my parents fought hard in the kitchen. It was rare for Mama to explode in rage. I was sitting on the stairs when Papa passed by me on his way to dress for the evening.

"Why don't you admit it? You have a mistress!" Mama shrieked as she hurled a bottle of tomato sauce at the stairs. The glass bottle passed one inch from my head, smashed onto the stairs, and splashed red sauce and broken glass all over my body. I sprinted to the bathroom, scared.

"Midlife crisis! You are possessed by *le demon du midi*!" Mama screamed, a French expression often used to mean "the noon devil." Then soon after, out of desperation, she implored him to stay while she sobbed.

Papa shoved her away. "You wanted this! You have it." Then he walked out of the house and slammed the door.

Over the years Papa continued to explode at Coco and me, often for the simple crime of laughing too loud. He would yell at us to go to bed. One time I refused to obey him.

"Why are you so wicked with us?" I asked him.

Papa seized me, smacked me against the living room wall, and shook his fist one inch away from my nose, saying, "I hate you!"

His angry eyes burned into my soul, but I did not cry. Lost in the intensity of his scorching eyes, for a moment I met the devil. I gasped, shaken to my bones. He released me and walked away toward the yard, seemingly overwhelmed by his behavior.

In the years that followed, Papa hit me many times. On one particular hot summer night, after Papa drank too many beers, he dragged me by my hair to my bedroom, unleashed the heavy metal buckle of his belt, slapped me with it, and smacked me against the walls as if I were a basketball.

I screamed, "Please, stop, Papa! I beg you."

Mama must have heard, but she said nothing.

I stayed in my room sobbing on and off all night. The following day, when Mama saw the wounds and dark bruises on my body, she shouted at Papa, "Don't you dare ever touch my daughter again. I will call the police!"

With time, I learned to repress how I felt so that I could survive—but the hatred that had started to enter my heart suffocated my spirit. Hatred is the most destructive poison.

I never once submitted to my father's abuse; my spirit refused to be treated that way. I confronted him each time, and all the while I dreamed of the day I would be free from him. Almost every night I dreamt that I was flying in the cosmos. I ran as I opened my arms, and took off into the blue sky to the Divine Mother. My spirit traveled into different dimensions beyond time and space. Another recurring dream I had was the sensation of falling deep into a bottomless pit. It would cause me to wake up in the middle of the night and jump out of bed.

If we listen deep to our spirit, we can hear it. Fire cannot burn it, wind cannot blow it away, water cannot drown it, and ether cannot diffuse it, says the legendary Bhagavad Gita. But the emotional trauma caused by such deep wounds to a child's psyche can have disastrous effects later in life.

The more we know and experience our ultimate nature, the more we become an instrument and expression of beauty, love, and compassion. Compassion is always the highest expression of love. If we learn as children that being authentic to our true nature means we will be punished, then we may grow to unconsciously lose that connection with our true essence. Part of the process of awakening is not only surrendering to inner guidance but also listening and dissolving all the conditioned imprints caused by our families, authorities, and society. One of the gravest maladies of our times is not paying attention to our profound inner cries.

As our family fell apart, my parents stopped playing music. What a tragedy to let our spirit suffer from a lack of expressing creativity and beauty. People can become insane when they do not allow themselves to express their devotional nature in creative pursuits. The creative process allows us to go deep within ourselves and reconnect with our ultimate loving nature. Creativity is the ultimate expression of the divine feminine energy. I am not referring to the female gender aspect here. I will go in depth on this crucial subject in later chapters. The creative process is healing, fulfilling, uplifting, and enlightening if we give ourselves to it completely. There is an artist hidden inside every one of us. The unfolding of the spiritual path allows us to discover and tap into this creative flow of the universe. When we do, exuberance and bliss burst from us—and we can live to our full potential.

On a hot, humid Saturday evening in August 1972, Papa returned unexpectedly from his weekend adventures to pick up his belongings. It was long after I'd gone to bed, near midnight, and I woke to screams echoing in the dark house.

"Wait! Stay with us," Mama and one of my sisters kept shouting.

I sat up, a jolt of fear devouring my stomach. I heard chaos: the wailing and yelling of my family fighting and slamming doors. Then, the wheels of a car squealed. The sounds were chilling. The commotion was coming from the street in front of our house, so I bolted out the front door.

My papa was clutching the wheel of our navy blue Ford, attempting to leave home. My sisters and Mama were trying to block his path by standing in front of the car and holding on to the hood.

"I am leaving for good. If you do not move now, I will run you over!" Papa raged.

Papa kept pushing down on the gas pedal with the brake on, making the tires squeal. Overtaken by rage, he pressed harder on the gas pedal and accelerated toward Rose, Jasmine, and Mama. With just seconds to spare, the three of them jumped out of his way in a fury. They almost fell to the ground. I rubbed my eyes, hoping I would wake up from this nightmare. The black tracks of his tires marked his final departure.

Papa left most of his belongings behind but took the family car with him. I was only eleven years old, and just like that, Papa had evaporated from my life like a puff of air. My heart bled.

I stood frozen in the middle of that emptied, cold, dark street for what seemed an eternity in this moonless night. Over the year, intense grieving and distress ravaged Mama's heart. Every day she sank deeper into the dark abyss of a major depression, buried in intense sorrow and pain.

Over the following year, Mama attempted to manage her business and household the best she could. Coco and I took care of ourselves; we often made dinner and helped clean the house while Mama popped Valium to kill her misery. Coco and I often heard Mama wailing in the night. The sound pierced my heart.

That fall, sunsets graced Mother Earth's golden curves, raindrops nourished my soul, and dewdrops whispered to my spirit as the red, orange, and violet leaves swirled. I was almost twelve years old. One Monday morning the phone rang. My oldest brother wanted to speak with Mama. Her salon was always closed on Monday; it was her day off. I told him Mama had slept all weekend, and we did not want to bother her.

"Go, Vivi. Force her out of the bed. I am coming home right away."

Coco and I entered her room. Mama's face was white as a dove, her look as serene as an angel's, and her hands cold as snow. We kept trying, but Mama did not respond. We got scared and began to cry. "Please wake up, Mama."

Within thirty minutes our big brother arrived and tried to rouse her, but nothing worked. Finally, he called an ambulance. As the paramedics entered my mother's bedroom, administered first aid, and placed her in the ambulance, a wave of anger toward my father filled my heart. I had never before experienced such hostility toward anyone. The ambulance took off, and our brother followed behind in his own car.

Within an hour he called from the hospital. "They have Mama under intensive care. She took a huge dose of Valium. Let's pray she makes it."

As those words vibrated into the core of my being, I remembered once overhearing Mama say to Rose, "I am going to take my life. I will bring Coco and Vivi with me."

Rose replied, "If you want to take your life, do it, but leave the children behind. They have their own lives to live."

When I went to bed that night, I invoked, "Oh, dear Mother, watch over Mama. Protect her, give her the strength, serenity, and peace to go on." At once I could feel Mama's presence in my bedroom. I opened my eyes. Her etheric form, some kind of transparent veil-like vision, floated toward me with her arms reaching out. I sat there in bed gazing, wondering what she wanted.

The doctors kept Mama hospitalized for three months. Coco, only twelve, and I were left alone in the large house. On occasion our big brother and Rose had meals with us. They would buy us groceries. At least once a week we visited Mama at the hospital. Seeing her in her gown, distressed, drugged out from the medications and drained of energy devastated our hearts. She was not the same Mama I had known. I was unable to cry, I felt numb, and anger at my father kept rising in my blood. I had to shut these feelings down somehow, switch them off by repressing them.

After her release, Mama continued to gulp pills every day. She was never seen by a psychologist, or had any form of psychotherapy. Our mama vanished in a sea of drugs and a severe depression that lingered for too many years. As she traversed the darkness of the soul, I accompanied her as her spiritual guide. I was no longer her baby. During those painful, turbulent times, my relationship with her shifted. I became the empowered mother who could face the challenges, and she, my vulnerable child to protect. I had learned to be resourceful.

I was unable to realize yet that we all are unique waves in the Divine ocean of love. Though, because of my sensitivity, openness, receptivity, and love toward the Divine Mother, loving energy still flowed through my heart. I became aware of a flaming hatred toward my papa trying to conquer my heart, and I did not want to experience those poisonous feelings toward anyone. Hatred is just a defense mechanism trying to alleviate the agonizing pain inside. A part of my being felt so deeply wounded, yet I could not stop loving my father. Because when love is present, it can never go away. It is eternal and boundless. Genuine love is just there like the sun radiating over the entire planet and all living beings. Its rays emanate without discrimination, without asking for anything in return.

The only boundary between our mastery and our dreams is ourselves. The conditioned and brainwashed personality that we accumulate over the decades can cause us the most intense misery and suffering. It would take many decades before I could break from the confinement of my self-made cage and become able to set myself free from it.

Three

INNER REBELLION

NOT LONG AFTER MAMA'S RELEASE from the psychiatric department, Papa filed for divorce. Rose and Jasmine came for dinner one night.
Mama threw the legal divorce papers on the table.

"That is what you get in return for twenty-seven years of marriage,
giving your heart . . . ," Mama hollered, slurring her words.

With all the medications Mama took to numb her pain, she couldn't
think clearly. Papa's lawyer took advantage of the situation and tricked her
into signing legal documents she would never have signed under normal
circumstances.

Mama told us that during a meeting with her own lawyer, he said in a
frustrated voice, "Madame, I told you not to sign anything before I looked
at it. You gave Monsieur the right to sell the house and your business.
According to these documents, all gain goes to him. Did you read these
papers carefully?"

Her face turned ashen, and Mama responded, "Oh, my God! What
happened? How can that be? My husband's lawyer told me you had read
and approved them. I worked my entire life to help my family and clients."

"I am so sorry, Madame. I am angry too. But there is nothing I can do."

Mama told us that she almost fainted in his office.

When Mama shared the news with us, we could not believe it. What
a nightmare! I was in high school and ready to rebel against any form of
authority while I searched for meaning in life. I could not concentrate on
my studies and missed most of my classes.

One time in the cafeteria, Calathea, an exotic brunette with a bold character, made a nasty comment about me. She pushed my shoulder and shouted, "You bitch! I hate you!"

It pressed my "self-worth" button. I grabbed her by the sweater. Calathea pushed me harder. I fell backward, straight onto my tailbone. Her words triggered an avalanche of rage within me. I got up, ran up to her, and pulled her hair hard while I dragged her down on the cement floor. She screamed and tried to grab my hair.

"You bitch! Let me go." She reached out and yanked my hair. By then the turmoil had attracted dozens of students who stood around us, cheering. We wrestled each other, tugging each other's hair like wildcats. The security guard arrived before any blood was spilled. He had to separate us. We caught our breath, sat down, and talked with him for a while; he wondered what such anger was all about.

Over the semester when Calathea and I ran into each other in the girls' lavatory we would ignore one another. One day as I entered the bathroom, she was alone in front of the tall mirror, fixing her hair. I could feel my heart pound, my cheeks burn. While Calathea was putting on lipstick, I said, "I love that color on you, Calathea. It brings out your beautiful features. I hope you've forgotten about our stupid fight." She did not say a word. "It was foolish of us, don't you think? I am sorry. Please forgive me. You and I are the same, so why are we enemies?" She turned her head and smiled back. I returned the smile, radiating love while I walked closer and looked straight into her eyes. We giggled. She offered to let me try her lipstick. Over the years our friendship flourished; we became close friends, just as I hoped for. I had allowed my true nature to take over.

Toward the end of summer, my mother received a phone call from my father's lawyer. "Madame Nantel," he said, "the house and the salon have been sold. You and your children must vacate by September 15."

By this time, almost six months later, Mama had forgotten she'd signed those documents and forgotten what her lawyer had told her.

"You are mistaken, sir. I did not sign such papers or approve the sale of my home," she exclaimed angrily while hanging up the phone. None of us took the threat seriously.

On September 15, a stranger banged on the door of our home. "Please open the door, Madame. This is an eviction. We are here to take the house and the salon."

Mama would not open the door. The man kept banging even harder.

"If you do not open the door now, we will call the police!" he shouted.

Mama hesitated. She unlocked and opened the door, but did not let him in. He handed her the legal papers. She stood paralyzed at the entrance. "Sir, to take my house you will have to walk on my dead body!" she declared, as she closed the door in his face.

The man called the police and continued shouting, "You and your children must evacuate immediately, Madame." The police arrived. Eventually, Mama let them in.

"Yes, these papers are legitimate, Madame. You must evacuate now. We are sorry," they said.

Mama began to hyperventilate. "I have a client waiting for me with her hair wet in my salon. I have been living here for over twenty-six years. This is my home and my salon! I paid for most of it. You can't throw us in the street just like that." I stood there in shock listening to them. The rest of my siblings were not home.

Meanwhile, in front of our house a moving company's blue-and-white truck waited, and a dozen men in overalls lined up by the door . . . an army ready for battle. The police took my mama aside and let them in. The movers invaded our home with their weapons: boxes, tape, scissors, and plastic bubble wrap. At that point Mama could not even lament; she looked like she was in excruciating pain, the kind that could kill her with a heart attack.

I invoked the grace of the Divine Mother. It was one year since Mama was released from the hospital, and she was still extremely fragile. I held her hand as I watched her crumble and fade. My mama could not stop sobbing and wailing loudly. I called my dear Calathea.

"How can your father do such a thing, Vivi?"

Mama mourned on and off all day and popped a few Valium pills to calm her nervous system. She was hiding in every corner like a wounded animal in distress. The movers took over our house and her hair salon, packing all our dishes, accessories, furniture, and clothing. Calathea and I stood there witnessing it all, still in shock while trying to process this nightmare. At one point, Mama fell to her knees in her hair salon and raised her arms imploring God for mercy. I held her tenderly. "It breaks my heart to see you like this," I said. "Calm down, Mama." Calathea and I hugged her in silence.

By five o'clock, the five bedrooms, kitchen, dining room, living room, hair salon, and large basement and yard had been emptied.

For several weeks, we were homeless; I had only one pair of jeans, a few t-shirts, and a few other small personal belongings.

A dear friend and client of Mama's let us stay at her house while our big brother searched for a bachelor apartment for us. After being evicted, Mama went to court to try to get alimony. Papa would not give up the fight, while she kept popping pills to calm her nerves.

Not long after, on one gloomy day, Coco and I summoned the courage to pay our father a visit at his workplace. We kept the visit a secret.

"Papa, why are you doing these wicked things to us and Mama? We are your children. We love you," I said.

"Go away! You're not my children," he shouted.

"Do you realize what you are doing?" I said. "One day you will regret it." We left.

"Mama did not deserve a tragic ending with Papa," I told Coco as we walked back to our tiny bachelor apartment.

The tragic loss of our home did not yet bring about the realization that everything in this physical realm is impermanent and ephemeral. This crucial realization occurred much later. The less resistance we have toward the events in our lives, the more we can accept the situations and process them—and the better we can detach and surrender to what is. Somehow, I did not feel attached to the material aspect. My mind was not in the way with its resistance.

The memories that haunt us either consciously or unconsciously can often become the most painful because they are recorded in our cells as karmic garbage. The unconscious, dormant level is the one aspect of our being that may cause the most pain and compulsion as we go on with our lives. At least if we are conscious of it, we may take actions to heal the wounds, purify the whole system and subtle body, and transcend duality.

I could feel my heart trying to close like a delicate flower withdrawing from the night freeze. Yet I longed to love even more deeply—and to be loved. How many millions of brokenhearted individuals feel they will never love again? Is it worth living without love? The great tragedy is that many people never have that love, and they concede by hating themselves. We cannot love when hate possesses our heart. Like sculptures with parts missing, pieces of our heart can be chiseled away, leaving ugly traces of what has been. This inner rebellion had to vanish before hatred turned against my being. My heart began to close—my spirit suffocating. I did not know how and where to begin.

Still, deep inside my being I held a mild, unconscious aversion toward the patriarchal system, and this would remain buried within me for many decades to come. I felt trapped in a tornado of duality. Yet I searched unconsciously for a gateway to transcend and liberate myself.

Four

CATASTROPHE AND MIRACLES

WHEN I WAS IN HIGH school, I met Beau, a tall nineteen-year-old with light brown hair, smiling hazel eyes, and a warm heart. In the years that followed, he became a gangster, loving the adrenaline rush. I was not aware of it until he got caught and put in jail. By then, however, I had fallen in love with him.

I had been taking ballet classes since I was a young girl, and to keep myself sane I danced four to five nights per week. Even so, by the middle of my third year, my studies and my mind became unbearable. Over four months had elapsed since Beau had been arrested and taken away.

One sunny afternoon I did not show up to my classes. I sought solitude. I lay down by myself in the yard of my high school and got high sniffing glue. I wanted to feel nirvana. Sitting there in the green grass beneath the branches of a majestic tree like Buddha, gazing at the leaves swaying in the hot breeze, I didn't flick an eye for three to four hours. It was an ecstatic voyage that felt like oneness. This feeling of unity was a false sensation; yet even so, a certain sense of self-transcendence occurred. I wanted more, a lot more, but without using any drugs. As it always had, a part of my being wanted to escape this life, hoping to transcend this physical realm and never return.

Not long after, I quit school and began working. Mama trusted my decision and never stopped me. I wanted to be independent and earn money, hoping one day to come back to my studies with a serene mind.

During the time Beau was in jail, he wrote me weekly love letters promising he would stop his illegal activities. Meanwhile, I worked in the finest beauty salons in town, helping Mama pay the rent and buy food, and continued to dance. Yet, I did not feel fulfilled. I did not want to repeat my mother's life story. "I want to explore what God gave me," I told her.

Beau was eventually released on parole, and while we were glad to see each other, it was not the same. I had grown so much in his absence. Not long after, our relationship ended. We remained good friends and continued to see each other.

On a dark night in 1978, Beau picked me up at my older brother's house, where I had been babysitting. He had borrowed his brother's van. I sat next to him on the hard plastic board between the two front seats.

Beau sped along at more than 80 miles per hour on a major highway divided by tall lampposts.

"Slow down," I said—once, twice, several times—but he didn't listen.

It was fifteen minutes past midnight. Only a few other vehicles were on the road. I had a premonition that we were going to crash and that I should prepare myself immediately.

It was like hearing a subtle voice whispering what to do to my inner being, yet I could not hear the words with my ears. These sensations vibrated within, but I was not afraid of the mystical experience, or of the crash. It was not my imagination. The message was so clear. I bent down to zip my purse as I invoked silently: *Dear Virgin Mary . . . oh my dear God, please protect us.* I specifically invoked the Virgin Mary this time.

I was just about to move over and buckle up when a car sped up from behind us, seemingly out of nowhere, and cut us off. Beau lost control of the wheel. The unknown driver disappeared in the distance, and we crashed head-on into one of the lampposts. The van rolled over several times. A case of empty beer bottles in the back of the van exploded along with the windows, sending glass flying everywhere. Beau, who was wearing his seat belt, stayed pinned to his seat; I was bounced back and forth like a Ping-Pong ball. The force of each impact crushed my bones.

Time and space ceased to exist. Broken glass pieces tore my body. No thoughts crossed my mind. Finally, the rolling stopped.

As we lay in the wreckage of the van, stunned, we could hear the sirens of police and fire trucks draw near. We crawled out through one of the broken windows. The twisted hulk of the van burned.

"Let's walk away," Beau said.

I wondered why he wanted to escape but did not say a word; I was too dazed. I walked with him for several yards, but then I turned back toward the scene and froze. I could not walk or move anymore.

I became aware of blood spilling through my hair, dripping into my eyes, and running down my cheeks and neck. My right leg was drenched in it, and my knee had swollen to the size of a coconut.

A police car arrived.

"Let's run!" Beau said, low and urgent, but I couldn't move.

The officers had us sit in their car. After they talked to us for a few minutes, my body went into shock and began to stiffen. They quickly took us to a hospital, while the firefighters put out the fire.

I remember being on a stretcher in the emergency room, then an operating room with huge blinding spotlights. Doctors and nurses were cutting open my jeans. While one doctor removed broken glass from my body, the others disinfected other areas and stitched up my wounds. They worked synchronized, like an orchestra, rarely talking. They ran a few tests and kept me under intensive care and observation for the following day.

Beau had fractured his left leg and was released not long after being admitted. My right knee's ligament and meniscus were badly torn. The van was destroyed. None of the people involved in the rescue and healing care could believe we walked out of that mangled vehicle still alive, conscious, and with relatively little bodily damage. This kind of brutal accident could have easily killed the passengers.

For the next five months, I walked on crutches, unable to put weight on my foot. An enormous amount of fluid remained trapped in my knee. Every night I slept with my knee elevated, Mama next to me in the bed, while Coco slept on the sofa. I often burst into tears of gratitude when I recalled the premonition I'd had prior to the accident. I could not stop wondering who the Divine force was who'd protected us. *Who is my Creator?* I wondered. *Who am I? Why am I here?*

During the following year, I suffered from post-traumatic stress symptoms. I did not want to get in a van, truck, or car. After over twelve years of dancing, my dream of becoming a prima ballerina was shattered like a crystal champagne glass dropped to the floor. My right knee would never be the same. I felt lost, but I could not mourn. A quiet sorrow lingered, buried deep within my being for many years.

Mama resumed seeing some of her most loyal clients again at home. She was filled with anger, sorrow, and resentment. Several years later we moved again into a bright, unfurnished three-bedroom apartment in a more peaceful part of town. We each had our own bedroom, so we retrieved our personal belongings and furniture from storage. Mama had stopped using medications but had grown bitter and extremely nervous. It was difficult for most people to be around her for long.

In this traumatic period, I stumbled onto a portal guiding me toward seeking deeper about the meaning of life and afterlife. A part of my being became more aware of my longing to know the truth, my intuitive abilities, and inner power. Yet I did not know where to go, what to do. I knew something was there beyond what I had known and experienced, and I wanted to know what it was. The veil had to drop one day. A sweet drop of Divine love and gratitude had entered my heart when the Divine Mother called to my being before the crash. But it would be a very long time before I was ready to explore what that meant.

Five

OBJECTIFICATION OF THE FEMALE

CHERRY BLOSSOMS, LILACS, AND YELLOW daffodils danced in the sun when I met Kiwi at the age of seventeen while searching for my beloved cat, Thisbe. Kiwi proposed we go out the following Friday to have a bite to eat with a couple of his friends who lived in the apartment complex across the street from him.

Kiwi was twenty-five and lived by himself in a one-bedroom apartment in a nice neighborhood. I did not hesitate because he and I seemed to have a good connection. He appeared to be a gentleman from a well-educated and trustworthy family. I trusted him and felt safe.

Kiwi picked me up at seven. The evening unfolded just as a young woman like me would have wanted. It was one of the first hot nights in early June. We drove through a few of the more scenic streets of downtown Montreal that were always lit up and filled with fashionable, attractive people. A romantic melody was floating through the streets, and the bouquet of fresh roasted garlic caressed our nostrils. We also passed the upscale boutiques and popular cafes where one could sit outside to sip a glass of wine or sangria.

We arrived at Kiwi's friend's place and enjoyed a good time together. When it got late, we left.

"Let's stop by my apartment across the street just for two minutes before I drive you back, Vivi," Kiwi said. "I need to pick up something. Plus, you can see my apartment."

I followed Kiwi to the eighth floor. His apartment was well organized, clean, and nicely decorated for a bachelor. It was all as I would have expected it to be. But when we stepped through the door to Kiwi's bedroom, he attacked me.

Kiwi threw me on his bed, tore my dress apart, and slapped my face. I wrestled as much as I could and screamed at the top of my lungs. I kept shouting as I fought back, hoping someone in the building would come to my rescue or call the police.

At last, I kicked him hard in his private parts, and he doubled over in pain. I escaped and ran, but I grabbed the wrong door and found myself trapped in his bathroom. I saw a rifle standing upright behind the door. I was horrified and did not dare to touch it. My heart beat so fast I thought it would explode. I felt nauseated and faint.

I closed my eyes and took a few deep breaths. I asked for help from the Divine Mother. Then, guidance clearly flowed into my mind. I summoned my courage, opened the door, screamed, and ran. This time I felt guided to a certain door, and when I reached for it, it was right. Flinging it open, I ran down the stairs in a fury, shrieking. Neighbors opened their doors, wondering what was happening. I ran out of the building like an arrow in full motion, never turning my head. It must have been around midnight, and the streets seemed deserted. I kept running, screaming, sobbing for help. My whole body quivered in terror.

A white Mustang stopped, and a young man got out. He was dressed as a nurse and worked at a nearby hospital. "Calm down, dear," he said. "What happened?"

I could not talk. I was trying to catch my breath. He sat me down in his car, reassuring me that I was now safe. He drove me back home; I sobbed all the way back to our doorstep. I could not understand what had happened to the charming Kiwi. Within a few seconds and without any warning signs, he had turned into a terrifying, wild beast.

I had never cried like that before, even when Papa beat me. I wondered why I hadn't seen the attack coming. Was I that naive? How could my intuition have failed me?

The following day I was too scared to call the police. I had no proof except for a few bruises and the emotional trauma. The experience, the violent assault, left me traumatized for months.

I never saw Kiwi after that. I have no idea what happened to him. I did not dare tell Mama or any of my siblings about this violent experience. I knew Mama could not handle any more stress and worry. But, I began to wake up from my ignorant slumber.

The assault by Kiwi made me reflect and meditate deeply on violence against women, animals, the elderly, and the weak. It is deplorable that in many societies, for centuries, women have been viewed as objects of personal possession or sexual pleasure and not as human beings deserving of respect, reverence, and compassion. This may be one of the reasons why rape is alarmingly common around the world. Consciously or unconsciously, this objectification is part of the collective dysfunction of our era, a subtle form of exploitation and violence. This desire to possess, exploit, and trap women into subservient and degrading roles has grown, and some women in many cultures allow and, passively or even actively, encourage their objectification.

The more influential the media, advertising, and social media have become, the more women have become increasingly objectified. This phenomenon has now become so ingrained in our psyches that it has desensitized us. Women of every age, and even girls, suffer from the grave consequences of this vicious trap.

Focusing only on one's physical appearance can become a dangerous trap that results in a false sense of power, an illusion for both men and women. The physical, emotional, mental, and spiritual stress that results from trying to fit into the box of female objectification is very destructive, not only for women but for men as well. Because of objectification, many women suffer from sexual assault and harassment, lack of self-esteem, low or nonexistent self-worth, anxiety attacks, and perhaps indirectly even depression.

Many individuals still have not yet realized that timeless beauty and bliss are our very essence, but they can only burst from within. Bliss—that ecstatic state of being alive and feeling absolutely and powerfully beautiful—is innate. That is our true nature. Divine love is our nature, and that is pure bliss.

~

A FEW MONTHS AFTER MY encounter with Kiwi, I decided to join a modeling program at a reputable modeling agency. Even though I was only five-feet-four-inches tall, I worked part-time in the modeling world doing TV commercials, fashion shows, and catalogue and newspaper ads.

I became obsessed with my weight. I had always tended to gain weight. My love handles had grown as I tried to bury a mountain of repressed negative emotions about my family and the crash under too much food. My siblings often teased me.

Over dinner one night, I heard Mama talking about a TV star who binged, then made herself vomit by shoving her finger down her throat. I was repulsed by the idea, but the notion got into my head. A month later, I found myself making myself vomit the same way. I could not believe I was doing it; as I puked I felt guilty and ashamed. Even so, the procedure gave me a false sense of control. Over the months, I became obsessed with the binge-and-purge cycle, a vicious habit that is hard to break.

This eating disorder, bulimia nervosa, is a compulsive behavior both serious and dangerous. It has dreadful physical and psychological consequences. It can become a lifelong battle for someone afflicted with the disorder to balance their desire to stay slim with their overwhelming compulsion to binge on food.

Although I prefer to avoid words that represent violence, I employ such words as "battle" and "fight" as metaphors, because they best describe the pull of duality, the many conflicts between our feelings, emotions, and conditioned beliefs—like how we are taught to think about our bodies.

For many people in developed countries, food has become a psychological crutch rather than a necessity and blessing for survival and well-being. People shovel down sugar and carbohydrates because they feel empty and unfulfilled. I loved to binge on many delicious unhealthy and fattening fast foods like french fries to bury my negative emotions. While this behavior may have given me the illusion of fulfillment and comfort, it did nothing to help appease my real problems: emotional and mental pain and stress.

Millions of individuals become bulimic yearly. It is a shameful secret no one wants to admit—not to themselves and certainly not to others. Like myself at the time, others who struggle with their weight fear being judged, rejected, and unloved.

Little was known about bulimia nervosa in those days. I had no idea how this dragon possessed me overnight. I certainly knew it was not a healthy behavior, but I could not stop. This monster became bigger than life.

When I finally told my family doctor about my struggle, he told me, "When you are older, you can seek help from a psychotherapist." I walked out of his office very discouraged. I had never shared my secret with anyone before, and he did not seem to take it seriously. I kept on praying to the Divine Mother to help me stop. Every day I resolved to put an end to it only to find myself back in the bathroom with my finger in my throat. Papa's ghost still tormented me, buried deep in the confines of my heart, and I had lost the key.

～

BY THE TIME I NEARED my eighteenth birthday, I had partly recovered from the van crash. I decided to move into my own apartment with a dear friend, Flora. I needed space away from Mama's bitterness and compulsive agitation. Flora and I rented a two-bedroom unit in a pleasant apartment building six blocks away from Mama. I became involved in modeling, theatre, and beauty pageants.

I won second position among the top finalists in a provincial pageant for Miss Personality, and first prize for talent. On the night of the final, I performed a sketch I had created. My character came out dressed like a vagabond with a tattered coat, black hat, and cutout gloves, talking about self-transformation. Then, mid-performance, the vagabond converted into an otherworldly light being, in a bright, flowing sequin top. This performance enacted a symbolic metamorphosis that I desperately sought. As I removed my hat, coat, and gloves to the sound of an upbeat song and revealed my dazzling new attire, I sought to transform myself, improvising a modern ballet.

While studying privately with a popular Canadian actress, I decided to move back in with my mama and complete my high school course work so I could continue on to a university. I wanted to become an actress and a singer, but I kept hearing a little voice in the back of my head telling me I could not do any of these things—that I was worthless, just a piece of shit, as Papa had so often said.

Back in school, even though I was doing a few things I loved, there was a part of me searching for a true Divine love beyond the physical realm.

Then I made friends with a girl named Ange Fleur who had a radiance I had never seen before. Her eyes emanated light. She was always positive and joyous. I loved being around her, and she felt the same about my being. She introduced me to the wisdom of Master Omraam Mikhael Aivanhov via our conversations and lending me his books. Perhaps without realizing it, Ange Fleur brought me the most precious gift of all: spiritual knowledge and a master.

I had been longing for guidance and seeking spiritual direction for a long time without realizing it. Even though I was not quite ready to embrace the spiritual path, this new information was a great blessing. Even though I never had the great honor of being in Omraam Mikhael Aivanhov's physical presence, reading his words soothed my broken heart, filling it with hope, inspiration, love, and insights. Without realizing it, a part of my being was looking for a genuine guru. Omraam became my first spiritual teacher when I was nineteen.

One of my favorite Omraam sayings is, "Learn to speak gently and lovingly, not only to human beings, but also to animals, flowers, birds, trees, and the whole of nature, for this is a divine habit. He who knows how to utter words that inspire and vivify possesses a magic wand in his mouth, and his words will never be spoken in vain."

His words penetrated within my being. A magical wand would be one of the greatest gifts one could get. *A voice that illuminates, inspires, and heals would be so wonderful to have,* I thought. Papa often used to tell me, "Vivi, when you were born, God injected you with the needle of a gramophone!" At the time I did not know whether he meant it as a compliment or criticism. However, today I realize perhaps this was the most beautiful compliment he bestowed upon me. Without realizing it, Papa might have meant his daughter was not afraid to speak the truth and be authentic to her true ultimate nature. Perhaps he could unconsciously foresee the magic wand in his daughter's voice.

I devoured all of Omraam's books, especially *Yoga of Nutrition.* It taught that on a spiritual level, nutrients that come from Mother Earth are filled with life-force energy transmitted from sunlight. This life-force energy is what the Yoga tradition refers to as *prana.* Energetic nourishment is a wondrous gift from our Source. We don't need a ton of comfort food to nourish ourselves. Just the bliss of being is our true feast, what we call *ananda* in the Yoga tradition.

As I absorbed Omraam's teachings, I started to have great reverence for my physical body. I began to see it as a temple where the Divine resides. A new dawn arose within my being. By 1980, after two challenging years on the roller coaster of bulimia, I claimed victory. Omraam's wisdom helped me conquer the disease, and through strength, will, and grace I was able to heal.

Most of us unconsciously develop a system of beliefs based on what our parents, siblings, peers, school, government, and religious authorities and the media have fed us about our bodies and our existence during our childhood and adolescence. We may call these brainwashed and conditioned accumulations, or just plain accumulations, which form the personality of each individual. We seldom question these accumulated beliefs until one day we are hurt so badly inside that we collapse. The objectification of women, which I was not aware of at the time, added to my struggle with bulimia. Realizing that we are not the body or the mind was essential to my healing. Emotional tornados like physical and mental illnesses force us to turn inward to listen, reevaluate, and examine our lives and the way we perceive our existence and the world. Part of self-realization, or enlightenment, is to free oneself from all limiting conditioning, brainwashing, and boundaries—especially norms or false views such as objectification that prevent the individual from blossoming to their true nature.

Objectification is no more than turning oneself into an object. Becoming objectified consciously or unconsciously can become a gigantic boundary to breaking free on the spiritual path, or even just to attaining well-being and happiness. It is most important to realize that embracing any forms of identification could put oneself in a self-made fabricated tiny cage. In other words, each time we identify ourselves with a gender, or a religious, socioeconomic, or ethnic background, we are confining ourselves in a box without realizing that we are not these identifications. Putting ourselves into any type of cage will suffocate our soul, spirit, and entire being and can only lead to suffering, pain, distress, and misery.

Divinity dwells within the very core of our being. Would you rather be an object or experience the boundless freedom, the Source, and the whole of what you are? Just see and realize that we all are a unique wave of the Divine ocean of love. If only each individual, including men, would treat their body as a sacred temple and their heart as a shrine, we would see and feel a phenomenal transformation within and around us. Do you treat your own body as a sacred temple, a shrine . . . or as a graveyard?

One of the greatest choices we have is to contemplate existence, live mindfully, break free from our limitations and any false view of ourselves, and to self-realize. Also, when we multitask we cannot be mindful. If we cannot be mindful, we can never be in the present moment. Everyone has a buddha inside waiting to burst and blossom. Have you ever stopped for a moment, smiled, breathed, and lost yourself in the magnificent blue sky? That moment is eternal. Experience the vast beauty of the Divine ocean of love that is inside you. The image you hold of yourself has the power to shape your course of actions and destiny, and ultimately to determine your happiness, success, and inner well-being. See and realize within your being that you are divine, and you will begin to transform and awake.

No other animal has this inner power and great privilege. By grace and free will, you can heal and blossom. Among all human values, compassion is the most treasured quality. I learned this from Omraam and my cat Thisbe. When compassion is followed by selfless actions, we experience our Creator at work, and beauty, joy, and pure love emerge.

We, like Jesus Christ, are capable of greatness. Jesus said we can do more than he did, for we have the kingdom of God within us. When I was struggling with my body, I wanted to experience the kingdom of God within my being more than anything; but I did not know how. This wisdom lay dormant within my being until I was introduced to Omraam's teachings.

Our spirits have all inner knowing and knowledge. Have you noticed when you hear the truth that it resonates deep within your being?

Throughout my early life, I spent a thousand and one nights wondering about my impermanence, the nature of things, and my existence. Some nights I could not sleep. I would sit in bed until two o'clock in the morning, pondering. I sometimes sat in the child's pose, not knowing it was a yoga asana, trying to calm my mind. The blessings of Omraam Mikhael Aivanhov stirred up a profound longing within my being. They helped me realize that the only obstacle between our mastery and our dreams is ourselves—our conditioned and brainwashed accumulations. Breaking from the confinement of our self-made cage, our conditioned beliefs about ourselves, especially the body and the mind, sets us free.

Six

THE BATTLE WITHIN

TWO YEARS FLEW BY. AFTER I received my high school diploma with honors and was accepted by a college in their dramatic arts program, I moved an hour away from home to live in a dorm near campus.

Within the first few weeks of the semester, intense loneliness, sadness, anxiety, and insecurity followed me like my own shadow. They were unbearable. The wounded part of my being wanted to escape the overwhelming repressed turmoil inside of myself and go as far away as possible to prevent a tempest of emotions from emerging. That haunting ghost of the past kept following me everywhere. I called a dear friend, Afrodille, who agreed to visit me for lunch while I shared my troubled heart.

"I can't concentrate on my studies when I feel so lost. I know one day I will find answers within. Right now, I can only live for this moment," I told her. "Let's go see Mama."

"Okay, Vivi . . . let's pick up your stuff! Forget everything! We'll go visit your mom, then go to the city and have a fun time!"

Just like that, without any hesitation, we drove to my dorm, picked up my belongings, and sped back to visit Mama. I never returned to the college. Unconsciously I was driven by my inner fears. I dropped out of the program without any regrets. I told Mama, "I have to conquer this dragon inside me first. I must find myself."

The following season I received a call from a friend who was a travel agent; she told me about a special charter trip to Acapulco, Mexico, she was organizing. While talking to her, I looked through our frozen windows to the streets piled up with snowbanks five feet tall. Long icicles hung from our roof, sparkling in the sunlight. It was almost 30 degrees below zero. To my surprise I blurted, "Yes! I will come!"

I had never traveled anywhere before. Now, overnight, I abandoned everything. My spirit screamed for me to run away like I had from my university—away from my fabricated cage, away from all the painful memories in Canada. I wanted to go as far as possible. I told Mama with jubilation, "I'm going to learn Spanish! Don't be surprised if I never come back to Canada!"

This turned out to be mostly true. In the years that followed, I lived in Mexico and then the US but did not return to Canada—except to visit Mama and my siblings, of course. By the time I was twenty-seven, I was living in New England and was working in the esthetics industry, both of which were mushrooming in the US at the time. I was earning a good income for a twenty-eight-year-old and traveling to many prestigious spas, day spas, and esthetics skin care conventions around the country.

I was at the Maplewood Health Club a year after moving to New England, working out on the treadmill, when a man approached me. We exchanged a few words, and he told me his name was Ian. I thought he was attractive with his pale blond hair and baby-blue eyes but realized he was probably fifteen years older than me. There was a certain restraint about him that hinted at his family and upper-class background.

A fragrant sweetness of his aura attracted me to Ian like a butterfly to a flower. He spoke a little French and loved when I spoke French to him. We met up for a romantic dinner over a bottle of French wine, and he told me he had been divorced for over a year. He had two sons, fourteen-year-old Eric and twelve-year-old Sam. Toward the end of our first evening after a long *tête-à-tête*, Ian held my hand and gazed into my eyes. He held me in his arms, and we kissed passionately. I felt a love I had never felt before. It scared me to death, but my heart could not resist him. Ian's innate shyness created a certain air of charisma and mystique.

We began to see each other regularly, and like a supreme lover, Ian lavished me with love, kisses, affection, romance, tenderness, and red roses. A few months later, he asked me to move into his spacious and beautiful townhouse in Maplewood. I agreed without hesitation. Over the weeks that followed, we spent many intimate nights at home lost in each other's eyes, holding conversations over bottles of oaky chardonnay, sometimes indulging in chocolate-strawberry or cheese fondue I made by the fireplace.

He introduced me to his children at an ice rink one night, and as I connected with his younger son, Sam, I became aware of how much I longed to have a family. I knew I could not be a mother to the boys, but I hoped to be at least a good friend. They lived with their mother in a lovely house Ian owned only a few minutes away, but they spent every other weekend with us.

I will never forget the morning of my thirtieth birthday. Ian placed seven gifts, all from Tiffany, on the kids' bedroom carpeted floor where we occasionally hung out to watch the big TV. I sat down to unwrap my presents. The warm autumn light penetrated the room and illuminated those precious moments.

"Baby, wow! All for me? One would have been enough. You're spoiling me. Thank you so much, *mon amour.*" I kissed him tenderly.

As he held me closely in his arms, Ian gazed into my eyes. "I love spoiling you, baby! You deserve it. You mean the world to me."

"I'm so grateful to have you in my life. I don't care about all these gifts. You are my most precious present!" I replied.

I thought of Ian as the love of my life and had hoped he would have asked me to marry him for my birthday. I wanted to marry him, grow old with him. Despite his conservative, stoic upbringing, when he was with me, Ian was a free and wild spirit.

～

ON A COLD JANUARY NIGHT, Ian and I dined at the most popular little bistro in Maplewood. We loved the simplicity of the space's tall bay window, the intimate ambience of candlelight on its white linen tablecloths. That night, though I rarely ate seafood, I ordered linguini with shrimp.

After a delightful evening, we returned home and lost ourselves in passionate kissing. Ian was holding me close when a violent, queasy sensation overwhelmed me. My body broke out in red hives that itched unbearably. My throat began to close up. I was soon gasping for air.

"Call 911. Call an ambulance. Something is terribly wrong. Hurry, baby!" I panted.

I saw Ian's saucer eyes and panicked face. I was panicked, too. My body felt as if I was under attack. Ian bolted out of bed and reached for the telephone.

"No," I gasped. "Too late. Hang up. Take me to the hospital. We can't wait for the ambulance. How far is it?"

"At least fifty minutes without traffic," he said.

We dressed in a hurry. My heart was beating twice as fast as normal. My blood pressure plunged, leaving me dizzy and weak.

Oh, God, I'm going to faint. Calm down, Vivi. You can do this, I coached myself silently. I could feel my pulse drumming against my lungs, ticking my life away. The sharp pain in my heart intensified as I attempted to breathe. I wondered if I was going to have a heart attack.

By the time we jumped in Ian's car, my throat, my face, and my eyes had swelled up like balloons ready to burst. My lips became a grotesque clown's mouth. When I saw my face in the mirror, I got so scared. I looked like some rare beast. My neck was almost as large as my head. I hid myself under my fur coat. In those years I wore fur, lacking awareness that the skins had belonged to magnificent living animals that had suffered tremendous cruelties at the hands of humans.

"Go faster, baby. Hurry up!" I puffed for air.

"I'm going 90 miles an hour," he said. "We're almost there, sweetheart."

I gasped for oxygen and wondered if these were my final moments. I sent a mental message. *I'm not afraid of dying, God. By your grace I know I'll be fine no matter what.*

Then I begged, *Don't let me suffocate, Divine Mother.* I could hardly breathe.

It must have been almost midnight when we reached the emergency room. The attendant took one look at me and picked up the phone for urgent calls. In less than a minute, a few nurses rushed me into a warm room while Ian stayed behind, waiting.

"Miss Nantel, what did you eat tonight?" the doctor asked as he looked into my pupils with a tiny flashlight.

"Linguini with shrimp," I answered.

"You're going into anaphylactic shock," he said, "We need an epineph-rine IV, quickly."

A nurse put an oxygen mask on me and took my pulse and pressure. Another one inserted an IV into my arm. I was about to faint when this life-saving medication began to enter my veins.

"Miss Nantel, you're having a severe, life-threatening allergic reaction," he said. "You must be allergic to shellfish. Do you realize how fortunate you are? If you had arrived ten minutes later, you might not be with us. We will keep you under observation until we feel it's safe for you to go home. Stay calm and rest." He gave me a reassuring pat on my shoulder and walked away.

While I listened to the physician, I marveled at how close I'd come to death. We may have the illusion that we have control over our bodies and life events, but at some level we don't. Still, we are responsible for every-thing in our lives. The freedom we have is in the choosing of our thoughts, words, perceptions, and actions.

The doctor kept me under observation for the night, and Ian picked me up the following afternoon. When we walked out of the hospital, I stopped and paused for a moment to look up at the blue sky. I smiled at the sun, filled my lungs with all the oxygen I could inhale in one breath, and thought, *This one is for you, my beloved Divine Mother. I offer this one to you. I love you so much.*

I looked at Ian. "I'm so grateful to have you in my life! I love you so much." I grabbed him and kissed him.

My face and neck were still swollen, but not as much as before. I did not care that Ian was seeing me in such an ugly state. I was alive and with him. It took a few weeks to fully recover from all my symptoms. This flirta-tion with death opened my awareness, revealing the mystical beauty of our existence and the preciousness of our breath.

The angel of death is always next to our shoulder, following us like our own shadow. Most of us are not aware and take our breath for granted. We never know when we are going to inhale our last one. Breath is the most cherished, blissful, joyous, and powerful gift, when we become aware of it. Breath is the link between the mind, body, and spirit, bridging infinity and earth. Breath allows life-force-sustaining prana to flow in through all living beings.

Are you afraid of dying? Have you stopped and wondered at the miracle of existence? Does the fear of death steal away your peace and joy? Most of us fear death, consciously or unconsciously, and this fear causes us pain, suffering, and anxiety. In many spiritual and religious traditions, including Mahayana Buddhism, Hinduism, and the Yoga tradition, a fear of death is considered a *klesha*—a Sanskrit word meaning "defilement" or "delusion."

In the *Yoga Sutras* book 2 (1, 2, 4), Patanjali, a great ancient *rishi* (sage), expounds upon the major klesha, which he identifies as ignorance (*avidya*), ego (*asmita*), attachment (*raga*), aversion (*dvesha*), and fear of death (*abhinivesa*). These can all become poisons that steal our peace of mind and erode our well-being.

The true nature of our intrinsic mind is pure. It is our accumulations and brainwashed, negative mindset that poison our lives. In many Eastern traditions, ignorance of our ultimate nature is considered the main affliction from which all other klesha breed. When we transcend the mind and awake to our true nature, we realize we never die. We are eternal consciousness. Living in the physical plane, we experience the pull of polarity, duality, and the illusion of separateness from our Creator—unless we transcend. How else could we experience happiness if misery did not exist? Joy from sorrow, love from hatred—isn't that what makes this world beautiful? There is nothing to stop us from becoming the hero or heroine of our lives.

Seven

FORECASTING THE TEMPEST

OVER TIME IAN'S CHILDREN BEGAN to turn away from me. I could not understand why my relationship with them was deteriorating.

Ian was at a business retreat for the weekend with some colleagues when Sam left me a nasty phone message.

I called Ian and wept. "I cannot understand why Sam is behaving like this. It breaks my heart. Can you talk with him?"

"Don't worry, baby. Go buy yourself a big bouquet of white roses . . . on me!"

Even though the message proved Sam's disrespectful behavior, Ian did not talk to his son, and Sam never apologized. Once I overheard Sam tell his dad that his mother often asked questions about me: "Isn't she a little too young for your dad? What is she doing with him? What does she want?"

It's common for women to sacrifice our fundamental needs for others in our families. It can be a very beautiful, devotional act of selflessness, but only if the gesture is performed without sacrificing our wholeness and integrity.

In our second year together, Ian told me he did not want more children. He felt obliged to focus 100 percent on Sam and Eric when it was his turn to raise them and when he would take them in as adolescents. This was the agreement he had with his ex-wife. My heart sank. Though I had wanted children of our own, I said nothing, willing to sacrifice.

The closer we got to the time for the kids to move in with Ian, the more I drifted into sorrow. Eric was only fifteen when he began to make comments about how he hated the Japanese. I wondered how hatred got into the mind and heart of such a young boy. What kind of adult would he grow up to be?

When I was growing up, I did not know discrimination existed in Canada, although it must have. I only became aware of it when I moved to the United States. I always viewed others, even animals, as my spiritual brothers and sisters. I began to watch what I said to Sam and Eric.

Seeing Ian's lack of authority with his sons and the way he showered them with love, attention, and gifts made me reflect on my own father's behavior toward Coco and me. The wounds of the past I had resisted for so long started to awaken from their tombs. A volcano started to boil within my being.

I had never opened my heart to any man like I had with Ian. Despite such painful challenges, our love continued to blossom. Later that year, Ian taught me how to sail. Our first major sailing trip was in 1989, exploring the British and American Virgin Islands. I became his first mate. I stood on the deck in the fresh breeze, enjoying the waves, the sun, stars, and sea creatures. I felt free from the worries I had about Ian's children and our future together; our trip made me feel deeply close to Ian again. Late one afternoon we docked our sailboat in a lonely cove near Tortola Island. The rippling sea enticed me, and I jumped in. Within minutes, dozens of gargantuan turtles' heads surfaced. Their mystical eyes gazed at my being. I swam with them feeling daring, yet vulnerable.

Many days later, on the way back to Virgin Gorda, gigantic black clouds began to roll in. We listened to the radio and feared being caught in the storm. Despite the warnings, we could not turn back. The wind roared; the sky turned black. Lightning lit the horizon and thunder vibrated. A fierce wind blew, and torrential rain pounded us. Colossal waves rose eighteen feet high and rocked our ship up and down as if we were on a roller coaster.

Ian shouted, "Baby, come here and steer the wheel in this direction for a few minutes while I go tack the sails. Hold on tightly, my love. You can do it!"

He fastened a security belt around my waist and tied it to the wheel. Nausea made me dizzy to the point of fainting. I clenched my hands around the steering wheel with all my strength. Ian attached himself to the ship and walked across the sailboat like an acrobat on a wire. My heart pounded louder than the rain on my yellow rain slicker.

As I steered in the direction of Virgin Gorda, my tiny body turned with the wheel more than 180 degrees first on one side, then the other. I could no longer see Ian or anything else. I froze there, lost. A good ten minutes or more must have elapsed before a ghostlike figure suddenly appeared in front of me. Ian took over the wheel. With immense relief, I ceded my post.

After forty-five minutes of turbulent weather, the storm subsided. We reached land and debarked. We had conquered the wrath of the grand sea. We dug our toes into the white sand, hugging each other with tears of joy. "We made it, baby. Yippee! Thank God. We're so grateful," I said. Many hours later I could still feel my body swaying back and forth.

For a time, I was triumphant, but deep within, a dark shadow lingered—that heavy black cloud persisted inside my being, announcing the forecast of what would be the most tempestuous chapter of my life.

～

AFTER OUR SAILING TRIP, IAN and I started couples therapy and worked with our therapist individually. One day she told me, "Ian has a fear of commitment. This is as much as he can give of himself for now. He's very conflicted. Ian told me about sending flowers to his mother for her birthday and how she complained that the bouquet did not come from the right florist! His stoic upbringing and his demanding mother have much influence over him."

I heard what she said, but I did not listen. I was too lost in love. I did not have the right family background, social status, age, or nationality for Ian's mother. Still I believed I was the right kind of flower for Ian, despite how his mother's ghost still haunted his choices and life.

In the meantime, I returned to my studies at a small private university and began studying art history and drawing. I contemplated a major in fine arts. I was alone at home one night when I saw a picture in a magazine of a statue of the Buddha; it spoke to my heart. I felt an overpowering need to draw a picture of Siddhartha Gautama, the Buddha.

Early the following morning I tore a large sheet of paper from my sketch pad, went outside, and began to draw a large, radiant Buddha sitting in meditation. Serenity engulfed my being, and something dormant began to awaken as I drew. Energetic sensations arose, and feelings deluged my being with elation, as if I was discovering something extremely precious—the beginning of an awakening of my true and ultimate nature, my buddha-hood. Buddha simply means "awakened one."

In some ways it was like what I felt in Montreal at the exotic bazaar when I glimpsed a past life. This time I became aware of my longing to know the truth and the beyond. I also realized that the act of creating art selflessly with love and devotion is a meditative practice. This large drawing was my first meditative practice, setting the tone for my artistic voice. My spirit longed to express the inexpressible truth.

In the Eastern philosophy course I chose that semester, I read the Bhagavad Gita. In my essay on the book, I wrote that like the warrior Arjuna on the battlefield, our most important triumph is to allow our ultimate nature to lead the way. Consciously or unconsciously, we must face our inner battle. As we become aware of it, our resistance starts to lose its power.

Our value system often sends messages that contradict what our heart, mind, ego, and our ultimate nature want and feel. To become aware of this inner battle is not only healthy but necessary. It is crucial to stick with the process of demolishing the false sense of self, no matter how painful or agonizing. This is a necessary surgery and recuperation that allows healing to take place. True healing emerges from our expanding consciousness, and it transforms us. The more our consciousness expands, the more we blossom.

This subtle inner battle, though common, was one of the major roadblocks on my path. A severe depression was slowly creeping into me, agitating the tempest of sorrow and pain already brewing inside of my being.

After my professor read my interpretation of the Bhagavad Gita, she gave my paper an A+ and invited me to her home for tea.

"Come with me to Washington, DC, Vivi. I'll introduce you to my beautiful spiritual master from India. He'll help you traverse the tornado," she said.

There is an ancient saying, "When the student is ready, the master comes." This was the second time a master had come for me, but I resisted again for fear of losing myself. I was too terrified of my own inner battle.

The more I grasped, the more I lost. The more my being held on, the more I suffered, sinking deeper into darkness. One night sitting alone on the porch, I became lost in introspection. I reflected, *I'm not a Buddhist, Hindu, Jain, Catholic, Christian, or Muslim, nor do I adhere to any other religious tradition. Yet I embrace them all, for the core essence of truth lies dormant within them. I'm just a spiritual being in a human garment.*

Without spirit manifesting in the physical realm, science and all other fields of knowledge would not exist. Spirituality can only be an all-inclusive, all-encompassing energy that connects us all as children of the one Source. The names that we all call this Source—Shiva, Divine Mother, Heavenly Father, Absolute Truth, Infinity, Holy Spirit, Cosmic Intelligence, Universal Power, Nameless One, Brahman, Allah, Yahweh, Nirvana, Tao, Oneness— ultimately all signify the same thing.

The process of awakening involves healing at all levels. The search for our Creator, or oneness, often comes in many disguises. Often we think we are searching for love, joy, happiness, and peace, but what we are deeply seeking is boundlessness and liberation.

~

BY 1990 IAN AND I had been together for over two years. He wanted to buy a large New England–style house for us and his children. We fell in love with one filled with bright sunny rooms in the most beautiful, quaint part of Maplewood. The home was near the ocean and had a large yard facing a stream. The attic was a charming room perfect for drawing and painting, with a cathedral ceiling and skylights that filled the room with sunlight. When Ian saw it, he exclaimed, "It's the ideal art studio for you, baby!" I was honored and touched.

He eventually bought the house. His ex-wife moved far away to pursue her studies. The following spring, we would move in.

For the holidays, Ian and I, with his kids, went to his chalet in Colorado for the first time. To the sound of Elton John's "Cold, Cold Heart," mine warmed. I adorned the magnificent twelve-foot-high Christmas tree with sparkling ornaments and garlands, a task I used to do every year. This time I held a special invocation in my heart for a loving and harmonious celebration with my new family.

On our first day, lost in the blue-green sky among titanic white peaks, we prowled the boundless horizon, looking for the slopes with the best moguls. There was almost nothing in the world like skiing with Ian, which gave me a thrilling sensation of freedom and exhilaration. To breathe in the cold, fresh air and commune with nature while we glided together on the slopes was nirvana. Our spirits soared as we zigzagged around the moguls. Like children, we often pretended that the bumps were balloons, and we popped them along the way with our poles.

With red cheeks, running noses, and growling stomachs, we made it to the lodge midway down the mountain where we were meeting the boys for lunch. Eric and Sam sat near the fireplace, sipping hot chocolate. "Dad, I hurt my leg. I want to go home," Sam said grimacing.

"Okay, Sam," I said. "We will go down to the clinic together. Your dad and Eric can ski together for the rest of the afternoon."

After lunch, Sam and I hurried to the clinic. A friendly doctor examined his leg. "Just a little pull! You will recover in no time. Just ice it, Sam," the doctor said with a pat on Sam's shoulder.

As we left the clinic, I thought this was a perfect opportunity to have quality time with Sam. I hoped he would open up a little. We walked through town and chatted like never before. We even laughed like we used to in the beginning.

When we were back in the chalet, I asked if he would like another hot chocolate. He sat down in the stairway and stared at the high ceiling. His mood changed. I approached him with two cups of hot chocolate and sat down beside him. He stood up. I looked lovingly into his eyes and said, "Sam, I know how you must feel. How hard it is for you to see your parents divorced. I can never replace your mom. Please give me an opportunity to be your friend again. What have I done to make you turn your back on me? I care about you. I love you, Sam."

He stood there with red eyes, tears rolling down his cheeks. Then he walked away without a word. My heart cried out to help him. I wanted to share how my own parents' difficult marriage had been a part of my childhood and adolescence. A sudden wave of pain emerged in my heart.

By the end of our vacation, the four of us sat down for our last holiday dinner together. I made pasta, and we ordered a pizza for the kids. Together we discussed our New Year's resolutions and plans. Eric and Sam talked with great anticipation about moving into the new house with Ian in the spring. Eric said, "What about Vivi, Dad? She's coming, isn't she?"

Ian still had not made a final decision about my moving into the new house with his children. We had never discussed it openly, but he always gave me the impression I would.

For a few moments Ian was silent. Finally, he said somberly, "Vivi will get her own place."

I remained silent with a heavy burden in my heart while I cleared the table and put away the dishes. Just like that, the tempestuous ghost of my past reappeared, and I could no longer resist it. I went upstairs to pack for our return to New England the following morning. I could not understand Ian's constant mixed messages. It never occurred to me to look at the situation with Ian's perception of his responsibilities and family demands, but even if I could have seen it with more clarity, it would still not have alleviated my pain and suffering.

Later in my life I realized that our own spirit attracts certain individuals into our lives for a specific purpose. We even attract these people unconsciously to help us heal, grow, and evolve. That is a blessing in itself, even though we might not recognize it at the time because it is too painful.

That night I went to sleep without talking to Ian. I fell asleep as a tidal wave of sorrow and anguish engulfed my heart.

The following day while driving to the airport, I sobbed. Eric and Sam mocked me, using phony French accents. At one point, Ian said, "You guys, be nice to Vivi." Ian rarely reprimanded his children. Like a snail, he would retreat into his shell in silence, never communicating his true feelings. The way Ian had intervened with only a weak voice, along with his lack of open communication and failure to discipline his children, caused me to sob even louder, as I wondered why he hadn't stood up for me and our relationship. I thought, *What is Ian teaching his kids by the way he treats his lover? How would Sam and Eric ever respect and accept me if their father did not stand up for his own woman and us?*

My heart descended deeper into the abyss of darkness. *I want to wake up from this nightmare. I beg you, our Creator. I want to wake up from this nightmare. I beg you God.*

~

A NEW YEAR HAD BEGUN. I asked the Divine Mother to help 1991 bring harmony and peace to our hearts. Ian planned to move out of the townhouse in February to his old house, while they transitioned to the new home in the spring.

When Ian began packing his personal belongings, it hit me like a hammer. For the following three weeks, he packed one box at a time without showing any feelings. Despite my inner turmoil, I helped him with a few of these tasks. On the gloomy day he moved out to go back to his old house to his boys, Ian's silence and the emptiness of the rooms tore my heart. When the movers stacked the last box in the truck, I stood outside in the cold winter wind, watching them depart with my beloved. Though Ian was not a father figure for me, when he left, I relived the abandonment and eviction of my past.

I called my older sister Rose. We spent over an hour praying together. I was inconsolable for days. I had anxiety attacks, along with heart palpitations. I had lost myself in the process of loving Ian, and now I was overwhelmed by the fear of losing him and grieving my past and the loss of Papa—all at the same time. I did not know what was happening to me. Ian and our precious love were slipping away into a nightmare.

Eight

THE URGE TO SEE PAPA

ABOUT A MONTH AFTER IAN left, I woke up with an intense yearning to see my father. I called Rose in Canada and asked if she knew where I could find him. "Papa came to me in a dream last night. I had a revelation this morning, Rose. I must see him."

"Oh, ma belle Vivi, I think I have a phone number. Papa gave it to me over nine years ago."

I called him with butterflies in my stomach. It had been twenty-one years since we last spoke. My heart pounded, and my voice shook. "Hello, Papa. It's Vivi."

"Vivi! Is that really you?" His voice sounded just as it did when I last saw him. I was eleven then. "What a surprise after all these long years. I'm doing fine, but my legs hurt. I have gotten remarried, you know."

Then Papa asked me a stream of questions. When he asked me if I had gotten married yet or had any children, I choked up.

"What is happening, Vivi?"

"I dreamt of you last night, Papa. I can't remember the dream, but I woke up knowing I had to find you. Please, Papa, I need to see you." I felt a pain in my throat, and my eyes watered. "I have a broken heart, Papa. I'm thirty-two now. I really want to see you. Can I come tomorrow? It's urgent."

"Come, we will have you over for dinner," he said.

While Papa spoke, a sharp knot attacked my stomach and throat. Painful stabs invaded my bleeding heart. I could not utter a word more. I refrained from exploding in a torrent of sobs while my spirit felt embraced by his invitation.

I could not believe I would be hugging my father after twenty-one years. At last, I would have the precious opportunity to express my love to him, help liberate our hearts, and reunite us. This could be a priceless time of healing for us.

After hanging up, I took a deep breath and looked through the French doors to where sparrows were chirping. I began to cry. At last, I was listening to my true Divine nature. My dream had revealed the necessary spiritual process for us.

~

EARLY THE FOLLOWING MORNING I flew to Canada. Rose drove me out to the serene white countryside. I could feel my blossoming heart opening wide. Rose began praying aloud. Over the years, she had become a devout born-again Christian. Her spirit sought to find solace in her religion. I closed my eyes and asked the Divine Mother for strength and courage.

"Rose, I am terrified of seeing Papa," I said shivering.

When we arrived, I saw an old man waiting in the tall window—it was Papa. He ran out the door with his arms wide open and squeezed me.

"*Ma petite fille,* my little Vivi! Here she is. Come, Muguette. Come see my baby!" Papa exclaimed with joy and pride.

Overwhelmed by emotion, I froze. Rose hugged Papa. When we walked into the dining room, Muguette, Papa's new wife, embraced me.

"Bonjour, Vivi. What a beautiful girl your daughter is!"

"Vivi, you are a grown-up woman now, but I still see your baby face," Papa said.

Muguette, a friendly woman, offered us something to drink. Papa showed us around their home while Muguette opened a bottle of Château-du-Pape red wine to mark our celebration.

Papa, Rose, and I walked around and chatted about mundane affairs. We could hear music in the background, which brought back tender memories. While Papa talked about his house, I wondered whether he understood the consequences of his past actions. *Had he forgiven himself, or did he have regrets? Had he forgotten the past and numbed himself like I had?*

Was he happy, at peace? My mind bombarded me with questions I did not dare ask.

At first, I was awkward. Old images returned: his fist against my nose, the welts and bruises, his malicious words of hatred, my throbbing heart, Mama's agony, the tragic eviction, the night Papa almost ran over Mama and my sisters, and the day Papa disowned us. I wanted to erase these painful memories.

We sat down for dinner. The four of us raised our glasses. The atmosphere was very tense. We talked because we were afraid of silence. By dessert and tea, when the aroma of Muguette's homemade apple pie flirted with our nostrils, the ambience had warmed. While Rose and Papa engaged in a conversation, Muguette shared with me about her childhood. Then Papa talked about their quiet lives together. Rose spoke of her newfound religion. Our family scandal never surfaced.

"Papa, I'm studying now at the university. I'm considering a major in fine arts," I said.

Papa smiled. "Wow! I'm proud of you, ma Vivi."

An eerie silence set in.

"Papa," I took a few deep breaths, feeling shaky. "I fell deeply in love with a man. He means everything to me, Papa. I want to marry him, but it is so complicated. He has two children. My heart is broken. I will never love again . . ."

I ran to the bathroom to compose myself.

On my way back to the table, Papa stood next to Rose at the table, reaching out for the teapot. Seeing him there still alive, I realized the blessing and beauty of this treasured moment. My heart burst in an explosion of Divine love. I grabbed Papa and hugged him close. I did not want my father to pass away without having the opportunity to mend our past. I wanted to help liberate us from our past and bring peace and light to our relationship.

"I thought I would never see you again. You'll always be my papa. I forgive you. I love you, Papa."

"I always loved you, my Vivi," he said weeping.

Rose rushed into our arms. "We forgive you, Papa. We love you. You are our father," she said crying.

The three of us intertwined as one, weeping rivers. For the first time, I saw a sparkle of light twinkle in my father's eyes. Muguette sat at the table in silence, witnessing the miracle of our Divine love.

When Rose and I departed, Papa stood in the window and waved at us. As we drove away in the snowy mist, he kept waving. I blew a big kiss and waved it with my hand like I used to when I was a little girl, knowing this was the last time I would ever see him. I felt a powerful, intuitive feeling beyond the logic of the mind. I began to sob again and could not stop. Our reunion had been the missing key to the secret gate of my heart, releasing two long decades of repressed negative energy. After our last encounter, I felt that our karma, meaning all the past memories embedded deep into our subconscious, was evaporating. A flood of intense emotions and feelings escaped from my wounded heart.

~

A FEW WEEKS LATER I called Papa, hoping we could develop a relationship. I was willing to try, but it was too much to ask from him. Our visit had awakened something deep within both of us. Papa had to face his inner demons. He drifted away from me.

Still, this experience was an immense gift. Not long after that, I came to realize that Papa's malicious conduct in the past was not his ultimate and true nature. His unhealthy behaviors reflected only his accumulated conditioned patterns and lack of awareness. Perhaps my grandparents abused him when he was a child. I don't know. It's common for abusers to have been abused by their own parents, repeating the same vicious circle over generations. Regardless of whatever the truth may have been, this time I had consciously ended this cycle. My heart overflowed with gratitude for the extremely rare opportunity the Divine was providing us. But it was a very intense spiritual process that would unfold over the ensuing years. The profound impressions of memories (karma) and repressed emotions started to release my energy flow and made way for the fresh beginning of my healing recovery. When forgiveness flows from a pure, loving heart, beautiful release occurs at all levels on both sides. Doing so can set us free from many potential compulsions attached to our past. When we heal and deeply let go of our accumulated baggage and surrender to what is, we take one of the most important steps to rekindle our true enlightened nature.

It was essential for my being to go through this intense spiritual process to face my upcoming tempest with Ian. It was time to return home. The blessing of seeing Papa empowered my being with courage to face the storm of my life. When our heart overflows with gratitude and Divine love, the whole universe dances with us.

Nine

IN SEARCH OF DIVINE LOVE

WHEN THE SPRING ARRIVED, IAN and his boys moved into the new home. Eric asked his father for the attic. Ian replied, "Well, Eric, there is a large, sunny bedroom just for you on the second floor." But Eric insisted, and Ian relented; he could never say no to his children, and they knew it.

I did not remind Ian that he had promised the attic would be my art studio. My heart melted like snow turning into slush. I slept at their new home on weekends but continued to live on my own in the townhouse. Ian and I were still dating, but I sensed I was losing him.

Without being aware of it, I started to slide into an acute major depression. I did not feel like I belonged in this world. I struggled with my feelings toward Ian and his fear of commitment. We seemed to be living in two opposing worlds. At the very beginning, I didn't realize I was trying to turn myself into Ian's ideal of a beautiful, submissive doll. Over the years I had resisted it, wanting to remain authentic to myself, but I slowly lost my identity. I wanted so badly to belong to his family. Feeling a sense of belonging is a portal to knowing our true being, realizing there is only One. Belonging is vital for reconnecting with the Divine within us.

I buried my paintbrushes, watercolors, art paper, and pencils in the back of my closet. I could not draw or paint.

After three years of being together, the thought of losing Ian forever brought unbearable anguish and sorrow, but I stood up and broke off our relationship. I did not know who I was without him anymore.

One night a few weeks after our relationship ended, I dozed off at the townhouse, hoping I could sleep forever and avoid the pain in my heart. Ian let himself in and tiptoed upstairs. He woke me, sat on the bed, and held my hand. "Baby, baby, please, don't leave me," he pleaded. "Let's work it out. I love you so much. Please let's get back together."

Tears were rolling down Ian's cheeks. I had never seen him cry before; the sight stirred a deeper love for him within me. Ian caressed my hair. We embraced and wept together.

His lips kissed mine. They traveled down my neck, shoulder, breast. He unwrapped the back of my white lace nightgown. We lost each other in physical ecstasy. The illusion of time and space disappeared. After what must have been a few hours, Ian whispered, "I don't want to let you go, my love."

We kissed good night. He left for his new home and his kids.

Like a virtuoso violinist, Ian had learned how to stroke the strings of my heart, whether he did it intentionally or not. The following day I realized our relationship had resumed at the old status quo. I had given away whatever inner power and strength I had left within me and done what he wanted so that I could belong.

Over the following two years, Ian and I broke up three times, only to return to each other again, dancing the same painful waltz. My feelings and emotions were constantly erupting like a blazing volcano, and I could not control them. I would be high on love one day and full of grief and mourning the next.

In a meditative process I would often do with my eyes closed, I thought of this wounded part of myself as a new baby that needed care. The feeling was intuitive, and I used it to help me process and be in touch with my authentic feelings and emotions.

The Divine Mother—or whatever name we attribute to God—can fill this hole within us. Whenever I felt confused and needed pure love and nurturing, I called out for the little Vivi within my being, and the Divine Mother showed up.

We live in an era in which many are obsessed with social media, physical appearance, money, status, fame, and sex. Our culture is overwhelmed with work, emails, errands, phone calls, and projects. The world is bombarded with wars, terrorist attacks, cruelty toward animals, and injustice. Our relationships with others and ourselves may include heartbreak, depression, neuroses, psychoses, divorces, disasters, and anxiety. In the face of all these things, I wondered, *Where can I find unconditional, pure love?*

Many people growing up in dysfunctional and broken families have a part of themselves that has been deprived of attention, affection, guidance, acceptance, belonging, unconditional love, and nurturing. Despite my difficult challenges, my heart continued to blossom with love. I would not let hatred enter my heart. Many individuals unconsciously use hatred as a strategy to protect themselves from intense suffering. Like cancer, hatred is a form of intense anger that eats us alive. With so much suffering in my life, I began to wonder about the nature of love. *Does it exist in this materialistic physical world?* Aren't we all in search of unconditional love, a pure energy expressing the truth of our ultimate nature—love beyond expectations, attachments, conditions, demands, and bondage? Such a love is both transformational and transcendental, beyond this physical dimension, a Divine love. *Where could I find it?*

The ancient spiritual Yoga tradition tells us that our ultimate and true nature is bliss, ananda. Isn't Divine love the same as bliss? Isn't one of the gravest maladies of our century to live solely in the physical realm, rather than expand and awaken to our ultimate true nature? How can we offer what we do not have? How can we use the spiritual process to manifest a harmonious and compassionate world unless we first heal our deep wounds?

Ian and I continued to see our family therapist; but our love did not recover, nor did it help with the tempest inside me. Though we got back together, we were not healing our deep wounds.

In June of 1992, I moved to 108 Miraculous Lane, a small, charming townhouse where I would live alone. I became friendly with my next-door neighbor, the charismatic Jacinta, a precious, compassionate woman of mixed Spanish and Italian blood. She loved animals, traveling, and the arts and sciences, like I did. Over time we spent many nights on her patio, talking and sipping glasses of chardonnay. Her endearing spouse, J.T., would sneak out to refill our glasses. He was not afraid to speak his mind. With his infectious sense of humor and laughter, J.T. often cut to the truth of situations.

"Vivi, you're a doormat!" he told me. He was right.

~

THAT EASTER IAN SURPRISED ME with a little getaway for the two of us at a Sandals resort in Jamaica during the Holy Week. But on that warm island, he was cold—miles away, lost in his logical world. By the look on his face, I knew something was brewing. I tried to reach him, but he would not open up. It was killing me.

Upon our return, we stopped by my place first. Jacinta had taken care of my cats and left a stunning bouquet of sunflowers with a card welcoming me back home.

At the last minute, before getting out, Ian murmured in my ear. "I need some time alone. We can't see each other while I make a final decision about marrying you."

I couldn't believe what I was hearing. We both got out of the taxi. Ian carried my luggage inside. "How can you do this now? You begged me to take you back. I can't go through this emotional roller coaster again. Not again. Please," I pleaded. I looked into his eyes. "If we break up now, it's the end."

My voice cracked. Part of my being did not mean my words. Ian hugged me and silently walked out the door. I ran upstairs and collapsed on the floor of my bedroom.

That night I descended into a dark abyss. I knew I could never take Ian back unless he put a ring on my finger in genuine, heartfelt commitment. I felt wronged and manipulated. Each time I had found the courage to let Ian go, he pulled my strings, and I reacted like a puppet.

"How could I have fallen for this?" I screamed at the walls. I banged on the floor with my fists, furious at him and myself. "How could I have let him manipulate me this way?" I wept on and off all night. There was excruciating pain in my solar plexus, my heart chakra. I had felt this unbearable throbbing pain on and off for years. This time it shattered into billions of pieces.

I had been blinded by a false sense of self, which I had created by trying to change my true nature to please Ian. I had also carried these false ideas from my childhood. As children we develop a self-image that is unreal and often unhealthy. We base our self-worth on this erroneous view. We emerge as adults thinking we are our body, our mind, our professions, a certain gender, our social status, our ethnicity, religious and cultural background, or that we are our possessions and wealth, or even our sexual orientation. These identifications prevent us from awakening and realizing enlightenment. We confine ourselves to limited boundaries, our own fabricated jails. My spirit could sense an intuitive and inner knowing telling my being that I was not any of these identifications. Because I had experienced a few drops of Divine love in my childhood, a faint echo still resonated within me.

In the act of shedding our old, worn-out garment filled with prejudices, conditioning, and assumptions, we can expand and break free from our cages. Divine love flowing within us is one of the keys to our freedom. We may call it by another name; that doesn't matter. The nature of this love is an intense, expansive, blissful, and ecstatic sensation of experiencing our Creator and all living beings within. That is to be in a state of union, of yoga. Divine love liberates the imprisoned heart and allows us to pierce the veil of false identifications and burst free from all boundaries. In this surrender, the master within becomes alive.

Paramahansa Yogananda, a venerated ascended master of the twentieth century, said, "The satisfaction of love is not the feeling itself, but in the joy that feeling brings. Love gives joy. We love 'love' because it gives us such intoxicating happiness. So love is not the ultimate; the ultimate is bliss. God is *Sat-Chit-Ananda*, ever-existing, ever-conscious, ever-new bliss. We, as soul, are individualized Sat-Chit-Ananda. True love is Divine, and Divine love is joy."

Divine love brings us back home, healing us from the illusion of separation from the Source. Our ephemeral journey on earth becomes richer, more beautiful, and more meaningful as the universe belongs to us. Without love we have no power over wars and negative acts committed by people on themselves and others, but we have the power to open up our own hearts and seek this transformational love within. By transforming ourselves in this way, we can help others, both human and animal. Where there is Divine love, there is compassion in actions.

In the middle of the night, I heard someone knock at the door. "Are you okay, Vivi? Is there anything we can do for you? Please let us know."

I opened the door. J.T. stood there in his pajamas. "I can't stand seeing what Ian did to you. We can hear you sobbing. It hurts us. You don't deserve to be treated like this," J.T. said. He shook his head and walked back next door. I closed the door, hyperventilating, and climbed in bed, sobbing again. Yet his unexpected visit made me feel so loved and cared for. I knew J.T. spoke the truth.

My being could not handle the blow of this intense pain, rage, and deep sorrow. Their shadows kept me paralyzed in the darkest and most frightening abyss, lost in a profound state of inertia and depression.

⁓

DURING THE FOLLOWING YEAR, I swore I would never love again. I was beyond angry and still in love with Ian, wondering how I could stop loving him. A part of me wanted to hate him, but I could not. Day after day I grieved, begging God to get me back home. At first, I did not fully realize that I was also grieving about my past and how it had conditioned me. I continued to wake up every morning with an unbearable pain that radiated from my solar plexus. All I could think of was Ian, as if his name had been stamped with a hot iron into my heart.

The anxiety and pain in my chest made it difficult to breathe. How could I function when my world had collapsed? I had built my life around him. I struggled to get out of bed. I was too lethargic, in distress. I had allowed myself to become too dependent on Ian. Now I had to stand on my own feet, alone, in the midst of a severe depression with a demolished heart.

After several months of feeling this way, I began seeing Dr. Violet, a new psychotherapist, twice a week. I desperately needed someone to hold my hand and listen to my torment. I walked around like a zombie, in a daze, dizzy, weak, and with sharp pains in my heart. Terror drained my life force. I could not function, paralyzed with hopelessness and helplessness. I was still obsessing about Ian. I wanted desperately to wake up from this horrible nightmare and did not understand I was suffering from major depression. I could not tell if seeing this therapist was working. I was too lost in the dark abyss to see anything.

The process of purifying and healing decades of emotional, mental, and physical abuse may take a very long time. It can be an extremely lonely, intense, and painful process. I longed for love and attention, yet never felt my love for Ian was love for a surrogate father. It definitely was not. I held Ian with great love and reverence as my supreme lover—the love of my life. But it was not a Divine love. Divine love is a certain state of realization and of being, expanded by experiencing it within every fiber of our being. It is all-inclusive. We don't need to fall in love intimately with an individual to experience Divine love.

Overwhelmed with such powerful emotions, complex and intense feelings, and pain, my nervous system began to break down.

Ten

SACRED LOVE

WHEN SUMMER ARRIVED IN 1992, it had been three months since Ian and I had seen each other. The weather was unusually humid and hot, yet I loved the embrace of the sun on my skin and could not get enough of the loving breeze. Ian and I had talked briefly only once over the phone. Despite my intense desire to be with him, I made a major effort to eliminate any contact with him.

Then one day in July we agreed to have lunch together. I don't remember who reached out first, but when we arrived at the restaurant, Ian looked at me with puppy eyes, his gaze melting my heart. He led me to believe he would marry me but left it vague. While nibbling our salads, he seemed confused as he questioned me. His shallow breathing and sighs made him seem nervous.

"What are your plans?" Ian asked. He was mostly silent throughout lunch. But by the look in his eyes, I could see he still loved and wanted me yet could not commit.

"I'm thinking about moving out of the state . . . most likely to Florida," I said. "I need to get away from here."

"Why? You don't know anyone there. Stay," Ian said, holding my hand. I could tell he was struggling between his upbringing and what his true self wanted.

The following weekend I called him on some light pretense. I felt guided to do so, and too, my heart longed to see him again.

"Hello?" a woman's voice answered.

Startled, I hung up the phone. Then I called a second time, thinking I'd misdialed.

"Hello?" Again, it was a woman's voice.

I jumped in my car and drove to Ian's house. I needed to know the truth.

When I arrived, I strode up to his door and knocked. Ian opened with an odd smile on his face. He was surprised to see me.

"Hi, Ian, can we talk for a moment?" I said. Just over his shoulder I could see a pretty young woman in tight blue jeans and a sexy top walking in the hallway barefoot, as if it were her home. She looked like a teenager.

"Is she Eric's new girlfriend?" I asked.

Without answering my questions, Ian said in an icy voice, "Let's go outside." He closed the door behind him and propelled me down to where my car was parked.

"What's happening, Ian? Please tell me. She's with you, right?"

He remained silent, but his expression and body language gave him away. I knew something despicable was happening. He looked at me dispassionately, but did not dare to look straight into my eyes. His eyes shifted from side to side, trying to avoid my gaze.

"Go back to your house," he finally said.

Tears welled up in my eyes. "Why can't you at least be honest with me?" I asked in a faint voice. "How can you have another woman move in less than a few months after breaking up with me? You told me you wanted to be alone to reflect and be with your kids." My whole body shook; my heart pounded. I felt faint.

For a fraction of a second, a part of me hoped I could be so mad at him that I would hate him. But, all I felt was love, deep sorrow, and hopelessness. I knew too well the devastating effects of hatred. I witnessed it in my childhood with Papa. Hatred manifests from those who lack the spiritual inclination and tools to transmute negative feelings and emotions into positive energies. And that is exactly what I did. Hatred never entered my heart. Yet we all have the capacity to make that transformation for our own inner well-being and the well-being of others.

"I always loved you no matter what, Ian, and I still love you," I said.

"You told me we would work out our problems together. Why are you doing this? I thought you loved me too."

Ian stood there for a moment, and then he opened the driver's door of my car. He turned to me. "I never loved you," he said.

His words lacerated my heart like a warrior's sword. I thought I was going to collapse. I sat down, grabbed hold of the steering wheel, and took several deep breaths. I started the engine and left without looking back, sobbing all the way home. The celestial beings (some individuals might call them angels or spirit guides) are metaphysical entities of the beyond. They can even be ascended masters. I always felt a very profound connection with many of them on the other side of the veil. They must have protected me, because I surely ran at least one red light and more than a couple of stop signs.

Later that afternoon, I lamented, "Dear Divine Mother, I don't want to love him anymore." I threw myself on the floor weeping, begging for mercy. I invoked, "Oh, dearest Mother, get me out of here. I can't take this pain anymore. I want to go home." I became so upset with God and at myself for everything that had happened in my life. I lost faith and could not connect with my celestial friends anymore. I felt abandoned, demolished by the Divine, lost in an abyss of hell.

～

EVEN MONTHS LATER, I WAS still in shock. I did not know who I was anymore. I had no sense of self. In my sessions with Dr. Violet, I shared how I had lost all desire, and struggled with lethargy and severe exhaustion. These symptoms were not only emotional and mental but also physical. The grieving process often kept me awake—hyperventilating, screaming with rage, sorrow, and anguish.

One lonely night around eleven during Thanksgiving week, my phone rang.

"Hi baby, it's me," Ian whispered. "How are you? I've been thinking about you a lot. I wanted to hear your voice. I miss you, want to see you."

A part of my being was glad to hear from him; another part wished I could erase him from my memory so I could say, "Sorry sir, you have the wrong number." Yet, I felt powerless. We spoke briefly. I did not mention the severe depression I had fallen into. He would not have understood. It had been almost four months since our last rendezvous. He shared that he was missing me, and he had gotten himself into "a pickle" with this other woman. I wondered if he was disgusted with himself and regretted his abominable behavior. *Was he trying to pull my strings again?*

It was inevitable their relationship would fail. He betrayed everything: his own spirit, my being, the other woman, and his children. He was trying to medicate himself with a pacifier so he would not feel the pain of our breakup or have to face his problems. I no longer trusted him. His lack of respect and his devious behavior disillusioned me even more. I had to let go but did not know how.

The shadows of our past continue to follow us until we are forced to face them. Problems, like solutions, are not outside but inside us. The healing process must manifest first in the depth of our heart. That is the path to heal the world. I did not fully realize it in those days.

In my next session with Dr. Violet, I told her sobbing, "I'm so scared of what is happening to me. I don't want to wake up in the morning to feed my cats anymore. That's not like me. I feel Ian has stolen my soul."

"Ian did not steal your soul, Vivi," Dr. Violet said firmly. "You're very strong. You can overcome this."

"Dr. Violet, . . . the symptoms are too heavy. I'm caught in this violent tornado," I said with a soft voice and tears in my eyes.

~

WHEN WE TALK ABOUT LOVE, it is inevitable the subject of codependency and interdependency arises. This relatively new term, codependency, was coined a few decades ago.

Codependency is a learned compulsive behavior and one of the gravest malaises of our time. Codependency makes it harder for people to unleash their true nature, causing them great suffering. There are many definitions of codependency, but they all come down to one thing: an addictive relationship. This addiction develops from the participants' learned behaviors and conditioned responses that leave the individuals unable to hold functional boundaries.

Codependency was first used to describe those who lived with an alcohol or drug abuser, but it has expanded to include all unhealthy, dysfunctional relationships—especially romantic ones. It includes anyone who has learned maladaptive behaviors to survive great emotional pain. These circumstances can arise from being subjected to drug dependency, chronic mental or physical illness, physical and emotional abuse, or other toxic environments. Codependency is the byproduct of the responses needed to survive traumatic stress.

A person who is codependent tends to become involved in toxic and painful relationships, enabling the individual to reenact their familiar dysfunctional behaviors in the new relationship. In many cases, codependency can lead to breakups, divorce, depression, and even suicide. Often a large part of the codependent's identity, self-worth, and self-esteem are based on the other individual.

This emotional and behavioral condition can affect anyone—a parent, friend, sibling, lover, spouse, or child—who has been emotionally or physically abused and neglected. Some relationships can stir codependency in an individual if one is not completely free from the ghosts of the past.

Ian and I played the codependency dance to a certain degree, but not entirely. When I would break off the relationship and stand up for my healthy boundaries and needs, he would compulsively run to get me back. Despite it all, I would fight back against Ian's emotional manipulation and control. But we also brought a full regiment of ghosts and wounds to our interactions. These invisible forces pulled us apart, affecting us profoundly. If we had both understood our tendencies and our wounds, and been willing to work to change them, we could have healed, grown, and blossomed together. We were both in love. Unfortunately, neither one of us was ready for that kind of transformation.

Being codependent does not mean individuals don't love one another. Contrarily, they may love each other deeply, but they don't know how to behave and interact in a healthy way. One or both individuals may unconsciously sabotage the relationship with obsessive actions, emotional manipulation, or submissive behaviors.

As a codependent, one gives power to external objects such as drugs, alcohol, food, sex, and other people, believing they will fill the profound void inside oneself. Most people are unaware of this void, yet it produces quiet desperation as well as the desire of always wanting more, of never feeling blissful by just "being."

Because of my deep longing to merge with the Divine, a part of myself must have hoped unconsciously that Ian would fulfill this spiritual void.

When a codependent relationship fails, both parties become lost and distraught; they experience pain and withdrawal. It is an addiction like any other. Most will seek distraction as Ian did with his new lover—seeking to continue the unhealthy pattern. Usually these new, equally addictive relationships also fail.

Our obsessive consumerist society reflects this void. So many people seem to want the latest of everything. This void comes from the depth of our being, which is longing. Believing that you are an identity based on certain socioeconomic, religious, or ethnic backgrounds, as well as prestigious labels, profession, and wealth, is a grand illusion. These things are ephemeral and transient as morning dew. These identifications can give only a false sense of self and lead only to bondage. They cannot nourish our spirit. When they go away, and they will, most people fall apart. They may add some spice to our lives, but they cannot be the ultimate source of our happiness. True power lies within the beauty of our ultimate, true nature.

Some spiritual traditions say this sense of "I-ness" is the source of pain, misery, and suffering, because it is the root cause of our desires. This sense of "I-ness," or what many people call the "ego," often comes with many identities, which were accumulated and conditioned over time leaving the individual believing that they are these things.

It's almost impossible to fulfill all desires in one lifetime. And it is the lack of fulfilling our intention that causes us misery. A suicidal person's wish to die is a desire. Wishing to stay alive when you are in the process of dying is a desire, too. It seems we are never free from desire unless we awake and expand our consciousness—whether it is Buddha consciousness, Christ consciousness, Krishna consciousness, Mohammed consciousness, or some other; ultimately, they are the same universal, Divine consciousness.

Unfortunately, the names we give create ambiguity that can lead to misinterpretation. Isn't that why we have had so many wars over the past millennia? Which name is the true name of God? It is the same Source, the same consciousness—one truth with so many different names.

A wise person who has suffered enough will look inward and take a long break from relationships to heal. That person will also begin to realize the dysfunctional nature, or a certain tendency in relationships, and seek help to start addressing those challenges. This process can be the beginning of a very beautiful and powerful spiritual awakening. Without awareness of compulsive, learned conditions, and without healing the wounds of the past, dysfunctional patterns will continue to repeat, leaving the afflicted to withdraw from relationships and feel even more alienated from the world and themselves. After a time, someone with a codependent personality may close their heart. Yet the heart will still long for love and belonging.

It is not unusual for many individuals in such cases to become averse to relationships because of the suffering they cause. When an individual closes their heart, every aspect of their being suffers and suffocates, like a flower deprived of water. Love is our very nature. It needs to be experienced and expressed. Unhealthy isolation and alienation lock the person in a self-made jail. We mustn't forget we all have wings that will help us soar.

The battle is half won when the individual realizes their codependency or tendency. The more the individual becomes aware, the more their consciousness expands. Some people say, "Ignorance is bliss." However, I believe ignorance is misery. But knowledge is not always power, for knowledge is useless unless positive actions follow it.

I had a genuine, deep love for Ian. But I learned from my experiences. There is a fine line between codependency and interdependency, where people depend on each other; yet the dynamics are very different. We are born to depend on others. Codependency is that need imbalanced. It can be healed. With the blossoming of our true and ultimate divine nature it becomes eternal, infinite, and whole.

Healthy relationships, those that are interdependent, can give us a sense of belonging. Within an interdependent relationship, individuals function at their best, complementing each other and feeling grateful. We can grow in these relationships. They provide us with great opportunities to evolve, heal, and expand our consciousness. Intimacy can allow us to blossom into our ultimate, true nature in unimaginable ways, freeing us from the prisons of our past.

It is hard to love and trust again after being heartbroken. Many individuals lock their hearts. Unless we are wise enough to learn from others' mistakes, evolving can be a roller coaster ride. Not everyone is humble and wise enough to learn from their own or others' mistakes. We all have our own journey and rhythm. Our spiritual growth and transformation depend on the intensity of our longing to seek the Divine.

There is a prodigious difference between true, sacred, intimate love and a relationship that comes with attachment and bondage. In true, profound love, there is no attempt to control or manipulate, no entanglement between the lover and the beloved. In a sacred loving relationship, genuine love stems from a very deep spiritual and energetic connection. It is one of the most beautiful connections, because the intimacy being created and experienced is beyond just physical. It touches all levels of our being: physical, emotional, mental, spiritual, and energetic. This profound love is not based on any conditions; it crosses all societal boundaries, such as age, tradition, socioeconomic background, and creed. Profound love is Divine and mystical because it is born from our true state of being and longing for ultimate truth. It is a sacred relationship dedicated to supporting each other's evolution on the spiritual path—in such a way that we want only the very best and highest for the beloved and do not harbor destructive, negative feelings. In true love, we are able to let go, uniting on a profound spiritual level. Genuine love can transcend to Divine love, a sacred relationship.

In love that comes with attachment, on the other hand, we create bondage and often hold on to what is not necessarily good for us. We all have some needs to fulfill in intimate relationships, but a sacred loving relationship will naturally and organically attend to these needs. Sacred love relationships come from the power of the energetic dynamic between the lover and the beloved; they allow each partner to abandon themselves completely in the loving, surrendering spiritual process of their relationship. Their connection is supreme; it is as if their hearts beat as one. Their love will persist no matter what and will overcome all obstacles, from passion to compassion, from compassion to ultimate Divine passion.

When two individuals who are sincere seekers on the spiritual path embark on a sacred loving relationship, detachment can be one of its most precious qualities. In detachment there is total abandonment and a surrender of self, interdependence, and the need for devotion. There is no jealousy, lust, or insecurity—only a grand sense of freedom to express a deep, expanded love that embraces the beloved as well as all living beings and life. Detachment does not remove or create a distance or separation between the loving couple. On the contrary, detachment allows a greater depth of freedom, trust, intimacy, consciousness, acceptance, and intensity. There is nothing greater than a sacred loving relationship when one is longing to be in a loving, intimate relationship. It is another powerful gateway to the Divine, to the Creator—to liberation.

Once we recognize and realize our interdependency not only with our loved ones but with all living creatures, we cannot continue to go on hurting other people, other creatures, and Mother Earth. Realizing this brings us harmony and inner peace and awakens us from the illusion of separation.

When Siddhartha Shakyamuni Gautama wandered the streets of India like a vagabond, seeking instructions for enlightenment from many teachers, he was not satisfied. He practiced six years of strict asceticism, thinking this extreme path would lead him to liberation. It was not until he meditated under the Bodhi tree that he realized the veils of illusion (maya) were tying him to the endless cycle of rebirth. He saw the interdependent links that keep one in the eternal bondage of causation (karma). When Gautama saw how everything arises based on causes and conditions, he awakened to his natural state of enlightenment. He became a buddha, an awakened one who has transcended his intellect.

Gautama the Buddha also saw how every sentient being and every phenomenon are fundamentally interconnected and interdependent, like the strands of a spiderweb. He realized that no independent existent self is real. He realized the emptiness of all phenomena, and inferred that the same links of interdependent origination also end the wheel of suffering (or *samsara*)—that countless rebirth into the physical realm of duality.

In quantum physics, the smallest known sub-particles have been broken apart, only to discover that matter is made of nothing, just as Gautama the Buddha realized more than twenty-five hundred years ago. Everything is pure energy. Yet that emptiness is filled with energetic intelligence, an ever-expanding consciousness—that universal Divine consciousness I talked about earlier.

Because a sacred loving relationship is all about self-actualization, self-realization, and liberation for the sake of well-being and happiness for all living beings, both individuals evolve together and start to expand their consciousness, awake, realize, and experience their interconnectedness and interrelatedness just as the Buddha; many other prophets, sages, saints, and ascended masters; and other buddhas have realized over so many centuries. Ultimately, there are no separations and boundaries between us, metaphysically speaking.

Having a sacred loving relationship was definitely an enormous part of my longing then, even though I did not realize it consciously at the time. I would have loved so much for Ian and me to grow into a sacred, Divine loving union. It is very rare—and a great blessing and grace—to enter into an intimate relationship and at the same time be in a Divine sacred loving relationship. Yet today it is very possible, since many more people are beginning to walk the spiritual path and/or are awakening. With our inner power of genuine intention and visualization we can attract this person into our lives.

Eleven

INTO THE ABYSS

AS THE FIRST SNOWFLAKES FELL in the winter of 1992, I was full of dread. I was not functioning well. I had put my studies on hold and fallen deeper into depression, not ready to face the holiday season. At one of my sessions with Dr. Violet I cried out, "Do you realize I'm not only mourning the loss of Ian, my lover and best friend, but also all my dreams for having a family and a life with him, and the loss of my father, and the trauma of my childhood abuse? It is such an extremely painful process to go through. My heart can't take all that suffering at once. I have been having suicidal thoughts." I wept. "I am in hell and don't know my way out."

She listened without a word.

A week before Christmas, Ian called. I agreed to have lunch. I knew it was foolish, but I still loved him. A part of my being did not believe that he did not love me. I wished we could just bring peace to each other so we could move on. He said he was going to spend the holidays at his chalet. When we hugged goodbye, I felt this would be the last time we would ever see each other. The holidays blew by, leaving me lost in darkness. A new year began.

By the week before Valentine's Day, I had plunged too deep into the abyss of severe depression; I could no longer resist my suicidal thoughts. I was beyond exhausted, and my longing to merge with God was unbearable. On February 7, I wrote a note, fed my cats, and left them extra food. I turned on the bathtub faucet and let hot water pour in. I placed a full bottle of Xanax and scotch on the rail and slipped into the tub. I lay there for several minutes; the hot water comforted my shivering, chilled bare body and soul. A presence hovered over me, enveloping my being. It was an energetic sensation that vibrated within every particle of my being.

"Dear Divine Mother, please bring me back home. I can't take this pain anymore," I whispered. I washed five pills down with nearly a quarter of the bottle of scotch. Within ten minutes, sleepy and drugged, I stumbled out of the tub, sat down on the bed, and swallowed the entire bottle of pills and the rest of the liquor. I collapsed.

It wasn't until four days later that I woke up—dazed and bleeding from my nose—at the hospital. Later, a second ambulance transported me to the recovery hospital center, where I spent the following three weeks.

During my second day there, I got a call from Dr. Violet.

"My dear Vivi, thank God you're still alive!" she said, sounding frantic. "What happened? I'm so sorry. You scared us. Your dear friend Lila came in for a session the day after your hospitalization. She was extremely disturbed and upset at you. She told me how she found you in a coma, blue, almost dead, with your arms crossed over your heart like an Egyptian queen in her sarcophagus." Dr. Violet kept going without even asking how I was doing. "I want to let you know I called Ian to tell him the news. I asked him to stop contacting you so you can let go of him. He must stop manipulating you, playing with your heart. His indecision and fears will not allow you to heal, Vivi. It would drive any woman insane. You must let him go."

I felt so dizzy and in a daze that I couldn't even think. I was just listening, feeling too drained and emptied.

Over the following three weeks of my recovery stay, I visited the facility's psychiatrist, Dr. Larose, several times for evaluation. At one of my visits I said, "I could not bear the excruciating pain. I wanted to go back home, be with the Divine Mother. My longing was killing me." While my attempt looked as if I wanted to die, I had really been trying to merge with God and be liberated from the confinement of my physical form forever. Deep down my spirit knew there was something in the beyond and wanted to fly there.

By his compassionate expression, I could tell Dr. Larose understood what I meant. He was a calm and loving presence. "Vivianne," he said, "after my evaluation, I can see you have been seriously and clinically depressed for too long. You have a chemical imbalance, my dear. Antidepressants will help you overcome these awful symptoms." He handed me a sample packet. "You can start taking these immediately."

Dr. Larose gazed intensely into my eyes and said, "Do you realize, *ma chère* Vivianne, God has given you a second chance at life? These reports say you were blue when they found you."

I continued to look at the barren trees outside the window, wondering where my spirit went while I was in the coma. "I'll take this second chance God is giving me," I murmured, wondering why I survived. The wounded part of my being still struggled with suicidal thoughts. I spoke silently to the Divine Mother while Dr. Larose talked on. *How am I going to move on with my life? Please guide me with all my steps. You have given me this second chance . . . why? I just want to go home.*

~

THE FOLLOWING DAY I WOKE up to a dazzling blue Sunday morning. I knew this day was not going to be like any other. Valentine's Day had just passed. My dear friends J.T., Jacinta, and Milo visited me that afternoon. A humble, attractive, and softhearted man, Milo radiated love and compassion for all creatures. He took care of Minoux and Pompom while I was hospitalized. My friends brought a bundle of love and an adorable teddy bear with them. Milo offered me a big chocolate heart and a bouquet of red roses.

After the three of them left, I lay back in bed, my mind emptied, eyes following the sunlight dancing through the window. I lost track of time and space. Suddenly, a supernatural warmth, an ethereal presence, nourished my being with renewed hope and strength. It was the same Divine presence and sensation I felt when I had attempted to commit suicide in the bathtub. It was as if the Divine Mother was reanimating me with new life-force energy. I could feel an extremely sweet, intoxicating presence hovering around and within my being. A blissful, serene, loving feeling surged through every particle of my being. Guidance flowed straight into my heart; a very powerful inner knowing emerged. I knew I was loved and protected and that I must move to California. These messages were so clear.

It was an otherworldly sensation like others that had touched me before, a presence I wanted to feel for the rest of my life. I felt I had arisen from the dead. The feeling that Ian had stolen my soul vanished. In this mystic moment, I was reanimated with a sense of hope.

~

AT OUR LAST MEETING, DR. Larose asked me, "Vivianne, have you forgiven yourself for what you did?"

I was surprised and did not respond. At first, I didn't realize he was referring to my suicide attempt. The truth was, I was still too shaken by all the events in my life to be able to process forgiveness toward myself in anything. I had not thought of it. Forgiving others made sense, but forgiving myself? I wondered why I should forgive myself for a failed suicide attempt. My mind was still too absorbed with overcoming my suicidal thoughts. I was still overwhelmed by a flood of intense feelings and emotions; my recovery was going to be a very long process.

Perhaps hearing Dr. Larose's question helped me reconnect with my spirituality. The process of forgiving myself would entail looking deeper, letting go of everything. Forgiving myself meant reconciling my spirit with my mind and my heart. It especially meant examining my entire life under a microscope—looking closely at my mistakes, my weaknesses, and my self-centeredness. Often self-centeredness derives from a very deep neediness. I wondered how I could take responsibility for my actions, thoughts, and words. These were my questions about forgiveness. Forgiving myself was going to be a very precious gift. On a deeper level, it meant I would have to accept and love myself in a Divine way. To do this, I would need to examine and assess the level of mastery over my being I had achieved or lacked and take a profound look and inventory of where I was and where I was headed. That was so scary, yet empowering. This was the kind of self-introspection I had resisted.

From the compassionate look in Dr. Larose's sparkling eyes, I could see he understood I needed more time to process my actions. He nodded his head. "Oh yes, Vivi, you will realize this and with time you will forgive yourself. Never forget you are a miracle, dear. Bring it to the world. Go do great things for God!"

~

ON THE DAY OF MY release, J.T. and Jacinta brought me home. When I entered my living room, my cat Minoux ran to greet me. I went outside on the back porch with him in my arms and called Pompom. She showed up at the door, purring. I fed them, made a fire, and the three of us cuddled. For a moment, lost in the flickering flames, I began to obsess about how I could try to take my life again. Then I became fully aware of what I was thinking and dropped on my knees pleading, "Oh, dear Mother, help me. Please forgive me. Fill my heart with healing, courage, strength, energy, wisdom, and serenity. Show me the path." I wept as I stared at the flames, feeling them pull me into in a meditative, trancelike state.

Then, I said, "I forgive you, Ian. I'm letting go of you now."

Later that night, I threw many of our photographs in the fire. A romantic relationship would not be the source of my future happiness and joy. True happiness and bliss would come from the joy of being, of living my true nature. I wondered how I had gotten into this mess. I had felt bliss when I was a very young child; I could remember feeling free in the St-Marie countryside. I thought this must have been what Jesus Christ meant when he said, "Let the little children come to me."

"Dear Divine Mother," I whispered, "I need to find myself, my true nature, and be that baby again. I'm so lost." The scent of the burning fire intoxicated me, reminding me that my life had changed forever. Dr. Larose's hope-filled words came to me: "You are a miracle, Vivianne. Bring it to the world! Have you forgiven yourself?" I pondered the mystical experience I had with the Divine presence and the message I received at the recovery hospital. Turning my attention inward, I could still feel the presence. I closed my eyes. "Move to California" resonated like a mantra.

I began to start the process of detaching from my life and my past, albeit slowly. My true healing would be a long journey filled with many spiritual revelations, mystical experiences, and processes. Part of my being wanted to give this physical existence another try. During the following years, I reflected on the nature of love. It took more than a year before I felt a sense of "I-ness," coming back to life, wanting to live life to its fullest and thrive.

Twelve

DISCOVERING OUR INNER GURU

IF WE ARE BLESSED ENOUGH to have the grace of a genuine and true spiritual master—or *satguru*—it would be his or her job to help us unleash our inner master. Our spirit has all knowledge, timeless wisdom, already within it because we are one with all things. When Jesus Christ said, "I and my father are one," he was alluding to our oneness, our interconnectedness, and interdependency. Siddhartha Gautama—the Buddha—and many other great beings and prophets have expressed the same message in different words befitting their own times.

Self-realization is realizing there is no self. The whole cosmos is one being. Our teacher is everywhere—in a bee, a cat, a blossoming rose, or an ocean wave. In our true essence, the Divine is enshrined within us. That awareness, that realization of our interdependency, our interconnectedness, our oneness, is by itself a transformation. On our spiritual journey, we must realize our inner guru, our divinity. Breaking free from our limitations and identifications is the infallible path to blossoming into a fragrant, intoxicating flower.

Within the intense suffering and pain I experienced through my relationship with Ian, one great blessing was that it accelerated my spiritual awakening because of the ton of karmic structure that fell away. My awakening had already begun when I was a young child, and I was able to return to it. The great Sufi poet Rumi once said, "The wailing of a broken heart is the doorway to God." A broken heart brings us to our knees with humility and surrender. This opening of the heart can become a grand majestic portal to the Divine. Every relationship, especially intimate, romantic ones, has the potential to become our teacher if we allow it. Our beloved may become one of our best teachers. Relationships and their unique dynamics allow us the opportunity to clean up some of the inner mess we have accumulated. The Divine is within us; there is no need to seek outside. Within the shrine of our heart is the supreme lover.

An intimate relationship can also be a powerful catalyst for hidden wounds to resurface. The closer, deeper, and more intimate the relationship, the more vulnerable we are. Vulnerability, too, can be a tool for growth. Some people use celibacy, work, or addictions to prevent them from being vulnerable. They hide from themselves, afraid to break free from their own limitations, wounds, and self-imposed barriers.

Unconsciously or consciously, many people are afraid of evolving, like I was. We feel too comfortable with our old ways and patterns. Change represents the unknown, and we fear what we don't know. Emotional, mental, and spiritual growth can be very painful and difficult.

Milo and I had become close friends. I loved him like a big brother. His sensitive and gentle nature toward people, the animals, and Mother Earth lit my heart. He had also suffered hardship in his youth, so we could relate and connect without judgment. Perhaps like no one else, he understood my profound sorrow and depression. I realized that Milo probably longed in his heart to be my lover and that I did not feel the same way, despite our mutual connection.

In fact, now that I was aware of the danger of falling in love with a dysfunctional man, I dated very selectively. Many suitors came along, but I only accepted a few. Even then, I always kept my distance and viewed them only as friends.

I never experienced any aversion toward myself, though I did not fully trust myself, nor could I self-medicate with another man. My heart was still possessed by Ian's ghost and my attachment to him.

One day Milo put his arms around me, pulling me close. He said, "My Vivi, you're like a wounded animal. Please let me help you. I love you so much. I am here for you."

His care, support, and friendship were beyond the call of a dear friend.

"I love you, too, dearly, Milo. You are such a wonderful and loving being. But I need time . . . a lot of time . . . to heal and find myself." Regardless of my words and actions, Milo continued to love me unconditionally.

While not fully realizing it then, I was seeking and longing for my supreme lover, for my true, Divine nature hidden within the shrine of my heart.

~

THE WEEK AFTER MY RELEASE from the hospital I returned to my part-time job at a high-end French fashion boutique. I was overqualified for it, but I needed the extra income and distraction. The position at the day spa had not worked out the way I had hoped.

Life had become a grand disillusionment. Even my attempt to escape this world had let me down. I could not find another position in the aesthetics industry unless I moved out of state. Because the skin care and spa businesses were well advanced in Florida, I had contemplated the idea that perhaps the sunshine and beaches of Florida would help heal my broken heart. But I knew now from the mystical experience at the hospital that I must to move to California, not Florida. So I sent out a powerful intention to find a good position in California and made attempts to visualize it.

The burning questions of my childhood resurfaced in rage. For months, I would drag myself out of bed, feeling so exhausted. Even part-time work depleted my system. I felt like a flower in the desert, perishing for lack of water. Every morning I would put on my sneakers and run the deserted roads of Maplewood. Jogging was something that Ian and I had often done together, and the fresh spring blooms brought painful memories of our relationship.

One day I discovered a tranquil stream in a woodsy area. From then on, I often stopped there, sat on a large rock, and listened to the birds. I meditated on the flow of the water rushing through the pebbles, losing myself in the sunlight reflecting on their ripples. The sun nourished my being. Sometimes hours would fly by without my realizing it. Time, space, and all boundaries melted away in the water's flow. My being kept searching and seeking for the Divine Mother. Even though the memories brought intense sorrow and distress, communing with the Divine and nature and breathing fresh air became my medicine. It became a powerful way to process my profound pain and let go. Letting go can be an extremely painful and long process for many people because of the karmic bondage that's still there.

I desperately longed for union with God, for liberation. My spirit cried out. This time I could hear it so clearly.

Sadhguru Jaggi Vasudev, a beautiful yogi and mystic, once said, "Liberation is not my idea; it is the fundamental longing in every form of life."* I wouldn't hear these words until years later; yet as I sat by the stream, the gushing water, singing birds, and sunlight caressing my face triggered a glimpse of hope, reminding me that life is ephemeral. Hope is a subtle yet powerful feeling. As I contemplated the fleeting nature of life as I watched the water, the disabling side effects of hopelessness and helplessness slowly disappeared. Then, a sense of inclusion overwhelmed my being.

Separation is the opposite of union, of inclusion. When one's heart longs for the Divine, it desperately longs for union with our Creator. When nothing else in the world fulfills us, our longing to merge becomes unbearable. Our spirit often cries out for liberation, yet most of us can't hear it. We do not recognize this fundamental longing within us.

My heart ached with this longing.

"I will never love again," I told our Creator. I believed I meant it.

While going through this major depression, and even during recovery, I had no sense of self. This type of identity crisis I was experiencing destroyed most of my conditioned beliefs and accumulations, if not all. Almost everything I knew about myself was dismantled, leaving me in a state of void. Everything about my childhood and my youth had been demolished. The illusion of being a certain personality with its identifications—of being Canadian, born to a Catholic family, in a female form, and my conditioning with my family—felt wiped out. I did not know who I was anymore. Though I did know one thing for sure: I did not want to spend my life in the beauty industry. I wanted to do something more meaningful. I had sought the Divine in the ephemeral pleasures of this world, but I longed for liberation.

I needed to take responsibility for my thoughts, actions, and emotions. By not being responsible toward my life, humanity, the animals, and our

* © Sadhguru

beloved planet, I was not living my life to its full potential and not using my inner divine power. I promised myself I would never give away my inner power—that intrinsic spiritual power that everyone possesses—again.

I had not heard from Ian in over four months, and I realized I did not need to be someone else or identify with any false identities to love myself or be loved. My spirit had always been eternally whole, perfect, and beautiful, because the Source created it.

My perception shifted. This new focus required great self-effort, mental and emotional strength, and positive energy. Being on a spiritual path that is all-inclusive is one of the key elements to our inner well-being and awakening. Whether or not we believe in a Creator, we need to hold a beautiful vision for the whole of humanity, nature, its creatures, and ourselves. With these new realizations and Divine grace, my false sense of self died. I burst from my chrysalis of false identity like a butterfly, reborn to a new level of awareness.

We also cannot underestimate the power of belonging. It was one of the major issues for me. Having a loving support group can provide much needed emotional, mental, and spiritual support. A *sangha*—a group of people who are walking together on the spiritual path and sharing—can be extremely important for support, healing, growth, and further expansion; for a depressed person, such a group can be the difference between life and death. While going through my severe depression, even though I had many dear friends, I still felt utterly alienated and separated. The symptoms of my depression were too powerful and overwhelming. What I desperately needed was to be walking on the spiritual path with a genuine satguru and a loving and supportive spiritual sangha. If I'd had a sangha to provide me with spiritual, emotional, and mental support, it would have helped me feel a sense of belonging and made a huge difference in my recovery.

One day, while driving in town, I saw Ian. It was a stab in my heart. Every red rose, cafe, quaint street, mutual friend, or song on the radio reminded me of him. Melancholy and unbearable loneliness settled in. Everything about this area resonated with this pain. If I was going to heal, I needed to move away as soon as possible. Every day I dreamed of California and invoked spiritual guidance on how to make my dreams become a reality.

After a few months, I got a call from my former employer. She told me that Zouzou, of the internationally known Zouzou Day Spa in Northern California, was looking for a spa director, and she had recommended me. Despite the fact I did not want to pursue my profession in this industry, I realized this could be the opportunity to move to California. I was willing to work until I was sure of my new direction and plans. I had met Mr. Zouzou, a jovial and handsome older man, at an international aesthetic trade conference in Miami years earlier and loved him and his wife. His company's renowned day spa had been one of our favorite accounts at the time. I could not believe how the celestial beings were working their magic.

In those days, I realized how awful my thought processes had been while I was struggling through this severe depression. I had not been mindful. It was almost impossible to maintain positive thoughts during that time before I had real help.

Now I began to make major changes in my thought patterns, sending nurturing and empowering thoughts toward myself. Every day I visualized my intentions and affirmed them aloud. Slowly, I became more mindful. At first it was very difficult. With patience, perseverance, awareness, and training my mind with mindfulness, the magic started to unfold, and my life began to turn around slowly.

~

EVERY LIFE CHALLENGE CAN SPUR us to our spiritual awakening. As we awaken, we begin to develop equanimity, magnanimity, and forbearance in the face of adversity and distress. As spiritual blossoming unfolds, we become more resilient. Life is transient. Our attachments, bondage, and delusions keep us in misery. In such circumstances one may ask, "How do I perceive these events and challenges in this moment? Is this the reality or just a projection? How can I bring harmony, peace, and love to a place devoid of it?" These are questions we need to ask ourselves often and learn to look at things from different perspectives. Supposedly Mahatma Gandhi once said, "Be the change you want to see in the world." I was more than willing. I longed for what seemed the impossible, but I knew that it was true. Only within the depth of your inner shrine can you know and experience the truth.

The message to go to California that I'd received in the hospital on that mystical sunny afternoon was about to manifest itself. I was still so far away from the truth, yet so close. As I prepared for my grand adventure, within my inner shrine I felt my true life beyond survival was about to begin.

Thirteen

THE BLOSSOMING OF THE HEART

I WAS DOWN TO SEVEN more big Xs on my calendar before I left New England for good. My cats felt the energy shift and enjoyed themselves by jumping from one box to the other. Over the past few days between packing, phone calls, lunches, and dinners, I hugged dear friends Jacinta, J.T., Lila, Milo, and others goodbye, feeling very grateful at how many precious friends I held in my heart. When the movers stacked the last box in their truck, butterflies palpitated in my stomach. The emptiness of the townhouse felt uncanny, sinister. It hit me. I was leaving forever.

Bluebell, a friend, had agreed to accompany me on the drive to California. We put Minoux and Pompom in the back seat, where they meowed from their carriers. I walked around one last time, standing there for a moment in the middle of the living room, overwhelmed with melancholy. I took a few deep breaths and walked away. I closed the door without looking back.

We drove away with a large map in Bluebell's hands. I listened to my favorite radio station, a swirl of memories flashing back. I became lost in long bouts of silence as I processed my emotions and feelings. Connecticut, Pennsylvania, West Virginia, Tennessee, Arkansas, and Texas passed by like a dream. Driving became part of my healing; but the more we drove, the deeper my sense of detachment felt. I was leaving my innocence behind. I was not the same person anymore, yet the essence of my being had not changed.

⌒

WHEN WE ARRIVED IN CALIFORNIA, I left Bluebell in San Francisco and headed north with my two kitty cats. While driving on the Golden Gate Bridge, I rolled down my front window for a moment, music blasting. My hair swirled up. Dozens of sleek sailboats sailed below me. "Yippee! Pompom, Minoux, we made it home! Thank you so much, Divine Mother!" I exclaimed.

Within the first week I found an adorable one-bedroom apartment located near the water in the charming town of Sausalito, less than a few miles from the Golden Gate Bridge. The building was perched on a hill with lush foliage and palm trees, and my apartment was bathed in sunlight from full-height windows overlooking San Francisco Bay.

On the day I moved in, my next-door neighbor, Iona—a lovely woman with long auburn hair, French-manicured nails, and an impeccably made-up face—walked in, smiled, and introduced herself in a rich Southern accent. "Dear," she said, "you have got to come over for a glass of chardonnay tonight. Let's celebrate your arrival!"

Later at dinner, Iona and I sat on her terrace overlooking the bay.

"Is it me or the place?" I asked her. "The energy seems lighter here. People are so open and receptive. The atmosphere is much more progressive, liberal, and spiritual. I love this free spirit, Iona!"

"Your energy, Vivi, matches Northern California!" she said, smiling. "Dear, you moved to the right place."

We laughed. I thought of Albert Einstein's words, "Great spirits have always encountered violent opposition from mediocre minds." The energy of a new place can trigger self-discovery and transformation. I felt myself transforming on the West Coast.

"Too many people—especially women—do not know how to assert their inner Divine power and are unaware of it. They allow someone else to exert power over them," I said to Iona. "I was one of them before I came here."

"I'm one of them too," Iona replied. "How can I regain my power?"

"The day we realize that we have inner Divine power is the end of other people's power over us, Iona," I said. "Our actions, our thoughts, and our words start changing. We begin to take responsibility for ourselves and stop allowing ourselves to become victims. I learned the hard way. We believe there are no other choices in our lives and make ourselves victims of our own words, emotions, and actions. There are always choices and opportunities. To see things as they are is the most difficult part, but that is the most empowering!"

Iona sighed. "Oh, Vivi, I never thought of relationships like that. Your words resonate inside." She paused in silence and sipped at her chardonnay.

After a moment, I raised my glass for a toast. "I feel free from Ian's domination and control. I've rediscovered my inner power, my authenticity of being. There is nothing like it. I love it, Iona! To our power!"

~

IT IS NATURAL TO WANT some measure of power in life. Certainly we want mastery over ourselves, but those who crave dominating power—power over others—seem to be those who are most powerless, insecure, and separated from our Creator. These power struggles may arise from a primal instinct to survive; dominate; and reign over other humans, animals, and Mother Earth; but this kind of power is destructive and archaic. It creates the illusion of separation.

Even power is an illusion. Our ultimate nature is naturally powerful because of its true essence. Inner power originates from the Divine. This inner power can only stem from the most profound expression of our spirit, from a stable emotional and mental state, with mindful and acute clarity. If we are willing and allow it to, our true nature will lead the way for healthy interactions based on mutual love, compassion, understanding, and equality. Inner power is expressed with loving, compassionate feelings for co-creation, cooperation, realization of our interdependence, and interconnectedness along with a reverence for all life forms. It is within all of us. Rediscovering this intrinsic, Divine power became one of my most important realizations.

Over centuries we have witnessed how the patriarchal system, a model of domination and control over other humans (women in particular) and animals, has caused tremendous suffering. It has destroyed lands, civilizations, people, and animals. Unfortunately, this patriarchal system is still ingrained in our psyche. We can still observe it in governments, civilizations, and even in relationships.

Consciously or unconsciously, this false sense of power is about conquering, annihilating, possessing, winning, and exploiting. How can we deny the deplorable effects of patriarchy over the centuries, when evidence everywhere proves them? Ask yourself: What kind of power do I exert in my life? What kind of power do people exert around me? How do they affect us? How do I affect them? We humans are the only animals on earth with the power to lock ourselves in our own fabricated jail, or to liberate ourselves instead. What do we choose: destruction, or creation?

~

NOT LONG AFTER I MOVED, I discovered the San Francisco Bay Area was filled with many eclectic artist communities. That August I attended the exuberant Sausalito Art Festival and its grand gala. A dear friend from New England flew in to visit. Together we dressed up and danced to the music of the Earth, Wind & Fire band until our feet hurt. The following day we returned to the art festival, strolled along the narrow paths filled with colorful canvases, intriguing sculptures, and mixed-media arts. The artist within me cried out, but my pencils and paintbrushes continued to accumulate cobwebs in the closet.

The months passed, and the California sunshine continued to exude hope and joy. I loved waking up to the bay view and the chirping sparrows while Pompom and Minoux lay on my chest purring their love songs. When I got the blues, I strolled along the bay in downtown Sausalito, conversed with the seals, seagulls, and pigeons, and fed them seeds and bread. I still felt lonely and melancholic. I was three thousand miles away from Ian, yet he continued to invade my mind and my heart. Sorrow could still overwhelm me. I attracted many potential lovers, but I was determined to stay single until I was healed and could find the appropriate lover.

A year later I joined a popular dating service. I became bored with it. On the last day of my membership, however, I decided to meet one last man—Joseph, a gregarious older gentleman who worked in music promotion at a record company and lived in the Los Angeles area. He was visiting San Francisco and wanted to take me out for dinner at a popular vegetarian restaurant.

Initially, I told him I could not meet him.

"Why?" he asked. "You don't want to see me?"

I was embarrassed to tell him I had just had a small chemical peel underneath my eyelids done at the day spa to test the skills of a potential colleague. The peel was shedding. I was not allowed to wear makeup and had to apply a thick layer of white cold cream underneath my eyes at all times. Going out slathered with cold cream would feel like walking naked down Fifth Avenue. But in the end, I decided to challenge my limitations.

When I met Joseph, he scooped off some of the thick cold cream with his finger, put it underneath his eyes, and declared, "Now we are equal!" Over dinner looking out at the bay, we laughed all night. Even though I didn't feel a romantic interest in him, I knew we would be good friends.

After dinner Joseph insisted I join him to meet a few of his dear friends, Nathaniel and Marigold. They invited us to their home for a glass of wine. Marigold showed me around the house. After the tour, she chatted in the living room with Joseph while I stood by the counter in the kitchen conversing with her husband, Nathaniel. Nathaniel looked like a movie star with his defined cheekbones and piercing hazel-green eyes. He was forty-nine years old but looked more like thirty-something, a handsome man with thick, black, wavy hair accented by a dash of silver. He exuded such an energetic aura; it pulled my spirit. His vibrant and high-energy personality thrilled me. But there was a fifteen-year age difference between us—and he was married.

"You look like a little raccoon, Vivi. So adorable! How long have you been in California?" Nathaniel asked as he pulled two wine glasses from the cabinet. I noticed the emblem logo and words printed on them.

"Over a year and a half." I pointed to the emblem. "I have been to that event. I loved it!"

"Thank you, Vivi. It's one of my events. I'm the executive producer."

As we continued to chat, our eyes met, and intoxicating bubbles of love soared in my heart. I blushed and turned my head away, wondering why, when I finally met the first man in California I felt attracted to, he was taken?

~

ON A THURSDAY EARLY EVENING just before April Fools' Day, my friend Mandara invited me to a cocktail party. "It's tomorrow evening at a restaurant opening," she said. "There will be a lot of cute guys there."

When we entered the restaurant the next day, it was so crowded we could barely move. Shafts of sunlight shone through its dozen skylights, making the tiny gold stars on my white tailored dress scintillate.

"So, where's my prince?" I whispered to Mandara. We giggled, grabbed two glasses of chardonnay, and enjoyed a few vegetarian dumplings. The restaurant was a blazing green, manmade jungle around us.

And then, suddenly, there was Nathaniel. He was sitting at the bar talking with an elderly gentleman.

I approached them casually. "Hi, Nathaniel, do you recognize me without the cold cream?"

"Vivi! How could I forget you? What happened to your raccoon face?"

Nathaniel and I engaged in an intense conversation for the rest of the evening. He had gotten separated after almost eleven years of marriage. He wanted to go to couple's therapy with Marigold, but she did not want to, so his marriage was over. As the hours passed, we moved on to other subjects— philosophy, culture, the universe, the Divine, love, relationships, traveling, and animals. The more we talked, the more our energy sparked and connected. Our noses almost touched; we could feel each other's breath.

The party was dying out when Mandara returned. Nathaniel and I were utterly taken with one another. From a few feet away, she tried to get our attention. Finally, she jumped right in between us.

"Whoa!" she said. "I think you guys have just met your match! Your energy!"

Nathaniel and I grinned.

Shortly after that, we began dating. Then, I grabbed my sketchbook and started to draw again. Over the months that followed, my life took on a joyous routine: my daily eight o'clock step aerobics class, then work as a consultant at the fine art gallery, classes at San Francisco State University, and time with my loving, supportive boyfriend. I threw my bottle of anti-depressants in the garbage.

In June of 1996, almost four years after the nightmare with Ian, Nathaniel and I stood in front of an enormous fountain in the romantic front garden of a hacienda resort and committed to one another in front of a small group of our closest friends and relatives. The fragrance of hundreds of roses added to our joy. I cried as I recited our personal vows. Jacinta, my matron of honor, also sobbed loudly.

After Nathaniel recited the last few words of his, we released two white doves into the sky. The lovebirds flew and then perched side-by-side on a branch of a giant oak tree, looking down at us. All eyes were focused on them, and everyone sighed and their eyes filled with tears. At the altar, hundreds of rose petals rained down on us. The professional dove trainer released a cloud of white doves from a large basket, and the beautiful birds flew back home in the sunlight.

~

TWO YEARS LATER, NATHANIEL AND I were looking for a new home. One day, we walked into a bright house overflowing with sunlight. I felt transported; it was the home I'd envisioned for myself when I first moved to California. We bought it, and I was thrilled.

I was about to settle in my fine art studio when I realized our home needed a facelift. Our budget was tight, so I decided to paint and decorate it myself. I worked on nearly every room, creating faux finishes on the walls.

On the last day of my task, I fell down the stairs, face forward, on my way to pick up the mail. I felt a pinch in my lower back but nothing more. Over the following week, however, my back began to hurt. Several well-intentioned friends recommended I see a chiropractor. My intuition told me that this was a dangerous move, but I decided to give it a try.

After being yanked and twisted like dough three times that week, I was pouring water into the birdbath one day when a sudden pain crawled up my lower back. I curved forward, immobilized.

"Baby?" I called. "I can't get back up."

Nathaniel ran out and held me by the arm, but I could barely walk. Excruciating pain radiated to various parts of my body.

A few weeks later, a scan at the orthopedist's revealed two herniated discs. The doctor recommended complete bed rest for one month. He told me it might take more than that before I would be able to move around comfortably. This meant no sitting—the worst thing for a back injury, he said. My studio and all my creative sparks had to be put on hold. I wished I had listened to my intuition and not gone to that chiropractor. All that twisting must have severely aggravated the herniated disks.

Misfortune always has the potential to be a blessing, depending on perception and surrender. Complete surrender is the ultimate healer; it reveals the magic of living in serenity and blissfulness. Only when you allow yourself to surrender to the Divine will your spirit fly beyond the blue sky.

I was forced to surrender. I was now completely dependent. I could not walk by myself. For the first week, Nathaniel helped me out of bed to go to the bathroom. My sister Rose flew to California and cared for me for three weeks. The physical pain overwhelmed me and left my being feeling extremely vulnerable. But soon my heart began to blossom in unexpected ways.

Staring at the ceiling for hours at a time, I could see little skeletons flashing in front of my eyes. They were the bones of underprivileged people and homeless cats, dogs, cows, and other animals; they were all starving to death in remote areas around the world. Overwhelmed by these intense images, I began to cry; I felt as if their misery throbbed in my own heart. I was overwhelmed with a wave of Divine love and compassion toward all living beings. This new heightened sense of sensitivity, awareness, and boundlessness permeated every fiber of my being.

I spent hours lost in profound self-introspection wondering about the meaning of this vision. As if it were a spiderweb, I could see our interconnectedness and how fragile and ephemeral our physical existence is. An epiphany arose—that what I had been seeking was to know the truth, to self-realize my true nature, to experience dimensions beyond the physicality of this realm, and also to express my Divine nature in overflowing compassion in my actions toward all living beings.

After I recovered many months later, I had become so much more sensitive, loving, and compassionate toward the suffering and pain of other people and animals. Something profound had shifted within my being, though I could not tell what that metaphysical something was. I only knew that my heart was blossoming in an infinite wave, and my being was experiencing an expansion of consciousness.

Fourteen

TUNING IN TO THE DIVINITY WITHIN

THE TWENTY-FIRST CENTURY DAWNED WITH a massive and collective paradigm shift in consciousness. Nathaniel and I loved to globe-trot. In January 2000, as in many years before, we flew to Puerto Vallarta, Mexico, for a dose of vitamin D.

On our last few days there, Nathaniel asked me, "Baby, how would you like to stay longer on the beach on our last day?"

"Yes! Absolutely!" I replied. "I want to see the sunset! Can we change our tickets to a later flight?"

Our original tickets were on Alaska Airlines flight #261. Only Alaska Airlines flights #261 and #258 were scheduled to return to San Francisco that day, so Nathaniel switched our tickets to flight #258, which was scheduled to leave one and a half hours later.

That evening, as we rode in the taxi on the way to the airport, I began to feel an intense, unpleasant sensation in my solar plexus, as if something catastrophic was going to happen. I wondered why. As we took off on flight #258, I sat in silence, haunted by an eerie feeling. Apprehension lingered in my heart. For the following hour, I lost myself in the vastness of the pink sky, gazing out through the tiny window, falling deeper into a meditative state. I envisioned a blue light circling around our plane and invoked the Divine for protection. *Was our plane about to fall into the Pacific Ocean?* I knew something tragic was happening or about to happen, but I did not know what.

When we reached the San Francisco airport, our plane circled for over forty-five minutes before landing. I could not wait to touch the ground, kiss the earth. I held Nathaniel's hand tightly. He appeared unaware of the strange energy in the air. As we landed, I was still wrapped in a contemplative silence.

"Passenger alert," the captain announced somberly. "Dozens of journalists and TV reporters are waiting outside the gates. We lost flight #261."

Before deplaning, I walked into the cockpit and asked, "What do you mean the plane is lost, Captain?"

He looked at me with a sorrowful expression and repeated, "The plane is lost." He kept saying it, like a broken record. I thought perhaps he meant the plane was lost somewhere in the sky.

We walked to the customs area to pick up our bags. The entire room was silent. While we waited, a woman who had been whispering on a phone hung up and exclaimed loudly, "Everyone died! All eighty-eight of them. The plane crashed into the Pacific Ocean. It's all over the news. My mother just told me."

Her words penetrated every cell of my being. In that instant, I realized it was the victims' energy, their cries, that I'd felt during our flight. My hands trembled, and my heart felt crushed.

One of the agents pointed to an exit door, "There is a private gateway if you wish to escape the crowd and the reporters."

Nathaniel turned and whispered, "Hey baby, do you feel good enough to go through the regular gate?" I nodded my head yes, although I was shaking inside.

We passed through the gate. As soon as we emerged, some of our dear friends came running toward us and hugged us. They had heard about the tragedy and were not sure if we were still alive. Moments later a flock of microphones, TV cameras, and tape recorders swirled around us. One journalist asked me, "How does it feel to be alive, miss?"

"I feel so incredibly grateful and blessed," I choked out. *We were supposed to be on the flight that crashed. How did we escape death?*

I felt as if I was having an out-of-body experience. In this altered state of consciousness, everything I saw, felt, touched, and heard was intensified. My usual way of perceiving the world had shattered, leaving my being in a lighter, expanded state. Something mystical had occurred. I didn't fully understand. It was beyond logic.

I learned never to doubt my sixth sense. There is a huge, though subtle, difference between fear and intuition. That day, I learned to make the distinction. Intuition comes suddenly as an inner knowing and bypasses our five senses. Often fears are what keep the mind chattering.

When we arrived home, Nathaniel insisted on opening a special bottle of French champagne to celebrate our survival. He wanted to watch the news. We sat, like kids, on our bedroom floor, leaning against our bed.

"Here's a toast to celebrate life, baby!" Nathaniel said. We clicked glasses.

"To all the people who perished and to their families," I added, feeling overwhelmed with gratitude. "May they always be in peace."

The next morning, we soaked in our outdoor hot tub and reflected. I felt frozen in an eternal moment: the trees were greener, the sky bluer, the air purer—even the birds sang sweeter. My sensations were still intensified and acute. Nathaniel did not seem affected. I couldn't understand how he was seemingly so fine with how narrowly we'd escaped a plane crash. I didn't judge Nathaniel for this; maybe he was touched in a subtle way. Everyone grows and evolves at different rhythms for reasons that may remain unknown.

Later that day I read the headlines. Alaska Airlines flight #261 was considered a major aviation tragedy. The plane crashed into the Pacific Ocean about 2.7 miles north of Anacapa Island, California. Most of the passengers on board were Alaska Airlines employees and their family members who had been vacationing in Puerto Vallarta.

How could I explain the mystery of tuning in to their energies in transit? Every day, I spent time on my knees in the tiny sanctum I had created in our living room. I could not understand how I could be grieving over this for so long, while at the same time I felt serene, grateful, and blessed to be alive. I uncontrollably vacillated from bliss to mourning. The experience had put me in a state of spiritual urgency, perhaps even emergency. Even though Nathaniel and I were not part of the tragedy, it had opened up a part of my being, creating an intense spiritual crisis.

This life-transforming experience became, in some ways, a spiritual process that propelled my being forward. Everything I did thereafter was in pursuit of truth, in a search for self-realization.

That year I started to realize, feel, and experience an expansion of consciousness that I call "the light of Oneness." It taught me how we, all living beings, are interdependent, interrelated, and interconnected by the same thread of Divine love, intelligence, and truth. We come from and return to the same Source—something I already knew on an intellectual level but had never truly experienced before I connected with the energies of those lost at sea.

Most of us live in a protective bubble wrapped in the limited perceptions of our five senses and governed by the limitations we have set for ourselves. This apparent physical reality is often mistaken for reality. Too many of us are still enslaved by our fabricated belief systems, our limited minds and perceptions, and ignorance of our true, ultimate nature.

How often do we make ourselves miserable because of our relentless demands and unfulfilled desires? How can we perceive a dimension beyond the physical realm unless we tune in, connect, and become aware of oneness?

I discovered that if I stayed open, receptive, and sensitive to all life, as happened in my bed rest vision, then I was aware of all creatures' suffering and more. The alchemy of transformation burned inside my being. When Divine love flowed through my heart, I experienced bliss, serenity, and compassion toward all living beings. I wanted to feel Divine love flowing permanently, but had no idea how that might come about.

My fears and desires arose from my ignorance of my true nature. Like many people, I was still enslaved by my own creations, attachments, and desires. We create our karma with our thoughts, words, and actions. Like a music composer, the personal song we compose can either be cacophony or melody, but its form depends on us.

The plane crash tragedy moved my being to search for something beyond the physical. I did not have a spiritual master then, nor was I reading books on the subject; yet even so, the process of breaking free from my personal bubble, of my false sense of enslavement, was beginning. The veil was collapsing. More old ideas, belief systems, fears, desires, and conditioned patterns started to dissolve. My attachment to false identity, especially the body and my mind, which prevented me from freeing myself, was weakening. I was awakening and realizing natural enlightenment.

Our physical body is just a garment. Our mind gives us the illusion we are separated from our Creator. In the act of shedding our conditioned accumulations from our past, we realize our true nature. It is like peeling an artichoke to reach the heart.

I could no longer rely on my five senses to experience the truth, nor did I want to be told any longer what to do or what was true by my family, religion, the media, or other authorities. We are conditioned by the beliefs we form in our youth; and the accumulation of these thought patterns and perhaps even brainwashing in certain cases may activate within us compulsions and unconscious mindsets. I had to explore what was true on my own. But it seemed the more I learned, the less I knew and understood. Nothing made sense anymore, yet everything seemed to make perfect sense.

A mystic is a person who seeks by contemplation and surrender to obtain unity with the absolute, a person who knows the spiritual truth beyond the intellect. A mystic taps into the Divine cosmic energy, experiencing life and the beyond. I wondered if I was becoming a mystic as I opened up to these visions and realizations.

All my recent traumatic life events had left me beyond thirsty to experience our Creator. I needed a genuine, living, enlightened master who knew the roadblocks on the spiritual path, someone who is called a satguru in the Yoga tradition. I wondered where I would find such a being of light and wisdom on earth.

When I went back to painting in my studio, I was surprised to witness how this process of breaking free affected my whole being. Overnight, my art transformed. My flow of creativity became stronger than myself. Without knowing anything about the spiritual Yoga tradition, I started to express profound yogic knowledge. Everything shifted in my art: the content, the color, and the style. It looked as if it had been painted by a different artist. What was most fascinating were the messages in my work. My art started to communicate on a spiritual, psychological, and metaphysical level about the human spirit, self-realization, identity, and evolution. It unconsciously attempted to demystify what seemed to be reality and truth . . . beyond the veil.

This new direction reflected my inner search for the Source and liberation. I often painted in silence, letting the spirit and energy flow through my being. My greatest inspirations became the Divine Mother, the Yoga tradition, the psyche, Eastern thought, and the life force that manifests and permeates creation.

One day as I splashed orange, red, blue, and violet oil on my canvas, I realized I was shedding my old skin like a snake. A shift of consciousness was manifesting within my core.

During this time, Nathaniel returned from a business trip with an unusual CD for me, *Buddha-Bar,* a collection of eclectic international music. I played it while working in my studio; and to my surprise, many of the songs uplifted my being to blissfulness. Even though I had never formally meditated before or heard Sanskrit chants in this lifetime, when I painted, I abandoned myself in this creative process, connecting deeply to the Divine energy as if I had heard them in a past life.

"Gururbrahmaa, gururvishnu, gururdevo . . ." chants Jai Uttal in one of the songs on the CD. In English: "My salutations to the guru (who dispelled darkness) who is Brahma, Vishnu, and Maheswara. The guru is Parabrahma incarnate." The satguru (enlightened guide) personifies the Divine in its highest physical form.

I had never heard this kind of music, and it was in Sanskrit; and yet the words flew out of my mouth as if I had chanted it thousands of times before. I was surprised, but I kept singing it with all my heart as my hands reached out for the Divine Mother with my paintbrush. Tears rolled down my face, neck, and chest as I expanded in an ecstatic state. I could not comprehend what powerful thing was happening. Each time I chanted, the same energetic sensations of pure love—a kind of loving energy that reminded me of childhood experiences—pierced my heart. Many years later I discovered the song incorporated some of the most important verses of the Guru Pooja, an ancient Sanskrit chant and ritual revering the lineage of ascended masters, starting with the root, the *Adiyogi* (first yogi) and first guru named Shiva. Chanting and performing the Guru Pooja with a devotional reverence, openness, and receptivity invites immense possibilities in accessing the energy of these great beings of light.

Creative expression through music, dancing, painting, crafting, and writing can be of immense value for healing, well-being, self-actualization, and self-realization. It is by creating that we emulate and invite the Divine feminine energy to flow through us. Painting became my spiritual ritual and meditation, an offering to the Divine Mother. My artistic work became a journey into the realm of the unknown, as well as a rediscovery.

His Holiness Sri Sri Ravi Shankar, a beautiful spiritual master and the founder of the Art of Living Foundation, says, "Enlightenment is like a joke! Like a fish in the ocean searching for the ocean.... Enlightenment is the very nucleus of our being; going to the core of our self and living our life from there."[1]

Can enlightenment be that simple? Our mind tells us it is the most difficult thing on our planet. After my major back injury and the Alaska Airlines crash, I realized any major life crisis, disaster, or tragedy can be a phenomenal spiritual process that can propel us on a journey of enlightenment. Still, I wondered what enlightenment was, if it even existed. The more I intellectually sought the truth, the more truth seemed a paradox. The truth needs to be experienced.

Scientists tell us everything is made up of energy that vibrates at different frequencies. Every particle of this manifested universe is made of the same energy, but not everything vibrates at the same frequency. Some scientists realize that at the core, science is spirituality. Quantum theory says the tiniest subatomic particle of the universe is energy. Metaphysically speaking, we are the waves of one cosmic ocean of energy, and we all breathe the same breath.

"Seek the kingdom of God first, and everything else shall come," Jesus Christ said. I knew intuitively that tuning in to the divinity within would connect my being to all living beings at the source. I started to understand how my suffering originated from my ignorance, my distorted mind, and the illusion that I was separated from our Creator. As Ramana Maharishi once said, "God is within yourself. Dive within and realize. God, Guru, and the Self are the same."

My being cried for expansion and boundlessness. One night I pulled out my journal. In it I had written my number one goal: to grow spiritually. I had no clue what that meant or how to get there. Religion was not my plan. In my heart I knew when one becomes passionate for the Divine, one opens their heart to all of creation, breaking down barriers and limitations. All religious, political, ethnic, socioeconomic, mental, and emotional walls may dissolve. That is the power of Divine love, our inner power. I had experienced glimpses of its bliss and wanted more.

Fifteen

DISCOVERING THE SCIENCE OF YOGA

ONE DAY I FORGOT TO bring my book to the gym, so I browsed the basket at the club for a magazine. I shuffled through what was there and pulled out *Yoga Magazine*, the leading international journal on all things yoga. It looked interesting.

An hour later, still on the exerciser, I was fascinated. I felt like I had discovered something ancient and sacred I had always known: the science of yoga. It rekindled a desire within my being to make yoga a part of my life. I was determined to start practicing the following day in a hatha yoga class.

In my first session, my spirit flew into a meditative state to the sound of haunting music. I loved being in this state of equanimity. When I lay on the floor in *savasana,* the corpse pose of relaxation, the pose offered at the end of a class, my body melted away. It is extremely hard for most people to let go and just be. Corpse pose allows us to practice being dead to our false identities by letting our ultimate nature be.

Lying on the floor with my eyes closed, not only did all the stress and tension dissipate, but I felt present and tranquil, like a pond in the moonlight. I sensed hatha yoga was only the appetizer to a grand spiritual feast.

~

THE SANSKRIT WORD "YOGA" LITERALLY means "yoke," to unite. This union aims to dissolve, liberate, and unite oneself with the pure consciousness often referred to as the Source, the Self, the Absolute, God, Brahma, Creator, Divine Mother, or hundreds of other names. I love to refer to our Creator as the Divine Mother. When the rishis (ancient sages) talked about *moksha* (or mukthi), the ultimate fruit of yoga, they referred to liberation from the endless cycle of rebirth, pain, and suffering in the physical realm.

Yoga is the science of union and the knowledge of the spine (related to the "kundalini" knowledge). So yoga is the union with the Divine in all its forms. Figuratively speaking, we can be in a state of yoga in every moment of our lives as we inhale and exhale.

Today we are witnessing a renaissance of this tradition, with yoga studios everywhere. Yet this trend is far from the genuine ancient and authentic yoga taught by the rishis for God-realization and liberation. Unfortunately, in the Western hemisphere many people still think of yoga as twisting one's body into some kind of knot. Yoga goes far beyond exercise. It is an extremely rich and powerful spiritual path that involves body, mind, and spirit. As the revered sage Patanjali expounded in the yoga sutras thousands of years ago, hatha yoga prepares one's body and mind for deep meditation.

This fascinating and ancient science of yoga is not a religion or a philosophy. Yoga does not fall into any category of an "ism." Faith is not a requirement. You will still get many benefits even if you don't believe in it. Yoga is a science. Anyone can test it and see the proof by having direct experiences with the Divine. However, to test it fairly, it is important to have the appropriate spiritual master, a satguru, at the right time. A spirit of inquisitiveness, patience, perseverance, and discipline is required to thrive on the yogic path. If one has longing and devotion for knowing the truth, success will surely come. In the Yoga tradition, the satguru or *sadhguru* is regarded as the highest embodiment of the Divine. It is with the grace and guidance of this true and genuine master that one reaches the highest state of ecstasy and liberation.

Yoga was brought from India by the popular pioneer and yogi Swami Vivekananda, one of the most revered yogis and spiritual masters of the nineteenth century, a close devotee of the highly reputable and well-known mystic, saint, and enlightened master Paramahansa Ramakrishna. Swami Vivekananda introduced yoga to the West when he came to America in 1893. He represented India as a delegate at the Parliament of World

Work
away. info

Religions in Chicago. That day brought a great boon to the Western hemisphere. Thereafter, Vivekananda conducted hundreds of public and private classes and lectures disseminating yoga in America and in Europe.

A few decades later, Paramahansa Yogananda set foot on American soil and went on to disseminate the knowledge of yoga in the West, especially *kriya* yoga, the yoga of mastering energy.

According to the ancient rishis and Sadhguru Jaggi Vasudev, a phenomenal being of light, the Adiyogi (also known as the Adiguru) was the first yogi and supreme guru. He appeared more than ten thousand years ago in the upper region of the Himalayas at Mount Kailash and transmitted the science of yoga and the power of self-realization and liberation to the first seven mystical sages (rishis) to help expand and transform human consciousness to a higher state of vibration. Sadhguru says, "The methods and technologies of how to experience that which is beyond the physical is what is known as the science of yoga."*

Predating all religious traditions, these seven rishis, known as the Saptarishis, spread yoga over Mother Earth. In the Yoga tradition, the personal form of "Shiva" is revered as the Adiyogi and guru, from which the lineage of gurus descended.

Over the centuries, yoga spread and infiltrated into many different traditions, and new branches of yoga developed. By the grace of the Adiyogi, today six major yoga branches have emerged: *Hatha* yoga (forceful) is the most familiar branch to Westerners; *Bhakti* (devotion-love); *Jnana* (right knowledge); *Raja* (royal), in which *Kriya* yoga falls; *Karma* (selfless action); and *Tantra* yoga (continuity) remains to be explored by many millions of seekers. "Kriya" from Sanskrit means "completed action," and the ultimate action of kriya yoga is to transform and master the energy. The words *yogi* (male) and *yogini* (female) designate those who experience the oneness of this phenomenal existence.

Spirituality means experiencing existence beyond the physical dimension of reality. Most people are trapped and limited within their five senses. As long as we continue to identify ourselves with the physical realm, we will remain caught in its boundaries. This creates the illusion of separation. As Jesus Christ said, "We are in this world, but not of it."

* © Sadhguru

~

IN THE SPRING OF 2000, Nathaniel and I decided to visit dear friends on the East Coast. While there I decided to take a class at the well-known Jivamukti Yoga Center in New York City. I invited Nathaniel to join me, but he said, "Yoga is not my thing."

So I jumped in a yellow cab to liberation on my own. When I entered the studio, I felt right at home. I loved the energy and all the tiny altars with candles, incense, statues of Buddha, Shiva, Krishna, and many other great beings of light. I revered all the framed photographs of well-known saints and ascended masters. After class, I tingled with bubbles of joy.

On my way out, I saw a single copy of the *Autobiography of a Yogi* by Paramahansa Yogananda. This classical saga is a poignant, personal account of Yogananda in search of his satguru. Later, I discovered his book brought thousands, if not millions, of seekers to the spiritual path. My inner voice told me, "Buy it now. You are ready for it." I had no idea this gem would propel me into the greatest adventure of my life.

I caught a cab and soon noticed the driver's words were muffled and hard to understand. I stretched my head closer and saw a tracheotomy tube protruding from his throat that enabled him to breathe. He related his story of lung and throat cancer caused by smoking. *What would I do if I ever got cancer?* I wondered. The thought terrified me. I shared my story about the Alaska Airlines plane crash with him, and we marveled at the great mystery of life. I rolled down a window and took a few deep breaths. "Ah! Breath is so precious and divine. It's the bridge between infinity and earth!" I exclaimed.

When he dropped me in front of our hotel, he said, "Goodbye, my angel. God bless you. Keep on breathing for me."

I smiled and said, "Stay well, my dear friend. God bless you too."

On the plane going back home, I read half of the *Autobiography of a Yogi*. I felt my sessions with yoga and this insightful book reconnected me with my beloved yogic spiritual path, which I had pursued in other lifetimes. A profound reverence for Shiva and all ascended masters' lineage and to Mahavatar Babaji Gorakhnath, also known as Shiv-Goraksha Babaji who revived kriya yoga in the nineteenth century, filled my heart.

"Shiv-Goraksha Babaji is regarded as a manifestation of Lord Shiva himself and the founder of the Nath Tradition," says Yogiraj Gurunath Siddhanath.[1] Something eternal inside my being knew yoga had a boundless, empowering divine force to transmit the truth to those who are receptive, open, and willing.

Once home, I signed up for a correspondence course of Paramahansa Yogananda's nonprofit organization, the Self-Realization Fellowship. It would take approximately ten months to complete before I would be initiated into kriya yoga. I spent countless nights reading until the wee hours every book I could find on his teaching. Even though Yogananda left his body through *mahasamadhi* in 1952, when I stared into his radiant eyes on his book cover I felt a profound connection.

$\mathcal{S}$ixteen

SAYING GOODBYE

EVEN THOUGH JOY BURST IN my heart with the practice of hatha yoga, I was also filled with a deep sadness to have to say goodbye to my beloved cat Pompom. I took her to the vet, and she was given a diagnosis of advanced liver cancer. I decided not to inflict any toxic treatments on her and to let her go with her dignity.

As the day of our last goodbye approached, she became a small pile of bones. She was not perky anymore and had not been eating. It had been almost eighteen years since the day we connected at the animal shelter. She did not seem ready to go, nor did she appear in pain. Every morning I took her in my arms, danced with her, and whispered love songs in her ears. My heart bled for her, but I could not find the courage to let her go.

One night Nathaniel and I were in the living room listening to music when Pompom stood gazing at something in front of her. Her gaze looked so radiant and beautiful. Anyone who had seen her would have detected a mystical aura around her. I could feel the Divine energy. After a while she padded away.

I had been reading *The Tibetan Book of Living and Dying* for weeks, preparing Pompom and myself for her departure.

The day I felt she was ready, I called our veterinarian. When he arrived at our home, I put Pompom on the island in our kitchen. I whispered to her as tears rolled down my face, "Pompom, you have been one of my greatest friends. How could I ever show you my gratitude? I will always love you. Go with the Divine." She could not stand up anymore, yet she turned her feeble head and looked at me with a loving light in her eyes.

Our vet assured us he would use the most humane way to euthanize her. Nathaniel stood next to me, his hand on my shoulder. I had never made a decision to put down an animal companion, and I struggled with it. The doctor gave her a tranquilizer, and then slowly injected a lethal serum into her vein. Her tiny head lay down.

In a flash, a blissful loving energy penetrated my heart. Pompom's spirit was passing through it. I could feel her energetic presence going straight through my heart chakra. I had never felt anything like it before. Pompom's subtle essence caressed my heart with Divine love, inducing a serene and blissful state.

I wrapped Pompom in her blanket and placed her on the floor of our sanctum. Within minutes, Minoux came and smelled Pompom's lifeless body. He stood there for a long time next to her, mourning in his own way.

I called to the Divine and called upon Paramahansa Yogananda to come get her. With my eyes closed, I saw a vision of a form smiling at me with Pompom in its arms. I felt their love radiate in my heart, embracing my spirit. One could think it was my imagination, but the pain in my heart went away. They vanished in a blaze of light. That night I slept with Pompom's body by my side one last time.

The following morning, Nathaniel and I conducted a funeral. In our front yard where the birdbath stood by a big rock, I placed a few lit candles, incense, a picture of us with Pompom, and a picture of Yogananda. Minoux stood by the grave while Nathaniel dug a hole. It began to rain. He put a large umbrella over our altar and Minoux. This area became our kitty graveyard. I placed Pompom's wrapped body in her favorite blanket and then in the hole and put our photo on top. I said, "We wish and bless you with peace, joy, and the highest rebirth."

Nathaniel shoveled a pile of soil over her body. Minoux remained there quietly. In that moment, I realized once more how ephemeral this physical life is, how we are made of Mother Earth's elements, and how eventually our physical bodies must return to her. One day we will all be free of the confinement of our decaying bodies, as our spirits fly away to the Source.

Self-realization is realizing there is no self. Enlightenment is boundless, like the wind in the blue sky and the beautiful flower in full bloom. Everyone can enjoy and benefit from the intoxicating fragrance. You need only be receptive and open.

$\mathcal{S}$eventeen

EMBRACING YOGA

IN SANSKRIT, "GU" MEANS DARKNESS and "ru" means dispeller. Thus, a "guru" is a dispeller of darkness that helps to remove the veil of ignorance.

"Of all the teachers," writes Dr. Georg Feuerstein, "God-realized adepts are even today given a special place in Hindu society, for they alone are capable of initiating the spiritual seeker into the supreme 'knowledge of the Absolute' (brahma-vidya). They alone are sadh-gurus (satgurus)—'teachers of the Real' or 'true teachers.' Here, the Sanskrit word *sat* connotes both 'real' and 'true.' These teachers are celebrated as potent agents of grace."[1]

A satguru is a fully enlightened person whose sole life purpose is to initiate the seeker in a relationship of *guru-shishya* (teacher-disciple). Satgurus have special mystical powers (*siddhis*) including the ability to transmit *shaktipat*, cosmic energy called *shakti*, to seekers. The ultimate goal of a satguru is to awaken the guru within the seeker and empower the individual to liberation (moksha), the supreme goal. It is the satguru who dispels ignorance for enlightenment, chaos for peace, gross for subtle, separation for unity, finite for infinity, individualism for oneness, bondage for freedom, and misery for bliss.

The satguru is abundant in energy, light, wisdom, knowledge, bliss, ecstasy, and consciousness. As Sadhguru Jaggi Vasudev explains, "A guru is someone who dispels the darkness in you. You can call him a light bulb if you want."*

The living spiritual master is an instrument of our Creator. He or she will empower seekers by helping individuals overcome delusion and

* © Sadhguru

bringing clarity. Satgurus are divine oceans of love who show sincere seekers how to access their own inner divinity, master energy, and help free
themselves from bondage. But to reap the benefits, seekers must be trusting
and ready to abandon preconceived ideas when they dive into this boundless sea of Divine love. One has to be ready to be torn apart and for the
accumulated personality to be demolished. The master–disciple relationship
is a very fascinating one, unlike any other relationship in the world. It is one
of the most precious and mysterious relationships on earth.

Longing is the cry of the soul that deeply yearns for the Divine and liberation. After Pompom's death, for the first time I consciously wished and
longed for a true spiritual master to enter my life, one who would guide
my being to God-realization (enlightenment) and liberation. Was I ready
for such a relationship and journey? Where would I find such a master?

~

THE HOUSE SEEMED EMPTY WITHOUT our Pompom. One night
after returning from a yoga class, I had an urge to pick up a vegetarian pizza
at a popular pizzeria in town. As I waited for my order, a tiny flyer on the
window caught my attention. It announced a *satsang* at an Asian art gallery
the following night with the founder of Hamsa Yoga Sangh, a Himalayan
spiritual and kundalini kriya master and yogi named Yogiraj Satgurunath
Siddhanath—I called him Gurunath.

The photo of Gurunath, with his silky white hair and beard and fiery
gaze, took hold of my spirit. I felt drawn to go. As soon I reached home, I
called my friend Mandara and asked her to join me.

When Saturday night arrived, Mandara and I sat on the floor in the
front row among a group of forty others. Tall statues of Buddha, Ganesh,
Shiva, Lakshmi, and other deities surrounded us. *Thankas* paintings hung
on the walls. Incense burned, providing an exotic aroma of faraway lands
where temples, poojas, mangos, and coconuts as offering are a part of life.

When Gurunath walked on the platform, he was dressed in a humble
white cloth. He bowed and sat down silently in a lotus position on a thin
orange pillow. His features were austere, yet exuberant. For a man in his

late sixties, he appeared robust. It was not what Gurunath said but the experiences he would be imparting that resonated within my being the most. He pursued the satsang as an experiential one, briefly touching on the meanings of shaktipat, *shivapat*, and *pranapat* transmissions. He explained that God or the absolute truth can't be understood on an intellectual level but must be experienced at a level of consciousness. He asked us to sit like five-year-olds. "Connect your heart to mine and form a bridge," he said, "the Golden Bridge!"

Mandara and I looked at each other, laughing. Gurunath's endearing, fun, and paternal attitude attracted my being, even though his powerful, fierce, and stern demeanor made me a bit uncomfortable. In any case, I was too intrigued by his presence—too thirsty—to run away.

~

SCIENTISTS AFFIRM THAT EVERYTHING IS made of the same energy manifesting and expanding in billions of different forms. This energy is prana, the infinite, omnipresent, and vital life-force that animates every living, sentient being and the universe. The cosmos is overflowing with it. Prana from Sanskrit can be translated as vibration, movement, or even motion and life-force energy. For this reason, *pranayama* (various types of yogic breathing techniques) extends beyond the control of breath; it is the grand portal to higher stages of consciousness, the universe, truth, and what we call God or Creator, the Source. Pranayama opens the door to endless Divine power and infinite possibilities. Controlling this life-force energy is the sole purpose of pranayama. Sincere seekers have to be initiated by a genuine satguru to experience, learn, and practice the ancient art of pranayama.

Swami Vivekananda said in his book *Raja Yoga*:

> *If we can succeed in controlling that little wave of prana, then alone can we hope to control the whole prana. The yogi who has done this gains perfection: no longer is he under any power. He becomes almost almighty, almost all-knowing. The world-movers, endowed*

with gigantic willpower, can bring their prana into a high state of vibration. And it is so great and powerful that it affects others in a moment, and thousands are drawn towards them, and half the world thinks as they do. The great prophets of the world had the most wonderful control of their prana, which gave them tremendous willpower. They had brought their prana to the highest state of vibration, and this is what gave power to sway the world. All manifestations of power arise from this control. Men may not know the secret, but this is the explanation.[2]

The higher we vibrate with prana, the more inner power we emanate. Most people have little idea of the importance of the spine—or, as it is called in yogic terms, the *meru danda*—but it is our spine that channels prana. Since our spine is the axis of our physical body, the meru danda becomes the bridge between earth and the subtle dimensions. According to the Adiyogi Shiva (first yogi/guru), the ancient rishis (sages), and Sadhguru, the meru danda is the great access to the universe.

Since ancient times the yogic tradition has viewed the human as a composite of five major sheaths. More precisely, over three thousand years ago the revered Taittiriya Upanishad scriptures discerned five sheaths. These are like envelopes or sheaths called *koshas*, which humans have and experience—many even identify themselves as these envelopes.

According to the ancient yogic tradition, each one of the five envelopes is composed of finer and finer vibrating energy. Many rishis and ascended masters have referred to these sheaths as peels of an onion, each layer representing a different substratum of our being—from the grossest to subtlest. However, many of them have said these envelopes are not our ultimate, true essence—that beneath them all permeates the bliss of the true eternal and absolute universal consciousness. The five sheaths are like substratum inhabiting within the gross body, the subtle body, or causal body.

Let's identify them with simple language, such as the physical, energy, mental, wisdom, and the bliss sheath. "Maya" from Sanskrit is referred to the word "appearance," which means what is perceived is not always the reality. So in many ways the word can also allude to "illusion."

The first envelope is *Annamaya* kosha, the physical sheath and is considered the grossest. It is made up of food (*anna*) we consume daily. The gross body is made up of five elements (*Panchamahabhutas*): *Agni* (fire), *Vayu* (air), *Prithvi* (earth), *Akash* (ether), and *Jal* (water.) To keep our gross body healthy, use a daily practice of ancient hatha yoga asanas, and consume an organic, vegan diet with at least 50 percent of fresh raw, nutritious food with a high content of pranic energy.

Pranamaya kosha is the energy sheath. This second envelope is composed of vital life-force energy (prana), and it is invisible. This is the vital life-force energy that holds the gross body together by sustaining and governing our biology; it regulates the functioning and the growth of our organism, and our respiratory, circulatory, digestive, and other systems. This universal life-force energy permeates throughout the entire cosmos, flows in all living beings, and animates everything in the existential plane. This energy sheath needs to be purified through daily practice of ancient pranayama (breathing). Because pranayama allows the pranic energy to flow and penetrate through every fiber of our being, as well as the subtle body (explained in depth later), pranayama purifies, energizes, replenishes, rejuvenates, and revitalizes our gross body and subtle body. Many individuals don't realize that pranayama is beyond breathing exercises, in that it expands our field of prana.

Manas refers to the lower aspect of our mind (thought processes) as opposed to our intellect. The mental sheath functions by processing sensory stimuli and perceptions through the awareness of our five senses, resulting in thoughts, volitions, doubts, emotions, imagination, etc. Manas describes the lower part of our mind that registers all the impressions and relates these experiences in terms of mental activity. The mental sheath is the third envelope and is called *Manomaya* kosha. A jabbering mind is the action of this mental envelope. The sincere seeker who becomes more aware of their mental sheath can free themselves from unnecessary mental fear, anguish, agitation, and unhealthy thoughts and can also better develop self-control to manifest their objectives and dreams. The health of our Manomaya kosha can be highly enhanced by the daily practice of potent and ancient mantra chant practices. Mantra yoga meditation calms the agitated wave of the mental sheath by appeasing the individual with ease and serenity.

Jnana from Sanskrit can be translated as knowledge, knowing, inner perception, and even inner-knowing tapping higher intelligence; another word for this is *buddhi*. *Vijnanamaya* kosha is the fourth envelope and is often viewed as the wisdom sheath because it corresponds and communicates to our direct experience of higher faculties such as discernment, intuition, wisdom, and insights. It acts as the golden bridge between the universal absolute truth and our conscious mind. It is through the Vijnanamaya kosha that mystical experiences occur—such as seeing different ethereal lights, deities, saints, and celestial beings; hearing otherworldly sounds; smelling intoxicating fragrances in meditation; or even experiencing certain altered states of consciousness. This wisdom envelope does not depend on causation, space, and time.

Vijnanamaya kosha is inherent in all of us, but not everyone has immediate access to it. Because this wisdom sheath is so related to the Tantra yogic tradition, it is often hidden away in many people unless they start to access it through genuine tantric yogic practices. Daily profound meditation practice is the doorway to Vijnanamaya kosha. The ancient rishis, mystics, and yogis placed great importance in developing and accessing it. Over the years as spiritual practices, contemplation, and meditation become richer and more profound, the wisdom sheath develops further—resulting in the blossoming of a greater sense of clarity, perception, guidance, intuition, wisdom, and insights.

According to Taittiriya Upanishad, the fifth envelope is the bliss sheath, the *Anandamaya* kosha. It is often viewed as the transcendental self in the yogic tradition. The word "ananda" from Sanskrit has often been misunderstood. It signifies intense bliss or ecstasy resulting from no apparent cause, though this word can't be literally translated. One has to experience it. In a state of ananda the mind remains in a calm, yet universal consciousness—in a quiet, intoxicating ecstasy regardless of duality, such as love or hatred. In other words, this bliss sheath leads us to experience our natural state of being. When the great sages, mystics, yogis, yoginis, and ascended masters speak of "bliss," they are referring to our Anandamaya kosha, not to the joy most people experience from a joyous state.

In addition, other yogic branches deem the bliss sheath as the last veil to pierce through to experience the magnificent splendors of our ultimate nature—or *satchit ananda*—absolute non-changing truth; consciousness-bliss. Ultimately all five envelopes (koshas) are manifestations of the divine power of shakti energy. One of the most important aspects to achieve with the phenomenal yogic practices is to align and harmonize the first three envelopes— the physical, energy, and mental sheaths—to access the magical gateways of the subtler Vijnanamaya kosha and Anandamaya kosha.

True bliss emerged from the realm of the Anandamaya kosha. One of the greatest blessings a sincere seeker may experience in his or her lifetime is the eternal and direct experience of his/her true natural state of enlightenment. Essentially, satchit ananda is the ultimate grace that can be bestowed upon a human being. No matter what the conditions, when an individual is experiencing satchit ananda, he or she remains firmly rooted in their divinity. My direct experience of satchit ananda is what I often call and experience as intense Divine love—exactly what the legendary ascended master Paramahansa Yogananda talked about.

Now let's talk about the phenomenal subtle body! It has an amazing network of seventy-two thousand or more astral tubes (*nadis*), pathways that allow the vital life-force energy to flow through our body and that play an extremely crucial part in yoga. The Sanskrit word "nadi" means "motion." The most important nadi is the *sushumna*, located in the hollow of the spine, where the spinal cord is. The *ida* and *pingala*, located on the left and right of this central channel, often represent the feminine and masculine energy principles in many tantric yogic paths. These two major nadis are often referred to as Shakti/Shiva and represent the duality of existence in the Yoga tradition.

In the various locations where the nadis meet, they form triangles and become chakras—energy wheels symbolizing dynamism and movement. Their triangular shapes make them look like lotus blossoms. For this reason, chakras are also called *padmas*—lotus flowers. Chakras are also invisible to the naked eye, but they exert tremendous influence over the gross body and our lives. We have 114 chakras in our subtle body, though most people may only be familiar with the seven most important chakras aligned along the spine.

Kundalini, which means "coiled" in Sanskrit, is the most significant psycho-spiritual force of our subtle body. Many traditions call kundalini by different names. In Japan it is "ki," in China "chi," and in Christianity "the Holy Spirit." Whatever you wish to call it, kundalini is the secret pathway to the divinity within us.

Over the centuries, kundalini—often called the "serpent power"—came to be regarded as Shakti, whom the great rishis of India worshipped as the Divine Mother (Kundalini Shakti). Shakti is accessible to all willing ones, anytime and anywhere. This dormant cosmic energy is often depicted as a snake coiled at the base of the spine in the sacrum bone of the pelvis in the *muladhara* chakra, the first of the seven most important and fundamental chakras.

The Sanskrit word shakti means "empowerment," or "to be able." In the Yoga tradition, shakti is regarded as a sacred, divine, and primordial cosmic force and is seen as representing the dynamic principle of the universe's feminine power energy. In the Yoga tradition, the creation is often viewed as a play of Shiva (masculine) and Shakti (feminine), symbolizing the duality of existence. Shakti represents the dynamic and creative aspect of the universe; Shiva, the male principle, represents the unmanifest supreme consciousness. These two principles can be observed everywhere. Their union creates astonishing forces, and our physical body is the microscopic mirror of the macroscopic play of the cosmos reflecting these two principles. Regardless of our gender, both the masculine and feminine aspect are within our subtle body.

The subtler our being is, the more expansive and freer we become. In this altered state of consciousness, the individual can transcend and go beyond boundaries. Yoga is all about enhancing our perceptions to experience and see things as they are. Ultimately the journey on the spiritual path is to move from the grossest to the subtlest, where boundaries are crossed—from bondage to freedom. Inner beauty is realizing and experiencing the oneness of existence. That is to be in YOGA.

~

BACK AT THE SATSANG IN the Asian art gallery, Gurunath started to impart the experiences to the willing seekers. He asked us to gaze into his eyes while he transmitted shaktipat, a transmission of shakti. As I looked deep into Gurunath's piercing eyes, waves of energy engulfed my being. Every cell tingled and pulsed. I had never experienced anything like it before, except when Pompom's spirit passed through my heart.

The more I gazed at Gurunath, the more he seemed to disappear, dissolving into minuscule particles, becoming a puff of light, even as other visages of what appeared to be prophets, saints, and other Siddhas emerged from his face. I sat, transfixed, as the faces transitioned from one into the other. The ones I was able to distinguish best seemed to be Jesus Christ and Sri Yukteswar, Yogananda's beloved guru. This spontaneous vision came from the universal consciousness and was authentic and divine. It was not my imagination. My jaw dropped; my eyes and heart remained wide open. It was an eternal moment.

After the shaktipat transmission, Gurunath took questions and shared his mission. Then he prepared to transmit shivapat. As we gazed at Gurunath, he suddenly clapped his hands—and in that instant, my mind ceased to produce thoughts. I felt mesmerized, frozen. The cosmos thrived within my being; my breath seemed suspended in air. The experience must have lasted only a few minutes, yet it seemed like eons. Spellbound, I was beyond the limitations of the box that had previously confined my being. My openness and receptivity were those of an innocent child, and this allowed me to experience his grace.

It's impossible to convey in words the intensity and subtle energies of any mystical experience or spiritual process. Seekers must experience them. And though it is everyone's birthright to fly high and know their true nature, not everyone is able to experience higher dimensions of consciousness at first. Experiencing the oneness of existence and interconnectedness requires more refined levels of awareness, openness, and receptivity than most people are used to, willing to, or trained for. One must be in a state of wonderment, like a child, capable of abandoning critical intellect, to experience consciousness beyond our five senses. These were my experiences with Gurunath on the first satsang at the Asian art gallery.

Gurunath closed the evening by inviting us to experience the Self at a deeper level during his upcoming initiation into Shiv-Goraksha Babaji's kriya yoga the following weekend. He bowed. We stood up in silence with our hands in a prayer position.

I felt irresistibly drawn to Gurunath. I was the first to walk toward the master and speak with him after he released the class. When I reached him, I was already bursting with joy.

"Gurunath, anytime you need a place to stay, please stay with us," I told him. "Our home is your home!"

I could not believe I said this without first consulting Nathaniel. An irresistible pulling inside of my being just wanted to be with Gurunath and be part of his mission. I could not tell exactly what it was. I suspected maybe it was the flow of Divine love I felt for him. He just looked at me, bowing and nodding his head, yes.

Mandara and I walked out of the venue laughing and elated. As we drove home, we shared our experiences with one another.

"Vivi," she said, jumping up and down in her seat, "did you see Gurunath's face transforming into other saintly ones? God! One looked like Sri Yukteswar! Did you see that?"

"You saw that too?" I asked, amazed.

We were both thrilled by the opportunity opening for us and decided to sign up for the upcoming initiation with this mystical Siddha.

When we got back to the house, we sat down in the kitchen with Nathaniel. Mandara and I could not stop talking about our experiences with Gurunath.

"Really?" Nathaniel kept saying as we told him about all that had transpired. He listened to us with a skeptical expression.

"Baby, I think I found my guru!" I exclaimed with joy.

"Wow! This is cause for a toast!" he cried out jokingly. He opened the fridge and grabbed a great bottle of chardonnay.

Eighteen

INITIATION

THE FOLLOWING WEEKEND, MANDARA AND I headed to a nondenominational church in San Francisco for our first yogic initiation. There, Gurunath gave us a mantra to use in his Kundalini kriya yoga's initiation. We lay on the floor and took our first step with our new *hamsa* wings. "Hamsa" means "swam" from Sanskrit, which signifies the soul.

In the minutes that followed, I did not experience the type of otherworldly occurrences I had at the first satsang, but a sense of peace, contentment, and gratitude enveloped my entire being.

Toward the end of the program, I watched a woman walk up to Gurunath and touch his feet with devotion.

"I could never bow and touch someone's feet like that," I whispered to Mandara.

⁓

THE FOLLOWING MONDAY I WOKE up feeling very depressed. I had not felt so sorrowful since my time in New England. For no apparent reason, tears welled up, and I could not stop their flow. Convinced that this was connected to my experiences in Gurunath's program, I called one of the Hamsa Yoga Sangh (HYS) volunteers and asked him what was going on.

He said, "Oh, don't worry, Vivi. It is very normal to have emotional and mental purging after being initiated by a satguru, especially after performing yogic kriya practices for a while. That is a great sign! Purification takes place and karmic baggage is eliminated from the gross body."

I hung up the phone feeling reassured by his words and encouraged to pursue my spiritual practices.

One night that week I woke screaming at the top of my lungs and sat up in bed covered in sweat. In my dream, an ugly, frightening face had tried to swallow me. I rarely had nightmares and was very shaken. *Why do I dream of the devil when I love the Divine so much?* I wondered.

A few days later, I spoke with my beloved Gurunath about my nightmare. He told me not to worry, that the idea of evil will often arise in the mind when one is newly initiated. He advised me to continue my daily yogic practices and said that eventually this "garbage" would disappear, and my blissful Divine nature would shine through. He was referring to satchit ananda.

"Satgurus are the world's premier garbage collectors!" He loved to make fun. Gurunath had such a loving sense of humor. I laughed when he said these words at our first satsang. Now I knew he was not just joking.

~

MY PARENTS NEVER INSTILLED DISCIPLINE within me as a child, but now I began the discipline of practicing ancient yoga in the soft candlelight of my art studio for several hours each day, often going late into the night. I never went to bed until I did my yogic practices, even after twelve hours of painting. I could hear Yogananda whispering in my head: "Give all your nights to God, meditate! You shall know your blissful nature."

Prior to my initiation into Gurunath's program, I had never sat down to a formal spiritual practice. My mind had long run wild. Now, as a witness, I began to be aware of all the rubbish inside me. Mundane thoughts popped up like stubborn weeds.

I created a small altar within the library of my art studio. I adorned the shelves with pictures of Gurunath, Yogananda, Jesus Christ, Shiv-Goraksha Babaji, and many great ascended masters, as well as a few photos of the beautiful female saint of the twentieth century, Sri Anandamayi Ma.

I stumbled across some photos of Anandamayi Ma at the local spiritual bookstore in town. When I saw her sunny face, I felt teary, and my heart expanded in bliss. There was a profound connection between us, though I did not know what. I bought the photos, framed them, and looked at her beatific face every day. Each time, I caught a glimpse of our Creator. That all-encompassing feeling of being One and blissful within encouraged me to continue on the yogic path.

Each time I tasted a drop of beatitude, I realized more the omnipotent and omniscient presence of the absolute intelligence, that supreme power we call "God." I knew in my heart that God was not an old, white-bearded man sitting up in heaven, looking down at us poor sinners. Our five senses could never define or describe what the Source is, whatever name we choose to attribute to what we call "God." From my experiences, if it must be put into words, one may say it is an ever-expanding consciousness. Supreme omnipotent, omnipresent intelligence and infinite consciousness vibrates and permeates all existence and beyond. Even these words fail to give a glimpse of what God may be. The absolute supreme Source can only be realized within the shrine of our being. What we call "God" can't be put into logical reasoning, especially not in words. The sincere seeker must experience it within.

After being in the presence of Gurunath, my longing to merge with the Source intensified.

~

OVER TIME, I CAME TO understand the complexity of our practice. I knew I would not have been able to experience these phenomenal experiences with Gurunath without the help and grace of my satguru and sadhana (yogic practices), and my own efforts, perseverance, patience, and trust. Having a satguru, a true master who knew how to guide me, became my daily nutrient. We cannot strive and blossom without the proper nutritious food.

When Gurunath toured California, I never missed an opportunity to see him at his satsangs. Once, after the satsang, he invited me, Mandara, and several close disciples for dinner at his son's home in the San Francisco Bay Area.

The day after our initiation, I had painted a profile of a mystical face emerging from the cosmos with a swan flying out of her third eye. I brought it to give to Gurunath.

Another of his disciples, initiated at the same time as me, also brought a gift: an elaborate architectural blueprint he designed of what he thought enlightenment was and how to reach it.

After the satsang, as a few of us sat on the floor near Gurunath, the disciple unraveled the plans and explained to our master his theory of God-realization and creation.

Gurunath stopped him. "My boy, my boy, cool your jets!" he said, laughing. We all laughed. "You must stop your intellect from going mad like this. God can only be experienced within, not intellectualized."

Then Gurunath looked at my painting and exclaimed, "Shivangani, look at what Vivi painted! A hamsa's flight!" This was the moment I met the radiant Shivangani, Gurunath's wife, a lovely Indian woman wrapped like a deity in an elegant silk sari. She spoke only a little broken English, but it didn't matter. We connected at the level of the heart and consciousness.

Soon after this, HYS posted my painting on their site with a poem by Gurunath.

~

THE FOLLOWING SUMMER, GURUNATH AND his wife, Shivangani, came to California with plans to stay at our house. Gurunath needed a quiet place to focus on writing his book, and Shivangani was working toward perfecting her own Indian recipe book.

The day they arrived, I drove to Palo Alto to attend Gurunath's satsang. For the first time that night, I witnessed his aura. An effulgent, diffused light emanated from him, which was thrilling to look at. I had never seen such ethereal beauty before.

After the satsang, I went to see Gurunath, and in a timid gesture, I bowed down and touched his feet. Perhaps seeing his aura propelled me to do so. Divine love flowed through my heart. I felt an altered state of consciousness. He looked at me strangely, as if to say, "Did you really mean that, Vivi?"

I nodded my head "yes," smiling. My heart burst in Divine love for my beloved Gurunath.

In the yogic spiritual tradition, it is customary to bow down and touch the satguru's feet with reverence, love, and gratitude if one feels devotional. Most Westerners don't understand its significance—grace flows in such a moment—and look down on it as submission. I, myself, had been guilty of that response when I saw Gurunath's follower touch his feet only one year earlier. Now I understood the true meaning and experience of "namaste." Namaste means: I bow to the true divine and ultimate nature within you— that which you may or may not have realized and experienced yet. I see your genuine radiant beauty and bow to you. Ultimately, namaste is like bowing to the absolute supreme intelligence that permeates the whole universe.

As Sadhguru says, "Bowing and crawling may not get you anything. To become receptive, one should become free of oneself—that comes from genuine reverence and devotion."[1]

The following morning before breakfast, I found the door to the guest room wide open. Shivangani was unpacking while Gurunath took a shower. I entered and greeted her. She pulled a small bag from her suitcase and looked lovingly at me, then said in her broken English, "Here, Vivi, Gurunath wants his daughter to have this." She placed a ruby pendant in my hand.

"Wow!" I said, amazed by its beauty. Then I shook my head. "No, no, that is too much."

Shivangani insisted, holding my hands. I was so touched.

I had created another oil painting for Gurunath, and I offered it over breakfast. Then I asked Gurunath to bless the pendant. He closed his eyes, put both of his hands on it, and placed it in my hand. From that day on, I wore it with much love near my heart.

Later that afternoon, when Gurunath entered our living room, he noticed my painting, called *Divinity*, hanging over the fireplace.

"Vivi, that is Shiva/Shakti!" he said. "Shivangani, come see!" he called.

Shivangani walked in and nodded in agreement, her eyes filled with admiration and light.

"This is the union of the feminine and masculine principles exploding in Divine ecstasy," Gurunath said. "That is the ultimate goal of self-realization, when Shakti merges with Shiva!"

"Look Gurunath! The female and masculine faces are sharing the same third eye," I said.

While painting *Divinity*, I had no idea my artwork expressed some of the ancient yogic knowledge such as kundalini awakening and ascension, and the ultimate marriage of Shiva/Shakti merging and dissolving in union. I had not even known this was possible, even though it was what I had sought my entire life, to be liberated, never to return to the physical plane.

I told them the story of flight #261 and the impact it had on my being. "These kinds of images have flowed in since the Alaska Airlines plane crash," I explained. "This painting was the first after that intense experience."

Because they both seemed captivated by my art and its significance, I offered to show them more. I took them downstairs to my art cabinet and pulled out several other paintings.

"See this one, Vivi, it's the trinity . . . Shiva, Brahma, and Vishnu!" Gurunath exclaimed, examining one. "In Christianity, it's the Father, the Son, and Holy Spirit. There is no difference."

I felt honored by Gurunath's interest in my paintings and fascinated by the explanations he offered. But it would take more than a decade for my being to fully discover, comprehend, and experience why these things were being expressed in my work.

~

WHILE GURUNATH AND SHIVANGANI STAYED with us, I sat with them every morning on our patio to meditate. I did not realize how blessed I was to practice with my own satguru at our home. Within the Yoga tradition, it is considered a great blessing and grace to do sadhana in the presence of the master, because doing sadhana in his or her presence can rapidly accelerate the individual's evolution.

Gurunath spent his afternoons working on his book at my office desk on the second floor. That week, a major heat wave swept over Northern California with temperatures reaching 100 degrees. We did not have an air conditioner, and the house warmed up like the Mojave Desert.

Gurunath had been a swimming champion in his youth, and he never lost the love of jumping in water. Shivangani preferred to work on her cookbook, so instead of joining us at the pool, she stayed in the house, preparing delicious Indian food for us. Nathaniel, meanwhile, left for his office early each day and did not return until late at night. So Gurunath and I went alone to the swim club to cool off each day.

One day, as we swam, I asked him playfully, "Gurunath, what about a little race?"

He looked at me. "Vivi wants to race with her guru!" he laughed. "Do you think you will win?"

"Why not?"

He kept teasing me. "Oh, Vivi's ego!"

We never raced. But after swimming, we sat cross-legged on the grass at poolside and meditated in the shade.

One of the pool supervisors, seemingly bothered by our session, decided to stop us by putting on the sprinklers. Big jets of water splashed—but Gurunath and I did not move. I opened my eyes and saw the man escape with a devious smile. I stayed focused on my meditation. I knew this person and understood where his behavior came from. I ignored it. Unless there is danger, it is preferable to ignore an individual when they do a foolish thing.

It is fascinating how some humans behave when faced with a situation they don't like or can't understand. Ignorance or lack of awareness of our true ultimate nature can impel people to do silly, stupid, and sometimes even dangerous things. In this case, luckily, it led to nothing worse than a bit of soaking.

~

ON SATURDAY, GURUNATH WAS GOING to conduct another experiential satsang at the same Asian art gallery where we first met. His children drove over and spent the weekend with us.

When Saturday arrived, Shivangani offered me her sapphire silk sari, the one I so admired. "Take, Vivi. For you," she said softly.

I could not accept. She insisted. Then she and her daughter-in-law folded me in its yards of fabric and taught me how to stylishly wrap it.

I repeated the same moves several times, making sure I mastered the art—but when I took a few steps, the whole structure collapsed, and I got entangled in a blue stream of silk. We all laughed. They rewrapped it around my hips and shoulder and put a *bindi* between my eyebrows on my third eye, the *Ajna*, one of the seven most important chakras. *Et voilà!* I was officially initiated into my new family.

While we were preparing for the evening, I washed and dried Gurunath's white cloth. When I gave it back to him he looked at me, saying sternly, "Is this the way you send your guru in public, wrinkled? Is this how you care for and love your guru? Please iron it, Vivi!"

"Oh, so sorry, Gurunath." I smiled and went to iron it. I took it as if he was just teaching me how to be more mindful and devotional toward my guru. When I returned the cloth, nicely folded, I said sweetly, "Gurunath, can I give you a big hug?"

Gurunath grabbed me in his arms and hugged me like he would his own child, demonstrating, not for the first time, what a rare yogi and master he is—one who proves that it is possible to have a household and still have a rich spiritual life dedicated to serving humanity.

Even though Nathaniel was never initiated by Gurunath and never embraced him as his satguru, he loved being around the couple and considered them dear friends.

When the time came for Gurunath and Shivangani to depart, we lingered for a while, hugging on our terrace. I had a terrible knot in my throat, and I burst into tears. I didn't know if I cried because I felt relieved after the intensity of hosting them, or because some karmic toxins or childhood emotional issues were surfacing, or maybe both: I simply knew that I would miss them.

Nineteen

LONGING FOR MORE

IN MANY WAYS, GURUNATH HAD become the father I never had, the one my heart had longed for. When Gurunath entered my heart, I did not realize how much healing I still needed. My closeness with him triggered many profound paternal wounds to come to the surface—wounds I thought had healed long ago. The loss and pain of my father were still imprinted into all my cells.

I had grown to disdain the patriarchal system—its assaults on Mother Earth, females, animals, and the matriarchal system. I still carried an underlying sadness and a bit of fierce revolt.

Over one year later at one of his evening satsangs, Gurunath made a few jokes about vegans, veganism, and animals. I was upset and disappointed by his comments. I could not understand how such a wise master seemed to trivialize veganism and the suffering of animals. I felt he was judging without knowing what the animal rights movement and veganism were about, and I decided that he must not be as enlightened as I had previously thought. Later in the satsang, I caught my mind saying, *same old thing,* as he led us. I wanted more.

I had always enjoyed seeing Gurunath, but over the past year, I had grown tired and restless. I could hear my heart cry out. I did not feel I was growing or making progress spiritually, when what I wanted was to evolve at rocket speed. Yet it did not mean that I was not growing.

I started wondering if Gurunath was my true satguru, or if his path was different from mine. Not realizing I had caused the golden bridge to collapse, over time I was unable to experience his shaktipat the same way I used to. I became frustrated and sad as my longing intensified. It was as if I had shut down the grand portal of the Divine. No one was to blame but myself. I had to learn to take responsibility for my thoughts, words, and actions. I had the key within.

~

WHEN THE HOLIDAYS APPROACHED, THE season weighed heavily on Nathaniel and me. We were trying to decide if we were going to have children. A part of my being felt hesitant. My heart tugged me to the maternal side, my head to my artistic career. I had been working on creating a body of art and launching my career as an artist, and I did not want to give up on that.

The battles between my heart, mind, and spirit seemed endless, but it was my heart that most often seemed to win. Our Christmas gift became our decision to conceive.

We started a tradition of buying a small live pine tree for Christmas and planting it on our property after the holidays. I hung a Winnie the Pooh sock on our tree for our future child.

After trying for a year, we took a different path. We went to a fertility clinic. But after another year of injections and intrauterine insemination, we were still childless.

Our frustration rose as we went through the routine of injecting my belly, checking my temperature, having to perform on the spot, and then race to the fertility clinic. The more we tried and could not conceive, the more I yearned for a baby. The more Nathaniel became exasperated, the more I became exhausted at all levels. I felt we were growing apart.

One night Nathaniel brought up the possibility of trying in vitro.

I shook my head. "Conceiving a child is a Divine and natural process. I don't want to force it to this point."

Not long after that, Nathaniel said, "I've had enough."

I immediately agreed. "Why are we forcing nature? There are millions of orphans who need a good home. Why don't we adopt? I would very much love a baby from India. What about you? It does not matter from whose womb a child is born, it's still a child of God!"

That day we put everything in the Divine Mother's hands. A burden lifted from our shoulders. Nathaniel understood my profound affinity with the Indian culture and the yogic tradition and wanted to support my vision. That afternoon I wrote a heartfelt letter to seventy-five Indian orphanages with different religious and spiritual backgrounds.

Over the year that followed, each time I opened one of the orphanages' letters, my heart tightened into a knot. One after the other expressed the same rubbish, turning us down. They said that one of us must be of Indian descent, that my husband was too old to be a father. There was only one orphanage that mentioned we could perhaps adopt a much older child. At that point, we were burned out, and let it go.

Meanwhile, when I wasn't opening a letter from an orphanage, I was reading a letter of rejection from the fine art galleries and national juried art shows saying my submissions did not fit their venue. Each time I read one of those stock letters, I threw it in the garbage.

～

I CHECKED THE CALENDAR ONE day in February 2003 and noticed that I had missed my period for many months. I had also been experiencing some nausea. Nathaniel and I stayed calm and somehow detached when we realized what was happening. We had tried so hard and too long. We needed to protect our hearts. I was not even sure if I could hold the developing fetus in my body temple.

Each night before falling asleep at night I put my hands on my belly and said, "Mommy and Daddy love you so much, my little one." I bought a tiny pair of pink knitted booties and often put them on my fingers and walked them around the bathroom counter.

Then, two months later, I was lying in bed one night when excruciating cramps attacked my abdomen. When I went to urinate, I heard an unusual splash. I saw a clot of blood the size of a Ping-Pong ball in the bowl beneath me. I flushed the toilet, saying goodbye to our baby and our dream. I ran to our bed, devastated. I knew getting pregnant again would be nearly impossible. It hurt too much to keep trying. Even though I had tried to remain detached, this loss was beyond what my heart could take. Not long after this, Nathaniel took me to Lake Tahoe for a four-day getaway with our two rescued Siberian dogs to help me heal.

We skied in the mountains and played with our huskies in the snow every day. Despite it all, over the following months I continued to mourn. I did not want to paint or do anything. I cried almost every day.

That following spring I saw a beautiful yellow bird lying on his back on our porch. He may have crashed into one of our tall windows. I picked him up in my hands, crying and caressing him while invoking the highest rebirth for him. "Why is life so cruel, Divine Mother? What is the meaning of creation? I want to know. Please send me my spiritual master if Gurunath is no longer the one, or if I need to be on a different path, or if the time has come to move on with another satguru."

I discovered that processing our feelings and emotions right on the spot instead of repressing and suppressing them is an important aspect of healing and a way to avoid accumulating karmic garbage. Because when a person processes what needs to be processed and sees clearly what is in that moment, they do not end up accumulating all the garbage that can cause much more suffering and pain for themselves and their entourage later in life. It helps them to free themselves from the burden of their unconscious, and their potential future compulsions and addictions.

Twenty

A NEW DIRECTION

NATHANIEL HAD BEEN ASKED TO produce a major festival in San Diego in late May. He kept asking me to join him, but I refused. At the very last minute, a prompt from my intuition changed my mind. It did not make any sense, but I had listened. The night before we planned to travel, I packed light, and we flew to Southern California together the following day.

At the hotel the following morning, Nathaniel rose at five thirty, kissed me on the forehead, told me he loved me, and left.

When I woke up, I went over to the tall window of our hotel room and admired the seagulls flying over the marina. I felt earthbound and wished I could soar like they did. Old feelings of loneliness returned, reminding me of my severe depression. I swore I would never allow myself to fall back into that pit. Still, it was not just the miscarriage and all the rejections that hurt so; it was something more profound, and the longing was unbearable. I wanted both Nathaniel and me to grow together on the spiritual path. We were becoming disconnected and heading in two different directions. I was concerned we could end up in divorce. For a long moment, I looked at the sky. I reflected on my gloomy days back on the East Coast and how I overcame that dark abyss. It is fascinating how powerful our mind is. Every thought and emotion has the capacity to change our body's chemistry. Some of my energy returned. I decided to go for a long walk by the beach, thinking the fresh air would lift my spirit. I felt pulled to go.

It was a cool day for San Diego. I put on a bulky knit sweater and headed for the marina. I had walked only a few yards on the boardwalk when I reached the back of the building next door and heard a mantra. An electrifying energy drew me to it. I knew yoga was happening inside.

I saw a man standing outside the door. "Who is teaching?" I asked.

"Guruji!" he said, lighting up. "You know, His Holiness Sri Sri Ravi Shankar of the Art of Living. Many of his devotees also call him Gurudev, a similar, reverential name. These are the last few days of his American tour before he leaves the States. Guruji doesn't teach the basic course anymore. This is a rare occasion!"

As he spoke, I had a vision of a radiant face with long, flowing black hair, a beard, and spirited black eyes.

"A face appeared to me as you spoke," I said. "Do you have a photo of him?"

"Just one moment," the man said. He disappeared through the door and came back with a large poster of Guruji.

"Oh!" I said. "Yes, that's the sweet face I just saw in my vision."

I stood there with chills, not knowing what to say next.

Eventually I said goodbye and kept walking along the oceanfront. For a while, I sat near the waves and wondered if this is what happened when you embarked on a spiritual path with a satguru. Did all your karma invade you only to wash away just as the waves crashed over the shore? I sensed I had reached a crossroads. I was not sure what it was, but something about my life and myself had to change, and fast.

I closed my eyes and drifted into a meditative state. A sense of boundlessness engulfed my being as the rhythm of the ocean rocked my heart. I inhaled the misty cool breeze deep into my lungs and breathed out my torment. When I opened my eyes to the beauty of blue sky, I sobbed. A wave of serenity overwhelmed my being.

Two hours had gone by. I strolled back along the waterfront, feeling empty and at peace. When I reached the boardwalk, an irresistible sensation gripped me. I walked to the front entrance of the building where I had heard the humming from earlier.

It looked deserted, so I assumed the program had ended. The front gates were wide open. I stepped inside the gateway. Silence reigned within the hall. Guruji sat on the dais in front of perhaps a few hundred participants.

All at once he gazed at me with a piercing glance and a mischievous smile. I stood still. His burning eyes enflamed my heart with a Divine love that enlivened my cells. He seemed to know I had come to him. I removed my shoes, sat down in the doorway, and listened with great reverence.

"Life is sacred. Celebrate life. Care for others and share whatever you have with those less fortunate than you. Broaden your vision, for the whole world belongs to you."

His words resonated deep within.

Shortly after I settled on the ground, Guruji (or Gurudev as I called him) departed, and his participants left for lunch. I hesitantly returned to my hotel, thinking what an amazing blessing it had been to be in his presence. I felt so awed by the Divine synchronicity of my arrival and realized that, after all, our Creator had heard my invocations. Grace had always fallen upon my being, but I did not always see or trust it. Grace can take the face of endless disguises. Misfortunes often turn out to be great blessings in disguise; we just need to stay open and feel abundant gratitude in our hearts.

~

THE AFTERNOON WARMED UP. CLOUDS yielded to the sunlight, and I decided to lie by the pool and read *The Yoga Tradition: Its History, Literature, Philosophy and Practice* by the amazing yoga scholar Dr. Georg Feuerstein. The section on Bhakti yoga caught my attention. I devoured every page, even the Bhakti sutra, which is made of aphorisms about devotion and love by two great rishis, Sage Narada and Sage Shandilya.

The Sanskrit word "bhakti" is derived from the root *bhaj*, which means "to share," "to participate in," or "to engage with affection," and is generally interpreted as love and devotion for the Divine. Dr. Feuerstein describes bhakti yoga as "the yoga of loving self-dedication to, and love-participation in, the Divine person. It is the way of the heart. Shandilya, the author of the bhakti sutra, defines bhakti as 'supreme attachment to the lord.' This is the only attachment that does not reinforce the egoic personality and its destiny. Instead, the bhakti-yogin consciously harnesses love in their quest for communion or union with the Divine."[1]

In bhakti yoga, the devotee (*bhakta*) is the lover, and the Divine becomes the beloved. As I read Dr. Feuerstein's words, I realized I had been a bhakta all my life. I had been born as a bhakta, though I had not known it. But there it was, in how I used the power of my emotions to connect and unite with the Divine either in chant, yogic practices, or with my art—and how I had even been doing this in my interactions with people and animals and nature. I had already been practicing bhakti yoga in everything I did, just by being—and also by how much I had suffered by not being able to express more devotion and longing toward the Divine and my spiritual master. I wondered if I had been on this spiritual path in previous lifetimes.

My devotional nature longed to express the inexpressible, to unite as One with my beloved. I realized that on various occasions and through several mystical experiences in my life I had experienced my true nature. When I did so, my ultimate true nature blossomed into a most lively exuberant, blissful, and ecstatic state, satchit ananda. Yet I did not know how to sustain satchit ananda permanently, which caused me intense suffering.

I wondered if the reason I could not feel more devotional love toward Gurunath was because I saw him as my surrogate father. As a bhakta, I needed and wanted my beloved. I wanted to feel my blissful true nature of satchit ananda twenty-four hours a day, seven days a week. Yet this desire was not an addiction. Wanting to experience our true enlightened nature is the most natural longing for a human being to experience consciously or unconsciously. It may take the form of many disguises—from drugs and all kinds of addictions, to seeking well-being and happiness. It is everybody's birthright to not only seek but also to realize our true enlightened nature. It is more than possible for sincere seekers. No professional success, child, or animal companion could fulfill my longing. I could see clearly that bhakti yoga was what I needed on my path.

I knew love could be the most powerful force of all. Love engenders love. Bhakti yoga is the only branch of yoga allowing us to immediately reconnect with the most powerful source of love—Divine love. That was precisely what I experienced when Gurudev gazed at my being for the first time. Bhakti yoga is the path of love, of devotion allowing the heart center—*anahata* chakra—to open wide, followed by the other chakras.

Dr. Georg Feuerstein writes in *The Yoga Tradition: Its History, Literature, Philosophy and Practice*:

> *The emotional force of the human being is purified and channeled toward the Divine. In their discipline of ecstatic self-transcendence, the bhakti-yogins or bhaktas ("devotee") tend to be more openly expressive than the typical râja-yogin or jnânin. The followers of Bhakti-Yoga do not, for instance, shy away from shedding tears of longing for the Divine. In this approach, the transcendental Reality is usually conceived as a supreme Person rather than as an impersonal Absolute.*[2]

In bhakti yoga, the most ordinary activity may become full of spiritual beauty, value, and significance if it is performed for the unfolding of self-lessness and the expression of Divine love. Mother Teresa illustrated this Divine love with her generous volunteer work when she said that she saw Jesus Christ in every face. Religious rites, rituals, spiritual practices, and even chanting become spiritual when they are magnetized by the energy of Divine love and are performed with utter awareness. The Source of creation is manifested in every atom of this universe. At the end, it does not matter who our sacred beloved is. The same thread connects us. When we hurt someone, an animal, or nature, we hurt ourselves. When we let someone down, we let ourselves down. When we become passionate for the Divine, we open our heart to all creation by breaking down man-made barriers. Inner beauty is realizing and experiencing the oneness of existence. That is to be in yoga!

When Divine love grows in one's heart, all human values flourish. Helping humanity and animals becomes natural. Isn't Jesus Christ's greatest teaching the simplest, the path of love? Love starts from within; it radiates and grows like a wildflower garden. When Divine love and joy flow from within, devotion, good actions, and knowledge will naturally sprout. The longing for meditation and truth grows. We start serving humanity as our beloved, realizing all knowledge is within ourselves.

When I put my yoga book down after a long afternoon of reading and introspection, the sun was descending. The time had come for a swim. While I swam, I thought about my love for Gurunath, and I felt torn. How could I leave my beloved Gurunath? Then, I realized it was by the synchronicity of the Divine Mother that Gurudev had entered my life.

~

BY EARLY EVENING, MY INTUITIVE voice nagged me to go to Gurudev again. I longed to be in his presence. I took a quick shower, dressed, and walked to the venue. On my way, I spoke to a couple outside the building. They told me they were about to have a satsang with him. They invited me to sit with them.

When we walked into the hall, their pillows were on the floor in the second row right in front of Gurudev's dais. We sat and closed our eyes.

The sacred chant of "Aum Namah Shivaya, Aum" began to vibrate in the room. I began chanting along. The words flew out of my mouth. Everyone chanted at the top of their lungs, jubilant. Every cell within my being vibrated, exuding ecstasy. I had never sung *bhajans*—simple yet soulful devotional songs or chants, often in Sanskrit, that express intense love for the Divine—with a group before. I did not know one person in the hall; yet everyone was a part of my being. I was overwhelmed with intense feelings of belonging and Divine love. I was intoxicated, weeping in joy and gratitude.

As we chanted, Gurudev tiptoed into the room and sat on the dais. Even with my eyes closed, I could sense his divinity. At times the chanting was fervent and mournful. Most of us were on fire with Divine love and Gurudev's shakti. When he at last opened his eyes and uttered a sound, high-pitched and bubbly, I was transported in bliss. I contemplated the beauty of this moment and marveled: I had discovered bhakti yoga just a few hours earlier, and now I was already able to give full expression to my devotional nature.

This divine star, Guruji played the strings of our hearts with a sublime melody that was eternal and universal and stirring. It was mesmerizing how this small, wise, amusing, and graceful white-robed man could move a crowd to pure ecstasy in just moments.

After the satsang, I bowed in reverence to him. I didn't want him to leave. Over fifty others rushed to his side and followed him outdoors. Gratefully, I hugged my new friends and exchanged cards. I trotted back to the hotel, chanting aloud and admiring the stars.

When we become aware of the intensity of our longing for the Source and invoke the Divine within, our cry is heard, I reflected. Expressing devotional love helped my being liberate my imprisoned heart. Realizing devotional love allows our true nature to emerge. We are spiritual beings dreaming a human dream.

It was already late evening when I walked into our hotel lobby and ran into Nathaniel. He noticed the change in my energy and asked what had happened. We sat in the restaurant and ordered a late dinner. I related the magical story. He could not believe it and seemed very surprised. He was skeptical, saying it was too good to be true. The following day we flew back home. By then, the negative energy that had plagued me lifted, and my black clouds disappeared, leaving my being at last full of lightness and joy.

Upon our arrival home, I checked out the Art of Living website— Gurudev's nonprofit educational and humanitarian organization. I opened the home page and saw an announcement that he had an upcoming visit and programs at their Canadian Yoga center. I was thrilled to discover this ashram was only a few hours away from Mama's home. Just a few months earlier Nathaniel and I had made specific plans to visit my family. Our dates coincided almost perfectly with Gurudev's visit to this center. He was going to teach the advanced program.

"Baby, I have to go," I said. "I can take the basic and advanced programs all at once! The synchronicity is too amazing!"

After some resistance, Nathaniel agreed.

In the weeks that followed, many of my friends asked me what had caused my sudden radiance and elation.

"I feel the presence of the master!" I told them. "Divine love is sprouting wild in my heart."

Only a few days later, I stumbled onto these words from Gurudev in one of his books:

The master is the doorway. To bring you to the doorway, it must be more charming than the world. Nothing in the world can give you as much peace, joy and pleasure. Once you come to the doorway, you enter the door and see the world from there; you see the world from the eyes of the master. The world looks much more beautiful. The master is the presence, just feel the presence of the master, that is eternal.[3]

It was only then I realized how symbolic the gesture of standing in the doorway had been in San Diego. I had entered the master's gateway that day and gained a whole new perspective on life through the eyes of Gurudev. I knew the time to move on had come. My burning heart and intuition screamed to be with him. It was obvious Gurudev was my new master. The Divine Mother had answered my invocations.

Following this realization, a storm of guilt and sadness tore me apart. I felt disloyal toward Gurunath. There was no question in my heart that I wanted to be with Gurudev, but I also wanted to keep Gurunath in my life. Still, I knew I could not follow two spiritual masters. I had to make a hard decision.

Later that week I received a call from Gurunath's daughter-in-law. "Vivi, Gurunath wants to speak with you. Please wait a moment." She put him on the phone. I was surprised.

"What is going on, Vivi?" he asked sternly, as if he already knew my torment.

"What do you mean, Gurunath?" I asked, startled. Then I sighed and admitted, "You're right, something is going on. I need to see you as soon as possible."

The following day, I drove to visit him. When I arrived at the home of one of his closest disciples, I walked in with my heart pounding and tears in my eyes. I bowed and touched Gurunath's feet and offered him his favorite chocolate truffles. We walked outside in the garden. I poured my heart out, crying and sharing my epiphany.

"Gurunath, I had never experienced this kind of deep sense of belongingness and devotional love. I must express my devotional nature with bhakti yoga! I can't help it. I love so much to sing, chant, and dance for the Divine Mother. I discovered that I am a bhakta. I feel like a *gopi* around Gurudev. I don't understand what is going on within me."

A "gopi" is a girl cowherd who demonstrated unconditional love and devotion to Lord Krishna. Gopis are legendary in sacred literature. Because of the intensity of their devotional love and emotions for Lord Krishna, many of them—perhaps even all of them—attained self-realization.

Gurunath was not a master known for his devotional nature. His focus had always been on kriya yoga. Still, he listened and understood. When I was done telling him everything, he threw his arms wide apart. "One wing is bhakti, the other is kriya!" he said. Gurunath meant that both yogic paths could be combined.

"Gurunath, it would be so wonderful if you added chanting in your satsang to loosen up people. Chanting mantras and dancing help people in so many ways," I said. I could always share my heart with Gurunath face-to-face. He always welcomed it.

When I stood to leave, Gurunath and I hugged each other for a long moment. Then I bowed and left in silence, overflowing with infinite love and gratitude for him and the immense blessings he had bestowed upon my being.

On the drive home, I wept. I felt like a little bird flying away from the nest. Was I mourning the father I had found in Gurunath? On occasion, he had scared me. I knew that was exactly what a genuine satguru is supposed to do: demolish one's old, false sense of self and disturb the seeker in profound ways by helping us break free from our limitations. This painful episode was about breaking free from my attachment toward him—Gurunath the father, Gurunath my master, my bondage with the patriarchal figure, and the residual issues toward my biological father. I was very grateful and relieved to know Gurunath would always receive me with open arms.

Our interaction and grace helped me move on. I knew I would always love him dearly and would very much miss his fun-loving divine presence and embrace. Yet part of my being also felt blessed, thrilled, and ready for the next step on my spiritual journey with Gurudev.

Twenty-One

INTOXICATED WITH DIVINE LOVE

MY LONGING TO BE IN Gurudev's presence intensified. At last, I signed up for the Art of Living basic and advanced programs to be held in Canada.

I would be staying at an ashram, though I had no idea what that meant. An ashram with a satguru is the place where one goes on a pilgrimage, a profound inward journey where one may get rid of accumulations, limitations, and karma. Ashrams also involve intense communal living. I was not fully prepared for this challenge.

I arrived at the Art of Living's lush green lakeside compound on a clear, sunny day in August. During my check-in, a volunteer showed me to my dormitory bedroom. I dragged my luggage to where three bunk beds were crammed in a small room and put my bags next to the bed by the window. My roommates had not arrived yet. A sweet, loving energy inundated my being. I spun around and said, "Yippee! Thanks to you, Gurudev. I'm so happy and grateful to be here!" I jumped up and down on the bed like a little girl.

During that first week, I experienced painful migraines caused by withdrawal from caffeine and alcohol. I never drank a lot of either, just a glass of wine on occasion, but my body craved and jittered for caffeine, alcohol, and sugar. There were no coffee shops or cafes around the ashram. I walked around like a zombie, exhausted by the three-hour time change and having to get up at dawn every morning.

One of my roommates slept less than three feet away from my head and snored like a trumpet. I used earplugs, but they didn't help much. I lovingly tapped on my roommate's shoulder several times asking her to turn on her side. She snored even more.

When Gurudev reached the ashram, I could feel his holy presence. My longing to see him grew stronger. But I would not see him yet. Gurudev says:

> *Protection simply means prolonging the time in a particular state; hence, protection also prevents transformation. And transformation cannot happen in a state of total protection. At the same time, without protection the desired transformation cannot happen. A seed needs protection to transform into a plant; a plant needs protection to become a tree. But too much protection can aid or hamper transformation, so the protector should have an idea to what extent he should protect.*[1]

Our initiation into the *sudarshan* kriya, our basic program, was to be held in a large open tent overlooking the lake. During our sessions, we performed a powerful yogic breathing practice, or pranayama, created by Gurudev long ago. His teacher, a handsome Indian swami with long salt-and-pepper hair and beard, led us into each step carefully.

We kept breathing to a special rhythm with our eyes closed while mentally reciting a mantra for almost forty-five minutes. I could not keep up. I wanted coffee! I feared I would collapse from exhaustion and my emotions. But I kept pushing my limits, expecting to erupt like a volcano at any moment.

As the class continued I began to feel a massive ball of energy in my midsection, and it was getting bigger, causing incredible pain and pressure in my chest. My breathing became very shallow and hard. What was going on? Frightened by what might come, when the time came to lie down in savasana, I strode out of the class.

One of the attendants ran after me saying, "Madame! It would be better to stay with the yogic process until the end."

I listened to her, feeling teary and overwhelmed. "I must go," I said. "I feel I am going to explode. There is a big painful ball of energy in my heart. I need time in solitude."

Earlier that morning I had heard that participants in the advanced program were to maintain silence for five days. I had never observed silence before and did not remember reading about it when I signed up. I was petrified to undergo such a long time in silence and did not think I could face the challenges of an advanced program with Gurudev right after my intense experiences in our basic program. I marched straight for the pay phone and called Nathaniel.

"I think I may have made a mistake, baby," I told him. "I don't want to take the advanced program anymore. I want to come home. Will you find me a flight, please?"

Nathaniel was annoyed. "Are you crazy? You just left and now you want to come back home? What's going on?"

"Baby, I don't understand. How can Gurudev's kriya work great, when I feel like I have been run over by a bus? It is way too simple."

I was judging it and comparing it to Gurunath's spiritual practices, not trusting my intuitive feelings and guidance. Our minds can get us in trouble with prompt conclusions and assumptions. I was holding on to my old mindset, resisting Gurudev's approach rather than allowing myself to remain open and receptive. How many of us have had to learn this valuable lesson more than once? This was one of the most priceless lessons I would learn with my Gurudev.

"I'll call you in the morning, sweetheart. I want to come home as soon as possible," I told Nathaniel, insisting, and hung up.

~

GRADUATION FROM THE BASIC PROGRAM was the following day. First the teacher made us repeat the long kriya once more. Oh no, not again, I thought. First . . . coffee, please!

"The mind is kept alive by cravings and aversions," Gurudev says. "Only when the mind dies does bliss dawn. Bliss is the abode of all divinity, all devas. . . . And having had a human life and having known this path, if you still do not realize this, you are at the greatest loss."[2]

After another forty-five minutes of intense pranayama breathing, at last I lay in savasana with my eyes closed in a state of profound abandonment. That excruciating gigantic ball of energy was trying to burst my heart wide open. All at once I witnessed a series of Indian faces flashing rapidly by, one by one. The first image was of a chubby and unadorned Indian woman with her eyes closed. I sensed she might have been me in one of my past lives or the most recent past lifetime. She lay there as if she had just passed away or was about to leave her body. Dozens of other Indian faces of both sexes kept popping up looking down at her. I could see them from her perspective and could clearly see their individual features. During this parade of faces, I was an invisible witness to the proceedings.

As I opened my eyes, I was overwhelmed by an urge to run away. I felt like a runaway bride fleeing Shiva for fear of being demolished! I wanted to scream at the top of my lungs. I stood up and dashed out of the room, overwhelmed by tears and terror.

Again the assistant volunteer called, "Madame!"

I ignored her and continued running, looking for a quiet spot. I hoped I would run into Gurudev. I paced around the ground for an hour, trying to let go of the fierce energy inside, but it was getting worse by the second. I called upon my master mentally. "I need your help, Gurudev. I can't do this alone."

He was nowhere in sight. I was petrified by the darkness inside me. I could not understand where these intense and overwhelmingly powerful emotions came from—maybe my vision of my past life in India had awakened some karmic unfolding. I feared coming face-to-face with this dark entity; I feared the confrontation it would take to purify my karma.

Finally, I decided to go back to my room. When I arrived, I looked at Gurudev's photo for a few minutes. I lay down in savasana on my bed and closed my eyes while calling upon him mentally. I could feel something epic was about to happen. This time I called Gurudev several times aloud, asking him to hold my hand. My profound love, devotion, reverence, and trust in him allowed my being to surrender to this very intense spiritual process of purification.

Gurudev says, "Surrender is not an act; it is a state of being. The purpose of sorrow is to bring you back to the Self. And the Self is all joy."

All at once I felt Gurudev's presence overwhelming my being. This time, at last, that huge energetic ball exploded in my heart region. I burst into an ocean of loud weeping while I held both of my hands tight against my heart as if preventing someone from pulling it out of my chest.

I lamented so loudly, Gurudev and parts of the ashram must have heard, and it went on for several hours. I had no idea why I was mourning so deeply.

When I started to calm down, with my eyes closed, I witnessed Gurudev and me holding hands, smiling at each other, and dancing in circles. I could see his white, silky robe flowing in the hot breeze and my hair bouncing to the rhythm of our hearts. In that moment, a sharp explosion of sweet, intoxicating energy traversed my heart center, vibrating along every vertebra of my spine. I did not realize then that this intense flood of energy inside me was the shakti energy purifying my heart chakra, the anahata, in its spiritual kundalini ascension.

Gurudev's cosmic shakti energy (shaktipat) penetrated my heart like a sharp, divine love arrow, and bubbles of ecstasy tickled every cell of my body temple. In that moment I became One with my Gurudev.

I smiled and lay on the bed for quite some time, relishing the intoxicating, blissful moments of my true ultimate nature in a state of satchit ananda. Afterward I slowly sat up, feeling profound gratitude for my master and his shaktipat transmission for releasing me from years, if not a whole lifetime of past-life karmic structure. That is exactly what a true genuine satguru does: They guide you to the light, to your true nature. My body temple was so light I felt I was floating.

Gurudev says, "Bliss cannot be understood and it is extremely difficult to achieve. After many lifetimes you finally achieve bliss, but once achieved, it is even more difficult to lose. All that you seek in your life is bliss, that divine union with your source, and everything else in the world distracts you from that goal."[3]

~

IN THE RICH AND PROFOUND tradition of Yoga, we find a magnificent living tree still standing tall after over seven thousand years. This tree has six major branches, each bearing fruit: Hatha (forceful), the branch most familiar to Westerners; Bhakti (devotion-love); Jnana (right knowledge); Raj (royal); Karma (action); and Tantra (continuity). All branches of yoga are viewed by the tradition as a science, because we can personally test them for ourselves.

Bhakti Yoga, like all yoga branches, is not a religion, philosophy, or cult. It is simply being filled with Divine love and having a profound reverence for the Source of creation. When we are in a state of Divine love, physical boundaries melt away. We expand that love to all living beings . . . to infinity. In essence, when we fall in genuine love with someone, we are in a state of bhakti yoga. The magical wand of the heart is revealed in bhakti yoga.

"When Bhakti is present," Gurudev says, "doubts do not arise. Bhakti gives the most energy. When your emotions get flooded everywhere, the mind is a mess. But when emotions flow intensely in one direction, that is Bhakti and that is powerful. A sign of intelligence is surrender or Bhakti. Love is not an emotion, it is your very existence."[4]

Bhakti yoga is the union of the lover and the beloved as the ultimate absolute One, the yoga of self-transcending love. At first this form of attachment becomes a sacred link where the mind and its demands melt away by the intensity of our burning heart. This yoga of love especially holds magic for those who have been heartbroken, and for anyone whose heart is still entrapped, repressed, and captured in its sorrow, fears, and limitations. Its practice opens up the heart center, allowing Divine love and bliss to flow in. Fall in love with Divine love and you become free.

In bhakti yoga, the devotee is the lover; the Divine is the beloved. When lovers hear the birds singing, it is God whispering in their ears. Every object and action is worshipped and sanctified as the manifestation of the supreme absolute. For the lover, the aroma of a rose, a cat playing, the laughter of a child, a deer grazing nearby, moss growing on a rock, dew dancing in a spiderweb, and even the sun rays sparkling on snowflakes can reveal the greatness, sacredness, and oneness of our Creator.

This transcendental reality comes from a personal divinity rather than an idea of an unseen, unknown, impersonal God up in the sky as has been taught by some religions to reinforce separation, dichotomy, and power over us. As long as there is a split between two entities, we will experience duality, exclusiveness, and hierarchy. Oneness is inclusive and boundless, transcending physical barriers. The ancient science of yoga leads to expansion, boundlessness, oneness, and liberation, no matter our background and life accumulations.

The ultimate goal of bhakti yoga is to merge with the supreme Source of creation. In the very process, the illusion of the ego loses its grip. We become intoxicated in the ecstasy of Divine love. Paramahansa Yogananda put it simply: "If you could feel even a particle of Divine love, so great would be your joy, so overpowering, you could not contain it."[5]

Prior to complete self-realization, the lover needs to regard God as a person or even a creature, so the Divine can be worshiped in ritual, actions, and art. There is also a meditative aspect to bhakti yoga. We become intoxicated with Divine love by focusing our energy into creative actions like chanting, dancing, composing, singing, painting, or even breathing; it becomes natural to lose oneself in a blissful state for the object of love. The subject becomes the object, and the two merge as One.

On the path of love, the devotee grows with intense passion (*rati*) for the beloved, whomever that representation may be—a beloved person, a spiritual master, teacher, Shiva, Jesus Christ, Krishna, Mohammed, Ganesh, the Buddha, Kali, Kuan Yin, the Virgin Mother, or even a companion animal. The symbolic objective of this sacred figure is that it helps the devotee expand and express the same Divine love to every being, animals, nature, and the entire cosmos.

The goal of any genuine and true spiritual master is to impart and transmit this wisdom so that self-realization naturally unfolds. This moment of realization, as the Bhagavad Gita describes it, is a complete love supreme participation (*para-Bhakti*). As Rumi so beautifully writes, "The minute I heard my first love story, / I started looking for you, not knowing / how blind that was / Lovers don't finally meet somewhere, they're in each other all along."[6]

Bhakti yoga is universal and can be practiced by anyone who longs for truth and is in search of genuine love. But this is not, as some may think, a path of emotional sentimentalism. The emotional force of rati transforms the lover, shedding all their psychological limitations. Bhakti yoga recognizes the amazing power of human emotions and encourages lovers to channel their energy to the highest Divine goal, the ultimate objective of life.

Devotion and love liberate the imprisoned heart to feel again by shedding life's conditioning and accumulations and the false power and illusion of the ego. Devotion and Divine love expand our consciousness to the Source of creation by allowing our all-encompassing ultimate nature to become realized. Only then can the intensity of our longing be felt and the cry resonating with the Source of creation be heard.

~

HALF A DAY AFTER MY mystical embrace with Gurudev, I walked back to class. In the midst of this emotional tempest, I forgot to call Nathaniel back.

The teacher welcomed my return with a smile without asking any questions. On that hot, humid afternoon, the air suddenly turned cool. I took a few deep breaths with my eyes closed, reflecting on the volcano of energy that had passed. Something inside my being had vanished, leaving room for sunshine to radiate in. I was intoxicated with intense bliss.

Torrential rain started to fall outside the ashram. The sound of it hitting the roof hypnotized my being into a meditative state. Once in a while thunder and lightning spread across the sky. I sat bewitched by the sound of the raindrops and the abundant fresh air.

In those final moments of our basic program, several participants shared their experiences with the group. I sat mute, lost in a lone shaft of sunlight. As people began to leave, I felt an urge to bathe in the lake. I went to my room and put on my bathing suit.

It was still sprinkling a bit when I returned to the lake. I tentatively put my toes in. The water felt cold and crisp; a refreshing change from the humidity. I dove into the pristine water, swirling and jumping in and out like a dolphin, enjoying the rain falling on my head. I was filled with bliss and gratitude. By the grace of Gurudev, I had survived the hurricane within myself.

After my swim, I went to the kitchen to help for several hours. While working, I realized how selfish and self-centered I had been. How I lacked the commitment to make the kind of contribution my heart and soul longed to offer to help all living beings. The time had come to transform myself. I vowed to make a positive difference for all living beings from then on.

It was time for dinner, but I was not hungry, filled as I was by Divine love. The clouds had disappeared in my mind and heart; they were as clear as the blue sky. I went down by the lake to sweep away the puddles of rain on the plastic platform where participants would sit for the evening's satsang.

As I swept, Gurudev passed me, with a trail of devotees following him. He turned his head, smiled, and placed his fist on his heart, moving it several times toward my heart, expressing his love. He seemed to be aware of what had occurred that afternoon. His gesture was his way of telling me he loved me while transmitting a shaktipat. This was our first in-person interaction. As he smiled at my being, his shakti energy pierced my heart once more, and I was lost in a heaven of pure love and bliss. I wished I could capture the moment in a bottle and never let it go.

~

AS NIGHT FELL, A WARM breeze blew, crickets sang their love songs, and the moon was pregnant with electric blue light. The musicians began to play bhajans. More than seven hundred people sat on the ground chanting at the top of their lungs, "*Om namah Shivaya*." The spotlights focused on the dais where Gurudev would sit. The lake behind the stage reflected the glory of the full moon on its still water. For an hour, I chanted while I assisted guests to their seats in the VIP section near the dais.

I chanted in delight, feeling serene and vibrating with blissful energy while my being throbbed in unison with the universe. I could not remember any happier, more exuberant moment. I thought, *I could do this for the rest of my life.*

Gurudev arrived and sat down on the dais while we chanted. He closed his eyes for the next half hour. I sat by his feet on his left. My good karma must have permitted the synchronicity of such an auspicious location.

Before the satsang began, he opened his eyes wide and began to sing. On several occasions, Gurudev gazed straight into my eyes with such intense Divine love that his regard penetrated to the very core of my being. The Source of creation pulsated within my being, overflowing with love and compassion. His loving energy made me feel so beautiful, humble, and beloved of the Divine.

At this point most of the crowd stood dancing and chanting. One senior teacher grabbed Gurudev's hand; moments later, I grabbed his other hand. Together we danced with him in front of the stage. After a minute, she let go. She smiled humbly and nodded her head in a gesture that said, "Go ahead, he's all yours." Gurudev and I danced, chanting as One under the moonlight. His shaktipat penetrated every cell of my being. Later I realized my mystical vision of dancing with our beloved master had become a reality.

"When you sing bhajans, the vibration of the sound energy gets absorbed into every atom of your body," Gurudev said. "This enkindles the energy in you and brings up consciousness. Your entire body gets soaked in energy. Transformation happens."[7]

During the satsang, all the terror I had about being silent during my advanced program vanished—and so did some of my limitations. Who needed coffee? I was intoxicated with the supreme nectar. I decided to stay at the ashram and go ahead with my advanced program. I knew I must always listen to my heart and that the path of love was the right one for my being.

The enchanting evening continued. Everyone's eyes focused on our beloved master and listened to his words of wisdom.

"Neither the body nor the mind is the Self," Gurudev says. "The only purpose for this body to exist is to make you aware of how beautiful you are and to make you aware that it is possible to live all the values you cherish. You can create a world of divinity around you. All the yoga asanas you do are for the body. All the meditation you do is for the mind. Whether calm or disturbed, your mind remains mind. Whether sick or well, your body remains body. Self is all-encompassing."

When the time arrived for questions, I raised my hand.

"Gurudev, if God made us in its own image, why aren't we perfect and enlightened yet?"

"From milk comes butter, from butter comes ghee," Gurudev responded in a very serene voice. The radiant light in his intoxicated eyes and his smile gave away his blissfulness.

I knew that ghee was clarified butter, but I did not understand the profundity of his words at the time. It was only much later I realized that movement from gross to subtle is the essence of creation.

Genuine masters often purposely speak enigmatically to allow seekers to perceive the reality on their own, and Gurudev was no exception; he often spoke in parables.

That night, I witnessed Gurudev's halo for the first time. I could see his aura as clearly as my own hand. This experience had happened to me with Gurunath, but Gurudev's aura manifested differently; it looked like something from a Renaissance painting. It was translucent light rimmed with a sparkling violet. I felt humble and transfixed by this phenomenon, absorbed in my devotion.

Around 10:00, Gurudev left the platform. I left the satsang dancing and chanting out loud. The air buzzed with blissful energy. Everyone was invited to go to the dining hall for vegetarian samosas. As I chatted with new friends, I realized I had not called Nathaniel back. I excused myself and trotted to the phone booth.

"Baby, baby, I'm staying!" I cried when he answered. "You won't believe what happened today. I'm so blissed out!"

Nathaniel asked, "One moment you're miserable, the next one you're blissed out! Can you make up your mind, darling?"

"That's the thing, baby, the mind is the challenge."

"Good," he said with an ironic tone of voice. "I couldn't find you a flight anyway."

~

FOR THE FOLLOWING WEEK, I walked around so drunk on bliss, an outsider might have thought I was high on drugs; but a look in my eyes would have revealed the truth. I was intoxicated with Divine love.

Everyone saw it. Some of the seekers even teased me. "Look at Vivi—she is a gopi—she has found her Krishna!"

The following morning about five hundred of us met in the main hall for our advanced silent program. During the first few days, Gurudev wanted to meet all of us in smaller groups at his *kutir*, or cell. We went in alphabetical order.

When my group's turn came, I sat near his feet again. All of us had been silent for two days. "It is okay to speak now during your visit. Are you all happy?" Gurudev asked.

Most exclaimed, "Yes!" or nodded their heads.

After a while I said, "I feel I'm with God when I'm with you, Gurudev. I want to paint you."

Gurudev gestured around him with one arm up in the air. "God is everywhere, so paint the trees, the sun, the stars, the mountains, the animals."

When our group left, I approached him as he was going out the back door. I whispered, "Gurudev, I want to give my life to you. Please guide me."

He stopped, looked straight in my eyes, and nodded yes.

~

AMONG THE MANY CHALLENGING PROCESSES we completed during Gurudev's advanced silent program, there is one that remains engraved in my heart and my being.

During a meditation, we stood in a very awkward position for over an hour. I never thought I could make it to the end. By the time we reached the last twenty minutes, most participants were screaming in pain, but I stood still and serene with my arms stretched, focusing on Gurudev, even though he was not in the room. With my eyes closed, I could see him smile at me and could also see Jesus Christ on the cross with nails through his feet and hands, his flesh dripping with blood. Somehow Gurudev's presence reminded me so much of Jesus Christ. My arms, shoulders, neck, and head hurt so much.

Overwhelmed by Gurudev and Jesus Christ's love, grace, and energy, tears of sorrow for Jesus kept rolling down my face and neck. Jesus was the perfect and ultimate embodiment of love and compassion. His life demonstrated the awesome power of Divine love. My heart filled with compassion and gratitude for him. I could not explain why. When the meditative process ended, I jumped up and down with exultation, then lay on the floor feeling blessed, bathing in Jesus Christ's healing energy.

Those five days flew by. Silence is the ladder to infinity within us. After we broke silence in our last hour, the teacher asked us if anyone wanted to share their experience.

I went onstage and took the microphone. "I feel my life has just begun since Gurudev has entered my heart. Such grace, I feel so blessed and grateful."

I went on to share the entire story of how Gurudev appeared in my life in San Diego, what I had gone through in the past few weeks, and how the program helped me break through many of my huge limitations. As I spoke, I burst into tears of gratitude. When I paused to take a deep breath, I noticed some of the participants also shedding tears.

~

ON THE MORNING OF THE day we were to leave the ashram, even though I was dressed and ready to go home, intense sadness lingered in my heart. I did not want to leave my Gurudev. My roommates had already left, but one of them ran back in to get me.

"Hurry up, Vivi!" she said. "The buses for the airport are almost full. You will miss them. Come on, honey, let's go!" Then she noticed I was crying, and a concerned look crossed her face. "Sweetheart, what's going on?"

"How can I leave Gurudev again when I have been waiting for him for hundreds of years?" I asked, sobbing. "I gave him my life."

For the first time, I was revealing my deep, intense longing to someone else. My roommate grabbed a tissue, cleaned the mascara running down my checks, and hugged me.

"Have you lost your mind, Vivi? You will leave everything behind, including your husband and your cats."

I stayed mute, overwhelmed by my deep longing. She hugged me and left the room in a rush. "See you on the bus!"

Everyone has a different rhythm and rides different energies. I knew no one in the world could understand and relate to my longing for the Divine better than Gurudev himself. Longing had been the underlying pain in my heart for decades. I knew returning home to California would present an enormous challenge for Nathaniel and me, but first I would stop at Mama's house in Quebec.

"Longing itself is Divine," Gurudev says. "Longing for worldly things makes you inert. Longing for infinity fills you with life. When longing dies, inertia sets in. But longing also brings a sense of pain. To avoid the pain, you try to push away the longing. The skill is to bear the pain of the longing and move on."[8]

~

AT THE LAST MINUTE, I grabbed my bags and ran as fast as I could to Gurudev's kutir. I wanted to say goodbye and express my deep love and gratitude to him. I had no idea if or when I would see him again.

When I arrived Gurudev was not in. I spoke with one of his attendants and asked her to give him a message.

"Please tell Gurudev I love him so, so much! I'm so grateful for everything! I feel so blessed to have him in my life. My heart longs; I'm in pain." I broke down sobbing.

"Go, Vivi," she said. "I promise I will tell him."

I thanked her, blessed her, and threw her kisses. She did the same. Then I ran as fast as I could to the bus.

Bodhi, a dear friend and senior teacher, was on the last bus, counting heads. I stepped in at the last second. Everyone was talking and laughing. The engine was humming. I caught my breath, gave Bodhi a big hug, and thanked him for holding the bus. As soon as I sat down, we departed for the airport.

Gurudev says, "Longing gives you the power to bless. Bless the entire creation . . . For the longing in you is God.[9]

Twenty-Two

BLOOMING PORCUPINE

MAMA AND HER COMPANION PICKED me up from the airport to bring me to her home. On our way, we stopped at a French cafe. Then we walked around the historical part of town, stopping by the Great Cathedral. I lit a candle and sat on one of the pews. I closed my eyes and invoked for all living beings' well-being and happiness, and expressed my love and gratitude to the Divine Mother for having Gurudev in my life. I gazed at the crucifix on the wall behind the altar and expressed my profound love and gratitude to Jesus for his presence in my life.

When we reached Mama's house, I was exhausted, but I went to Mama's bedroom and practiced my sudarshan kriya yoga. After, I was full of energy and bliss. Then we departed for the family reunion dinner.

Most of my siblings joined the celebration, along with their spouses and children. I sat next to Mama and shared a few of my spiritual experiences at the ashram—my silence, revelations, and Gurudev's wisdom. I kept laughing because I felt intoxicated with ecstasy. My bliss resonated in my family's hearts. It became contagious.

"I have never been so touched and nourished by such profound sense of unconditional love and belongingness than I encountered at the Art of Living. All the volunteers, teachers, and participants were from so many different national, cultural, religious, and socioeconomic backgrounds, but we were as one," I said enthusiastically.

I started hugging everyone around the table. I exclaimed laughingly, "I belong to you! We belong to each other!"

My elder brother hugged, teased, "We belong to each other, my little sister!"

"That is exactly what was missing so desperately in my life, belonging-ness!" I said to everyone. "I was the one creating separation without real-izing it, because I was afraid of being hurt for loving again. My heart is as open as the blue sky, by the grace of Gurudev." Tears welled up in our eyes.

I read them Gurudev's words on belongingness: "You should have belongingness. Silence is mother of all creativity. Silence is mother of inven-tion. Silence is basis for love. You know when you love somebody and you sit and talk . . . blah blah blah. You know while you're talking that you're not enjoying the communication that could have come with silence. So you need to create a belongingness with silence or for silence. That's very precious in life. This realization, I belong to the whole universe, will give us an insight into something that is so stupendous, magnificent in life."[1]

We paused for a moment, silent, and relished our belongingness. By the end of dinner, we stood up and hugged one another again, saying, "We belong to each other!"

"I belong to you! I belong to the whole universe!" I said, dancing and laughing. My oldest brother grabbed me by the hand and we danced like I did with Gurudev.

For the first time in my life, our family reunion turned out to be the most precious healing and loving spiritual process for everyone. We danced and sang together by the table. The restaurant was almost emptied by then. This magical moment will be forever treasured in my heart.

$\sim$

WHEN I RETURNED TO CALIFORNIA, Nathaniel picked me up at the airport. I told him all about my phenomenal journey with Gurudev. I said one of the most significant discoveries I had made was that when I put awareness in my heart, a Divine exalted presence throbbed inside my shrine. I had never felt that kind of pure ecstatic love before.

"It's not the kind of love we feel when we fall in love with a person. It's more of a sublime and Divine nature. No words can describe it. Baby, you have to experience it for yourself!"

Nathaniel kept saying, "Really."

He seemed skeptical, though it was always hard to read his feelings.

Back at home I put my favorite Art of Living music CD on, grabbed Nathaniel's hands, and pulled him toward me, dancing. I began to swirl around him. At first, he just stood there, not knowing what to do. Then he tried to keep up with my steps, yet his expression revealed his worry and concern about losing the Vivi he had fallen in love with.

Returning home was very painful and powerful all at the same time. My heart longed so much to be with Gurudev. I did not feel like working. His sublime presence continued to invade my thoughts and heart as if I were an addict. For the following few months, I was too serene and still to be able to paint. I only wanted to meditate—to be alone, feeling emptied.

～

ONE HOT DAY NATHANIEL AND I headed to my favorite beach about forty-five minutes from home. This little-known oasis is mostly deserted, the perfect sanctuary for self-introspection and solitude. I chanted Alleluia all through the drive until we reached the rolling hills, saw the blue ocean, and heard the songs of the seagulls.

The sparsely populated beach seemed to stretch to infinity. I practiced my sudarshan kriya, meditated, and contemplated the reflections of the sunlight on the waves with both of my feet buried in the sand. Nathaniel read the newspaper nearby.

In the weeks that followed, I returned to the same beach on my own many times, feeling thirsty for solitude, silence, and fresh air. I was no longer sure about what I wanted to do with the rest of my life. Gurudev's presence had shifted many of my priorities and views.

Every day I processed my experiences and feelings, and meditated. Soon new horizons opened up before my eyes. More of my old, false sense of self crumbled and disappeared. I had to learn to reintegrate all this new energy into my core self. The numerous blessings flowing in my life were

Divine grace. My heart was full, and I wanted to give back. I wondered what I could contribute with my talents and skills.

I started to embrace everything in nature, animals, people, and creation. My sense of belongingness expanded to embrace the whole universe. I realized when you see and feel the world as part of yourself, your love becomes all-inclusive, and the illusion of false boundaries and sense of separation begins to vanish. A profound sense of oneness and belongingness dawned within my being.

Gurudev says: "Stretching the Sound is Music / Stretching the Movement is Dance / Stretching the Smile is Laughter / Stretching the Mind is Meditation / Stretching the Life is Celebration / Stretching the Devotee is God / Stretching the Feeling is Ecstasy / Stretching the Emptiness is Bliss. . . . Emptiness is the doorway between the material and spiritual worlds."[2]

My only desire to return to work was so that I could paint Gurudev. This project brought me back to my studio after a month and a half of absence. I knew that what I needed to express in art would emerge.

I spent an entire month painting Gurudev's portrait with oils and mixed media. First I meditated on his photo and then drew many sketches, followed by a single major drawing. I wanted to capture not just his resemblance but his essence.

Each time I drew or painted Gurudev I felt empty. I would find myself in a meditative trance, focusing on his features, especially his eyes. On my canvas, I included an aura of beatitude around Gurudev's head to complement his holiness, just the way I had witnessed it during the satsang.

When I completed the portrait, it resembled an ancient wall fresco. I loved it so much I wanted to keep it, but I decided to overcome my attachment and give it to Gurudev on my next visit.

~

FIVE MONTHS LATER, I FLEW back to Canada for my second advanced silent program with Gurudev. I arrived well prepared for the harsh winter in Quebec. I walked around the ashram with my long faux-mink coat, big hat, and boots, while Gurudev walked around wrapped only in his shawl, wearing his sandals with socks. I wondered why he never caught the flu.

Prodigious snowflakes fell, sparkling like jewels in the sunlight. The yoga center glittered with light and shakti. Everyone felt the festive atmosphere of the New Year still in the air.

During the first satsang, I sat in the third row among perhaps eight hundred participants, all crammed together. When Gurudev entered, we stood up in reverence, and the room exploded with a happy clamor, many participants tooting holiday noisemakers. As Gurudev passed by, I blew a whistle flute that reeled out to a feather at the tip. Unexpectedly, it touched his nose.

My breath caught in anticipation. I wanted him to know I had returned again to see him; I had brought along his portrait to the ashram and planned to offer it to him after the program. Perhaps he would notice me now.

But Gurudev did not even flinch at the feather's touch. He kept smiling and walked on, without looking my way. I was so disappointed. Perhaps he ignored me purposely just because I was seeking his attention. Masters have many mystical ways to interact with their seekers, often to accelerate their seekers' transformation.

During the previous five months, I had contemplated becoming one of Gurudev's full-time teachers. I had already accomplished many of the requirements, including following a vegetarian diet—in fact, I was almost a vegan. I was determined to fulfill the other requirements and be admitted to his teacher-training program in India. Only one concern still lingered: One of the requirements was abstinence from alcohol. I wondered how I could overcome my craving for a glass of wine with dinner. I wondered if there was some flexibility there.

That first night at satsang, the opportunity arose to ask the master himself. With the microphone in my hands, I said, "Gurudev I would love to become one of your full-time teachers, but do you think I could still have one little glass of chardonnay with dinner?"

Gurudev threw his head back and laughed. After a few moments, he exclaimed, "You have cornered me! If I say yes to you, all the teachers will be jealous and envious. If I say no, then some of the teachers will feel guilty!"

I laughed with the crowd.

"But, Gurudev . . . Jesus turned water into wine and gave it to all the people!"

Gurudev continued to laugh as the crowd laughed with him, then he paused for a long moment. "Jesus also talked about overcoming temptation. Temptation comes because of the pleasure it brings, but pleasures are immediate and ephemeral. They can make us miserable in the long run."

Gurudev went on to speak of the nature of the universe, and how certain laws of nature operate—specifically, the three qualities called *gunas* that govern us: *sattva*, *rajas*, and *tamas*. To put it simply, Gurudev said that sattva (*sattvic* or *satguna*) is based on the principle of lucidity and consciousness; raja springs from the principle of action; and tama stems from the principle of inertia. I sat attentively listening to our master, feeling humbled that he took the time to share such important, timeless wisdom.

The sattva quality includes such examples as spiritual practices and rituals, meditation, pranayama, prayers, invocations, contemplation, eating an organic vegetarian or vegan diet, and not drinking alcohol or doing drugs (not out of moral obligation, but because alcohol and drugs impair our lucidity, consciousness, introspection, and shift one's perception of existence to a very limited view, or even false view). Even though there may be some misery in the beginning, in the long run, sattva will bring long-lasting pleasure, joy, peace, happiness, and bliss.

Someone who is dominated by rajas (*rajasic/rajoguna*) could be considered compulsive; for instance, a workaholic who takes on too many projects would fall into this category. Such individuals tend to live an overactive and out-of-balance life. Having a dominant rajoguna quality often brings short-term pleasures but also conflicts and afflictions.

Someone who tends to be dominated by tamas (*tamasic/tamoguna*) will exhibit a lot of inertia, such as laziness, extra sleep, or rest. Someone who is an alcoholic or drug addict would likely be dominated by tamas. As it brings immediate pleasure that does not last, this quality will, over time, bring only misery and pain.

There are many examples of the three gunas. Gurudev explained that they affect all areas of our lives; this is why it is important to become aware of these qualities and how they affect us and dominate our state of being and our lives. We all have these three tendencies within us. The question is, which one is dominant?

"One of the three gunas will dominate," Gurudev explained. "Sattva is always there in everybody, as is rajas and tamas. All the three gunas always exist together. But what dominates is what makes the difference. If tamoguna dominates, there is misery. When rajoguna dominates, there are conflicts. When satguna dominates, there is awareness, knowledge, and happiness."

Once Gurudev had fully explained the three gunas, he tied in the spiritual knowledge and timeless wisdom regarding temptation. He emphasized that overcoming temptation is crucial because it ultimately will bring long-term pleasure, whereas yielding to our temptations brings pleasure but leads to misery over time.

I realized in that instant that one of the most beneficial and important parts of awakening was to increase my sattvic tendency. The beauty about spiritually blooming as we evolve is that our sattvic will naturally dominate. Our lucidity, awareness, and consciousness expand in every aspect of our lives. The benefits of a more sattvic lifestyle are priceless. We will become filled with Divine love, light, serenity, bliss, and ecstasy. There is a distinctive radiance, a bright light emanating from the eyes of a sattvic being filled with light. Individuals who are attuned and receptive to it can feel the vibrations of shakti this person can emanate if she or he has that *siddhi*—spiritual power.

As I reflected on these sattvic characteristics, I thought about how the other gunas expressed themselves. Generally, a strongly rajasic individual tends to be more self-centered and selfish and ultimately causes pain to himself and to others. A very tamasic person may be more primitive and self-destructive. On the spiritual path, as we awake to our true ultimate nature, our being naturally leads the way to a more sattvic lifestyle.

At the end of the satsang, Gurudev stood up onstage. The musicians played in unison as we all chanted, "Hari Bol!"—"Speak of God."

When he was about to depart, I found my way to his side and gave him a letter I had written. "I love you so much, Gurudev," I whispered.

He grinned, put his index and middle finger on his heart, then turned them around, pointing them toward me. I interpreted it as "I love you twice as much." His subtle shakti pierced my heart with a Divine love arrow. I could never get used to his presence. It had such an intoxicating effect on my being. This was the first in a series of many letters that followed over the next decade. I wanted to share with him what troubled my heart the most about the animal kingdom, our world, and the future of our beloved planet.

～

TOWARD THE END OF OUR program, a small group of us, mostly teachers and close devotees, received the great blessing of visiting with Gurudev in his kutir. We had been waiting for ten minutes in the hallway when Bodhi walked in and hugged me. He had been a long-time, close devotee of Gurudev and full-time Art of Living teacher for decades.

I was holding the painting I'd made of Gurudev in my arms.

"May I see it?" Bodhi asked.

I showed it to him. At first sight, tears rolled down his cheeks.

When we entered Gurudev's kutir, it was already packed with devotees and teachers. I tried to find a small spot in the back where I could fit in. During most of the visit, I remained silent. Eventually, some individuals left, and one of the teachers said, "Vivi, go ahead! Now is the time."

I saw a tiny space next to Gurudev's feet. I carefully moved in, saying, "Gurudev, I painted this for you." I offered him the portrait, which I had gotten beautifully framed.

He looked at me with a loving gaze; his shakti permeated my heart. He smiled. "Oh! You painted this! Very, very, very good," he said rolling his r's. He started knocking on the artwork, touching it as if he was feeling and reading its vibrations with his fingers.

"No, no, Gurudev, please be careful," I said softly. "It's fragile. It may crack or break."

Gurudev was fascinated by the painting's textured bas-relief and its vibrancy. He seemed to love it very much, for he took his time and explored it like a child. I believed he could feel the energy of my devotional and vibrational love in the canvas.

"Gurudev, you're welcome to auction it for the poor children in India," I said. "The money can be used to build a school in a poor village."

Then I presented Gurudev with a small signed reproduction of one of my limited-edition giclée prints of my painting *Garden of Love*.

"Gurudev, here is a small self-portrait." I wanted to tell him that the inspiration for this painting of myself flowed in because of him, my beloved master. Its golden tone and serene introspective expression depicted the transformative effect he had awoken in my being. On the canvas, a gigantic bouquet of sunflowers emerged from my scalp as growing branches with needles wrapped around my arms and my neck, and a white dove is perched on my left shoulder. I wanted to tell him this artwork signified my spiritual blossoming and my oneness with all of nature. Yet I could not express one word. I was too overwhelmed with emotions, too awed and silenced by his exalted presence.

He looked at it closely, taking his own time. "You look a little pale in this," he remarked.

"It's a portrait of my etheric body, Gurudev," I whispered.

"What are those things coming out of your head?" he asked. "Porcupines?"

Everyone laughed. My face turned red. After what had occurred at the first satsang with the blowing of the feathered Christmas whistle flute, I did not want his attention anymore.

"No, no, Gurudev, these are blooming sunflowers! If you continue teasing me, I'm going to crawl under your coffee table," I said with a little smile, feeling humble as I attempted to do just that. Gurudev and everyone kept laughing out loud, though I was not trying to be funny. I laughed too and relished with great joy every moment of our interaction since it was so unexpected. Gurudev often says that expectation reduces joy. I felt deeply honored, humbled, and very loved by Gurudev's attention. He loved to have fun and tease. He would often say jokingly—God loves fun! Ultimately it was his shakti energy in his loving gaze that was so transformational for my being.

~

UPON MY RETURN HOME, I began to experience Gurudev's wisdom in all aspects of my life. Nathaniel became more surprised by my transformation. Gurudev's presence lingered in the shrine of my heart, and just by putting my awareness in it, I became filled with bliss. I meditated on his wisdom about the essence of Divinity buried within us all. At our cores, we are unique expressions and manifestations of the Divine—microscopic mirrors of existential phenomena.

I was able to return to my art studio and attended the weekly satsang. My creativity exploded. I often painted ten to twelve hours a day while chanting bhajans. Each canvas became a meditative process. I offered all my work to the Divine Mother.

I always asked Nathaniel to join me at the satsang, but he never wanted to. His resistance often drained my energy. He kept building a big wall between us while I was trying to demolish it. A few months later, with the holidays approaching, I spoke enthusiastically to him about the benefits of taking the basic Art of Living program and practicing yogic techniques. I had never insisted that he participate this strongly before, but this time I asked him to take the program being offered in San Francisco during December. It would be taught by a senior teacher I knew and loved, a male physician with considerable insight. I sensed he could reach Nathaniel in ways I could not.

"Baby, just forget about the spiritual aspect. Do it for the sake of our relationship and your well-being," I pleaded. "I'll even take it with you."

Nathaniel became very defensive. He said with an annoyed tone, "I will never meditate. What a waste of my time. I tried Zen meditation a few times when I was younger and could not sit still for a single moment."

"I understand, baby," I said, "but the past is the past. There is an even greater reason why you need to meditate—to calm your agitated mind. You are judging meditation and our relationship based on your past experiences. I live in my heart, you in your head. That creates tension and conflict between us. It pushes me away. Often couples who grow in separate ways end up in divorce, and I fear we're heading in that direction. This big wall growing between us could destroy our love and intimacy."

"You and your guru!" Nathaniel snapped. "I don't want anything to do with a guru. That's your thing."

"It's not my thing—it's everybody's thing!" I said. "Everybody needs to wake up at some point. If that happened we would live in a much more compassionate, harmonious, and loving world for all living beings, for sure." I took a deep breath. "Come on, baby, wake up! How can we communicate when you're so defensive and critical, constantly building this wall of resistance? One minute I demolish it, the next, you build it back higher."

Nathaniel stood up and walked away infuriated. Harsh words flew out of his mouth. He could not, would not hear his beloved wife. Or was I incapable of reaching and hearing him? Or both?

He had never yelled at me before. I raised my voice so he could hear better. "Why are you so closed-minded?" I demanded. "What do you have to lose? Please open up and be a little more receptive to new ways of experiencing and seeing life. It means so much to me. Doesn't our relationship mean anything to you?"

I didn't want to discuss the matter any further at that point; we were both too upset. "Let's continue this conversation later when we're calmer, more centered," I said firmly. I ran upstairs to our bedroom, crying.

～

A FEW DAYS LATER I realized Nathaniel must have felt threatened by my growth, by Gurudev, and by my awakening. I was transforming rapidly, and my newly ascending energies were changing the dynamics of our relationship. He was a witness to my spiritual awakening, and that was frightening for him. Perhaps he wished to keep his little Vivi just the way she was when he first met her.

Resistance to change and transformation is extremely common. Most people fear change because it brings the unknown, which can trigger insecurity and anxiety. I felt Nathaniel might be unconsciously afraid of transformation because his belief system, identity, and preconceptions would have to collapse. It is threatening for people to face their limitations; that is human nature. He would have to turn inward, face and heal his buried wounds.

This experience revealed to me how hard it is, for men especially, to feel and become sensitive to others' feelings and emotions. They must allow themselves to become vulnerable first. Many men equate vulnerability with weakness. This means having to open the grand portal of their heart and needing to destroy many self-imposed boundaries, an extremely painful and difficult process for most people.

I wondered how Nathaniel and I would overcome such enormous challenges in our intimate relationship. He remained snoring in deep slumber while I was awakening. I was determined not to go backward on my path, but I did not want to leave him behind. I tried to wake him up a little by poking him, but he seemed to be merely turning over to his other side and giving me his back.

Twenty-Three

THE LION'S ROAR

SINCE THE TIME I WAS a little girl, I had always perceived other living beings as equals. When I looked into animals' eyes, I saw the Divine in them. I believe that simply by existing, they must play vital roles in our lives and our planet. I am sure God created animals for a good reason, not for us to exploit and abuse.

This connection was natural for my being as a child. I loved animals and insects and have always been intrigued by their precious essence, intelligence, and unique personalities. Can you imagine the planet without them?

For years after Pompom left us and my beloved Minoux passed away, I was beyond devastated. After my heart had healed, Nathaniel and I decided to rescue a cat from our local shelter. We were painfully aware of the millions of dogs and cats who ended up being euthanized each year in America and didn't even want to imagine the numbers of unwanted animals in third world countries.

We went to our local humane society planning to look at the cats, but when we arrived we found ourselves moving toward the dogs. We had been contemplating the idea of rescuing a dog so that our dog, Jessie, would have a new friend. As we walked, a snow-white dog with soulful blue eyes, thick black markings around her eyes like eyeliner, and a few sparkles of light blonde on the tips of her ears came forward in her pen to greet me. Her majestic presence and intense gaze were filled with overflowing love.

I caressed her head. The card on her pen said, Snow Ball, one-year-old husky mix, and deaf dog. I ran to get Nathaniel. Both of us bonded with her and decided to inquire further. I thought she looked more like a snowflake than a snowball and began to call her that. Although she was deaf, I felt she could hear and feel everything we were saying. Each time I looked into her eyes, I melted more.

The volunteer told us there was already a waiting list of three people who wanted to adopt Snowflake. "You can always put your names on the list," the attendant said. "Just . . . don't get your hopes up."

We agreed and asked if we could spend time with Snowflake. We took her out in their garden and played. Her sweet and gentle aura captivated my spirit. When we put her back in her pen, I said goodbye with tears in my eyes, hoping she would one day come home with us but aware the chance was small.

We crossed over to the cat section, and I immediately fell in love with an apricot blond tabby that looked like a mini lion. Nathaniel said he looked like Simba in *The Lion King* movie. I wished we could adopt all the cats there. Sadly, there are too many homeless animal companions for the number of responsible, willing, and loving guardians who can care for them.

I could not decide between Simba and a small frisky calico girl I named Leela, a sacred name from Sanskrit meaning "play of God."

"Can we adopt both?" I asked Nathaniel while playing with the kitties. "The insensitivity of so many people makes me so sad, baby. When I see people abandon their animal companions when they move away, my heart hurts. It's cruel and irresponsible. At least bring them to a rescue group, a friend, or a shelter instead of letting them starve alone in the street."

He was trying to hold Leela in his arms. She jumped all over him. Nathaniel looked at me, smiling, and said, "Let's bring them both home!"

"Yippee!" I said and kissed him.

We left the shelter with our cats. I renamed Simba "Simba Krishna." I said he deserved a godly name. Nathaniel agreed.

~

WEEKS LATER THE LOCAL HUMANE Society called to tell us we could adopt Snowflake. After I hung up the phone, I exclaimed out loud as I jumped up and down, "Yippee! Wow! My invocation has been answered!"

When we went to pick up Snowflake, her tail wagged and her ears stood up. By her intense gaze, we could tell she knew we had come for her. I held Snowflake in my arms and whispered my love in her ear. My heart overflowed with Divine love and gratitude. My inner knowing kept telling me she would be a very special spirit in my life.

Nathaniel took photos of us rolling together on the ground in the garden. I kept gazing at her electrifying blue eyes as she remained mesmerized by mine. Our spirits soared together in this intense loving embrace. I kissed Snowflake on her head several times while I caressed her snow-white coat. Tears welled up in my eyes, yet I kept laughing.

Later we brought our other dog, Jessie, in the garden, and he started following Snowflake everywhere. She seemed indifferent at first, but not long afterward they became close friends.

Nathaniel and I decided I would train Snowflake, teaching her a combination of dog training signs, sign language for humans, and signs that I created for her. I told Nathaniel I felt Snowflake had much to share, teach, and give. Because of her rare inner and outer beauty, she would be an ideal therapy dog to help others open their hearts and be more sensitive.

After spending over a year with Snowflake in advanced dog training at our shelter, I decided the time had come to volunteer, and I took her in for the official animal therapy examination. I knew she would succeed and impress the staff. A therapy animal is required to be calm, gentle, loving, patient, and absolutely nonreactive to any situation or emergency. The strict therapy-test checks for these behaviors.

Over time I took Snowflake to different establishments designated by the Humane Society in our neighborhood. There was one nursing home we went to every Friday morning. Before we left the house, I made sure Snowflake was well groomed and wore her red animal therapy bandanna. I often bathed her in my own bathroom. Snowflake looked like a pure white fuzzball and smelled of lavender. People were always stunned by her majestic beauty and the intensity of love in her eyes. I often teased them by saying I had applied her black eyeliner and had painted the tips of her ears with a dash of gold pigment from my studio.

In the nursing home, there was a ninety-five-year-old woman who was always grumpy and miserable. She didn't speak to anyone and remained in her room. She would shoo me and Snowflake away with a wave of her hand. One day as we were walking past, I noticed she was in bed, motionless.

"Are you okay?" I asked her.

She responded, but I couldn't make out her answer.

I went in and saw she was very near death. "May I sit by your bed?" I asked.

She nodded yes.

I held her hand and caressed her hair. "The celestial beings are here, waiting to take you home. Can you feel their energy, dear?"

She smiled and tried to speak. I could not understand her, but words seemed insignificant. I looked deep into her eyes for a long time, caressing her head. Snowflake sat by my side.

"I brought you a special angel. Snowflake would love to connect with you," I said to the woman as I took her hand and placed it on Snowflake's head. "See how beautiful all the creatures of the Divine Mother are! There's no reason to fear anything, not even death."

As I spoke, Snowflake's eyes began to glow with an intense, ethereal light. I lifted Snowflake a little higher so the woman could see her eyes. On her own, the old woman attempted to fondle Snowflake's neck. Her hand trembled, so I helped her. Snowflake remained angelically calm.

The old lady mumbled again. Her joy and the light in her eyes illuminated the entire room; her smile was like sunrise. I became blissful and fell silent, awed. I thought, *this moment came from the magic of animal therapy and the grace of the Divine Mother. Our Creator is always within us. We never know when we are called upon to be an instrument of the Divine helping another.*

The old lady moved her gaze from Snowflake to me, making feeble sounds of joy. She pointed to my necklace, touched the medallion, and said, "Who?"

"You want to know who is in the photo on my medallion?" I asked.

She nodded yes.

"That is my beloved Gurudev, my spiritual master. His real name is His Holiness Sri Sri Ravi Shankar. He's a holy man. Isn't he beautiful?"

Her eyes said yes.

"He's with us now," I said. "He will help you transition to the other dimension. It will be so good to go home. You can let go now, dear."

The air exuded a Divine presence. Our spirits melted into one. Bliss emanated from us as we silently connected, lost in this boundless moment.

An hour must have gone by with us in that ethereal state. Then, I put my hands on the old woman's head and blessed her. She closed her eyes. I left the room feeling our Creator working through my being like an instrument and through Snowflake. I was awed and humbled by the great mystery of living and the magic of animals.

The old woman passed away that afternoon. I could only hope that one day I, too, would pass into the beyond as sweetly as she had.

~

THE DIVINE IS IN EVERY particle of creation. Every living being is sacred. Like humans, animals are endowed with innate intelligence. Love, emotions, and feelings are in all living beings; animals manifest these things in a different form. We must walk the path of loving compassion. We cannot talk or ask others to have compassion for all living beings if we don't have compassion ourselves. There is no other way. Violence engenders violence. Love engenders love.

It was on one of our vacations to Puerto Vallarta, Mexico, that I howled the great powerful roar of freedom—that roar of courage that arises from our heart. That inner cry emerges from our true and ultimate nature. True compassion is boundless love overflowing for all living beings and expressed in positive actions. True compassion is doing what needs to be done when the opportunity is presented to us without any expectations and rewards.

That is exactly what happened to me with the suffering homeless cats in Puerto Vallarta. They offered me this priceless opportunity to give back by expressing boundless loving compassion.

Nathaniel and I were on our way to dinner at a trendy restaurant, and when we arrived at its front door, we found a pregnant tabby cat waiting close by. She looked hungry, and she meowed. Her belly was close to bursting; she seemed to be due within a few weeks.

"Wait for me, mommy, I will bring you something very soon," I told her.

When we entered the restaurant, I asked the hostess about this friendly cat. She told me the pregnant cat did not belong to anyone, that I was welcome to take her home. She confided that not long ago, there had been more than fifty stray and feral cats on the island. Then a great tragedy had occurred: In the middle of the night, someone had poisoned most of them. The following day, bloody, dead cats were everywhere—among flowers, under tropical bushes, on the street, in front of restaurants, and even a few appeared on roofs. I was shocked by the cruel massacre, and the tabby's cries reached deep into my heart. I burned inside.

The hostess had taken me outside to tell me this story, as she was prohibited by her employer from speaking about it in public. This issue was very controversial in Puerto Vallarta. She confessed she was still angry and devastated by the crime.

"Killing is destruction," I said. "Taking the life of another living being is an act of violence. We don't have the right to do that."

The hostess went on to share that most of the feral and stray cats had been abandoned by locals. When people got rid of their animal companion for whatever reason, they had simply dumped them here. There were only seven left in the colony, and most of them had been sterilized, vaccinated, and received vet care.

Most people favor baby animals. Unfortunately, when an animal companion grows older, some people lack awareness and compassion for their well-being. They don't think about the consequences of their actions and may treat the animal as if it were garbage.

I remembered my beloved Thisbe in his final moment and told her how Thisbe had died horrifically from poisoning in front of my eyes, a scene carved in my heart. I felt the same about these cats. "More of us need to speak out for them!" I said. "They don't have a voice. We are their voices."

We went back inside. I sat down with Nathaniel but could not eat. Nathaniel asked what happened, and I told him what I had learned. He was shocked by the barbaric approach to solving a simple social issue. We ordered a few dishes, and I returned to the garden to feed the cats.

When I called them, a friendly little orange-and-white tabby was the first to come running and rub against my legs. I picked her up and petted her and decided to call her "Puja," a Sanskrit word meaning adoration, reverence, and worship. Within seconds, Puja won a unique spot in my heart.

Not long after Puja came running, the rest of the cats showed up at my feet. While talking to and feeding them, my courageous and compassionate voice exploded within. I told the kitties how much I loved them and that I would do everything I could to help them. The roar of courage arises from our heart . . . that powerful roar of freedom!

When I went back to our table, I told Nathaniel, "I don't care what people will say. I'm going to speak up for the cats that died horribly—for all the injustice. If we're going to raise consciousness and see transformation, we must all speak up, take compassionate and effective actions to end violence against animals, children, women, elders, and the weak. I want to live in a world filled with beauty, love, and compassion for all sentient beings!"

I told him I would write an article about the cat tragedy, compassion, and awakening. "It'll be published in all the newspapers around Puerto Vallarta!" I declared. "I'll have it translated into Spanish."

After we finished dinner and left the restaurant, I called the kitties again so Nathaniel could visit with them. Again, Puja charged up first to greet us. I placed her in Nathaniel's arms, and she kept purring and rubbing her face against his chest. He fell in love with her on the spot, just as I had.

$$\sim$$

THE FOLLOWING MORNING, WE BOUGHT cat food and returned to the area. When I called the cats, Puja came running, happy to see us.

I held Puja in my arms and whispered in a baby voice, "Little Puja, you are coming home with us! Just stay around. We will be back for you."

I wished we could take all the homeless cats home with us.

An old Mexican woman was lingering in the area, watching us. She seemed to be keeping an eye on the cats. She came to us and explained that she was one of the concerned neighbors who loved cats. She told me that a group of American animal lovers had founded a nonprofit animal welfare organization to look after these cats. Nathaniel and I were delighted.

As we spoke, a few of these volunteers arrived. We introduced ourselves. I told them of my intention to write an article and to adopt Puja. They were delighted to connect with us.

A day later, the leader of the organization, accompanied by a few volunteers, met with me by our hotel pool. They had become disheartened and needed help. They had been trying to work with the local government, but the municipality was not very responsive. The organization told us that they wanted to build a cat sanctuary. We agreed it would be a wonderful, compassionate, and powerful tool to bring awareness to the issue. We thought tourists would love it, and the sanctuary could offer cats for adoption. I gave them a donation and assured the organization they had our support.

~

A FEW DAYS BEFORE THE end of our trip, Nathaniel and I picked up Puja, put her in a pet carrier, and brought her back to our hotel. The concierge noticed, so I related the story of what had happened to the abandoned cats. He was horrified and told me about a blue-gray female cat who lived in the bushes around the hotel.

That night after dinner I walked around the area calling, "Kitty." I heard a few faint meows and then a delicate girl cat came out of the bushes and rolled over at my feet.

A noise scared her, and she ran back into the bushes. I walked after her through the bushes with a bag of food I'd brought from dinner. When she saw me, she rolled on her back, purring. I sat down and caressed her belly. Her abdomen was so big.

"Oh, you are so beautiful and pregnant too," I whispered. We gazed into each other's eyes, connecting. Infinite love and light emanated from her spirit.

I lost myself experiencing oneness with the cat as I became more and more transfixed by the glow of the full moon reflecting in her soulful, loving eyes. In that eternal and mystical moment, I entered into a certain state of samadhi—a trancelike state of profound expansion, equanimity, and unity. A sense of boundlessness immersed my being, as if I did not have a body anymore. My heart overflowed with Divine love, serenity, and bliss. When I snapped out of this transcendental trancelike state, I looked at my watch. It was after two o'clock in the morning. Almost four hours had elapsed! I could not believe it. It was time to go to bed, and yet I did not want to leave her there alone. The word "Isha" came to mind, as if someone had whispered it into my ear. So, I named her Isha. I discovered much later Isha has many meanings in Sanskrit, the main one being "of God." Today I realize Isha had become a phenomenal gateway to the Divine.

Nathaniel was asleep when I returned to our room. When I slipped underneath the sheet, he woke up and asked where I had been. Puja ran across our bed and lay flat on my chest, purring. I explained about Isha and our transcendent spiritual process. I thought about her being exposed to danger outside and knew I could not sleep if I left her there alone. "Baby, I want to bring Isha home too."

"Not another cat, darling," he said, but then he sighed. "Ah, it doesn't matter what I say. You will do what you want."

He was right.

It was almost four when I got up, dressed, returned to the bushes with the pet carrier, placed Isha inside, and brought her to our room. That accomplished, I sat on our bed and called our airline for an additional reservation for Isha in the cabin with us. While I spoke to the agent, Isha sat on my lap, purring loudly.

I had set up a litter box in our room and displayed a sign in Spanish on the front door warning the housekeepers about our new cats. With only two days left before our departure, we bought another cat carrier and took the girls to a vet, because a health certificate was required by the airline and customs.

When we picked up our girls, both had passed the test and vet exam and had been vaccinated. The vet said Isha was not pregnant but that she had gotten sick from the shots. He wanted to keep her for another day. He hadn't explained why Isha had such an enormous abdomen, and I thought I would take her to our own trusted vet upon our return to the States.

When we returned to the clinic for Isha, I asked the vet if she could travel.

"Sí! Sí!" he assured me.

We were so glad, but I felt something was wrong.

When we got to the airport and onto the plane, Nathaniel placed Isha's carrier underneath the seat in front of me and Puja's in front of himself. I noticed Isha seemed to be having difficulty breathing. I took her out and held her. She was very weak and lethargic. I was alarmed and told Nathaniel we needed to take her to the animal emergency hospital immediately when we got to California.

After a plane ride that seemed to take hours, we were finally able to get Isha to the emergency vet. At this point, she could barely breathe on her own. The team placed her under an oxygen tent. I felt distraught, sensing the worst was going to happen. The doctors performed several tests and took x-rays of her abdomen.

The head veterinarian called us into his office and told us that three-quarters of Isha's lungs had been eaten away by some kind of fungus or organism. Based on his x-rays and expertise, Isha had only a slim chance for recovery. The more advanced tests and potential treatments could cost thousands of dollars.

"You have the choice to humanely let her go. Take the time you need to think about it," he said compassionately.

Nathaniel and I looked at each other and asked to discuss it privately. We decided we would have to let her go.

I asked to be left alone with Isha. I looked at her innocent eyes, gazing at mine with so much love and trust. I was responsible for this creature's life, a very beautiful and precious one. I held her in my arms. "It's too unfair, Isha," I said. "We just found each other. Now I must let you go. One day we'll be back together. I'll find you again. I promise. I'm so sorry. You have shown me the way to the Source . . . to the Divine Mother. I'm so grateful to you and always will be."

We left the hospital with an empty carrier and my broken heart. We let Puja out of the carrier to stretch her legs then drove back home in silence while she ran wild in the back seat. Nathaniel held my hand while I mourned. In silence, I invoked the Divine Mother that Isha would reincarnate as a beautiful, enlightened human being filled with light.

～

OVER THE FOLLOWING MONTH, EVEN as I mourned the loss of Isha, Puja's flamboyant, exuberant spirit inspired my creative spark. As I painted Puja in her full glory, a goddess was born! I gave her a feminine human body with a feline head. Her orange tabby fur gave way to her ultimate divine spirit, meditating upon transcendence and world peace. Puja's third eye appeared on her forehead, wide open and all-seeing, just as a *dakini*—a goddess or deity with spiritual powers. I decided to call the artwork *Puja Blossom*. Over the decades, Puja lived to become a true little goddess.

During this time, I wrote the article on the cat massacre in Puerto Vallarta and had it professionally translated. Soon it was published in the three main newspapers of the state that Puerto Vallarta was in—*Vallarta Tribune, Tribuna de La Bahia,* and a popular tourist periodical in English. It was very well-received by the public and the local government.

Eventually the grassroots nonprofit organization I had spoken with during my time there implemented a solution with the municipality. Within a year, the local government opened a small shelter farther away from town. It was not what we hoped for, but it was the first baby step toward humane progress. Over time the main volunteers and leader of the grassroots organization helped improve conditions at the shelter.

This experience taught me that we must always speak from the heart, not out of compulsion and anger, but out of love, compassion, conviction, understanding, and commitment. We must always speak for the voiceless, whether it is a vulnerable child, an older woman or man, a neglected cat, or a bee. I sensed the article had helped raise consciousness and awareness. Hopefully it opened the hearts of a few individuals toward compassionate love for all living beings. Humility is bowing in reverence to all living beings while realizing there is One supreme intelligence behind it all. Ultimately this was exactly what Isha showed my being with our moonlight transcendence, and I also recognized the true significance of *Puja Blossom*. I realized that an inner roar of courage can lead us to freedom. Never refrain from speaking the truth, even if your voice shivers and your body trembles; but speak with loving compassion, otherwise no one will hear you.

Twenty-Four

THE POWER OF SENSITIVITY

WHENEVER I PAINTED, I CHANTED. Often, a few does lay with their fawns on the small hill near my studio's window to listen; they seemed to love spending their afternoon by my side.

I felt one with the deer. They reminded me that creation is all around us and within us. I frequently poked my head out the window and sang to them. Nathaniel called them my audience. After the first small group began to gather, others soon joined them.

Even though the deer visited me often, I never tried to tame them. I had my close ones in the herd, such as a fawn I called Mimi and with whom I felt a profound connection. After she had grown, when she was almost two years old, Mimi showed up injured. Deep layers of the skin on her shoulder were torn out. The wound was large and deep; bone showed through. It was infected; flies and other insects flew into it.

Mimi needed a friend who cared, and she came to me.

I closed my eyes and asked for help and guidance from the Divine Mother and ascended masters as I always do. If there is a pure and intense heart, these celestial beings are always there to assist us. At once I could feel energy rushing through every cell of my body temple. I felt guided to feed Mimi a mixture of oats, corn, and barley made for deer. As she ate, I carefully sprayed her large wound with an antibacterial solution my vet had given me long ago. I placed my hands not too far from the wound, stroking her ears and nose. She returned the next several days for treatment and affection. I was the only one she would allow to touch her. A week later, not only was the infection gone, but her skin had grown back without a single scar. I could not believe it . . . all by the grace of the Divine Mother.

Mimi was not the only deer that gave me the opportunity to express loving compassion in my actions. Compassion is in all of us when we are in touch with our true spirit. Another time a few years later, a tiny sick fawn appeared in our front yard. His eyes were rolling, and he kept turning his face into the dirt. I placed a cotton sheet over his head, and Nathaniel and I placed him in the back of his SUV to take him to our wildlife rehabilitation sanctuary. As we drove, the fawn cried in pain for his mother. I had never heard such a cry from an animal before, and the distressful sounds tore my heart.

Animals may be governed by their instincts, but they also have feelings and emotions; they feel pain and suffer like we do. These innocent beings have no voice to defend and protect themselves except for ours. Grave injustices and atrocities are committed against them daily. How can we not see and feel their pain and suffering? People who can't see and feel this have not yet connected with their ultimate nature, or made the connection with the spirit within the animal. Far too many people are not aware, sensitive, or receptive to the magnificent beauty of our Creator in all creatures and nature.

We can become a voice for the voiceless. It is our responsibility to do everything we can to transform our planet into a more harmonious and nonviolent world for all its creatures, not just for humans.

The unawakened human can be crueler than the wildest beast. Open your heart to animals, for they can be a gateway to the Divine. Cherish, love, and care for them, but not as objects or possessions. The spiritual connections that you forge with them can begin your journey of awakening. Ultimately you will burst with joyful ecstasy, when you get to know the universal spirit that animates all creation.

His Holiness the Dalai Lama says, "The future will be in the hands of those who belong to the twenty-first century. You have the opportunity and responsibility to build a better humanity. This means developing warmheartedness in this very life, here and now. So, do whatever you do, but ask yourselves now and then, 'How can I contribute to human beings being happier and more peaceful?'"[1]

～

AFTER ALL THESE MYSTICAL EXPERIENCES with the animals—and many more not in this book—my heart was full of Divine love and compassion for all living beings. I wanted to help them in any way I could.

In 2004, I participated in a three-day seminar, Helping Animals 101, put on by a nonprofit animal welfare organization. The seminar offered tools, strategies, suggestions, and discussions about many animal issues, and training so that participants could become an effective voice for animals. It would also be presenting documentaries showcasing animal exploitation and cruelty from around the world, to help raise our awareness of these problems.

Not long before attending this program, I thought of my dear friend Eos—a beautiful, tall woman of Greek descent with a long golden mane, and I flashed back to the day I met her in New York City in 1995. In some ways, she was like the ancient Greek goddess of the dawn, bringing the hope of a brand new day. She had been a longtime friend of my husband, Nathaniel. She let us stay in her loft apartment during our short trip to the city.

When we arrived there, it was a cold, snowy night. I wore a mink fur coat my ex-boyfriend Ian had given me. Although I had not met Eos yet, I immediately felt a kinship. She had many photos of her travels on her desk, but one affected me strongly. It showed a very beautiful and radiant Indian sage or sadhu with long silvery hair and burning eyes. I could not tell what it was about the magnificent being of light in that photo, but he transported my being into a world of transcendence. I knew at once he, or what he represented, was what my soul had been searching for.

After returning home from that trip, I opened our mailbox and found a compelling letter from Eos asking me to join the organization, along with a copy of their newsletter. The magazine contained many photos depicting the atrocities and abuses inflicted on animals by many different commercial and industrial sectors for profit, and called for us to help them. I thought how compassionate Eos was to extend such a kind and caring gesture. I had been blind to the world of horrific suffering and pain we inflict upon animals. I became a loyal member and supporter.

Neither Eos nor I had any idea she and the organization would inspire me to join a movement of compassion that would eventually influence my spiritual growth. Advocating for animals requires immense courage; an open, sensitive heart; and the compassion to look at all these issues from within. The more we expand our consciousness and awareness, the more compassion we express in positive actions.

Throughout my years as a student at San Francisco State University (SFSU), I always read newsletters, even created a few art projects exposing injustices to animals. When the initiative to stop trapping wild animals appeared in California, I participated by collecting hundreds of signatures in front of pet shops. It was Eos's plea that opened my eyes and the animals who made my heart blossom. The animals' cries naturally guided me to become an advocate and an environmentalist, though I rarely call myself that. All who care about our planet and its creatures must play a part in transforming our Mother Earth into a more harmonious and compassionate world for all of us and for future generations. We must walk this path together.

~

AFTER REFLECTING ON MY EXPERIENCE with Eos, gratitude overwhelmed my heart. I realized that almost nine years had passed like a single breath, and I was not helping the animals as much as I wished to.

Out of respect and love for the animals who suffered these horrors, and for the individuals who risked so much to capture the evidence of cruelty and horrific confinement, I kept my eyes and ears wide open while we watched the documentaries such as *Meet Your Meat* (focused on factory farms). I forced myself to bear witness. I wanted to know the truth.

I was overwhelmed with sorrow and horror. The films laid bare what some humans are capable of doing when they lack consciousness and compassion. Documentaries showed countless atrocities: cows and pigs being decapitated while still conscious; chicks whose beaks were seared off with a hot blade; foxes, raccoons, minks, and bobcats skinned alive; dogs and cats roasting on sticks on grills; and so much more.

All of this was done in the name of convenience and profits by producers of food, pharmaceuticals, garments, cosmetics, games, and entertainment. I sobbed, wondering how people could eat meat when it comes from pure misery and torture. I almost fainted. Greed, selfishness, arrogance, and lack of awareness had created a world of misery and injustice for these animals.

Together our group mourned the billions of animals who suffered this treatment. I knew that human beings could be the cruelest and least intelligent of all the animals—destroying our planet, ourselves, its creatures, and its beauty.

Pope Francis says, "It is contrary to human dignity to cause animals to suffer or die needlessly."[2]

Animals are supposed to swim, crawl, walk, run, and fly free. These are their natural behaviors—not to be confined, decapitated, boiled, burnt, cut, tortured, torn, scalped, poisoned, trapped, grilled, toasted, and turned into commercial products. I wanted to scream so loud that the world could hear my roar.

These were not the gentle and sweet images I grew up with in my youth in the countryside of St-Marie. My heart was torn into billions of pieces as I realized that my parents, schoolteachers, and the media had lied to me. I felt profoundly violated and enraged.

Back at home that night in our bedroom, I sobbed to Nathaniel, "How can I live in such a world? My heart breaks for those suffering animals. I feel their cries and their pain."

Over time I realized how these profit-driven industries spend billions of dollars yearly in advertising to keep consumers in the dark. Many of these industries hire powerful lobbyists to affect the laws regarding such behavior and counter the initiatives that protect and defend the rights of animals and their lives.

Over the following decade, I learned to take action. I participated in many demonstrations; signed hundreds of petitions; wrote many major articles on spirituality for other periodicals and magazines; and participated as a guest speaker on TV and in documentary interviews on the subject of spirituality, awakening, and animals. In 2006, my first major feature article was published in *Yoga Magazine*, which was followed by a series over the next six years. I also began networking with other animal advocates, humanitarians, and environmentalists. Nathaniel and I became loyal members, supporters, and donors of many nonprofit animal welfare, environmental, and humanitarian organizations.

Compassion without actions is not genuine compassion.

Maha karuna means great compassion. Individuals may not realize that choosing not to eat animals or use their by-products is a way to express great compassion. Your personal resolve can save hundreds of animals from the cruelty of confinement and pain at farm factories and slaughterhouses. Maha karuna will explode in your heart. You can't be sensitive if you are not allowing yourself to be vulnerable.

Sensitivity is not a weakness. It is one of the most precious qualities of the heart. It reflects your openness and receptivity to all life forms, just as a blossoming lotus thrives in the mud. The more sensitive you become, the more you will tap into the ultimate power of vulnerability. Vulnerability is essential for experiencing a dimension of reality beyond the physical realm. One must break free from the gateway of resistance and logic to experience the light. That is the power of sensitivity. This will allow you to express maha karuna. And great compassion is the way of the light.

Changing the world is about transforming oneself. Change, harmony, and peace start from within and are furthered by practicing awareness and being mindful of our daily habits, words, thoughts, actions, surroundings, and influences. Being compassionate is about loving life, feeling a reverence for its source and beauty. Compassion is the most beautiful expression of love.

As Mahatma Gandhi supposedly said, "The greatness of a nation and its moral progress can be judged by the way its animals are treated."

The lifestyle of "veganism" is widely misunderstood. A vegan is simply a vegetarian who does not eat animal products of any kind (including dairy products), does not wear animal skins, and abstains from using or consuming products which may have caused animals to be exploited and hurt. A vegan also avoids those products that affect our environment negatively. They do so because they do not want to support exploitation and oppression of animals as a commodity in any form. It is very hard to be

100 percent vegan in today's world. There are often tiny traces of animal components in many products without our realizing it.

Veganism is not an opinion, philosophy, a religion, or a cult. An individual who embraces veganism as a way of life is one who embraces nonviolence (*ahimsa*), compassion, and kindness by becoming aware of his or her own footprint and decides to make wiser and healthier choices that affect the well-being of the environment and all living beings, including themselves.

Most people do not realize the low level of prana and intense negative energy released by animals into their flesh before they are slaughtered. On the physical and metaphysical levels, animals emit hormones such as adrenaline and feel intense emotions such as terror, anger, hatred, and distress before they are killed; these can affect their bodies. So when individuals eat animal products, these kinds of energy and chemicals enter their own bodies and keep them at a low vibrational level. People can choose to be vegan for any number of reasons, including having concerns about their health and the environment, or for ethical or even spiritual ones. Yet often the underlying motivating factor for adopting a vegan lifestyle is a desire to show more love, compassion, reverence, and awareness for other life forms.

Like many people, I was once unaware that raising animals in farm factories around the world results in a great waste of natural resources; adds to global warming, air and water pollution, extinction of other species of animals; and affects starvation in developing countries. Think of all the tons of grain grown yearly and the resources required to grow it—such as water, land, fossil fuels, and the like. Imagine these foods redistributed to the starving poor of the third world. Of course, food redistribution alone is not the only answer to poverty and famine. We need many more creative humanitarian programs that empower underprivileged countries to thrive, especially for women, who are the core essence of the family nucleus. Everywhere, it is mostly the women of our world who have shouldered the primary responsibility of nurturing, creating, caring, loving, and attending to the children, elders, and animals.

Twenty-Five

COMPASSIONATE AND NONVIOLENT LIVING

FOR A VERY LONG TIME after the animal cruelty program, I didn't even feel like getting up in the morning. I could see no way to end the atrocities suffered by animals, or the perpetual violence and oppression toward women, children, and the weak.

I cleared my closet; I pulled out a fur coat, my bags, belts, shoes, and other accessories made with leather. I did not want to wear them, knowing another creature may have suffered torture just for my pleasure and comfort. I was already a vegetarian, but now I stopped drinking milk and eating dairy products.

During my studies, I had become aware of the violence and destructive cruelties of past civilizations, including how women and children had been oppressed. I remembered weeping about it then. Yet these issues had not prepared me to find the same things going on in modern society all around us. I felt like humans should have evolved since the Stone Age, and while on the surface it appears we have, anyone who is aware can see that violence and aggression are still very much alive, though now in different disguises.

The archaic mindset of the caveman, with its precepts of dominance and power over women and animals, came to my attention again. I could clearly see their influence in my own time. I felt I was drowning in a sea of destructive energy. I could also see how lacking we are in the feminine energy principle, and how it may help save us and our planet.

This mindset of conquering and dominating those perceived as weak and vulnerable may have served its purpose in centuries and millennia gone by, but we are now in the twenty-first century. In today's world, masculine dominance is still much in evidence, although it's subtler and often deliberately disguised.

We must all, men and women alike, raise our consciousness and expand our efforts to change things for the sake of our children, future generations, and the survival of our precious planet.

Even though I had already begun to speak out about the importance of nonviolence and having compassion, part of my being still felt paralyzed and despondent after discovering the immensity of this truth. For a while, my only solace came through creating art in my studio. I buried myself in painting, feeling guided to express the inexpressible on canvas. My urge to create beauty in all its forms continued to grow.

After this period of intense grieving and distress, I began to wonder how I could reach millions, even billions of people who, like myself, longed to evolve and contribute to a harmonious, loving planet.

One night in bed, I said to Nathaniel, "The whole world ought to know the truth about how animals suffer. I can't remain silent. I can't sleep with this pain in my heart. I must take action—help the animals who have no voices! We all must."

That year, in 2004, I joined the National Animal Rights Conferences organized by the Farm Animal Rights Movement (FARM) in Washington, DC, and Los Angeles. The following year I was invited to be a guest speaker and even led an opening night ceremony in front of a thousand compassionate people and conducted a meditation for them.

In my heart, I had to forgive those who harm, exploit, and oppress the most vulnerable among us. I realized it was their ignorance, dysfunction, and conditioning, their lack of consciousness and awareness that keeps them locked in such negative behaviors. In a profound way, humans suffer the greatest confinement by enslaving themselves with narrow-minded views.

Evolution needs to take place deep within each of us, so that we realize our true ultimate nature. We are not just bones and flesh. Truth and knowledge are dormant within us. Ignorance of our ultimate nature is the source of so much of the injustice in the world. Awakening and raising the consciousness on our planet are among the most effective, important tools and solutions.

Over the years I have observed that those people who are involved in helping, protecting, and speaking out for animals tend to be drawn to the animal advocacy movement because of their own accumulated emotional background.

The call to help animals and other vulnerable beings tends to attract individuals who also have been abused and suffered from oppression and aggression. It is wonderfully cathartic and healing for wounded individuals to help others who have been oppressed.

It was very beautiful to witness people starting to wake up and trying to change the status quo. In some ways, one of the blessings the animal advocacy movement provides is the opportunity for people to work out their dysfunction, heal, and rediscover themselves. It also offers the chance to serve other living creatures selflessly. When we awake spiritually and see the suffering of animals and others, our hearts start to blossom and feel again as we let go of the negative energy inside. In this way, one can connect, relate, and empathize with oppressed animals at many levels, including the energy level.

Of course, the opposite can also happen when an individual remains unawakened. Children who have been badly abused may learn from their abusers and become abusers in turn. There is a correlation between adult physical and mental cruelty to people and youthful perpetration of animal cruelties. Studies have found that for many people, violence and domination began first with animal abuse. I suspect that individuals who may have lacked love, compassion, and proper guidance in their childhood abuse animals to get rid of their anger and negative energy, and to assert dominance over a weaker, more vulnerable being. It may give them a false sense of security, power, and control over their lives, but it is a very dysfunctional way to cope with stress.

As I became more involved in helping animals, I began to notice that most of the spiritual masters and teachers of our era spoke often about humanitarian issues, but they rarely spoke on behalf of suffering animals or Mother Earth. Animals need our help in initiating new laws, rescuing, protecting, defending, and caring for them and, most crucially, in raising people's consciousness and awareness—but not enough people in positions of power were helping this happen. It occurred to me that if I could reach a few of the most influential masters, they could speak up about these injustices and help create nonviolent solutions. Together, we could transform our blue-green planet for the well-being of all living creatures and future generations. I resolved to do what I could.

It is crucial to hold a beautiful vision for Mother Earth. The power of loving compassion is infinite when it flows from a pure heart. Together we can transform our world into a harmonious planet regardless of our various backgrounds. Every moment we have the inner power to see and experience our ultimate nature and make choices through our actions, words, and thoughts. Why lock yourself into a fabricated jail? Smile and breathe . . . the entire universe belongs to you!

Over the years I wrote numerous letters to His Holiness the Dalai Lama and Gurudev about animal rights, the environment, and vegetarianism and veganism, asking them to speak about these crucial issues within their communities around the world.

Once I also dared to ask my Gurudev, His Holiness Sri Sri Ravi Shankar, in front of more than seven hundred participants, what could be done to help our fellow creatures. We were in Lake Tahoe for Guru Purnima, a special celebration honoring the lineage of all spiritual masters and the Source within all of us.

"Gurudev, would you speak to all your followers about the well-being of suffering animals, so we can raise awareness and do something to help them? What should we do to stop these horrific animal cruelties?" I asked.

Gurudev responded, "You are more sensitive than others. You should be teaching!"

I was disappointed with his answer. I thought he would elaborate and give us a wise discourse; instead, he had barely said anything.

From that experience, I learned it is best not to have any expectations or assumptions, especially with one's spiritual master. Assumptions often lead to disillusions, conflicts, and suffering, because most of them do not take into account the objective reality. Forming high expectations can reduce joy and may also lead us to disappointment, misery, and more suffering. I learned it is preferable to remain in a state of "I don't know," unless we know for sure. That way we remain very open and receptive—it is the fastest way to grow and evolve.

A few months later, I decided to write Gurudev another letter, this one like the one I sent the Dalai Lama. I asked him to be a voice for the voiceless, and for the Art of Living family to help all living beings, not just human ones. I thought perhaps Gurudev was unaware of these animal cruelties and exploitative issues, as they are well hidden from the public.

The Dalai Lama says, "Compassion, forgiveness, these are the real ultimate sources of power for peace and success in life."[1]

I have seen those words validated hundreds of times. Most of the time we are too blinded by our own garbage to see clearly the reality of existence. The truth is always there, however, though it may be buried deep within us. Reverence and compassion for all living creatures, humans, and nature is the way of the blossoming heart.

The Dalai Lama also says, "If you want others to be happy, practice compassion. If you want to be happy, practice compassion."[2]

Gurudev, meanwhile, says, "When you revere all relationships, then your consciousness expands. Then even small things appear to be significant and big. Every little creature appears to be dignified."

The instant we are unafraid of the crowd, the roar explodes in our heart, and we are no longer frightened lambs. May our roar of freedom, compassion, harmony, and reverence for all living beings vibrate in the entire universe. Genuine kindness and compassion are as mesmerizing as the petals of a blossoming cherry tree swirling in the springtime breeze.

Twenty-Six

A JOURNEY TO MYSTICAL INDIA

IN 2006, I WAS READY to take the Art of Living teacher-training program offered at the International Yoga Center in the south of India. I had invited Nathaniel, but he chose to stay behind. I would be going alone.

This program was going to be special because it was followed by various multicultural and spiritual events marking the Art of Living's twenty-fifth anniversary. Over two million visitors were expected to participate in the three-day Silver Jubilee celebrations, including prominent dignitaries and diplomats from around the globe.

When Nathaniel kissed me goodbye at the airport, he seemed uneasy. I had never been to India, and I would be traveling there for a month alone. A part of my being was simmering with great joy—or was it agitated butterflies that twisted my stomach upside down? I was as ready as I could be, looking into the unexpected.

~

WHEN I ARRIVED AT THE old Bangalore airport almost forty-eight hours later, it was past midnight. Through my jet-lagged body's aches and pains, I could feel the ethereal land's vibration. Its aura of spirituality and mysticism vibrated into my being. The sensation told me my love affair with this land and its people would flourish.

Many other Art of Living trainees arrived on this flight, and volunteers were waiting for us in the small lobby. They informed us that a political uprising was taking place, and Gurudev encouraged everyone to go directly to the ashram. In the bustle and chaotic unrest of the moment, the volunteers rushed us to the taxi stand, carrying our luggage.

I was herded into an old, beat-up taxi with another woman. During the next several hours of driving, we kept silent. She dozed, but my eyes remained wide open. Outside the window, I saw dozens of crumbling shacks and poor older women dressed in bright saris washing their clothes in the streams in the late night. Dozens of gentle cows roamed and blocked the streets as they ate garbage, pulling plastic bags from the side of the road into their mouths. Half-naked, dirty children ran wild along the filthy streets. Dozens of homeless dogs foraged for scraps and begged for a loving gesture.

Occasionally, I caught a glimpse of emaciated cats perched on top of a fence or running through an alley. How did they survive the army of homeless dogs in the streets?

It was a shocking reality to process. My heart ached for all this suffering, and I wished I could do something.

Amid a sea of large, colorful billboards, many small bonfires glowed, while people huddled around them, rubbing their hands for warmth. The smoke released a distinctive perfume of sweet and spice. It combined with the land's energy and permeated every cell of my body, intoxicating and seductive.

Closer to the ashram the scenery changed. Monumental palm and mango trees perched on top of verdurous rolling hills. Monkeys ran free, and night birds chattered. I sensed I had lived here before, that I knew India in the depth of my being. I felt ecstatic to have returned.

When the taxi stopped in front of the reception building, a stray dog greeted me, tail wagging. I caressed her head and chatted with her for a while. Her face ignited with joy. I gave her a French name—"Bougie," meaning "candle"—and promised to visit her soon.

I dragged my heavy luggage to the second floor of the dorm building and through the long corridor. *Why had I brought so much?* When I opened the door of my room, there were three women already asleep inside, snoring. *Oh, no!* I thought. *Not again!* Luggage crammed the little bedroom, covering almost every inch of floor. As I tiptoed around the dark room dragging my bags, my foot caught someone's bags and I almost fell.

When I'd made my way to the last available bunk bed, I climbed the ladder. It was mid-February, summertime in India, when heat can top over 103 degrees some days. The room had only one very small window, on the opposite side of my bed, and the humidity near the ceiling was stifling. Even so, after I crashed on the top bunk, I fell asleep quickly, with all my clothes and makeup still on.

~

A FEW HOURS LATER, AROUND 6:00 a.m., I woke feeling exhausted and groggy. My three roommates had already left for the Vishalakshi Mantap, the grand meditation hall, to do their yogic practices. I showered and headed to do my sadhana with the rest of the participants. As I walked along the pathway, the sun rose.

In its light, the splendors of this tropical paradise were revealed. The ashram, which spread over sixty-five acres across the top of the Panchagiri Hills, twenty-two miles southwest of Bangalore, spread before me in humbling, magnificent vista. Its beauty and energy struck wonder and awe.

Walking toward the Vishalakshi Mantap, down a winding pathway bordered by blossoming foliage, a profound sense of serenity engulfed my being. A few homeless dogs, including Bougie, were sleeping on the pavement. She was curled at the foot of the Ganesh statue at the front entrance of Gurudev's kutir. I stopped to pet her. She rubbed her face against my leg and then fell right back to sleep.

The majestic Vishalakshi Mantap grew on the horizon with its perfect balance of geometric Vedic architecture and modern technology. At the foot of a long stairway, two colossal white stone swans guarded its gate. An enormous golden brass bull protected the gateway from atop the main entrance. The edifice emanated a serene and feminine energy.

The campus already buzzed with activities. Approximately one thousand international teacher-trainee participants had already arrived and were waiting inside the lotus-shaped structure, meditating on its pink-and-white marble floors.

After my sadhana, I felt energized, ready to face the challenges of the program. On my way to the cafeteria I passed Gurudev's kutir, when suddenly he walked out alone.

Gurudev always had a long trail of people behind him, something to be expected because he had about twenty million or so followers around the world. To find him alone was surprising, rare. Only a few of us stood by the curb to greet him.

Gurudev turned and walked toward me. As our eyes met, he stopped in astonishment, grinned, and exclaimed, "Whoooo!" He seemed very enchanted to see me there for the teacher-training program. I reverberated with Divine love. I seized his hand and pressed it to my cheek, enraptured in that cherished moment.

His presence filled my body temple with humming. "Gurudev! I will be writing about you, your life, the Art of Living, and the Silver Jubilee in a major feature article for *Yoga Magazine*."

"Good, good, good!" he said, rolling his eyes blissfully.

"*Jai Guru Dev*," I said in reverential greeting, letting go of his hand and bowing.

"Jai Guru Dev," he replied, and he then walked away.

As we spoke, he gave me his loving intoxicating gaze. I stood there blissfully vibrating with his shakti energy long after he had disappeared.

Gurudev says, "Jai Guru Dev is victory to the big mind in you that is both dignified and playful. That is what Jai Guru Dev means: Victory to the greatness in you."[1]

~

LATER THAT AFTERNOON, THE TEACHER trainees met at the Vishalakshi Mantap for a welcoming introduction and instruction. We gathered in smaller groups according to the continent we came from. Two teachers were assigned to each group. We were instructed to arrive at the meditation hall every day in silence before 5:30 a.m. for the daily Guru Pooja and then to go immediately to our sadhana.

I felt the program would be very draining; we had to wake up at 4:00 a.m. every day, and sessions would last almost until midnight some nights.

How will I manage with only a few hours of sleep every night and a snoring orchestra in my bedroom?

One day later, someone from the administration knocked on our door, saying they were going to add a fifth person to our shoebox.

"How are we going to walk around safely in this crammed room?" I asked. "We can't accommodate another bed. We can't even unpack! It's impossible! Find another room with space, please."

"There is no other room," the man said.

This new roommate, a woman from Russia, did not speak a word of English. None of us spoke Russian. How were we going to communicate?

After a few moments, I become aware of my selfishness. I heard Gurudev's words as if he were murmuring them in my ears, "Yes! Yes! Yes! Say 'Yes' to life!"

Okay, I thought, *by the grace of the Divine Mother, we will find a way to make it work.*

Gurudev often says, "Be a big 'Yes' to life, and doors will open up." Life is so much more painful and difficult when we put up resistance.

I tried to communicate with our Russian comrade in English, French, and Spanish, but we could not understand each other. We were now five females in a room no larger than a luxurious American master bathroom.

After each one of us did our midnight toilet, we collapsed in bed.

Within a few minutes I heard loud snores. Earplugs did not help much. A few hours went by while I gazed out at the moonlight, my thoughts on all the requirements I had to meet to be accepted to the teacher-training program. The room was stifling hot, without a breeze. I was drowning in sweat and my body ached. My watch read 2:00 a.m. I wondered how our new Russian roommate was feeling. She was alone, far away from her home, and unable to communicate. Perhaps she felt uninvited. I remembered my own need to belong.

I looked down and noticed she was not asleep. She did not have a pillow. I pulled out the extra pillow I keep beneath my knees and held it down to her and whispered, "Hey, sweetie, here is a pillow for you."

She took it, smiled, and placed it under her head, mumbling a few Russian words.

"We belong to each other," I sighed. I hoped she felt my loving energy.

~

EVERY MONDAY MORNING, GURUDEV CONDUCTED a *Rudra Pooja* (also called a *Shiva*) open to the public that attracted thousands of seekers to the ashram. Rudra Pooja is an Indian practice dating from antiquity. A pooja (also spelled *puja*) is an offering. This pooja honored Shiva, a word that means "that which that is not." The Rudra Pooja is recognized by Vedic scriptures as one of the greatest of these offerings; it replaces negative energy within and around us with joy, bliss, and peace. The Rudra Pooja's vibrations may also have a cleansing effect on the subtle and physical bodies. One can attain great inner peace and serenity from experiencing the Rudra Pooja's vibrations.

On that first Monday morning after our arrival, I sat in the back of the grand hall near the open gate, absorbing the fresh morning breeze and waiting for the Rudra Pooja to begin. Today, Gurudev was conducting it just for teacher-trainee participants.

After we had all completed our yogic practices, Gurudev walked through the main gate with a trail of hundreds of Vedic students and pundits chanting in unison. They sat on the platform, and he began the ceremony. As I listened quietly to this powerful evocative Sanskrit chant, I drifted into a profound meditation for over an hour, never reopening my eyes. My entire being reverberated as I melted into the hypnotic sound of our beloved master performing offerings of fire, water, flowers, coconut, camphor, and incense. These offerings represented our overflowing gratitude for things we often take for granted.

After the Rudra Pooja, everyone lay in the corpse posture. This time I abandoned myself completely without resistance. An epic volcano erupted from my being. I began to wail loud and painful moans. My cries echoed through the grand hall, which, except for a few occasional sobs from others, was silent. On and on I kept grieving, not knowing why. Lost in a sea of wailing, I felt I had become a vortex sucking in the negative energies from all the suffering around our planet.

A loving feminine presence came to my side, but I could not stop grieving. The pain in my chest was so excruciating. The woman held my hand and caressed my hair.

An hour must have passed, but then I slowly opened my eyes. The woman sat there silently beside me, gazing into my eyes. She struck me as an exceptional being of genuine compassion and unconditional love. I knew the Divine Mother had put us together. We remained lost in each other's eyes for a while, and then eventually, I let go of her hand. She handed me a tissue, stood, and left without a word.

I gathered my belongings and strolled to the cafeteria, reflecting on my first Rudra Pooja experience and this gentle woman. I could not understand why I had exploded into this intense, painful wailing for so long. I felt shaken by it. And yet, among all the thousand future teachers, that woman had reached out to me in my intense distress. I had never seen her before, but it felt like we had known each other forever. She must have noticed the gratitude and love overflowing from my eyes, but I wanted to express it in person.

The following morning I woke up to an ocean of serenity within myself. It dawned on me that this wave of wailing must have surged up from previous karmic lifetimes. My grief had nothing to do with this life; I had already done that inner work.

~

LATER THAT AFTERNOON, I RAN into Gurudev when he walked out of his kutir to feed his elephant. I could not believe the synchronicity of our encounter, just as I could not the first time. I stopped, smiled, and bowed to him, feeling his abundant grace. A while back, one of his devotees had offered him this elephant. Gurudev named him "Maheshwaren." His face and head were painted in intricate and colorful patterns and he was very big . . . even for an elephant. Only a few other devotees, Gurudev's attendant, and his sister, Bhanu Didi, stood near. She held a stack of bananas.

I approached the tiny group, greeted them, and stood next to Bhanu Didi and Gurudev. Maheshwaren was in front of us with his feet chained;

his mahout, or elephant trainer, used a sharp whip to control him when necessary. I reflected how there must be a better, nonviolent way to train the elephant. I refrained from saying anything, since the mahout had not used the whip yet.

"Gurudev, may I take a few photographs of you feeding your elephant for my article?" I asked our master.

He nodded his head yes, but before I could take a picture, Bhanu Didi placed a banana in my hand and showed me how to feed the animal.

"Offer it to him like this," she said, stretching her arm forward.

I mimicked her actions, holding the fruit. Maheshwaren grabbed it with his trunk and put it in his mouth. Then he walked one step closer toward me and smelled my hand and arm with the tip of his trunk. Then suddenly Maheshwaren twined his trunk around my arm and attempted to pick me up.

"Maheshwaren! No!" his mahout shouted a few times, and after a little while, the elephant let go of me.

We all laughed, but I could feel my heart thump. I was glad the mahout had not used his whip.

That was how the beautiful Bhanu Didi and I met the first time. The next half hour we spent together with Gurudev, feeding Maheshwaren. In the excitement of the moment, I forgot all about taking photographs.

Twenty-Seven

BREAKING THE RULES

AT THE FIRST OFFICIAL SESSION of our American teacher-trainee group, I saw the woman who had sat next to me during the Rudra Pooja. I hugged her and expressed my heartfelt gratitude. We were delighted to be together in the same sangha. She introduced herself as Angelica.

Any group that walks the same spiritual path together is a sangha. Within our sangha, we promised to take responsibility for one another's well-being and committed to complete the teacher-trainee program together. If for any reason one of us quit or was expelled from the program, the whole group would not be allowed to graduate. If someone arrived late at a session, he or she could be expelled from the rest of the program. So, in between these fine, rigid lines, we had to find our way. I wondered how I was going to be able to keep up.

Although I grew up in a family of seven children, the building of team spirit was foreign to me. As our program unfolded, I lost track of time and space. Most days lasted up to twenty hours and were filled with dozens of processes. I did not feel a sense of self.

After a week of eating only Indian food, many of us began to crave fresh fruit. After our daily two hours of sadhana, a few of us would sneak off to the local merchant kiosk in an alley by the cafeteria building. We were told not to buy from outside vendors for hygienic and health reasons, but we could not resist their juicy papaya, mango, and pineapple in that infernal heat. While I was out there, I became aware of how many homeless dogs and cats roamed the ashram. My heart ached for them. Many of them were starving and had mange or other ailments.

Many stray animal companions and cows roam the streets of India. A few individuals and animal welfare nonprofit organizations were trying hard to educate the populace about these humane issues in India, but for the most part there appeared to be little concern from the locals.

I could not remain blind and mute. I had brought pet food in my suitcases, expecting something like this. I embarked on a crusade to feed as many animals as possible, since no one else would feed them or even offer them water in the blazing heat. My mind became consumed with the search for solutions, wondering why those who were on the spiritual path were not more sensitive to animal pain and suffering. In my heart, I hoped future teachers in our international program would wake up and take positive actions for their well-being. Everyone grows at their own pace, but I wished the blossoming of their hearts could be accelerated.

After one week of feeding stray animals, I ran out of supplies. I could not leave the ashram to visit a store; how could I eat without feeding my little friends? Feeling I had no other option, I began to fill up my bag with leftovers from the tables. I may have looked like a thief, but nothing would stop me from bringing food to the starving animals.

Every day after brunch, I fed the dogs around the cafeteria building. A dozen friendly strays would often wait for me. Along the arduous twenty-minute walk I took through steep terrain to reach my sangha's sessions, I would make several stops along the way to feed the kitties and have a brief "meow" with them. When Bougie spotted me, she would come, tail wagging. So sweet. I wondered: *Why did so many people in India look down on animals with contempt? What was the point of studying and reciting all the ancient Sanskrit scriptures for hours and days if the individuals did not practice them?*

One blistering morning I poured water in a bowl on the side of the cafeteria for a few puppies and their emaciated and dehydrated mother. Many little Indian children around the village happened to be there. "Look, children," I said, gesturing. "The animals have bellies like us! They're also thirsty, hungry, and need love. They feel pain and suffer like we do. What do you say? Let's care for them now."

~

FROM THE VERY BEGINNING OF our program, we were instructed to share any problems with our teachers by discussing it in front of our group. My grief at the treatment and neglect of the local strays made my being burn inside. I dared to ask during one of our sessions, "Teacher, can I feed the homeless animals as my *seva*, or volunteer task?"

Our teacher responded with an annoyed tone, "It is not allowed. You should focus on the program and your designated seva instead."

"I have been doing my volunteer work in the kitchen," I said, "while still giving 100 percent to the program. But I also want to do more to help the suffering animals around the ashram without compromising the rules and our safety. Please?"

She never responded, and somehow her nonchalant attitude triggered my inner roar.

All at once I stood and addressed her and my classmates. "Why can't my seva be caring for homeless animals? What about compassion for all living beings? No one seems aware of their suffering and pain—some even look down on them with disdain! I see Gurudev in their faces. God is every-where . . . in every particle of this creation. It's in them, too!"

Everyone remained silent, stunned by my outburst. The teacher looked at me wide-eyed.

"They need our help," I continued. "Soon we're going to become teachers and role models. We'll be in a position to inspire and influence many people. Please open up your heart with compassion to all creatures and act for them."

The teacher blushed. My classmates applauded.

~

THAT NIGHT I STARED AT the ceiling thinking while my roommates indulged in a snoring contest. I had figured the purpose of being on the spiritual path was to awaken to our ultimate nature by experiencing the oneness of existence in all its forms. But still, compassion would be useless unless positive actions were taken. I realized that compassion combined with the right actions allows us the opportunity to transform ourselves and help others. The fundamental expression of love and compassion is at the very core of our true ultimate nature. I was on fire. I resolved to speak up on this issue with Gurudev in front of all the future international teachers and assembly during our next satsang.

The following night our group received the blessing of an audience with Gurudev. He had to be at other Silver Jubilee meetings, so he had squeezed in only twenty minutes for us. He was gleaming with love and wore an elaborate garland of orange marigolds with white and violet flowers over his draped white robe. It is the custom in the yogic tradition to offer a garland of flowers to someone you honor, especially a holy individual or spiritual master like Gurudev.

Most of our sangha had questions for him that night, so I bit my tongue, thinking I would wait for a better opportunity to speak. When Gurudev departed, he left his gorgeous garland hanging on the arm of his chair. No one else seemed to notice, so I grabbed it and ran after him, calling out, "Gurudev, you forgot your garland!"

He turned around and gazed into my eyes with an expression that seemed to mean, "It's yours."

"Do you mean I can keep it?" I asked.

He nodded yes.

~

DURING THE FOLLOWING MORNING'S SESSION, my sangha's teachers announced that there would be a celebratory day at the ashram the next day. They asked us to dress and act in any way we wished, and even to wear a costume if we wanted. Gurudev came to mind right away. I wanted to be him.

Gurudev exuded an aura of elegance, gracefulness, beauty, and ecstasy. To embody this, I wore my elegant white chiffon sari embroidered with golden thread and one of Gurudev's shawls I had bought at an auction at the Canadian ashram. I placed his garland around my neck, pulled my hair back into a ponytail, put an ornate bindi on my forehead between my eyebrows, and walked around the ashram imitating Gurudev throughout our entire celebratory day. Many even would say, "Jai Guru Dev!" when they saw me. Someone even exclaimed, "Oh, see, she has been garlanded by Gurudev!" I responded, "Jai Guru Dev!" in a high-pitched voice, raising my left arm and twisting my head to the side like he often did in his ecstatic moments. People seemed to be enjoying my demeanor as Gurudev. But I wondered if most people knew that I had turned myself into Gurudev for the day. What mattered the most to my being was feeling empowered and radiant with Divine love.

That evening everyone gathered at the grand meditation hall as customary for daily satsang. The Vishalakshi Mantap was packed with thousands of people attending Gurudev's talk. When I walked in, I thought, *I don't care if they expel me from the ashram. I must speak my heart tonight. I'm Gurudev!* The satsang seemed the perfect occasion to speak to him about animal suffering in front of all the teachers, trainees, swamis, pundits, and the ashram's staff.

Music made the grand hall vibrate, as most of us sang at the top of our lungs, "Om Namah Shivaya." Gurudev sat on his dais, meditating. I sat there thinking, *If I don't raise my question right after the music stops, I will miss the opportunity and will never find the courage to speak again.*

When the last bhajan faded away, the crowd fell silent. Gurudev opened his eyes and emitted a high-pitched hum. I stood and with a pounding heart raised my arm. He turned his head, gazing at my being with anticipation.

My heart was pounding, but I did not even wait for his gesture or a microphone. I said, "Gurudev, something is burning in my heart. I enjoyed so much feeding bananas to your elephant with you and Bhanu Didi, but why can't we feed the stray cats and dogs too? They are suffering and need our help. Why can't future teachers express compassion with positive actions to all living beings? I have noticed, even here in the ashram, that some people look at the animals with disdain." I continued, "For instance, Gurudev, there is this dog who has lost almost all his fur. His skin is burning red. He has mange, an ailment that can be easily healed with proper antibiotics, but untreated he could die from the infection."

I can't remember every word I spoke, but Gurudev listened for ten minutes without interruption. Then he gestured for me to sit down and said, "Yes, of course you can feed the animals! It must be done down near the cafeteria area." He signaled for the musicians to play again. Then he closed his eyes and meditated again through another song.

After the satsang, all the teacher-trainee participants returned to their designated groups for the evening session. As we walked out, a female participant passed by me and said angrily, "How dare you speak to Gurudev like that. So disrespectful! You're not allowed to speak after bhajans until the master speaks the first word."

"I didn't know that," I said. "I don't feel I was disrespectful to Gurudev. If he didn't want to hear, he would have stopped me."

She walked away with her nose in the air.

I returned to my sangha's classroom for our evening's session. As soon as we all sat, our teacher stared at me and said harshly, "What is wrong with you? What happened tonight?"

I stood again and looked her straight in the eye. "There is never a good opportunity to speak for the suffering animals. They don't have voices. We are their voices! Most people don't want to hear or see their misery, because it will shake their belief system. We must seize the opportunity. What's the point of becoming a teacher if I can't express my love and compassion in actions here at the ashram? If I can't speak my heart and express compassion and love for all living beings, then I'm in the wrong place, I don't belong here!" I said firmly, ready to walk out of the program for good.

Her face turned red. She remained quiet.

～

THE FOLLOWING DAY THE CAMPUS was overcrowded and chaotic. Thousands more visitors had arrived from around the globe. The ashram was filthy, filled with garbage and plastic bags. There was a lot of gossip about my words to Gurudev. Some people even spoke to me about the animals and started calling me "the animal lover."

The truth is, I had never considered myself an "animal lover." I was simply in love with love, the creation, and my Creator. I never made the distinction among species of who is deserving of love and compassion and who is not. But, I was realizing that this was not true for many of my fellow teachers-in-training.

One of the Indian teachers from another group approached me. "Weren't you the courageous one who spoke to Gurudev last night at the satsang? Everybody knows about you now. You're getting a reputation!"

Good or bad? I wondered—but I did not really care. I had no regrets and knew my efforts would not be in vain. I believed Gurudev enjoyed my heartfelt initiative and might have even used me as an instrument. Sometimes masters have mystical ways of operating a situation for the greater spiritual outcome for the disciplines and devotees involved. Gurudev was known for that. I did not know if this was the case. I may have lacked protocol, but it was better to seize the moment and be authentic than let a great opportunity slip away.

~

AS THE DAYS PASSED, THE tension intensified within the teacher-trainee groups. I tried to keep up with all the demands, rules, daily tasks, feeding the stray animals, and trying to do some research for my article at the ashram's archives. It did not matter if I slept only a few hours; I managed to barely arrive on time to our sessions.

One afternoon I volunteered to interview participants we were filming for an Art of Living video. I had been there several hours when an American woman showed up with a three-week-old kitten in her hands. "I have been looking for you everywhere!" she said. "We found this kitten crying inside a garbage bin near the administration building. I don't know what to do with the little fellow. Can you help us?"

I completed the interview I was on, picked up the tiny fur ball, and caressed him. "He's very hungry and cold. See? He's trembling. Kittens need to be fed every hour and kept warm all the time, otherwise they can die." I asked her a few questions, wrapped the kitten in my kurta, and left to get some warm milk at the public cafe located a few steps away in the ashram.

I sat and fed him with my finger and called him "Minoux" after my beloved black Persian. He needed intensive care and a good home. I wondered who would throw a living animal into a garbage bin, or perhaps the mother brought him there for safety.

I knew I would get in trouble bringing him to class, but I had no choice; I could not leave him behind. As I ran back to our session with the kitten cuddled against my chest, I tried to come up with a plan.

When I walked into the classroom, Angelica saw us, snapped Minoux from my hands, and exclaimed, "Oh, my God, what a beautiful kitten! Vivi, you know the main teacher will pick on you for this. He could expel you for good! Hurry up! We must hide him." She ran out the door holding the kitten, not saying where she was going.

Within a minute the male teacher walked in and began our session. Ten minutes later, Angelica walked back into the classroom. The teacher stared at her and asked in a firm voice where she had been. Angelica said she had taken a rescued kitten to the Art of Living doctor at the clinic nearby and that the doctor had agreed to adopt him.

Knowing what would happen to Angelica, I stood and said, "Teacher, I take responsibility. Angelica has nothing to do with this. I brought the kitten here. She did this just to protect me and help the kitten."

"What would you do with a kitten if you were the one teaching this class?" the teacher asked.

"Nothing would change, teacher," I responded. "I would keep the kitten safely tucked away until the end of the session, then find him a good home. If we can save a life at the same time we teach a class, why not? His life is very important. What a great opportunity to inspire people to take compassionate action!"

The teacher didn't reply, changed the subject, and continued with the session. Angelica and I looked at each other, smiling.

AFTER A WEEK AND A half into the program, I was still burning inside. A part of my being felt like it was about to explode again. Every day the pressure intensified. Between the tension and pressure of my personal situation and how my own karmic structure was rising, I had a host of extremely intense feelings and emotions.

Only now, after years of being with Gurudev, do I recognize how often he let a situation unravel without his intervention, depending on the circumstances. I had heard from many people over the years that Gurudev also had a habit of creating mischief and chaos so that his followers could evolve faster. I had experienced this firsthand.

One day, I sensed another volcano would erupt soon. I wanted to run away again, but I was too depleted to go anywhere. During brunch, I dragged myself to our bedroom feeling dizzy, heavy with sorrow, and needing solitude.

When I arrived, I stood facing the wall in the direction of Gurudev's kutir, lost amid the mountain of luggage. I began wailing, "Why are you putting me through so much, Gurudev? I need a break!" I banged on the wall with my fists, sobbing, "I hate you!"

I was like a little child angry at her parent. After grieving for a long time, I climbed up into my bunk and collapsed there, beyond exhausted. When I woke up, I marched over to the cafeteria building, hoping to have a last-minute bite. It was still packed with thousands of visitors finishing their meals. In silence I grabbed a few spoonfuls of food and sat, hidden away from the crowd toward the end of the gargantuan hall.

I was still nibbling at my meal when Gurudev walked in through the grand entrance alone. Everybody dropped their conversations, stood, bowed in silence, and gathered themselves near the end of the tables, forming a pathway for him to walk.

At first, I did not know what was happening. I felt too giddy and empty to think or move. I remained seated, lost in a daze. Gurudev continued to stroll along, as if he was searching for someone. When he was close to the end of the hallway, only a few feet away from my table, he stopped and turned in my direction. I froze and dropped my fork. I stood in shock in front of my seat, remembering and regretting my harsh words about Gurudev. He looked at me for several seconds with a mischievous smile. Then he turned around without saying a word, walked slowly away, and left the hall.

A part of my being felt Gurudev had heard my deep cries, and he was demonstrating he was there for us. His physical presence felt encouraging. It reminded me to be more aware as I walk upon Mother Earth while remembering he is always inside my being. It is always a great blessing to be in his physical presence, no matter what the circumstances.

Everyone had been still as a statue in Gurudev's presence, but the moment he walked out, the noise level erupted, buzzing like a hive. I sat and stared at my plate for a while. By the time I left, the hall was almost deserted.

As I lay on my cot after midnight, I marveled at the mysterious ways of the masters. I would never know for sure why Gurudev showed up at the cafeteria the way he did, or even if he came for me. I often could not comprehend him, but I trusted my beloved guru. A genuine spiritual master never does anything without a purpose.

～

A FEW DAYS LATER, A general meeting was called in the Vishalakshi Mantap for all teacher-trainee participants and teachers. They announced the ashram was expecting many more thousands of international visitors. Gurudev wanted all teacher-trainee participants to make space for them and move with our belongings from the dorms to the cafeteria building. The men would occupy the third floor, the women the fourth. That would be our living quarters for the following two and a half weeks or more. The cafeteria building did not have an elevator, or hot water. Each floor had a large public bathroom with a few dozen showers and communal sinks. Several of the resident volunteers had built temporary light wooden partitions dividing the space into smaller compartments on both floors. Each of these compartments held fifteen to twenty cots, an inch or two away from the next.

That afternoon in the blazing sun, almost five hundred of us women dragged our luggage from one side of the ashram to the other with the help of some of the men. Upon our arrival on the fourth floor, I decided to camp in one of the compartments that faced the tropical rolling hills opposite the noisy center of the ashram. I did not notice that this side faced a chimney emitting thick, black, suffocating smoke that was coming from the kitchen through our windows. On that first night, the smoke began to irritate my throat and lungs. I started to cough. Everyone had settled in. It was too late to move to a different compartment.

In less than two days, crisscross ropes sprung up over our heads, filled with wet underwear, dresses, and pants, while huge piles of luggage surrounded our beds. With five hundred roommates all crammed on the same floor, it was nearly impossible to get anything done at dawn. You had to have a good bladder and hold it in! I thought back to our previous arrangements with nostalgia. Four roommates was a bargain! I tried every kind of earplugs I could find. Nothing worked.

The roommate on my right was an African-American reverend. On the first night, she could not fall asleep and confessed to me how scared she felt.

I whispered, "It's often just our own thoughts and assumptions that trouble us. We need to practice being more aware of them."

I shared some of my experiences with her. While we were talking, a tiny lizard crawled on the wooden panel above her head. She screamed, terrified. I laughed. "It's just a little creature of God, sweetheart! She's more afraid of you than you are of her. Don't worry, she won't eat you up."

The reverend laughed, too, realizing how her mind, not the lizard, had caused her fright. After that, we both slept like babies.

Twenty-Eight

MOMENT OF EPIPHANY

THE ASHRAM, NOW HOST TO over ten thousand international visitors, was overflowing. Since we could not use the Vishalakshi Mantap anymore for our sadhana, it had become impossible to find a quiet spot to meditate. We had no choice but to do our spiritual practices on our cots in our compartments.

One morning I woke up with a fever and painful sore throat. I knew it was turning into bronchitis. I was concerned because in the past few years, I had contracted bronchitis and it had turned into severe pneumonia. I had been breathing the black smoke coming from the kitchen and wondered if it had caused a relapse of this bronchitis.

I went to see the doctor at the ashram's clinic, the one who'd adopted our rescued kitten. She put me on an antibiotic and loaded me up with cough syrup. "Vivi, you need rest, plenty of rest," she said.

"Do you realize I'm a participant in the teacher-trainee program? How can I get rest? It's impossible unless I quit." I had to laugh at the irony.

At this point the thought of becoming a teacher did not even exist in my mind. I didn't know anything anymore. I missed being with Nathaniel, cuddling in bed with all our rescued cats. Still, the upcoming Silver Jubilee inspired me to stay around. We expected over 2.5 million visitors. I had never experienced meditating with such a massive number of sincere seekers before. On the second day of the Silver Jubilee, Gurudev would be conducting a meditation for the multitude. I wanted to be there for this rare experience.

~

ONE MORNING, JUST A FEW days before graduation, I did not hear the alarm, and my roommates did not wake me up. I rushed out of bed, dressed, and ran to our session. I entered the classroom like a ghost and sat in the back.

The main teacher had not started the class yet and was chatting with a few participants up front. He dropped everything, stared at me, and asked sharply, "Where have you been? You're five minutes late!"

"I'm so sorry, teacher," I said. "I take responsibility. It takes so long to walk here with my injured knee."

He stared at me with a sneer, then addressed my classmates, "Just ignore her! She's not allowed in class anymore." He asked everyone to gather into smaller groups for a process. I tried to join my peers, but he raised his voice. "No! Don't let her in."

I tried to approach him and sat near his feet. "Listen, teacher, I'm truly sorry. I apologized. Please let me in the class. In a few days, we will be graduating."

He did not look at me and pretended I did not exist. I closed my eyes, sat in lotus position, and meditated while the small groups worked. An hour later I opened my eyes. Participants asking questions surrounded him. After everyone returned to their seats, I tried to speak with him again and begged to be allowed to return. "Please, teacher, understand. I slept in out of exhaustion, and I felt too sick to get up. I saw the doctor yesterday."

He ignored my petition.

I closed my eyes and meditated for another half hour while he continued with the class, then approached him again, saying, "I have been very sick. Please let me back . . . Gurudev wants me here."

I could see the issue had become a personal matter. It was nothing specific, just the dynamics and karmic structure unfolding. I stood, walked out of the classroom, and went to find Gurudev.

Two of the young male trainees ran after and reached me outside the building. They grabbed my being and prevented me from leaving. They must have been concerned over the rule I was breaking. They knew too well the program would end there if I did not come back to class. We had to graduate together. It was my responsibility to wake up and to show up on time no matter what. I did not blame anyone and did not care anymore about graduation. In the fire of the moment, I just wanted to go home. "Let me go," I screamed. "I'm going to speak with Gurudev about this. I'm going back home!"

They attempted to pull me back into the classroom with force.

The teacher ran out yelling, "Yes, yes, let her go!"

The boys released me. I ran off wailing and feeling sick to my stomach. My fever and sore throat had gotten worse. I was hyperventilating, trying to catch a deep breath, when I reached Gurudev's kutir.

I knocked. He was not there. So I knocked on Bhanu Didi's door, sobbing.

When her attendant answered, I told her, crying, "I urgently need to speak with Bhanu Didi. I am going back home. I quit the teacher-training program."

"Bhanu Didi and Gurudev are at an event this afternoon. Please come back later, Vivi. I will tell her you stopped by," the attendant said kindly.

I left Bhanu Didi's room and walked around the campus for a while, weeping. It was time to go home.

~

THE PHONE BOOTHS WERE LOCATED off campus, a good thirty minutes down the road from the ashram. As I walked there, I realized I had flown thousands of miles just to be at the ashram. And then there was the article I would be writing on the life of Gurudev. I wanted to include the Silver Jubilee celebration in it.

When I got to the phones, I dialed Nathaniel. We hadn't spoken in three weeks, and he seemed surprised to hear my voice.

"How are things going, baby?" he asked.

I hardly knew where to begin. "An entire lifetime has happened here, sweetheart," I said crying. "I just want to come home as soon as possible. I'm so homesick. I can't take it anymore. I have a fever and bronchitis again. Please, find me a flight."

"Not again," Nathaniel said.

"Wait a minute," I urged. "You don't understand. I'll share the story when I see you. Please don't judge me. I don't have the energy for that now."

"I know you can do it, baby! There is only one week left. In no time you will be back home. Stick around," he pleaded.

When I hung up the phone, there were tears in my eyes once again. I headed back to campus wondering why being on the spiritual path was so painful.

As I wandered on the main pathway leading toward the cafeteria, I noticed our classroom's building had emptied. The main teacher was outside, talking on his cell phone. When he noticed me, he rushed his call and hurried after me.

"Where have you been, Vivi?" he asked. "The whole class has been looking for you for hours."

"I went to see Gurudev and called my husband to arrange for my departure," I said. "No matter what your personal issues are, teacher, I still love you and accept you the way you are. I see the Divine in you. Why can't you see the Divine in my being too?"

He stared at me, frozen, not knowing what to say. A long moment elapsed in silence. Finally, I turned and walked away without a word.

I made my way to the cafeteria, which was almost vacant. I served myself a little food left over from brunch and sat feeling so drained that I barely nibbled at my meal.

As I ate, two of my Indian classmates appeared at the table.

"Here you are, Vivi!" Chandani said. "Where were you? We have been looking for you everywhere since morning. We were worried about you. Can we sit with you?"

I nodded yes.

"We both agreed to take the lead and speak with you," Ganesh said as he pulled up a chair. "The entire group cares for you. We want you back! After you left, we all agreed that we see you as a great leader. You have amazing and rare qualities. You can save billions of animals if you want. Please don't give up now. Don't let the teacher's personal issues make you quit. Don't let him win. You have it in you to be such a wonderful, powerful teacher and leader!"

"We love you and want you back with us so we can all graduate together as a sangha," both said.

I remained mute, but my heart was bursting with Divine love. After conversing with them for over an hour, it dawned on me why I had such difficulty facing the challenges of life. I realized I had trouble accepting where individuals were on their spiritual path and accepting their dysfunctions. For most of my life, I had given up when situations got too painful to face, trying to run away from my accumulated garbage and limitations, trying to bury my childhood. Yet life kept bringing these kinds of challenges back and reopening the wounds. I knew I had to surmount my fight-or-flight instinct. How could I quit now, with only two days away from graduation? True leaders never give up, no matter what. They inspire always. If I wanted to lead, I had to transcend my habits and break free from the boundaries that held me back. I had to stay and finish the program; this was my path.

"So, Vivi," Ganesh finally asked, "are you coming back with us?"

I nodded my head yes, stood, and hugged them as tears rolled down my cheeks. "I'm not coming back because I don't want the teacher to win," I said. "I'm coming back because of all of you and Gurudev."

It was mid-afternoon when the three of us entered the classroom. Silence dropped like a bomb. Everyone turned toward us.

Ganesh and Chandani sat. I stood looking at everyone for a moment. My classmates burst into applause. I blushed and sat in silence feeling Divine love in my heart. A sense of belongingness overwhelmed my being like never before.

~

THE FOLLOWING MORNING IN CLASS we performed the Guru Pooja, honoring the lineage of all the great ancient masters who had transmitted spiritual knowledge throughout the ages. In the yogic tradition, it is customary for the spiritual master to offer the *prasad*, the blessed sweets from the puja.

Our female teacher asked me to offer the prasad, which was a great honor. Sitting on the ground in lotus position, honored and humbled, with a large bowl filled with savory Indian sweets, I placed one in the hand of each of our beloved sangha members.

I was still walking around like a zombie feeling sick and drained, my throat and chest hurting. I wondered if Gurudev was aware of what some of us had had to surmount during this program. I decided I would write him a personal letter after my return to America.

In the last moment of my sangha's graduation, I asked for the microphone. "I want to express my love and gratitude to all of you and both of our teachers," I said, my throat tight with emotion. "Through all of you and the teachers, I learned the power of the sangha, belongingness, transcending through many obstacles and my own limitations, no matter what they are. Never give up!" I closed my eyes and took a few deep breaths. "I bow down to you all."

~

ON THAT FINAL EVENING OF our program, Gurudev sat on the dais while each of us paraded onstage to pick up a rose. When it was my turn, he turned his loving, smiling gaze on my face as he offered me my rose. I held it tenderly in my hand and bowed down, touching his feet.

After the ceremony, the grand hall exploded with exuberant energy as we danced, jumping up and down and chanting to the music. Overflowing with gratitude, I enjoyed it all.

By late in the evening, my fever had returned, and I could not stop coughing. Everywhere around campus, filled with laughter, singing, and dancing, a magical energy reigned. Part of my being wished I could celebrate longer—but my body temple cried out for rest. I returned to my room and collapsed in exhaustion.

When I woke up around 10:00 a.m., my entire floor was vacant. Over twelve hours had elapsed while I was in deep slumber. I showered alone in the public bathroom. I skipped brunch and my sadhana. I did not want to breathe black smoke anymore. I headed to the phone booths while doing my rounds feeding the stray animals. Only a few days remained before the grand festivities would take place. I hoped to feel well enough to make it. I remembered what my doctor told me: *Rest.*

I called Nathaniel and told him what had been going on. He said, "I knew you would make it! I could not find a flight for you anyway. In four days, you'll be back home. Miss you so much, baby."

It was already blazing hot. I bought pineapple juice and sat alone in the shade outside, sipping it and contemplating my voyage. I listened to the birds sing, the dogs bark, the children laugh, my heart beating to the rhythm of my breath, in and out. Then I walked into a neighboring salon to greet my friend, Flower.

Flower persuaded me to let her paint my hands with henna in the Indian traditional style for the Art of Living's Silver Jubilee. I sat on her chair, mesmerized by the intricate patterns she formed. Within a few minutes, I dozed off.

When I awoke a few hours later, Flower had almost completed her masterpiece. She explained that it would take the whole afternoon to dry and that I should not do much with my hands until then.

I sauntered to the ashram listening to the silence within while admiring the monkeys playing in the trees. I reached the Vishalakshi Mantap and was surprised to see how empty it was. I had forgotten everyone was sitting with Gurudev underneath the enormous tent near the grand meditation hall. I would always try to create an opportunity or never miss one to be in the presence or at the feet of my beloved Gurudev. I had signed up for this silent program but decided not to go. This time I felt free from my attachments; I didn't need to be there in person, because he was throbbing deeper in my being.

I entered Vishalakshi Mantap, thinking what a great blessing solitude can be when one needs tranquility far away from sensory stimulus. I sat, did my sudarshan kriya, and meditated for a while till I collapsed on the marble floor.

Loud voices woke me. It was too dark to read my watch. At a snail's pace, I rose, walked wobbling to the terrace, and noticed hundreds of participants headed to the cafeteria for the seven o'clock dinner seating. Another six hours had disappeared while I slept. I dragged myself to the nearest washroom feeling too groggy to talk to or look at anyone. The henna was peeling off. I washed my hands and discovered a world of beauty underneath.

~

THE FOLLOWING MORNING I ROSE like the sunlight. The enormous bathroom was deserted. I took a cold shower, and lingered, combing my hair while I watched through the window as the villagers made a bonfire around their crumbling shacks. Homeless dogs roamed, begging for a morsel. I exploded with joy to be alive and feeling better and sent blessings to those outdoors.

I met with Kuvalaya near the mega tent. She was Indian, and a longtime resident. I had been told Gurudev had assigned her to care for the animals at the ashram, including the peacocks, rabbits, and birds. We sat on chairs outside in a shady area far from the crowd. Bougie spotted me from far away. I called her, and she came running, rolled over my feet, and sat there content during our meeting. I had heard numerous times over the years that Gurudev put particular individuals in certain positions to help them overcome their specific limitations. I wondered if this was the case with Kuvalaya.

"It would be helpful if we could work with a local nonprofit animal welfare organization, if we can find one, and do an animal birth control (ABC) clinic at the ashram," I proposed. This kind of clinic is a sterilization program for stray and feral dogs and cats and includes vaccinations and vet care. I explained that option was the best solution to eliminate unnecessary suffering and pain for the animals and reduce the number of strays. I volunteered to sponsor the whole project. She agreed and mentioned they had done a tiny clinic with the group Compassion Unlimited Plus Action (CUPA) from Bangalore a very long time ago. I inquired why they did not keep it up. I stressed the importance of doing regular clinics to maintain a very low and healthy population of animals.

We called CUPA and set up a date to provide a more elaborate clinic at the ashram. A sense of joy overcame my being. I knew this initiative would help alleviate suffering and many future problems, not only for the animals, but also for the community. I hoped this would be the first step of something much bigger for animal welfare and advocacy in India—a rise in consciousness filled with love, reverence, and compassion for all creatures.

Giving back to all living beings in whatever way you can begets a wealth of joy and grace in your life. Is your heart overflowing with gratitude and compassion in actions? If not, have you wondered why? It seems religions create division and separation among people. Yet just walking the path of loving compassion is enough to transform you—to help you realize your true nature is divine. The more we experience our ultimate nature, the more we become an instrument and expression of beauty and loving compassion.

Twenty-Nine

ONE WORLD FAMILY

ON THE FIRST MORNING OF the Silver Jubilee festivities, I woke up filled with elation. These celebrations were about to take place at two different locations simultaneously during the following three days. Gurudev was to conduct his grand meditation at the Jakkur Airfield Aerodrome for the enormous crowd on February 17, 2006. This was the day I had longed for since landing in India; nothing was going to prevent me from going unless God took my last breath away.

Only one thing shadowed the big event: My high fever kept coming back, and the bronchitis and extreme fatigue had settled even deeper. I wondered why my immune system was so weak.

I woke alone in my compartment that day with a fever of 103 degrees. I was coughing and having difficulty breathing, and my voice was faint and hoarse. Undeterred, I swallowed my pills and cough syrup. I had only three days left before my departure, and today was the big day—and if I did not make it to the ten o'clock bus leaving for the aerodrome in Bangalore, I would miss the entire day and night of the Silver Jubilee, including the meditation. My body temple craved only rest and healing, but my heart cried out to be at the Silver Jubilee.

"I'm not the body. I'm not the mind," I told myself. I crawled out of bed, pushing myself.

I lingered in the shower, the cold water rejuvenating my aching body. As I combed my hair, I lost myself again watching the villagers and stray dogs behaving as before. Suddenly an intense feeling of profound gratitude overwhelmed my being. Tears rolled down my cheeks. I felt so blessed by the abundance in my life and for having Gurudev, my beautiful spiritual master, in my life.

When I made it to where hundreds of buses had lined up on the far side of the ashram, most had already left. I dragged myself toward them, trusting I would make it for the last one. I thought, *I never want to rush anymore. If I miss the bus, so be it. I will take a taxi.* When we rush, we don't remain tranquil or aware and do things with lack of consciousness. Our actions can easily become compulsive behaviors. When we rush and multitask, we often make mistakes, break things, even hurt ourselves and others. When I arrived, the last bus was about to leave. The driver gunned its motor, but he waited for me.

I jumped in, walked to the back, and sat in silence, my eyes closed, preserving energy. My sore throat and laryngitis provided me the perfect excuse to remain silent. I was too sick and exhausted to be with millions of seekers, yet here I was, heading to the biggest celebration I had ever attended in my life. I longed to retreat somewhere in the Himalayas, somewhere in a yogi's cave. I wondered if I had lost my mind. I imagined Gurudev saying, "Good, good, good!" and something inside pulled my being. Ah, devotional love may move a genuine seeker to do many crazy things.

When we reached the dusty, burnt-sienna grounds of the aerodrome, hundreds of buses lined up like dominos. The aerodrome covered 256 acres and was already filled with visitors. Dozens of giant TV screens separated the terrain into sections. Merchants in the bazaar had set up camps around the circumference. Its 3.5-acre stage had transformed into the International Faith Conference, a global forum where spiritual and religious leaders of all faiths would share their wisdom and exchange ideas.

I walked half a mile before arriving at the front stage where all the teachers and teacher-trainee graduates sat together. Gurudev had reserved these front rows for the media and for us. We were given special VIP access to a large tent on the side where a sumptuous buffet of Indian vegetarian delicacies and refreshments were served all day long.

As I sat in the third row facing Gurudev's dais, I was awed. Lost in a vast sea of people from more than 150 countries, I watched a Pakistani flag wave in the hot breeze to the rhythm of an Indian flag, and an Israeli flag dance to the cadence of a Palestinian flag. Over thirty thousand volunteers joyfully orchestrated these once-in-a-lifetime events. I stayed there, silent and still as a Buddha statue, my eyes closed much of the time, as speakers and musicians took the stage and shared their message of peace.

Late in the afternoon, as the sun bathed the area in an orange-violet glow, a helicopter circled the stage and landed on it. No international rock or pop star was arriving; instead, I heard someone say, "His Holiness Sri Sri Ravi Shankar!"

"Gurudev!" I sighed. When I saw him debark from the helicopter, my face lit up. I marveled at this divine star who knew how to play with the strings of our hearts, who stirred us to the core with his sublime melodies—ancient, eternal, universal, yet familiar.

Among the numerous bits of wisdom Gurudev shared with us that day, these words reverberated most deeply within my being: "Life is sacred. Celebrate life. Care for others and share whatever you have with those less fortunate than you. Broaden your vision, for the whole world belongs to you."

Eighty gigantic video screens projected the depth of Gurudev's infinite, loving gaze and words to the crowd and the world as he spoke, "Vasudhaiva Kutumbakam or 'One World Family' is a call to move from tolerance to love, from self-centered success to selfless service, from being exclusive to being all-inclusive."

He continued, emphasizing the urgent need to globalize wisdom by honoring the oneness of the universal spirit in all living beings and restoring human values in all walks of life. These cherished values of compassion, love, kindness, cooperation, friendliness, integrity, empathy, enthusiasm, benevolence, generosity, patience, respect, and reverence for all life forms are at the heart of most religious and spiritual traditions and paths.

One of the guests onstage—a mixture of spiritual leaders and dignitaries—asked Gurudev, "Why have you done all of this?"

"For you," he said, "to get a sense of belonging. The only true security that can be found in this world is in the very process of giving love. Love is seeing God in the being next to us. Meditation is seeing God within us."

Following Gurudev's timeless wisdom, millions of us closed our eyes and meditated as one in a massive sudarshan kriya, a powerful breathing practice created and taught by his teachers. As we meditated, I fell in a zone between heaven and nothingness. I experienced oneness with millions of other seekers. I felt blessed for having this opportunity.

The night fell upon us like a lover's embrace. Enormous colorful spotlights illuminated the stage and the vast terrain. Hundreds of musicians began playing the theme song of the One World Family. At this point, I stood on top of my chair as others did to wave my arms in a "V" shape that signified, "Victory to the big mind." I whispered, "Jai Guru Dev!"

Dust from the ground had covered the bottom of my long white skirt turning it rusty red, but I didn't mind. Joyous energy transported my being. I felt triumphant. Everywhere I looked, I saw radiant smiles. Vibrations rippled along my spine while millions of people sang in unison to the echoes of "Vasudhaiva Kutumbakam."

I wondered how one little wise, bearded man could bring together such a massive number of people from various religious, cultural, political, and socioeconomic backgrounds in the largest peace gathering ever manifested on earth. What was the secret of his magnetism, his charisma, his power to move the world?

During the intermission I remained seated and pondered the life of Gurudev. I felt his aura. Being in his presence for my being had been cathartic, like a soothing balm that helps heal a painful wound.

The Art of Living Foundation Silver Jubilee celebrated twenty-five years of love, devotion, and selfless service for the well-being and evolution of our planet, with Gurudev leading followers from five continents through practical and timeless wisdom.

The essence of wisdom is always timeless, universal, and expansive. The heritage of all diverse religions and spiritual traditions belongs to everyone, regardless of our backgrounds and ages. There is only one truth, one Source of creation manifesting in billions of different forms.

~

AFTER LISTENING TO GURUDEV SPEAK, I considered how we might teach our children these precious human values without imposing strict morality. We cannot teach morality, but we can inspire others to blossom into beautiful human beings. I knew role modeling and positive vibes were important to inspire the world, but were they enough for spiritual transformation? How can we nurture these precious values in people's hearts when most societies are focused on survival, power, or economics? The practices of altruism and nonviolence are the seeds. Our thoughts, words, and actions are the sun and water that nourish or deplete our growth.

Most people are still in a deep slumber and do not realize their ultimate nature. The Source of creation is the absolute artist of all. But we are co-creators of that world. Love or hatred, the choice is ours. Everything in nature has much to teach us.

Gurudev often points out that religion is the banana skin, spirituality the banana. He said most of us have thrown away the fruit and kept the old, rotten skin. Spirituality has the potential to unite individuals from all religions, even atheists, for spirituality is beyond religion and creed. Spirituality is at the very core of our true nature and is all-inclusive. The thread of love, that Source of creation, interconnects us all.

As the celebrations unfolded, the ether was filled with an intense, loving energy. Receptive and open visitors could not miss it. At the end of the festivities, a few of us climbed on the stage holding hands and chanting, feeling awed and blessed by Gurudev's grace. When the volunteers began to wrap up the flags and equipment, I strolled back to the bus area alone, lingering a little while to look at a few booths while I marveled at Gurudev's phenomenal life and his power to inspire so many millions. I sat in one of the buses by myself in silence with a worn-out body, closed eyes, a full heart, and an emptied and hollowed mind.

~

THROUGHOUT MY STAY AT THE ashram, I had been persistent in requesting an audience with Gurudev, but I had given up the hope of an interview. After the Silver Jubilee, I thought he must not have slept in days, with all these thousands of people always wanting something from him. How was he able to give so much of himself, his loving energy, wisdom, and guidance? Only a great, enlightened being could be that selfless. I aspired one day to be just like him and His Holiness the Dalai Lama.

Then, on my last morning in India, I woke up with no fever and an amazing surprise: The Art of Living's public relations director contacted me and told me I was to meet with Gurudev that afternoon at his home. I could not believe it.

Later that day, a tiny group of us from the media sat outside by the lake with Gurudev. He radiated Divine love and was beautifully dressed in a long, silky white robe. He gestured for us to come closer. Several individuals began to ask questions.

I sat by Gurudev's feet and bowed down, feeling so blissful and serene. I fell deeper into this noble silence, no thought crossing my mind. Noble silence is not just absence of words. It is a profound stillness, a silence from within. No agendas, no thoughts, no judgments or assumptions arose. I was just there, lost in an oasis of tranquility, a piece of life breathing in and out in the oneness of existence.

During the month, I had put together a long list of questions for Gurudev, but in his presence, all my questions evaporated. All answers were revealed within. There was no need to ask him. I sat in lotus position and merged with him as his divinity beat within my heart. In the yogic tradition, the state of being in "yoga" is to experience the ever-expanding consciousness beyond all physical limitations, encompassing the oneness of all existence. I entered this state in Gurudev's presence, lost in the oneness of creation.

Forty minutes must have passed before Gurudev stood and told us he was going to rest. I got up and stood next to him, beaming with Divine love. I raised my left hand as I had done many times in the past. Gurudev bestowed his penetrating shakti gaze upon my being, and it flowed straight to the shrine of my heart. I could see the whole universe in his eyes.

"Your article is going to be very good!" he said. Then I raised my hand, and he gave me a high five. I felt deeply humbled by Gurudev's words. My heart just overflowed with an ocean of gratitude.

When he took his leave, I bowed, touched his feet, and watched him go back inside his home. I left there with the most profound sense of expansion I had ever experienced. I knew no matter what occurred in my life, he would always be in my heart.

~

I RETURNED TO THE ASHRAM around five—with just enough time to eat a bit, carry my bags down from the fourth floor, and jump into a taxi for the Bangalore airport.

On my way back to the cafeteria building, I stood near Gurudev's kutir hugging a few friends goodbye when Bougie dashed over to see me. She had brought with her the homeless dog with the severe mange infection. Bougie wagged her tail with gratitude as if she knew I was departing from the ashram.

"Bougie, I'll do everything I can to help you. I love you so much. I know others will take care of you doggies; I have arranged for it." The other dog came right to me, wagging his tail, too, as if he understood everything I had said. I patted both their heads. They responded with kisses. Soon I noticed that people began to gather around. A scene like this was a rarity in India.

Someone asked, "Aren't you afraid to get bitten?"

I answered this stranger, "This is a miracle of love. I have been feeding these dogs for a month, and all that time, this dog with the mange infection would not get near me or anyone else. Bougie brought him to me now for the first time!"

I walked away from the dogs and remembered what Gurudev often said. "Go out there, make new friends every day." *No matter what the species is,* I thought.

As I took off in a tuk-tuk for the nearest taxi station, I looked behind at the glorious pink lotus meditation center, the rolling hills, the dogs running free, the cows and grazing goats. In this eternal moment, the Divine within was revealed.

I sat in the taxi whispering, "Jai Guru Dev!" While we rode to the airport, I reflected on my journey. I realized how true unconditional love and compassion can transform the most impossible situations and people. Seekers who take the time to listen and discover the depth of their true nature not only have the inner power to transform their being but also the world!

I recalled a beautiful saying by Mahatma Gandhi, "Truth alone will endure, all the rest will be swept away before the tide of time. I must continue to bear testimony to truth even if I am forsaken by all. Mine may today be a voice in the wilderness, but it will be heard when all other voices are silenced, if it is the voice of Truth."[1]

As we drove faster through the deserted road on that late Sunday afternoon, the scenery unfolded before my eyes. Cows strolled along the sides of the hazy freeway among dozens of homeless dogs, cats, and poor souls searching for food, happiness, and liberation. Everything was the same, but I was not. Yet the core of my being remained the same—free, eternal, and boundless. A load of karma and limitations had melted away during my training. A sense of lightness and a profound sense of homecoming uplifted my being. I could only bow down to my beloved Gurudev, feeling infinite gratitude and Divine love for him and for all living beings.

Thirty

BLESSING IN DISGUISE

AFTER A GRUELING FORTY-EIGHT HOURS of travel, I landed at
the San Francisco airport. Nathaniel embraced me with a sigh of relief. We
headed to one of our favorite Italian restaurants for a late lunch. I sat there
quietly picking at my angel hair pasta. My eyes often rolled on their own,
drifting into a meditative state. I wanted to share with Nathaniel the intensity of my journey, how I was feeling, but words failed me.

Weeks later I still had a deep cough and decided to see my general physician. He put me on stronger antibiotics. The bronchitis had already turned
into pneumonia. Exhaustion settled in. I often woke up after sleeping ten
to twelve hours feeling drained. Something wrong was going on within my
body temple. Painting had been my life for decades, but now I no longer
had any interest in my art studio. I could not understand why. It felt as if
everything that needed to be conveyed through my canvases had already
been expressed. I deeply yearned to help others transform themselves on
the path of enlightenment, as a solution to resolving many challenges on
earth, and indirectly to get them to help animals.

One day while taking a shower, I noticed a large lump snaking from my
left breast to my armpit. Lumps are familiar occurrences for women like me
with fibrocystic breasts. This time I was sure it was cancerous. In the next
few weeks, it continued to grow. One day I summoned up my courage and
went for a biopsy.

A few days later the phone rang. "Vivi, I have the result of your biopsy in front of me. I'm so sorry to have to announce this . . ." my gynecologist said hesitantly.

"I have breast cancer," I said, feeling courageous that I was finally going to face the reality. A part of my being knew I would be completely healed from the cancer. This inner-knowing throbbed within every particle of my body temple.

"How do you know?"

"I've had that premonition for some time," I said. "I just did not feel ready to face it." On many levels, I was relieved. I could not put it off anymore.

"I'm worried about you, Vivi," he said. "The tumor is very large and growing toward the lymph nodes under your arm. Dr. Columbine is an excellent surgeon."

"Please don't worry, doctor, I'll be fine. I'll get through this journey beautifully, trust me." I sensed the upcoming battle would involve not only the disease but also something much deeper and that I would overcome it by the grace of the Divine.

I hung up the phone and called Nathaniel. He didn't say much, but when he got home he held me close for a long time. In his eyes, I could see he was afraid of losing me. After dinner, he researched cancer treatments online until three o'clock in the morning, while I meditated upstairs.

~

MY SPECIALIST, DR. COLUMBINE, HAD been medically following my case closely for many years, periodically checking my breast for potential harmful lumps. The day we went to see her at her office, Nathaniel sat opposite her asking questions while I stared out the window at the blue sky, stupefied.

"Vivi will walk around for at least one year without her breast before we can do reconstructive surgery on her," Dr. Columbine said.

My Creator had given me this precious body temple, and I was resolved no part of it would be amputated until I left it. I couldn't imagine going through such a traumatic procedure. I did not want to fall into the trap some cancer patients feel when they are diagnosed and make decisions out of fear.

All at once I started to cry. "How can this happen to me?" I demanded. "What did I do to cause this cancer?" I could not comprehend why someone who practiced hatha yoga, performed breathing exercises (pranayamas), ate a vegan diet, did not consume drugs or alcohol, and walked the spiritual path could be diagnosed with advanced cancer. I told my surgeon I did not want to interrupt my work—that I wanted to be of service to humanity and to animals, not fight cancer. But reality settled in. I could not ignore this anymore. I had to do something to stop the cancer from growing.

A few days later we landed in the office of Dr. Davidson—the chemo-oncologist. Nathaniel again took the lead as my health advocate, while I acted as if this nightmare belonged to someone else, wondering what was going to happen to our lives.

Like Dr. Columbine, Dr. Davidson recommended a mastectomy, but he proposed neo-adjuvant therapy—intense chemotherapy for six consecutive months to reduce the tumor size prior to surgery—as well.

"If the tumor is reduced enough after the chemo, Dr. Columbine might be able to perform only a lumpectomy," he said.

While we were running from specialist to specialist, I felt torn apart. The diagnostic process turned our lives upside down, consuming all our energy and time. Overnight I dropped all my projects to focus on this healing crisis. I was frightened that I might fall into a major depression again, but I knew these were negative thoughts, and I had the inner power to transform my perception. For most of my life, I had been longing to go home and merge my spirit with our Creator; I wondered if this was my opportunity to cross over and be liberated. Where would I find the strength, will, and courage to fight a battle I did not want to fight?

Arjuna, the prince warrior in the Bhagavad Gita, does not want to fight an inevitable battle, and so he chooses Lord Krishna, a Divine incarnation, a *mahavatar*, to be by his side on the battlefield over the grand army he could have received. The word "avatar" comes from the Sanskrit *avatara*, which means "descent," a fully God-realized incarnation of the Divine, and *maha* means "great." I decided, like Arjuna, I would choose God to fight my own inner battle.

⌒

ON OUR SECOND VISIT WITH Dr. Davidson, Nathaniel continued discussing details while reviewing statistics of cancer survivors. I stepped out of his office to go to the restroom. On my way, I stopped by the chemo room where the nurses injected these drugs. I peeked in and saw a middle-aged man sitting with his eyes closed while a red liquid traversed his veins from a large tube. Part of his face had been removed. I sent him blessings of healing while realizing after all that I was blessed.

Before we stepped out of the doctor's office that day, I said, "Dr. Davidson, no matter what we decide, not only will I survive cancer, I'll thrive with my breast unharmed. We'll see a miracle by the grace of the Divine Mother!"

We returned home, and the pressure mounted from all sides, even from well-intended acquaintances and friends. Nathaniel insisted we take the conventional road of Western medicine. I saw these cancer treatments as barbaric and archaic, but I could also see another wall of resistance rising in my husband. I did not want to debate with him and waste my energy. He was afraid of losing me. How could I fight cancer with alternative medicine and the Divine if my beloved was too worried and scared? His resistance depleted my being. I knew if I did not take the conventional path, it would be harder to heal because of his insecurity and fear. Over the following days, we discussed our next steps. At last, I yielded and agreed to pursue Western treatments, not fully realizing the reality of my decision. Though, I held firm in my desire to pursue a holistic approach for wellness as well.

⌒

THE FOLLOWING SUNDAY NIGHT, NATHANIEL flew to Boston on a business trip, leaving me alone to face my own mortality. As I washed my face in the bathroom sink, I looked in the mirror and it hit me that my hair, eyelashes, and eyebrows would soon fall out. I screamed and fell to my knees, sobbing. "Why have you forsaken me, God?"

My whole body trembled as I met my terror face-to-face. In this mystical communion, burning sensations engulfed my abdomen as if flames flared up inside. The sensation was very physical as well as metaphysical. The fear of death blazed, leaving me in a silent void of eternal Divine love.

I was no longer afraid of dying. My attachment to my body temple seemed to have disappeared. In that instant of emptiness, a portal opened up to another dimension, as if my personality had been burned to ashes. It was a complete surrender.

Tingles of blissful bubbles tickled all over my being. A great sense of lightness and serenity engulfed every cell of my body as if I was floating above the floor. In this profound surrender, I felt the splendor of my true ultimate Divine nature. No words could ever describe such a mystical and boundless experience. It lasted only a few moments, yet an eternity elapsed. Something of what is called "Vivi" evaporated in the ether.

When I went to bed that night, I wrapped myself with the blanket feeling a wave of Divine love and grace. Within a few minutes, I drifted off to sleep in a deep state of serenity and blissfulness, feeling a supreme, loving presence.

~

DURING THAT EASTER HOLY WEEK, Nathaniel drove me to the cancer center to receive my first chemotherapy IV infusion. The nurse prepared my arm with a warm compress, tapped on my vein, and poked it with a thick needle. As the drug oozed into my vein, a very painful burning sensation traveled through my arm, shoulder, and heart.

"Oh miss, it is hell in my veins! Ouch, it hurts so much. Is this normal? I can feel the drip going toward my heart, burning. Can you slow it down right away, please?" I asked my nurse, feeling alarmed.

In silence, she flew to my side to adjust the big red tube entering my veins, heart, and lungs. I asked her what this chemo was exactly and to tell me more about my treatment.

"This medication, Vivi," she paused, hesitating, "is considered the most intense and powerful of chemo drugs. If it is injected improperly, it can kill."

Suddenly, I remembered the releases and the dangerous warnings I had read and signed during my visits with Dr. Davidson, giving them the right to inject me with these drugs. I sat there for many hours feeling very buzzed, weak, and dizzy.

When we returned home, I began to feel weaker by the second. My body was overcome with sweats and chills. As I passed by a mirror in our kitchen, I glanced at myself and gasped—I saw a dead body. My face was a whitish, gray-blue color. By the time I reached the living room, I was about to faint. I collapsed on the sofa and was trying to call out to Nathaniel when extremely violent spasms of excruciating pain attacked my abdomen and stomach. It felt as if dozens of large sharp knives were cutting my intestines into morsels. Aggressive pulling sensations attacked my reproductive organs as if someone was extracting them from my body with their hands.

I had my period on that day, and the trauma of the chemo stopped the flow. It never returned. My reproductive system entered an abrupt, shocking menopause. My head hurt as if it had been split wide open and my brain pulled out. My heartbeat was faint, almost nonexistent. I curled into a fetal position, feeling like I might vomit all my organs out. My blood pressure kept dropping, dropping, and dropping.

Nathaniel rushed to my side, applied a cold compress to my forehead while calling the oncologist on staff. Nathaniel tried to explain what was going on the best he could.

The doctor responded, "Vivianne is having an adverse reaction. Call an ambulance and bring her to the emergency room within the next ten minutes if she is not improving."

That doctor must not have realized the magnitude of the emergency, but I knew. I was experiencing an acute anaphylactic shock reaction, and it was in the process of killing me.

While Nathaniel was on the phone, out of love and compassion for Jesus Christ, I invoked him. I know that sounds religious, yet my call was purely energetic and spiritual. My systems were shutting down extremely fast. My life force was draining away. I could not even cry or moan. I whispered, "Jesus Christ, my pain is insignificant compared to your suffering on the cross, but please take this unbearable pain, spare me."

The moment the words left my lips I felt an energetic light and loving presence by my side, and in a flash the severe pain and death agony disappeared. My blood pressure slowly came back, though I could not get up for over eight hours, feeling too weak to even raise my arm.

Our cat Krishna, who spent most of his time outdoors, seemed to know what had happened. He came in and lay next to me, purring and comforting me. He stayed on the sofa, next to my chest, until Nathaniel helped me get up and carried me upstairs to bed.

I am not sure what to call this mystical experience. A miracle? Miracles are daily occurrences, yet most people are not aware of them. Every day we inhale and exhale life-force energy, the bridge between earth and infinity. Isn't that a miracle? One day, just like that, we take our last breath.

After sleeping for over fifteen hours, I woke up very dizzy, weak, ill, and shaken. I was no longer sure what course of action to take. I should have been hospitalized. I needed intensive care. Only by His grace had I survived this life-threatening attack. Only later would I discover the extent of the damage that had been inflicted to many of my organs and systems.

~

A FEW WEEKS LATER, GURUDEV happened to be in the US for a brief visit. I was still too ill to travel, but at the last minute I felt guided to go. Nathaniel booked and bought my ticket. I flew by myself to Utah the following morning, planning to stay for a few days.

That afternoon, Gurudev gave a public talk at the hotel. Right afterward, a dozen of us visited him in his suite. While waiting outside in the hallway, the male teacher of our teacher-training program happened to walk by, and I greeted him. It had been almost one year since I had last seen him—in India, at our graduation—and I shared a little about my diagnosis and my life-threatening experience. He seemed shocked, filled with regret and compassion. I asked him if I could see Gurudev for a few moments alone. He walked into the suite and just a few minutes later opened the door and let me enter.

Just as I entered Gurudev walked in from the adjacent room, set his eyes upon my being, and said, "I heard you're in trouble. How are you feeling now?"

"Now that I see you, Gurudev, I feel much better," I replied genuinely.

He paused. "Where is everybody?"

He opened the door and let the rest of the small group inside without another word. He walked toward the large chair on the far wall, and halfway there he turned his head and looked straight into my eyes. "Don't worry," he said with a knowing smile.

Just seeing his radiant face and feeling his energetic, loving presence, I knew I would be healed. It was a strong inner-knowing. His Christ consciousness was so alive! I remembered the first time I sat by his feet in his kutir at the Canadian ashram, thinking it must feel like this to be in the physical presence of Jesus. That is how I felt, and still feel, about Gurudev's presence. Over the decades, I had also heard that in certain cases great ascended masters can take on some of your karma if appropriate. I don't know if Gurudev did that. I just simply trusted him so much. His personal words soothed my soul and appeased my mind.

We all sat on the floor near his feet. A few of the devotees asked him questions. He offered a prasad of sweets to everyone except me. When we walked out, one of the aspirants gave me a little piece of her sweet to signify his gesture, seemingly wondering, as I was, why Gurudev had not offered me any. I put the bite in my mouth—but removed it at once. Masters do certain things for good reason, and it is crucial to revere their unfathomable ways.

In bed that night, from nowhere, Christ's words came to me: "Your faith has saved you, go in peace." As I turned these words over in my mind, I realized that we have the innate divine power to heal anything within us, just like Jesus Christ did in his lifetime. That universal consciousness is within us all.

I never read the Bible, nor do I call myself a Christian. I have never called myself anything, in fact, since I feel beliefs and all identities create separation. It is a rather naive view to believe that our blind beliefs equal the truth. Jesus spoke in parables during his time; if he were physically among us today, he would use language more appropriate to our era. Gurudev also had his own mystical way to speak and reach us, often not telling us things directly.

The following afternoon I flew back home feeling very serene and grateful. Gurudev and I had exchanged only a few words, yet I was filled with a sense of great empowerment. I was not alone on the battlefield. In some ways, my Krishna, my master, was with my being.

I have always experienced infinite veneration and deep love for Shiva, Jesus Christ, Krishna, Mohammed, Gautama the Buddha, Shiv-Goraksha Babaji, and all the lineages of mahavatars, ascended enlightened masters, rishis (sages), other buddhas and bodhisattvas (awakened ones), such as the legendary Kuan Yin and others. Upon my return from Utah, I felt guided to call and work with them on a subtle level. Perhaps it was Jesus Christ who opened up the grand portal for my being, I am not sure; but suddenly I was able to tap into a new dimension beyond the physical realm. I trusted the guidance I received. Mystical phenomena exist that logic can never explain. Our intellect and our five senses are too limited to physical boundaries to experience the beyond.

Within that week, inner guidance emerged on how I should continue with my journey. I started acupuncture and Chinese herbs at a holistic center that specializes in treatment for cancer patients. Somehow I knew intuitively that I also needed to proceed with the Western medical treatments Nathaniel was advocating for.

Thirty-One

EMPTINESS AND LOVE

THE FOLLOWING WEEK AT THE cancer center, my oncologist told us they had been praying for me. I was touched. Dr. Davidson was very reluctant to try chemo drugs again, but I assured him I knew how to protect myself this time. We decided to reduce the pre-medications, but the chemo infusion quantity remained the same.

When I sat for my second chemo treatment, I invoked the Divine Mother, Jesus Christ, the mahavatars, and the ascended enlightened masters for their healing and protection. I placed my hands over the drugs and chanted a potent mantra in Sanskrit. My body vibrated with the energy of those celestial beings, and I could feel that our Creator was blessing the medication. Through the mystical power created by the high sound-frequency of the mantra and Divine energy, the chemo liquid turned into blessed liquid.

"Now we have holy water! That is the alchemy of the Divine!" I told the nurse. "You may inject it."

This ancient mantra, and others like it, have been chanted for thousands of years by the yogis, yoginis, great masters, and rishis in the most remote corners of our planet and have been transmitted to sincere seekers.

The ancient mantra I had chanted was imparted to me by my first beloved guru, Yogiraj Gurunath Siddhanath. I have been told this is Shiv-Goraksha Babaji's mantra. Babaji is the great avatar identified by Paramahansa Yogananda for having revived the science of kriya yoga in past centuries. It is a mantra of protection, and it remained in my heart for decades, allowing my being to invoke Shiv-Goraksha Babaji, who has been regarded as the manifestation of Shiva himself by many great enlightened masters. It was only later that I realized I was invoking Shiva himself when I chanted that mantra over my chemo drugs.

The power of sound to affect water's molecules is a mystical phenomenon, one of the greatest secrets of our Creator. The work of Dr. Masaru Emoto has shown that water has memory and the capability to transform its chemistry when exposed to specific sounds and words. Dr. Emoto discovered that when specific thoughts, sounds, and words were targeted directly at water, different vibration frequencies caused different crystals and geometry patterns to form. In his *New York Times* bestseller, *The Hidden Messages in Water,* Dr. Emoto shares his intensive research. There is even photographic evidence of these crystals in the book. He writes:

> *Existence is vibration. The entire universe is in a state of vibration and each thing generates its own frequency, which is unique. The fact that everything is in a state of vibration also means that everything is creating a sound. Now the science of quantum mechanics generally acknowledges that substance is nothing more than a vibration. Water is so sensitive to the unique frequency being emitted by the world, it essentially and efficiently mirrors the outside world.*[1]

Water has the power to absorb the energy of certain vibrational frequencies to which it is directly exposed; so I figured other liquids must also hold this capacity, even chemotherapy drugs.

The synergy between water and other liquids, sounds, words, thoughts, feelings, and individual energy creates unique phenomena. Ancient and authentic mantras have the power to transform the molecular structure of liquid. Our thoughts, words, and even our feelings have the power to affect the molecules of water and liquids, even more so with potent mantras. Since our body is made of approximately 75 percent water, our brain over 80 percent—can you imagine the power of transformation that ancient Sanskrit mantras have over our entire being? They are like magical spells!

~

AFTER SEVERAL HOURS OF MY second chemo drip, I returned home. I lay in bed feeling nauseated, weak, and drained, but no life-threatening shock reaction occurred. All our rescued kitty cats joined their mommy with their loving, healing, purring presence.

I was practicing healing visualizations daily during my meditation to help my being recover from the chemo and fight the cancer. One visualizing meditation I often practiced was imagining the cancer cells being shattered by the light of the Divine Mother. Another was a meditation that invoked some of the ascended enlightened masters, buddhas, and mahavatars, and also Gurudev and the Dalai Lama. On this day, I chose the second. I lay on the floor of our sanctum in corpse pose, visualizing this:

> *I hold Gurudev's hand while we walk together in silence on a deserted white sand beach with enormous palm trees over us. Our bare feet soak in the turquoise water as we stroll along to meet the celestial beings at the far edge of the reef. Both of us wear white robes that flutter in the warm breeze. From far away we see a dome of bright blue light where they await us. When we reach them, Gurudev disappears.*
>
> *The beings surround and enter my being. The life-force energy light descends through my spine, spreading through all particles of my subtle and physical body. I can feel it flowing in every cell. One of them reaches out for my hand, brings me in the ethereal ocean of Divine love, and pours water over my head. No words are spoken. Overwhelming feelings of Divine love, gratitude, tranquility, blissfulness, and serenity emerge.*

These visualizing meditations seemed to take on a life of their own. Sometimes I wondered if I was going through some kind of initiation, ascension, or spiritual process with them. In my meditations, I always experienced the energy light field, and afterward I always felt rested, protected, and guided for the next step.

~

IT IS COMMON IN SOME religious and spiritual paths such as Buddhism, Hinduism, and the yogic tradition that individuals shave their head as a symbol of renunciation of the individual self in a ritual called mundun. The aspirant offers his or her hair to our Creator or to any manifestation of the one Source. It has also been said that 108 years of karma is lifted when a genuine mundun offering is performed with love and devotion.

When I began chemotherapy, just the thought of being bald terrified me. Most people don't realize how a woman's hair is universally imbued with notions of beauty, femininity, and sensuality. Losing their hair can allow some women to let go of some of the personality accumulations and gender role identifications they have been burdened with. The illusion of the ego can vanish if the individual is in total surrender. It is often these identifications with the body or the mind that prevent us from going beyond the physical, to experience other dimensions of reality. If the seeker is receptive and open like I was, facing my own mortality in front of the mirror, many false identifications of the physical body can be demolished in the process of losing one's hair.

My experience taught me that chemotherapy combined with the potential of dying can act as a major catalyst in helping a woman relinquish a sense of false self. I learned how intense doses of chemotherapy over a period of many months can dehumanize you, strip you to the core, weaken you, and deplete you physically, emotionally, and mentally. You are left only with whatever spiritual strengths, weaknesses, and limitations you have. The drugs do not differentiate between the good and the bad cells; instead, they kill both.

On the afternoon of my mundun, I drifted in a profound meditation for a few hours in our sanctum. I heard Nathaniel's voice calling me to depart for the salon. On the way, I told him I would begin a period of silence right after my mundun. He was originally against it but soon realized he needed to drop his resistance for the sake of my healing and our relationship.

When we reached the salon, my stylist held me in her arms then led us into a private room in the back. She silently prepared her razor. Nathaniel took out his camera and began to record. I took a few deep breaths as she brought the razor to the back of my neck and turned it on. Tears welled up in my eyes. One by one, clumps of my golden hair fell to the floor. After she had shaved my entire head, my spirit soared like a white dove flying high. I smiled feeling free. Nathaniel snapped a few more photos. We gathered my hair and put it in a plastic bag. It was still chilly in April. I was not used to having a bald head. I wrapped it in a silky white shawl. This act marked the beginning of my first ten days of silence.

Nathaniel and I had made an agreement that if something needed to be communicated, I would write a brief note on a piece of paper. If there was an emergency or urgency, I would call him on his cell phone, wait for a few seconds, and hang up.

When we reached home, I climbed up to our sanctum, prostrated myself, and offered my hair to the Divine. I placed it in the lotus petal of our Buddha statue. I bowed down to our Creator, Jesus Christ, the maha-vatars and ascended masters, all buddhas and bodhisattvas, to my previous masters from past lives, Gurudev, the Dalai Lama, and to all my ancestors. In my heart, I forgave everyone for the harm they may have caused me in this life and in past lifetimes, and I asked forgiveness for all the harm I may have caused to others.

For the following ten days, I remained silent and meditated four or five hours every day. Our white Turkish angora cat, Shiva, curled up on my lap while I meditated. When I spent time in bed, all nine rescued cats gathered around. Nathaniel kept snapping photographs, recording these cherished moments.

In the evening of day eight of my silence, I lay in bed with our kitties, feeling exhausted. I called Nathaniel's phone in his office. I had never called him before. He rushed to our bedroom, alarmed, and asked me what the emergency was and when I would come out of silence. He complained he could not take my silence anymore. I burst out laughing. I was the one in silence, not him! I wrote: *Please, would you bring me a cup of mango sorbet, baby?*

He looked at me with a serious expression. "This is your emergency!" he exclaimed. "I'll bring you the sorbet only if you come out of silence right now."

I kept laughing at how he was trying to bribe me. At last, he let his guard down and laughed too. I got my mango sorbet in bed and still completed my ten days of silence.

~

DURING THE LAST FEW DAYS of my silence, Nathaniel told me he had read that His Holiness the Dalai Lama would be in San Francisco to expound on the Buddha's highest teaching on the sacred text Dependent Arising (also called Dependent, or Interdependent Origination). Nathaniel suggested I write an article on the life of the Dalai Lama and his teachings.

I loved the idea and emailed my editor in London, who approved my proposal. Twenty-four hours after contacting the organizer of the Dalai Lama's event and submitting a comprehensive application and proposal, I received the marvelous news that they had chosen me as one of only five press members to be allowed to attend.

I was beyond honored and humbled, also filled with jubilation—but I wondered how I was going to attend feeling so weak. I had never met His Holiness before, although I had written to him many times and had always received answers to my letters. I wished I could hold his hand and express my love and gratitude to him.

This rare seminar was scheduled for the day after I came out of silence. How auspicious! But on the morning of the program I got out of bed feeling nauseated and weak. It had only been a few days since I received my second dose of chemo. I was no longer sure I would be able to attend the seminar.

Then Nathaniel's ex-wife from his first marriage offered to drive me to the auditorium, as she was also going to attend the program. I was touched by her compassion and filled with the sense that every detail of the day had been synchronized by an invisible hand. I knew I had to go.

The organizer had reserved an area for press members on the second floor, but I wanted to get a closer glimpse of His Holiness. Since his schedule was too tight, and I was a last-minute invitee, I could not obtain an audience with him. I was a little disappointed and would have loved so much to meet him. Still, somehow, I knew in my heart that I would one day meet him under brighter circumstances.

Before climbing to the reserved area, I walked straight to the front of the stage area where only the Dalai Lama's entourage was allowed to stay while he entered the stage. Somehow the police and his many bodyguards let me stay there.

A rich, luminous tapestry of deep red, burgundy, orange, yellow, violet, blue, and green from the sacred flags of the Buddha, Avalokiteśvara (also known as the feminine form as Kuan Yin in other traditions), White Tara, and Green Tara, hung in the background of the stage, creating a tranquil atmosphere. A majestic throne stood at the center. Everything was as sublime as a sunny autumn day in the countryside. I was as hypnotized by the setting as if it were an intricate mandala. I stood at the bottom of the ramp of this grandiose stage with closed eyes, invoking the Buddha and Awakened Ones.

A stunning procession of several hundred monks in orange and maroon robes, and wired bodyguards, entered the stage, led by the Dalai Lama. They exuded a serene energy. In the audience, seven thousand people, Buddhists and non-Buddhists alike, stood out of respect for His Holiness, ready to receive the highest teaching of Gautama the Buddha on the Dependent Origination.

Everyone was silent, awed by the sheer beauty of the moment. I was elated.

Before I was diagnosed with cancer, I had created an original piece of artwork, with mixed media and broken glass, and had inserted into this jewel-like piece a museum-quality reproduction of one of my original paintings of Gautama the Buddha entitled *East Meets West*. I was holding this artwork within a white *kata* as a symbol of love and reverence, extending my arms high toward His Holiness. The Dalai Lama's playful and blissful demeanor with his laughing, tiny, curled-up lips; smiling eyes beneath his glasses; and bald head reminded me perhaps of how the original Buddha might have emanated the same kind of intoxicating sweet energy. When he came near and was about to make the final turn toward his seat, I spoke in the silent auditorium, vibrating the echoes of my love. "Your Holiness, here is a gift on behalf of H. H. Sri Sri Ravi Shankar."

Even though I had created it, I felt guided to offer this piece as if it was coming from my own guru. Both men are dear friends who love and honor each other and their traditions. The Dalai Lama stopped and turned to face my being. He moved his arm in a wide gesture, signaling his acceptance of my gift. Then he bowed and graced my being with his loving gaze before walking on, sitting down, and beginning to chant.

With His Holiness, we studied the sacred text *In Praise of Dependent Origination,* which Je Tsongkhapa composed during his lifetime between AD 1357–1419. This book explains the middle way, called Madhyamaka, a school of Buddhist philosophy and part of the Mahayana which His Holiness has adopted. The Madhyamaka is a system of philosophy and analysis founded and expounded by the great Indian sage Nagarjuna, based on the Prajnaparamita (transcendent perfection of wisdom) sutras of the original Buddha, and is considered the supreme wisdom on emptiness (sunyata).

The middle way embraces the fundamental philosophy of the inter-dependent origination that holds that all phenomena are interconnected and arise from causes and conditions and are, therefore, impermanent. All phenomena participate in a relationship of mutual dependence of cause and effect. Thus, all things are empty of inherent existence because of the interdependence.

The word Buddha means "awakened one." Over the ages, thousands of buddhas have populated our planet, and many are here among us. Most people do not perceive them. Siddhartha Gautama, the original Buddha, did not say that phenomena do not exist. He simply stated that things do not inherently exist independently. There is a huge distinction between these two statements. The aggregates make the whole. Without the parts, the whole cannot exist, like a chair without its legs. Just as a coconut sprouts into a tall palm tree, it also depends upon other favorable conditions such as fresh oxygen, water, fertile soil, and sunlight to grow into a magnificent palm tree. Each cause with its own conditions creates its unique effect.

His Holiness said this aspect of Dependent Origination only becomes completely clear after one realizes sunyata. Realizing emptiness brings a profound sense of peace and serenity. Rain falls, trees blossom, fruits grow, humans and animals are born, and nebulae form in the cosmos. These phenomena are all interrelated with causes and conditions that are brought about by them, and they disappear as the causes and conditions change and pass away. Gautama the Buddha compared all phenomena to illusions or mirages (maya), but did not say they were. Our perception distorts the truth because most people see the world from their brainwashed mind that is filled with delusions, and most do not live in the present moment.

As the program unfolded, my fried brain could not follow. I returned home that night feeling entirely exhausted and depleted of life force. I collapsed in bed without eating, wondering how I would write such a major article when I could not even balance my checkbook. My mind was lost in a thick fog.

~

TOWARD THE END OF OUR second day, the Dalai Lama said something that spoke directly to my concern—that we shouldn't worry if we did not understand one word of the teaching, because with deep meditation, it would come. Upon hearing these words, I gasped in relief. He also recommended meditating on emptiness and emphasized it could take many years or more to fully assimilate, understand, and realize Dependent Origination and sunyata because the emptiness of inherent existence and Dependent Origination are closely related. His Holiness encouraged us to test the knowledge, not take the words for granted, just as we do in the yogic tradition. One must experience the ultimate truth. As Je Tsongkhapa said, "Mindfulness and introspection are the foundation of the entire dharma."

Self-inquiry, *vichara*, is rooted within the knowledge of many masters, such as Bhagavan Sri Ramana Maharshi. In vichara, one goes deeper into introspection, asking the truth about everything. The most important point is to see existential phenomena as they are, not filtered through our own preconditioned minds. I was touched by the ideal of the bodhisattva. Mahayana teaches the altruistic, benevolent, and compassionate way of the bodhisattva. I realized it may be just an ideal for most people, but oneness, love, compassion, and nonviolence toward all sentient beings sang to my heart. Bodhisattvas are enlightened beings. Like the blossom of lotus petals in the mud, *bodhicitta* is the awakening and opening of the heart and mind to the altruistic and compassionate wish to awaken one's Buddha-hood for the sake and benefit of liberating all living creatures.

Bodhisattvas take vows to return for eons even if they can transcend this physical realm. They postpone their own nirvana to help liberate all living beings from suffering and misery. As a result of the awakening of the bodhicitta, we get rid of karma. That is why Shantideva, another great Buddhist saint, said that in the instant we awake the bodhicitta, we will be called a bodhisattva and a child of the buddhas. It is not enough just to have compassion. By cultivating great love and compassion, a natural altruistic state of mind develops, a sense of responsibility for helping others and all creatures.

The Dalai Lama says, "I believe that to meet the challenges of our times, humans will have to develop a greater sense of universal responsibility. Each one of us must learn to work not just for one's self, one's own family, or one's nation, but for the benefit of all humankind. Universal responsibility is the key to human survival; it is the foundation for world peace."[2]

I hoped such a beautiful thing could be possible for many thousands of humans on our planet. His Holiness told us it is very important to have an affectionate attitude toward all living beings, to realize all living creatures have been our mother (or father, or a beloved surrogate parent) at one point on the continuum of existence. He also recommended meditating on love and on the mother's genuine kindness. When we develop a deep sense of indebtedness to our mother, then we can start extending this warm feeling of gratitude toward all living beings, even to our enemies by remembering that at one point they were also our mothers or fathers. In this way, we may expand our consciousness to the oneness of all creatures. There are also other ways to expand consciousness, such as the practice of intense daily sadhana and different yogic paths.

Throughout the ages, it has been said by many awakened ones that meditating on love, even for an instant, far exceeds the merits accumulated through making endless offerings to all the buddhas. Meditation on love is one of the ultimate protections. This practice clears the aura by emanating luminous vibrations. Our loving vibrations emanate harmonious frequencies around us and through the universe. Just as the sun emanates its rays upon all living creatures, just as the rain falls over the planet nourishing the trees, plants, and flowers, the bodhisattvas shine their light, love, and compassion upon all living creatures with equanimity and magnanimity.

Then His Holiness quoted Je Tsongkhapa, who said, "If you have an authentic aspiration to enlightenment, then any act of goodness, even something minor like giving grain to a crow, becomes a bodhisattva deed."

The Dalai Lama added that one might make treasured offerings to all living creatures, but if the individual lacked an authentic aspiration to enlightenment, it wouldn't be the deed of a bodhisattva.

These words brought tears to my eyes. I was awed not only by the sheer beauty of these words but also by their relevance. I realized I may also have taken these bodhisattva's vows in past lives.

Much of my artwork testifies to my fascination with the ideal of the bodhisattvas. I wondered if some of my art was an unconscious attempt to remember. I had known only that I had to paint them. Doing so had been a sacred act of revering, honoring, and recalling the bodhisattvas. My work is filled with images of all sorts of bodhisattvas and goddesses, even some with wings.

At the completion of our seminar, together we recited these words along with the Dalai Lama: "For as long as space endures, and as long as living beings remain, until then I too abide to dispel the misery of the world," a promise and prayer composed by Shantideva to generate bodhicitta.

Even though I did not follow the Buddhist path, I took the vows of the bodhisattva, this time in a different human garment, and in the presence of His Holiness the 14th Dalai Lama. I was not sure if I could keep such an eternal promise, but my heart longed to help other suffering creatures. If many hundreds of thousands of us around the earth were able to perform a deed of bodhisattva every day, can you imagine the kind of energy we would generate on our beloved planet?

We stood. His Holiness blessed us, bowing. The flock of monks onstage began chanting, "Long life to His Holiness." My heart's song was filled with praise, love, and veneration to Gautama the Buddha, Avalokiteśvara, the bodhisattvas, the ascended masters, all the buddhas, the Dalai Lama, and my Gurudev. I infinitely bowed to them as I fell into a profound meditation.

When I opened my eyes, over thirty minutes had elapsed. I walked out of the nearly deserted auditorium. The sky was a light, clear blue. I could hear the birds singing to the rhythm of my heart. The warm rays of spring penetrated my soul with Divine love. In a humble gesture, I pulled off the white turban wrapped around my bald head. A grand sense of freedom overwhelmed my being. There was no longer any need for a scarf. "Long life to His Holiness, long healthy, happy, and joyous infinite voyage to you," my heart sang.

~

OVER THE WEEKS, I CONTEMPLATED the words of His Holiness the Dalai Lama and the teachings of the Dependent Origination and continued to meditate on emptiness and love.

Our mind is limited by our five senses and our biases. It does not mean if one cannot prove the existence of God, the Source or Creator, that it does not exist. It depends on the meaning of our interpretation of the words "God," "Goddess," "Divine," or "consciousness." Meanings of words are rooted within the culture where language has evolved. Just like space in a box is limited by its size, words are loaded with beliefs, assumptions, and traditional ideas, and they often lose meaning in translation. We need to consider that other religious and spiritual traditions are perhaps talking about the same thing but perceiving it with different angles and using different words. What is the original cause of all phenomena? Until we desperately long to know and seek the truth, it will never be revealed to believers, only to sincere seekers. Once the Buddha said, "Your work is to discover your world, and then with all your heart, give yourself to it." The Buddha meant the world within us . . . that world is boundless and infinite.

I realized that the Source of this existential phenomenon called "life" can't be boxed in by the logical mind. Because I have experienced the flow of the Divine within my being too many times, I feel the Source must be experienced and realized from within in profound meditation.

Self-realization is realizing there is no self. The whole of existence is One being breathing. Our teacher is everywhere—in a bee, a cat, a grazing deer, a cow, a blossoming jasmine flower, the waves of the ocean, the raindrop, the ephemeral morning dew, the fruit trees, the sun radiating upon Mother Earth. The eternal book of nature has so much to teach us.

Thirty-Two

OVERFLOWING WITH GRATITUDE

AFTER BEING ON INTENSE CHEMO for over five months, my tumor was reduced to less than a quarter of its original size. We were thrilled. Dr. Columbine now felt more comfortable about performing a lumpectomy instead of removing my entire breast.

A few weeks prior to the surgery, another MRI was required by the diagnostic cancer center. The result confirmed another suspicious area in the opposite side of the tumor, toward my heart. This news meant I would most likely lose my breast. The team of specialists decided to perform an invasive, guided MRI biopsy, a more advanced technology. I would have opposed it if I had known the dreadful consequences.

When Nathaniel and I arrived at the hospital, I was wheeled to a special MRI room and laid out prone on a table with my breast hanging down. Although they had anesthetized the local area, when the specialist pierced my breast from side to side with a long, thick needle the size of a meat skewer, I screamed at the top of my lungs and nearly fainted. This was torture! They anesthetized the area again.

The acute pain reminded me of what animals may endure on farms, in fur factories, laboratories, and other sectors where they are viewed not as living beings but as products for profit. When we develop compassion, expand our consciousness, and become aware of these injustices to animals, knowing pain and suffering, why would we want to eat them? Wear them? Experiment on them?

I left the hospital in the wheelchair, dizzy and in pain. When we got home, and I looked at my breast, I became very concerned. I applied more ice packs and a holistic gel that helps with inflammation. My breast had swollen to three times its size. The bruising spread over on my rib cage and part of my abdomen.

The next morning I woke with dark blue bruises over ten inches long on each of my sides. Nathaniel was shocked. Later, the specialist called us to announce the specimen was benign. I knew it had been all along and wondered why I had not listened to my intuition again.

Several days later, Dr. Columbine called me unexpectedly. She had seen me for an office visit not long after that procedure. "I'm terribly sorry, Vivi, to tell you . . . " She paused for a moment, hesitating. "I will be relocating my family within a few months to a different state. I have accepted a new position there at the hospital. I won't be able to do your surgery. The damage to your breast is too severe. I can't operate any longer as we had planned. So sorry, Vivi."

"Oh, Dr. Columbine, I can't believe it. I have so much trust in you. Who will be my surgeon now?" I said with a soft fainting voice. I started to cry, feeling as vulnerable as a newborn.

"I would have done it before leaving, Vivi, but this situation makes it impossible now. It could take up to three months before you are fully recovered. I feel for you and understand how you must be feeling. We will make some good recommendations and find you a great surgeon. Don't worry."

For a moment a part of my being felt devastated by the shocking news. I was losing my beloved doctor who had been with me for many years, the one I trusted and loved. She was right, and I knew healing would take many months. That was an enormous setback to accept. Despite my loss, I realized after hanging up the phone that many events occur in our lives for some good reasons, often for higher reasons we can't logically understand. Many times they are blessings in disguise. Only with emotional and mental distance can we see things with clarity, seeing the truth in a specific situation.

~

THE NEXT MORNING I WAS in much pain, standing in the kitchen in the process of feeding our kitty cats. Suddenly, I lost it. I sobbed like an infant.

Nathaniel stared at me. "What is wrong with you?"

His words broke my heart. My beloved could not see me, nor could he understand my pain and sufferings.

"What do you mean? I'm in intense pain. I lost my surgeon. I almost died; my system is so weak, so exhausted. I'm fighting cancer, and I might lose my breast. Where have you been the past five months?"

I kept sobbing. My whole body shook from the pain and sorrow. I felt demolished. I drew in a few deep breaths, trying to find my equanimity again. I extended my arms, to reach out to my husband. "Why don't you take me in your arms? Hold me. I'm suffering. Be here. I need you right now."

After a few minutes, Nathaniel realized the effect of his clueless reaction. He stopped everything and held me in his arms gently while I kept grieving aloud. He whispered, "I love you, Baby Buddha."

Nathaniel was not used to seeing me so vulnerable and frail, and it must have hurt him. His presence in this moment meant the universe to my being. It empowered my being to blossom even more.

The beautiful Vietnamese Zen master, poet, and peace activist Thich Nhat Hanh says in *The Art of Communicating*, "To love you have to be there. The tree outside your window is there, supporting you. You can be there for yourself and your loved ones, just like the tree. Mindfulness practice is the foundation of your love. You cannot love properly and deeply without mindfulness."[1]

~

NOT LONG AFTER THIS EPISODE, the coordinator at the cancer center helped us find an accomplished surgeon, Dr. Eliseo, who turned out to be a lot more experienced with cancer patients.

When we met him, I knew intuitively that he would do an amazing job. On the day of the lumpectomy at the main hospital, Nathaniel snapped many photos of his Baby Buddha parading down the hallway to the surgery room in her sexy hospital gown and kitty cat paw socks. Like some kind of seraphic being with no hair, no eyelashes, no eyebrows, I was not recognizable to anyone. I laughed.

When I was on the operating table, I invoked the help of our Creator and my celestial friends; together we blessed the hands of Dr. Eliseo and our anesthesiologist. I told the team to be aware of their words while I was under since I knew I would hear everything and still be aware. I said to Dr. Eliseo, "If something goes wrong during the surgery, even bleeding, talk to me directly. I'll still hear." Then I became unconscious.

In the recovery room, the nurse tried several times to wake me up. Nathaniel stood next to the bed smiling, holding my hand. "Baby Buddha, when they rolled you out of the surgery room, you were chanting in Sanskrit, laughing out loud while you were still asleep."

I smiled, half-conscious. "Really?" My head fell to the pillow, and I went back to sleep.

~

A FEW DAYS LATER AT my surgeon's office, Dr. Eliseo told us to his surprise he had removed what turned out to be a much deeper, larger, and longer tumor than what had been anticipated. Among the four lymph nodes he'd had to remove underneath my armpit, one tested positive. "The cancer has already metastasized. It can be anywhere in your body and grow," he said somberly.

Nathaniel and I just looked at each other. I sighed. "Are you confident, Dr. Eliseo, about removing the rest of the tumor?"

He said, "Yes."

More than a quarter of my small breast had been chopped off, and now more needed to be cut out. Most of my doctors believed I would need major reconstructive surgery after the second lumpectomy, especially since I would have to be exposed to three months of daily radiation on my chest. Except for my surgeon, they all voted in favor of the mastectomy. At this point I had no more attachment to it, yet I wanted to do everything possible to alleviate more trauma to my body temple that would require enduring many more months of recovery time.

One week later we were on our way to the hospital for the second surgery. While Nathaniel drove, I chanted aloud in the car.

Upon our return after the second surgery, Nathaniel said smiling as he drove, "You did it again, baby! Are you aware that you were chanting aloud in Sanskrit again when they rolled you out of the operating room?"

I smiled and said, "Really! Are you serious? A second time! That is the power of potent mantras! They heal and protect us."

I laughed at it again, feeling blissful and content. It validated how interconnected I was with the yogic spiritual tradition, all ascended masters, and our Creator. A part of my being also felt deeply grateful for having Nathaniel by my side.

We returned to Dr. Eliseo for the verdict one week later. He walked in the room with a smile and said, "Clean!"

Nathaniel and I looked at each other, smiling. He reached out for my hand. All margins were now clear of cancer.

Dr. Eliseo removed the bandages. Tears of triumph welled up in my eyes. My surgeon's meticulous artwork was a masterpiece! We could not tell I had just had two lumpectomies back to back. You could barely see the scars. In the process of letting go of my breast, the body, that life, some personality, and limitations, a sense of freedom had emerged. A new gate had opened.

Not long after recovering from the surgeries, I started radiation at the same institute. My radiation oncologist was convinced the treatments would dry up and wrinkle my breast like a prune, so that reconstructive surgery would be inevitable. The nurse wanted me to apply thick animal fat on my chest after each daily session. I refused, telling her I would not use animal products because I did not support animal exploitation. Instead I applied pure aloe vera and a mixture of essential oils twice a day, which I blessed.

"Watch," I told my oncologists. "We will witness another miracle!"

In my last two weeks of radiation toward the end of November, we lost our beloved Dad to a massive stroke, and also our little Tina La Ballerina cat. Dad, as we called him, was not our real biological father. He was Nathaniel's father-in-law from his first marriage. Nathaniel had enjoyed a very close relationship with him for twenty-five years. Dad was more than a beloved father for us. Over the years, he naturally became the loving dad I never had. He always showered my being with unconditional love and comprehension. They were buried one day apart. These life events reminded me once more of the importance of realizing our true nature before dropping our garment and the gift of our precious breath.

~

DURING THE NINE MONTHS OF intensive medical procedures, I had embraced my big "C" journey with the majestic "D" for Divine. In the midst of suffering and facing my mortality, I rediscovered the eternal Source within my being. I realized there is profound humility in surrendering, in abandoning oneself completely. In that surrender, an inexplicable sense of serenity and bliss exudes from within. That presence is the Source shining forth.

One lit candle has the potential to light thousands of candles. The energy, frequency of vibration, aura, and presence one being can emanate around the globe has boundless possibilities. Humans are overdue to wake up to their ultimate nature. Every day I witness miracles. Do you? We all have the same full potential and Divine power dormant within us.

Although we live at a time when many of us have all the comfort, convenience, and technology we need, we still live in a time of chaos, disease, and natural and man-made calamities. As a global family, there are a few crucial things we must do to eradicate war, poverty, many more diseases and extinction of many species, and the massacre of many billions of animals. All these things have a devastating effect on our spiritual unfoldment. To raise consciousness is of utmost importance. That is the vision for the seeker, the lover, the visionary, the compassionate warrior, and the awakened and enlightened ones.

That is why it is essential to meditate every day on our ultimate nature, love, and emptiness or oneness. If more people looked inside, more would awaken into buddhas, enlightened beings. Meditation helps nullify negative vibrations in the universe and creates a harmonious energy in the atmosphere. We cannot win with a lash, only with compassion . . . and rose petals! Even if we lose in love, there is always victory. A victory won out of selfishness, violence, and greed is a great loss for the individual, humanity, and future generations. Together let's raise the consciousness and unite the world by One spirit, One heart, and One breath. That is the call of our era.

~

THE LAST TIME I SAW my oncologist Dr. Davidson for a checkup, he was astounded by the excellent result. "We can't tell you had breast surgeries and intense radiation."

"All the praises go to the Divine and my surgeon!" My heart was overflowing with gratitude for our Creator, Shiva, Jesus Christ, Shiv-Goraksha Babaji, the ascended masters, Gautama the Buddha, Kuan Yin, the mahavatars and all celestial beings, and to Gurudev, the Dalai Lama, Yogiraj Gurunath Siddhanath, Nathaniel, my doctors, and everyone else who had assisted my being on my healing journey.

"Vivi," Dr. Davidson said, "you've taught me a lesson."

I was touched by his humility.

In December 2007, after six months of intense chemotherapy, one traumatic biopsy MRI, two invasive surgeries followed by three months of daily radiation, all my treatments ceased. I was elated as I geared up for my recovery and physical rebuilding. The healing journey was not over; I was merely at the very beginning of a seemingly endless recovery, an amazing, insightful odyssey. When our heart overflows with gratitude and Divine love, the whole universe dances with us.

Thirty-Three

OUR BODY IS OUR TEMPLE

IT IS CRUCIAL TO VIEW our physical body as a temple. When we do so, our demeanor can help transform our entire being at all levels by affecting our ways of behaving in all arenas of our lives, and of others' lives. Our behaviors become more holistic, reverential, and mindful. This process can become very spiritual and healing for some individuals, like it was in my youth in overcoming bulimia. To embrace our body as a temple does not mean to get attached to it, to become vain, or obsessed with it.

On the contrary, the individual can move through life more gracefully with warm-hearted dignity, integrity, respect, gratitude, compassion, kindness, and reverence toward oneself and all living beings. When you realize the Divine permeates every cell of your body temple, the shrine of your heart can rapidly blossom to embrace all living beings as oneself. The body temple is our vehicle to travel through this physical realm—to grow, to ascend, and to experience this existence as well as other dimensions of the beyond.

The physical body is the most phenomenal instrument, so to treat it as a temple is to express great love and gratitude to God, our Creator, who ultimately is the source of it. To love our body temple is to love the divinity enshrined within it. Therefore, to take care of it in a holistic, compassionate, and reverential way is ultimately to be of great service to others. When we are in top shape at all levels, we can reach our full human potential and realize enlightenment. In return, we radiate light and loving compassion everywhere we go. We become the light.

People around us will feel the emanations and vibrations. Also our health affects all of our sheaths (koshas), even the subtle body that I talked about in earlier chapters. Because the physical body can experience so much pain and suffering, viewing it as a temple, in my experience, helps transcend negative conditions. In the yogic tradition, some schools regard the physical body as a hindrance in order to attain liberation. They don't give it any concerns, attention, or care and want to move as fast as possible. On the other end of the spectrum, there are yogic branches, such as hatha yoga, that regard the physical body as an important instrument.

Do you treat your own body as a temple, a shrine . . . or as a graveyard?

To nourish the body temple well is essential on the spiritual path if one wants to flourish. It involves many aspects at all levels. We must cultivate holistic habits by nourishing our body temple with the highest pranic food and liquids, maintaining positive and harmonious words, thoughts, and actions with mindfulness, daily meditation, and chanting mantras; we must feed it with the highest vibrating energy from practicing daily pranayamas and hatha yoga, combined with the right outdoor exercise regimen.

During my lingering and very challenging recovery period, I realized even more the importance of viewing and treating the physical body as a temple. That embrace—the realization that our body is a temple that the Divine inhabits—empowered my being to a new level with immense will-power, determination, patience, and perseverance. Without it I would not be alive today.

It all started about a year later at Cafe Gratitude, a casual restaurant serving vegan live (raw) foods, that opened in a nearby town. Nathaniel and I loved their healthy, nutritious food and regularly ate there during and after my cancer treatments. The cafe had a friendly family atmosphere, which created a sense of belongingness in our community.

Shortly after opening its doors, the cafe became the community hub for those who strived to obtain or maintain a healthy, consciously holistic, and spiritual lifestyle.

One day in late December when my hair had grown back enough to make me look like a baby chick, I bought a little book from the cafe. It was someone's story about how he healed from early-stage cancer by eating an organic, live vegan diet and by keeping his body alkaline. Even though it was very early-stage cancer, the science behind it fascinated me. I was willing to explore more of the natural healing processes the Divine has given us. This story opened up a new horizon. I was determined to discover what had caused this advanced cancer to grow in my body temple. Deep within my being I knew intuitively it had to be an environmental cause, and that one day I would know precisely which one. It was just a matter of time.

Through reading other books and magazine articles at Cafe Gratitude, I discovered two internationally renowned and empowering holistic and educational centers. I was eager to visit both. The Hippocrates Health Institute was in West Palm Beach, Florida. The Tree of Life Rejuvenation Center was in Patagonia, Arizona. With this information in hand, I was empowered and propelled into a deep, holistic healing journey, which is crucial on the spiritual path. This new knowledge motivated me to recover from the damage caused by the harsh medical treatments I had undergone. I needed to rebuild many of my vital organs, systems, and glands, and to detoxify my body temple.

At this point the most important endeavor in my life was to gain and maintain vibrant health. People debilitated by major illness or medical problems often can't do their spiritual sadhana, meditate, and be benevolent to others. I did not expect that this holistic voyage and embracing even more my body as a temple would help empower my spiritual path. Good health is one of the greatest blessings and privileges from our Creator. Like most people, I had always taken my health for granted. Now I treasured it beyond anything else because I knew when we are sick and debilitated by any major illness, we can't function and can't grow at our full human and divine potential. It is a tragedy to live a life unfulfilled.

From my experiences and experts' advice, I learned that sugar feeds cancer and many other diseases and ailments. A significant amount of scientific research has been conducted on the biochemistry of our body and its balance between acids and bases (alkalines). In increasing numbers, populations are addicted to animal flesh, dairy products, and junk food. As a result, more people than ever are becoming sick and obese. These diseases of affluence reflect the lack of awareness of the masses.

Human biology is a great miracle. Our body has the Divine power to heal itself if treated with care and knowledge. Our body is like a swimming pool. Because it is about 72 percent water, the pH of its fluid is extremely important. If the water in a pool is left unattended and becomes too acidic, then microforms such as yeasts, bacteria, and molds start to grow, which create mycotoxins—metabolic waste products that are acidic. The same is true for our biological fluids, especially blood. If our body is too acidic, it becomes a fertile ground for sickness and disease. Over time our system becomes out of balance and vulnerable, especially since we are constantly bombarded by toxic chemicals, heavy metals, and pesticides in our food, water, and the environment.

~

ONE DAY I MET WIZARD, a health consultant at Cafe Gratitude. We shared our stories over green juice. I told him about my cancer journey, and he recalled how he had jaundice and was sick for many years. "I'm living proof of what the holistic approach can do, and how our body has the wisdom and power to heal with the proper healthy lifestyle, nutrients, and a natural, holistic approach," he said.

Wizard had a beautiful spiritual quality about him. I hired him on the spot. The synchronicity of the Divine is never an accident but always the orchestration of the Divine Mother, I told him.

A few weeks later Wizard came to our house, and we sat on the floor barefoot in lotus position in our sanctum, feeling very happy to connect again. He would call me Devi, my spiritual name. He said, "Devi, you need to do the live blood cell analysis as soon as possible, what is called dark field and dry field. It's the science of looking at blood while it is still alive, under a microscope, and checking to see whether your pH is healthy. It is just awesome to see your own blood alive under the microscope!"

I replied, "I can't wait to have it done!"

"This science allows us to witness our blood's biochemistry and its decomposing condition. Remember, Devi, when I met you, I shared my story. My health crisis propelled me in this profession for this reason, to help people like you! Today I'm thriving and very grateful. I know one day you will be too," Wizard said, smiling.

"I completely agree! Yes, I always felt that the body has the wisdom and power to heal itself, Wizard. My body temple is screaming for help now," I replied.

After we talked for a few hours, I paused for a moment with tears welling in my eyes. I became overwhelmed with sadness. Despite how very grateful I was for my new discovery and direction, a part of my being felt totally demolished and so exhausted. Just for a moment I wondered how I would find the courage and strength to go on with this journey. Wizard hugged me in silence before departing.

~

OVER THE FOLLOWING MONTHS, I had several gentle detoxifying treatments until I could find my way to the holistic health institutes that Wizard had told me about. He recommended a program at the Hippocrates Health Institute and several green-juice detox programs at the Tree of Life Rejuvenation Center. He had called them life-changing. I yearned to learn more about this healthy way of living and do more intense detox.

I decided to go for a local consultation with a technician for the dark field and dry field. As I looked into the microscope, I said, "Oh my God! So many microforms are swimming in my blood. My blood looks awful, not surprising given the barbaric treatments I had undergone with cancer. Wow! I have some serious work to do."

As we spoke further, I realized it would take many years to get back to a healthy pH balance and that my vegan diet was not a nutritious and well-balanced one conducive to excellent health. I had a lot to learn. The next time I went to the microscope, I wanted to see luminous cells forming perfect circles with rings of light emanating from within, like the pictures of the super healthy cells I saw in books.

That first visit made me think about what I ate and drank daily, and I realized I had an unhealthy diet. It was filled with too much cooked, fried, and processed food like tofu, mock meat, and pre-made frozen food. I was eating dead food lacking prana, vitamins, minerals, and enzymes. I lacked fresh greens like kale and sprouts, legumes, and raw veggies, which all have phytonutrients. I wasn't eating super foods like maca, chia, and hemp.

After several years of effort and dedication, my pH and blood became well balanced, and I always strive to keep them that way.

~

ONE DAY A FRIEND FORWARDED an insightful article on detox from Dr. Cousens, which greatly inspired me. The following week I started a detox program with herbs I bought from his natural dispensary. For six months, I followed the "Phase 1" diet Dr. Cousens recommends in his book *Rainbow Green Live-Food Cuisine.* This is an extremely low-glycemic, healing, holistic, and organic live vegan cuisine without any form of sugar or fruits. Among all the fruits, I had a weakness for juicy berries, especially blueberries and strawberries. On rare occasions, I snuck a strawberry!

Dr. Robert Young says, "Just as our body temperature must be maintained at 98.6 degrees Fahrenheit, our blood is ideally maintained at 7.365 pH—very mildly basic. Maintaining the alkaline pH of the body's fluids, including blood, urine, and saliva, is critical for good health."[1]

I embarked on a quest toward wellness as I discovered the joy of eating pure, fresh organic vegan live food rich in prana, energy, enzymes, phytonutrients, minerals, proteins, and vitamins. This way of eating is low-glycemic, and it also helps balance hormones. This way of living keeps the body baseline slightly alkaline, balanced, and cleansed. Eating live organic vegan cuisine also positively affects our environment, animals, and people, and it has a powerful impact on our spiritual unfoldment.

~

FULL RECOVERY AND PERSONAL TRANSFORMATION after cancer or any other major disease is crucial because our bodies and systems are so weak and vulnerable. Yet most people with cancer or other major diseases never bother to change their way of living, and many die within the first few years after treatment. What does it take for most people to wake up and pay attention to their food consumption, thoughts, words, and actions? The wise ones learn from others who have walked the path. They don't wait until something grim happens to them. Our health is priceless. I call this way of living "Divine medicine!"

Both food and drink affect our pH and have an impact on our health. Every morning I made three ounces of wheatgrass juice and a large pitcher of fresh organic green juice. I wanted to learn everything I could about this wellness lifestyle. I devoured every credible source I could find.

Nathaniel was still not convinced of the tremendous benefits accruing from the holistic programs at those two centers. He put up a wall of resistance. I sensed my adrenal glands were completely burned out, and my thyroid glands were not working in harmony with the others. I had never realized before how fragile the adrenal glands are, and how important they are to our overall health and vitality; but now I was experiencing what it was to be consumed by adrenal fatigue. With the amount of stress in our modern societies and the inability for most people to cope with it, adrenal fatigue (hypoadrenia) has become a major problem and epidemic, according to Dr. James Wilson in his book *Adrenal Fatigue: The 21st-Century Stress Syndrome.* He explains: "People suffering from adrenal fatigue are much more likely to develop a host of other common diseases and syndromes in which fatigue is one of the primary symptoms." He refers to the adrenal glands as "the glands of stress" because "the purpose of your adrenal glands is to help your body cope with stresses and survive."[2]

∼

ON A WARM SUNNY MORNING in December, I was helping Nathaniel roll in the garbage cans from our driveway when a sharp pain radiated from my ribs to my entire torso. I felt as if I'd just broken my ribs. I knew what the pain was like. I'd already broken them once when I tripped over Snowflake several years earlier and fell down the stairs with her.

We called my general physician and were able to get an emergency visit. While Nathaniel drove, I could feel a rash creeping over my torso. I saw huge blisters growing. By then my skin was on fire. My doctor took one look and said, "You have shingles." He explained that the zoster virus that causes shingles lingers in the body of anyone who has had chickenpox.

I remembered I had contracted chickenpox from an infectious child when I was a little girl. Immense stress can activate the virus, which bursts forth as shingles, and it had been only one week since I'd completed all my cancer treatment. Common effects are extremely painful rash with blisters, severe pain, and nerve damage that can linger for months or years. Shingles can appear anywhere on the body.

My doctor prescribed prednisone for the first three weeks along with a strong painkiller. The pain was already so bad that I had difficulty moving and walking around.

When we arrived home, I went straight to bed. I still had not written my article on H. H. the Dalai Lama, Gautama the Buddha, and their teachings. I wondered when the heavy fog in my brain, the severe adrenal fatigue, and this excruciating pain would go away. Tears welled up in my eyes. I didn't know if I could handle any more pain and suffering.

For over a month, I was too sick and weak to do anything except meditate, rest, and sleep. The nerve pain I was suffering felt unlike anything I had experienced before—as if a truck had run over my whole body.

Besides the severe pain from the shingles and feeling my body temple and system totally demolished, drained, and beyond exhausted, many times a day sharp currents of shooting pain similar to electric shocks shot through it, causing me to sweat so profusely that my clothes were soaked in minutes, thus debilitating my entire being. I believed the shocks and hot flashes were related to the abrupt menopause caused by chemotherapy.

I also discovered that although the cancer treatments had ended, they had left a destructive, lingering effect on my digestive and elimination systems, not to mention my immune and reproductive system, glands, and major organs. My whole system was a monstrous mess. How was I going to rebuild it? How long would it take? At what price? I reminded myself that my body is a temple. I had no idea of the intensity, efforts, patience, cost, perseverance, and spiritual strength my full recovery would require in overcoming so many health obstacles and challenges. My recovery had just begun, and here I was, hit again.

Mahatma Gandhi said, "Strength does not come from the physical capacity. It comes from an indomitable will."[3]

During that challenging time, our dear friend Leilani was bedridden with a severe episode of lupus. I called her almost every day to cheer her up. On weekends, her boyfriend would bring her to our house to watch comedy films.

Leilani and I would lie in bed while our men sat on chairs next to us. I called our soirées "laughing therapy." Laughter helped us heal and manage the intensity of our journeys.

After several months of rest, I sat in my meditation chair in our sanctum and began to research the life of His Holiness the Dalai Lama. I mused deeper on his teachings and on Siddhartha Gautama the Buddha's life and teachings while experiencing intense pain from the shingles and many other symptoms from my cancer recovery. I would get very exhausted from thinking; my brain felt fried and fogged up. Often, even after only an hour, I would drift into a meditative state.

Once during a profound meditation, I heard a phrase echo: "Self-realization is realizing there is no self." Days later I jotted down these words:

> *Self-realization is realizing there is no self. The whole cosmos is One being. My teacher is everywhere: in a bee, a cat, a deer, a blossoming rose, the waves of the gigantic ocean, the falling raindrop, the morning dew, the sun shining upon every green curve of Mother Earth, and in the essence of you. I bow to the Goddess enshrined within my being and you.*

When we tune in, life events synchronize to support our evolution and ascension. My body temple was in a state of collapse, so feeble, exhausted, and in pain. I was experiencing how ephemeral our existence is, the body constantly aging, decaying, and dying, exactly what Siddhartha Gautama the Buddha realized. Through this experience, I was awakening like the young prince Siddhartha Gautama did in his era.

Upon Gautama's first visit beyond the confinement of his palace, around 600 BC, the young prince noticed a very old person, a sick person, a corpse, and a renunciate *sadhu* (a renunciant). In that instant, he realized that all living creatures seek happiness and do not want suffering or pain. Except for physical pain, most human beings suffer because of their undisciplined minds. This wild mind is often afflicted by negative and toxic emotions, susceptible to conflicts based on a false perception of reality.

When Siddhartha Gautama saw how everything arises based on causes and conditions, he awakened to his natural state of enlightenment. He became a Buddha, an enlightened one. He saw how every living being and phenomena are fundamentally interconnected and interdependent. He realized that no independent, existent self is real. Siddhartha Gautama the Buddha saw that sickness, aging, death, famine, and drought are external conditions related to the nature of our impermanent existence. Based on his own realizations and experiences, he turned the first wheel of teaching, the *Four Noble Truths*. He saw what the true nature of conditioned existence is.

The first noble truth is that suffering does exist.

The second noble truth is that the cause of our suffering originates in our desires and delusions. Because we are mistaken by the notion of a permanent and independently existent self, ultimately the real cause of suffering is ignorance of our ultimate and true nature.

Anyone can end this endless cycle of suffering. The cessation is called nirvana. It is the third noble truth. Like moska or mukthi (liberation) in the yogic spiritual tradition, nirvana is a state of freedom from suffering and pain where the being is merged in supreme ecstasy into emptiness, or the Source. Buddha stressed it is crucial to recognize suffering to eliminate its origin and bring its cessation.

When we see suffering and recognize its effect, we seek the cause. Walking the eightfold path serves as a guideline for our lives (right understanding, right intention, right speech, right action, right livelihood, right concentration, right mindfulness, right effort). Whether we are Buddhists or not, the eightfold path is a guiding light shining through darkness for everyone. That is the fourth noble truth.

All the pain throughout my life shed a new light on my existences by allowing my being to become more aware of it. I knew the cause, and it helped my being to transcend the conditions. I allowed my pain to become my teacher, leading my being to continue to seek the truth, to full realization, and to deeply listen to the wisdom of my body temple. I also had allowed the duality of this physical realm to tear my being apart and demolish what needed to be destroyed in me. Most importantly, my suffering helped me realize even more how all living beings suffer and experience pain, and how imperative it is to help other suffering beings. It is much more than empathy—it is a deep realization of our interconnectedness and oneness.

My suffering helped me transform my entire being into a more loving and joyous, compassionate human being who is active in the world. If you allow your suffering and are receptive to it, your heart will blossom in unimaginable ways. It will render you very humble and grateful by rekindling in you a great joy of being, especially when you realize that most of our suffering and pain is self-created. So we have the choice—either we carry our wounds as a load of garbage or as a guiding light to shine the truth to help us liberate ourselves and others.

Thirty-Four

PREMONITION AND
THE HEALING POWER OF SINGING

AFTER MY CANCER JOURNEY, I never touched a paintbrush again.
My desire to paint vanished. My inner knowing was guiding my being to
the next level of my life. It was hard to believe. Painting was my breath, but
I had to listen. For the next three years, I focused mainly on recovering,
rebuilding my organs and systems, and attaining vibrant health.

It took over a year of recovering before I could focus. I was not able
to write my article on the Dalai Lama and his teachings for a year after my
cancer episode.

In mid-August of 2009, I had an intuitive feeling I should visit my
mother in Canada. Although she was eighty-seven years old, she looked
more like a radiant, young seventy, exuding vigorous health. Mama continued dancing with her longtime boyfriend, Ives, almost five times a week,
and was still active doing hair for many of her old-time clients and friends.
An inner knowing constantly nagged that I must go see her. I could not
ignore this intuition.

A few weeks later Nathaniel and I flew to Quebec. Mama had been
very worried by my illness and challenging recovery. She was still afraid I
might die. I thought the only way for her to accept the miracle would be
to see her daughter in person. Mama prayed none of her children would
pass on before her own death.

During our visit, Mama was filled with serenity and joie de vivre. She
kept saying, "My baby's face looks so beautiful and radiant! She's healed!"

When we were about to leave, Mama and Ives met us at the curb. I held her tenderly. As our car pulled away, I smiled and waved goodbye with a knot in my throat. I knew it would be the last time we would see each other. I did not know why. She had never suffered a health crisis. The intuition felt too strong to ignore.

A few weeks after our return to California, during one of my meditations, a vision flashed before my eyes. Mama lay in her casket at a mortuary with all her children and grandchildren surrounding her. In the vision, my sister Jasmine was on my left, mourning, grabbing my arm, and trying not to fall apart. My childhood friend Gardenia stood on my right, crying, and I stood like a pillar, serene between them, witnessing the moment. Nathaniel was behind me with a hand on my shoulder. The reverend father stood by the coffin addressing us before he closed the casket and began the ceremony.

Over the decades, I had learned to discern between genuine premonitions and my projections of fears and feelings, or imagination. I kept this premonition to myself. I knew Mama would be leaving us very soon.

I had never thought of myself as a singer, but that week I started singing "Ave Maria" many times a day. It was not a rational action. The spiritual energy flowing through my being propelled me to sing, and this song overwhelmed my being with many feelings. I could not understand exactly what was happening.

~

DURING THIS TIME, NATHANIEL AND I attended a spiritual concert of Deva Premal and Miten at a magnificent cathedral, a *kurtan* event where everyone may sing along to ancient Sanskrit chants. When we arrived, a long line of people had already gathered. Nathaniel parked the car while I waited. An angelic woman in front of my being engaged me in a conversation, asking my name and what I did in life.

"Who cares what I do? All I want to do is sing praises to the Divine Mother in all its forms!"

"Why don't you?" she asked.

"I can't sing. I have no voice."

She laughed. "Of course you have a voice, a beautiful one too! You can learn how to sing. You must!"

The woman gave me the phone number of a spiritual voice teacher. After talking with her, something profound clicked inside. I had been wanting to sing all my life, but felt I could not. Papa's poisonous words were still stuck inside me. "You're just a piece of shit!"

During the concert, I didn't hold back. I sang along with Deva Premal through the entire concert, with tears of gratitude flowing from my eyes.

~

THE FOLLOWING MONDAY, NATHANIEL TOOK off for a business trip to the East Coast. I called the voice teacher and phoned one of my yoga friends who was also a voice teacher. I set up classes with each of them for that week and registered for a basic music theory course at the local college. That afternoon I found a Yamaha keyboard. I gave it to myself as a birthday present along with my first voice classes. I could not wait to share the exciting news with Mama.

When Nathaniel returned from his trip, saw my keyboard in our sanctum, and heard about my voice classes, he looked at me as if I was out of my mind. "How could you give up all these long, challenging years as a painter?" he exclaimed. "You studied the violin, the *erhu* (Chinese violin), and you gave them up. Now . . . singing?"

He couldn't understand what was going on inside my being. I did not blame him, because I could not understand it either. "Baby, I must listen to my inner guidance. I long to sing and compose music. I know it is hard to understand. You must trust, my love."

I related to him what had occurred at the cathedral.

Genuine guidance cannot be comprehended by the intellect. I remembered how my first melody came out of my violin in 1999. I notated it on a music sheet and guarded it like a treasure. Now I pulled it from my cabinet and saw how I could add harmony. I named it "Compassionate Heart." I turned it into a vocalization. I studied the violin and the erhu because these instruments seemed the closest to the human voice. My longing always had been to sing with my own instrument, the voice our Creator gave me.

The following Friday, my birthday, I attended my first voice class at the home of my friend Belle Fleur, an amazing jazz singer and spiritual being. I could not sing one note; a giant knot caught up in my throat. A torrent of tears flowed out of my being during the class. She understood. A deep string had been touched. I could hear music and wanted to notate it. I was grieving for all the decades I had not sung and composed music. I wondered why I had not listened. Nathaniel may have thought it was a whim. I knew it was not.

Later that afternoon when I returned home, Mama and my elder sister Rose had left me a voice message expressing their love. Together they sang a French "happy birthday" song. I played it six times. I almost called Mama back but decided to wait for our usual Sunday night chat since Nathaniel and I had plans to celebrate my birthday.

The following night during dinner, we received a call.

"Vivi, Mama is in grave danger," my sister Jasmine lamented frantically as she sobbed.

"Calm down, Jasmine. Take a few deep breaths, ma chérie."

"Mama was watching a film with Ives when all of sudden she fell into a coma. The paramedics immediately put Mama on life support and took her by ambulance to the emergency room. The doctors are not sure if she is going to make it."

I remained tranquil listening to her and did not tell Jasmine about my premonition; it would have terrified her, and she had to drive several hours to reach the hospital. I told her I would meditate and try to connect with Mama's spirit. I promised to call her afterward. She calmed down and hung up.

I went upstairs to our sanctum. When I closed my eyes, I felt Mama's presence right away. I saw her serene, emanating light. It was clear that she had already left her body and crossed over. After an hour of meditation, I returned to see Nathaniel.

I hugged him for a minute and whispered, "Mama has already passed on to the other dimension. I should not have waited to call her back."

Oh, I was so glad I had not deleted her voice message. I played it again and again. It made me smile while tears filled my eyes. Once again I realized I hadn't trusted my inner guidance. "How many times will I have to learn this lesson?" I asked myself. It was a hard lesson to swallow. Yet I radiated serenity. I was in a complete state of abandonment, surrender, and detachment. I was bathing in an ocean of calm with no emotional outburst, yet I was in touch with my feelings. A part of my being felt a Zen state, hollow and emptied.

I waited several hours and then called Jasmine. She had just reached the hospital. I told her about my vision and connection with Mama's spirit. She was in denial. "I'm with her now and her heart is beating. She'll make it!"

~

A CALL FROM ROSE WOKE me the next morning around 7:00 a.m. She had returned to the hospital to see Mama and speak to the neurologist.

"Mama died," she mourned. "She had a brain aneurysm."

"Rose, I knew a while ago, because Mama's spirit came to my being last night in meditation. Mama is not dead. We never die. Consciousness is eternal and infinite. Rose, please, realize death is an illusion. Our bodies are just like clothing."

She interrupted me.

"Stop, Vivi! I don't want to talk about death people, spirits . . . such things! It's against my religion."

I stopped talking out of respect for Rose. It is futile to speak with someone who cannot hear.

The following day Jasmine phoned to say the family had gathered at Mama's bed and disconnected her life-support machine. The neurologist said the life-support machine had kept her heart pumping, but Mama was gone not long after the brain aneurysm exploded. We had been very close to Mama throughout our entire lives. It was fascinating that Mama unconsciously chose to leave her old garment the day after my birthday. She was celebrating in her own way.

I spent part of that afternoon on my computer composing a French poem for Mama's eulogy. The following morning I flew back to Canada to be with my family and Ives, giving them love and help.

~

ON THE NIGHT OF MY arrival, Ives picked me up at the airport and drove us to an elementary school near Mama's house. They had attended dancing classes in its gymnasium. When we entered, I was transported. The school's smell, architecture, and its walls covered in children's drawings reminded me of when Mama used to bring me to my kindergarten. In silence I sat in a corner of the gymnasium, admiring the elders joyously dancing in their elaborate square-dancing costumes.

Ives danced a few steps forward in front of me pretending to hold Mama's hand. "Here, Vivi, this is where your mother and I danced together for many years," he said. Then he roamed among the large group and disappeared. Not long after, the music stopped. Over the loudspeaker, someone announced Mama's passing and asked for a moment of silence. After the silence, he announced my presence. Ives reappeared, grabbed my hand, and brought me on the floor among fifty or so individuals. They began to circle my being. Many hugged us while praising Mama.

I could not hold back my tears. I fell silent, treasuring this moment. In that instant, I realized that despite her many decades of deep suffering, she had attained some sense of serenity and contentment in the last decade of her life. My admiration for her overwhelmed my being, leaving me speechless and humble. As the group held my being, I could see Mama's life with us unfolding before my eyes. All the sacrifices Mama had made for us. All the pain she had experienced, and how she traversed through the other side without holding hatred, bitterness, or anger in her heart at the end of her life. As Ives and I left the school, I recalled my last moment with Mama, holding hands and hugging her tightly by the curbside. Nothing had changed. I still felt like she was my precious child to protect and care for. I was overflowing with gratitude that I had followed my intuition to visit her in August.

Mama had turned away from the Catholic faith and was not religious, though she always loved Jesus Christ and felt close to him. I had noticed over the past decade that she was no longer the bitter, nervous wreck she used to be. I could see a certain blossoming had begun within her. She must have let go of much of her karma.

~

ROSE, JASMINE AND HER BOYFRIEND, my brother Coco, and one of my elder brothers were already at Mama's house, drinking tea and eating when Ives and I arrived.

The atmosphere was somewhat tense and sad. Ives had told Rose it was her fault our mother died. Rose was overwhelmed with grief, guilt, remorse, and resentment.

A week prior to Mama's passing, Rose had stayed for a week at Mama's house recovering from surgery. I had convinced Mama over the phone that Rose should do that. Ives believed Rose took advantage of the situation, and Mama's cerebral aneurysm burst because taking care of Rose was too much for her. I knew Mama took care of Rose out of devotion and love. Ives was convinced Mama could not handle such exhausting physical activities at her age. Rose had just returned home after having dinner with Mama and Ives on the night of my birthday when they called to wish me happy birthday. Now, full of grief, he was putting the blame on her.

Ives became so upset at Rose that he could not grieve. It is a human tendency to accuse others for what happens in our lives, rather than realize we are responsible for our reactions to those events. Turning ourselves into a victim is poison. Taking responsibility is always liberating.

Despite the unresolved issues between Ives and Rose, we managed to have an enjoyable evening together. We sat at the dining room table to look at photographs and share childhood memories. It was past midnight when one of my elder brothers decided to go to bed in Mama's guest bedroom. Everyone else departed except for Coco. We sat together in the living room. I read him my poem for Mama's eulogy entitled, "Ma Belle Mama." I wanted to practice reciting it before the funeral service.

As I recited it, I felt Mama's loving spirit. Her energy was among us. Coco looked at me with beaming eyes and said, "Do you feel her too? Wow!"

I smiled. "Oh, my God, ma belle Mama, you love the poem!" After experiencing her spirit for a while, Coco said my poem reflected Mama's beauty. He was touched by it and gave me a few tips. We hugged and said goodnight.

I got ready for bed. When I entered Mama's bedroom, it was a gorgeous warm night with no breeze. I left the curtains wide open and opened the window several inches. I lay in her bed feeling comforted by her sheets. I could smell her everywhere. My luggage and a plastic bag with goods in it lay on the floor.

Suddenly, I heard a crackling sound coming from my plastic bag as if someone had walked over it. It startled me. Mama did not have any animal companions, nor were there mice or rats in the house. I sat in bed. The streetlight outside the window cast light on the floor. I could see that no one was there. I asked out loud in French, "Is that you, Mama? Please come, give me a hug." I lay back, putting my head on her pillow.

Within a few seconds, I felt her presence again by my side. All at once the bangs on my forehead moved, as if Mama was caressing my hair with her fingers. In the last decade of her life, Mama had often made that affectionate gesture. Chills ran through my entire being. Then her spirit passed through my being, a feeling of Divine love caressing every cell of my body.

I received a communication from her. It was pure energy, an instant inner knowing. This telepathic communication derived from my heart, not my imagination.

Mama's message was clear. I was to help bring peace between Rose and mother's beloved Ives, and also within them.

I communicated in French to her spirit, "I'll try to help them, Mama. I love you so much." I tucked myself under her blanket, my eyelids closed, and I drifted, like an infant in her womb.

~

THE NIGHT BEFORE MAMA'S FUNERAL, Nathaniel arrived. He picked me up from Mama's house to stay with him at a hotel. By then, Rose and I'd had many meaningful talks. She was processing her feelings, peacefully letting go of the issue with Ives. That night a group of us met for dinner in Mama's favorite restaurant on the left bank. Ives sat next to me. I approached him. Toward the end of our conversation, he broke down crying like a little boy, realizing his behavior had been a cover-up for his loss. I was relieved, and I held him for a long time.

On the day of her funeral, many people paid homage to our beautiful Mama. Her casket had been opened for the past three days during visiting hours. Mama looked splendid in her favorite peach chiffon dress. Nathaniel and I had given it to her to wear for our wedding day.

I sat alone by her casket. She had done her very best despite all the incredible hardships and adversities she had to face, always devoted to us and her grandchildren. I would be forever grateful. I sent invocations for the highest blessings for her spirit. When the time arrived to close the casket, the reverend father addressed us. Explosions of wailing filled the room. Each detail was as I had seen it in my vision. When Nathaniel and my four brothers carried the coffin to the chapel across the hall, I held Nathaniel's arm and whispered, "It's too mysterious. These last moments were exactly as I saw them in my vision, like a déjà vu."

The service started with an address from the reverend. Then I recited Mama's eulogy. I could feel Mama's spirit with us, hovering over the hall. Midway through the poem, I choked up, took a deep breath, and resumed reciting. Toward the end of the service, all children and grandchildren put our hands on the closed casket. Together we released Mama's spirit into the beyond as the reverend guided us. Then he asked us to clap our hands and cheer for a life well lived, like an actor whose performance had exceeded the expectations of the audience. A hundred and more of us applauded so loudly the roof vibrated. Heaven shook. I said out loud, "Brava, Mama! *Bravissima!*"

Not long after, Mama's body was cremated. How ephemeral is this physical existence! One second we are here, the next we are gone. Losing a beloved one always reminds us of our own mortality. It is an opportunity to go deeper in truth and on the spiritual path.

This was a woman who did not have many wishes, but I realized one of her dearest desires had been granted. She did not have to bear the loss of one of her beloved children. I was grateful for that.

My siblings and I decided to gather at a restaurant in Old Town to celebrate our *belle* Mama. We toasted champagne in honor of her life, beauty, courage, spirit, and her endless love and devotion for us and many others. Even though I don't really drink, I lifted a glass and drank a sip for a beautiful being who lived a selfless life.

Thirty-Five

DREAMING OF LOVING COMPASSION
FOR ALL LIVING BEINGS

EIGHT MONTHS AFTER THE FUNERAL, I received a small amount from Mama's will. I closed my eyes and tears welled up. She had worked so hard all her life to earn a scant income, saving every penny she could, to leave us something after her passing. I used to tell her, "Don't worry about us. Enjoy life, Mama!"

I wondered how Mama would want me to spend my inheritance. I paid a few bills and signed up for the three-week life-changing program at the Hippocrates Health Institute.

Nathaniel even helped with an upgrade for my room. I was grateful and surprised.

When I arrived in West Palm Beach, the Institute was a tropical Mediterranean oasis filled with green foliage and sculptures. I broke into tears and continued to cry many times during my stay. I was alive with a grateful heart. Mama's presence was everywhere. I knew this was the most cherished gift I could get to honor her spirit and mine. My recovery journey would challenge my being at every level. It would last for over ten years, during which many of my dear friends would die from cancer.

~

AFTER A LONG ABSENCE, IN February 2010 I decided to go back to India and the Art of Living International Center. My heart longed to be with Gurudev. Nathaniel did not care to join me, but he supported my return.

Upon my arrival at the ashram, I donated a sum to rescue a cow from the slaughterhouse. This cow was a gift for Gurudev from Nathaniel and me. She would live at the Goshala, their cow sanctuary, not far away from the campus, near the lake.

I had never been to the Goshala and yearned to visit the cows. Late afternoon on my second day at the ashram, I went. Many of the cows were eating. When I got near, most of them stopped and walked over to greet my being. I stood behind the wooden fence of the enclosure and rested my arms on it. A dozen tongues began to lick my hands and arms. Many more of these precious creatures tried to get to me, gently pushing to embrace my being with unconditional love.

"Oh, I love you too, all of you. Soon you'll have a new friend living with you!"

Together we sent love and blessings of well-being to all living beings around the world who suffer.

All at once, Krishna's presence overwhelmed my entire being. His energy intoxicated me with bubbles of bliss. Deep silence is hearing and feeling with all the particles of our being in the ultimate ecstatic state of oneness.

～

ONE NIGHT DURING SATSANG GURUDEV elaborated on the meaning of oneness and love. Toward the end of his discourse, the hall exploded in exultation. Thousands of us danced, chanting with our arms toward heaven as music played.

When Gurudev exited the hall, hundreds of individuals followed him. Most gravitated to the front of his old kutir, chatting about the evening's wisdom or gossiping. The atmosphere buzzed. I stood among the crowd, caught in the fire of this cherished moment. A stray dog came to greet me. I petted him and gave him a little piece of chapati (flatbread) I had in my bag.

An Indian man I had met a few nights prior stood next to me. He was the director of the Complaint Department of the ashram. He stared at me coldly and said, "Don't feed the dogs! We don't want them here."

"We have permission to feed them," I replied. "Gurudev gave it to us in 2006. I personally asked him during a satsang in front of a thousand future teachers when I was in the teacher-training program."

"How could you use Guruji's name!" he snapped.

I looked him straight in the eye. "Why would I lie? What about all the precious wisdom Gurudev just shared with us tonight. Weren't you there?"

He fumed, "If I see you feeding the dogs again, then I will request you to leave."

I laughed. "Gurudev would never allow that to happen. Anyway, as long as I'm here, I'll continue to feed the dogs and express compassion and love to them!"

He turned away.

I was more determined than ever to do something to help the animals in India, especially at the ashram and in the surrounding villages. It was then I remembered Gurudev had said to feed the dogs at the bottom of the hill around the cafeteria area. I wondered if there was an easier and more practical solution than having to go all the way down to the cafeteria to feed them.

~

A FEW DAYS LATER, GURUDEV invited our American group to his new kutir for an intimate audience with him. The fifty of us entered the room in joyous silence.

Somehow I landed next to Gurudev's feet. I offered him an elaborate garland of flowers I bought in the alley near the cafeteria. I bowed, beaming.

He asked us if we had any questions. "Are you all happy?"

Most exclaimed, "Yes."

I raised my hand. He signaled for me to speak. In that instant he gazed at my being with his most loving gaze. I became so intoxicated with bliss, his shakti tickling every cell of my temporal shrine.

"Gurudev, have you read the letter I gave to Bhanu Didi this morning?"

He nodded yes, smiling.

Then I related the incident with the director of the Complaint Department.

"Gurudev, we need to do something for the homeless dogs and cats around the ashram and surrounding villages. I'm willing to put up two thousand dollars and raise the rest of the funds for an animal sanctuary and veterinary hospital at the ashram. I already have several friends here in this group who are willing to contribute."

I pointed out that an animal sanctuary would be a wonderful tool of compassion and love, and it could help open the hearts of thousands of followers and children who visit the ashram from around the world each year. I suggested we could even have an animal advocacy department to help the suffering animals and Mother Earth.

Gurudev listened attentively and said, "Write a proposal. I'll look at it."

I also asked him again to speak on behalf of the suffering animals to all his devotees and followers, as I had asked him to do on other occasions in my letters over the decade, and to help expand the circle of compassion and love for them in his discourses. "Gurudev, together we can all help raise consciousness by bringing the awareness of the billions of suffering animals on our planet."

He nodded his head yes. "Art of Living will do its very best for the animals!"

I was overjoyed at his words. I knew when Gurudev says something like this, it was a promise.

Thirty-Six

CATALYST TO BENEVOLENT ACTIONS

ONE WEEK AFTER MY ARRIVAL at the ashram, Dr. Fury and his wife became my next-door neighbors. I knocked on their door to introduce myself and greet them. They were both long-time devotees.

Bougie, my long-time animal companion at the ashram, had slept on my doorstep for many nights. One moonless night she followed me to our building again. I often tried to discourage her from following me to my room, since I knew the issue with homeless animals was a controversial one. She was extremely thirsty; the temperature had been in the high 90s every day. When I reached my room, I poured water into a bowl and set it outside.

Suddenly Dr. Fury and his wife appeared at the building's entrance. He tried to kick Bougie away and said, "Don't bring these filthy creatures here. They're filled with diseases!"

It was only later in the night that it occurred to me to say human beings are also carriers of diseases, and many times humans are very destructive when they have not awakened to their true nature. I also had forgotten to tell him this stray dog had been sterilized and vaccinated years ago.

Over the following days when we crossed paths in the hallway of our building, I was not yet in silence in my program. Once I reminded him of our spiritual master's wisdom and engaged him in a brief discussion.

"Dr. Fury, Gurudev talks about universal responsibility, oneness, and compassion all the time. Why not expand that circle of loving compassion by embracing all living beings?"

Dr. Fury replied with an arrogant attitude, "Ah, you have the teaching all wrong."

He slammed his door behind him.

I sensed we had entered into some kind of spiritual process. I reflected and asked for guidance from Gurudev.

The following day we participants began a five-day silence. I wrote Dr. Fury and his wife a note and passed it under their door.

Dearest Dr. Fury and wife,

Here is an important message flowing in from Gurudev: If you had the misfortune of being a homeless dog, or any animal for that matter, how would you like to be treated?

1. Neglected, deserted, viewed with disdain and hatred, and cruelly beaten.

2. Treated with love, compassion, kindness, respect, care, and viewed as part of the Divine, the web of life, oneness.

Please meditate on it. Mahatma Gandhi supposedly once said, "The greatness of a nation and its moral progress can be judged by the way its animals are treated." Krishna tells us in the Bhagavad Gita in verse 5.18: "A humble person by virtue of true knowledge sees with equal vision a priest, a cow, an elephant, a dog, and an outcaste."

Much love, Vivi

Several days went by. There was another friendly stray dog following me to our building, even though I fed them at the bottom of the hill by the cafeteria. I tried hard to trick them so they would not come all the way back.

Toward the end of our program, Bougie followed me on another night and once again lay at my doorstep. I told her no and sent her away, but she kept coming back. Her eyes beamed with love and said, "Why? I just want to be with you."

When I entered my room and closed the door, within less than a minute I heard loud yelping. I ran out to see what was happening. Dr. Fury was quickly walking back toward his door with his chin up, not daring to look in my eyes. I don't know if she got hurt, because I did not see her for many days. I took a few deep breaths and did not confront him. I felt tempted to break my silence, but I remained calm and mindful.

~

ON THE LAST NIGHT, WHEN we broke our silence, another affectionate female dog followed me home. She had also been sterilized and vaccinated by CUPA. I figured if I closed the gate to our building, she could not enter. She would be protected from Dr. Fury's aggression. Still, she lay outside waiting for me not far from the building. I told her many times to go away.

As I was shooing her, Dr. Fury rushed out of his room in a rage. He grabbed whatever he could—stones, branches—and threw them at the poor animal.

I could not believe my eyes. A part of my being felt responsible for the situation. I thought, *There is no excuse for anyone to behave in such an abusive manner toward a gentle creature, or any defenseless creature.* I said nothing, knowing it was useless to speak to anyone who did not have ears to listen.

Later that night, however, I decided to bring the issue to Gurudev in a letter. But then, I let it go and sent Dr. Fury and his wife love, light, and blessings. I meditated in my room until 3:00 a.m. before I left the ashram for my early-morning flight back home. On my way out, I dropped another little handwritten note under Dr. Fury's door.

Dearest Dr. Fury,

The Divine loves fun, as Gurudev expresses often. I had fun having you as my neighbor. I love you both and wish you well.

One day you will understand and feel the suffering of animals, and will awake to your ultimate true nature and see yourself in the animals as I do. Have a safe trip back home.

Jai Guru Dev, Vivi

In the middle of the night I dragged my luggage to the taxi station near the gate where one of the guards stood. One of the stray dogs spotted and greeted me. I whispered to this fluffy apricot beauty while caressing his face, "I promise I'll do my very best to help all of you." He looked at my being with despair in his eyes. Tears rolled down my face, and my heart ached as I sat in the taxi in silence. I remembered the inspirational words, "Be the change you wish to see in the world."

At the airport in Bangalore, I started to develop a high fever and deep cough. I could feel another bout of bronchitis invading my lungs. I slept through both of my flights without eating until I reached New York. Nathaniel met me there, embraced me, and wrapped me in my winter coat. I was overflowing with gratitude to be back to America safely and back home with Nathaniel.

~

AFTER OUR RETURN TO CALIFORNIA, it took my being several weeks to recover. At last, I was able to do some research on international nonprofit animal welfare organizations and ask them to help with a massive ABC clinic at the Art of Living International Center and its surrounding villages in India.

Angelica, my new dear friend from my teacher-training program, gave me the email address of Mr. Rahul Segal, the director for the Asian branch of Humane Society International (HSI). She had recently met him at an animal welfare conference in America and heard rave reviews about their homeless dog program.

Within a few days after contacting Rahul, he responded. He knew of Gurudev and Art of Living and was very happy to let us know that the HSI would help. Rahul wrote that he had also had an audience with Gurudev many years ago and made the same requests I had presented to him for almost a decade.

We worked together to make the big ABC clinic happen. There was a lot of resistance, however, and obstacles within the ashram's political red tape.

Almost one year later I started to feel down about the situation, but I refused to give up. I had just come out of meditation when I stood in the sanctuary at home and said out loud with a powerful intention, as I looked at Gurudev's photo, "Gurudev, this ABC clinic needs to happen! Give me a sign. Please help us!"

That afternoon I received a call from the ashram in India. Magic happened! It was Violet, an American woman who was a long-time devotee and a full-time Art of Living teacher. She expressed her grief over the situation with the animals at the center in India and said she had heard of my animal projects from my dear friend, Lotus.

Violet was our missing link to help coordinate efforts at the international yoga center. With a team of volunteers, we were soon able to sterilize over eighty stray dogs. All received their vaccinations and appropriate vet care. Without Violet's love and compassion, the massive ABC clinic would probably never have happened.

I envisioned a day when we would celebrate all creatures with love, kindness, reverence, compassion, and dignity. This day could become the first official day, perhaps it could even be called "Day of Compassion for All Living Beings" or just "Day of Compassion," where many events around the world would take place raising consciousness and celebrating ahimsa—non-harm—for all living creatures.

I kept dreaming of love and compassion for all living beings, free from abuse, neglect, and indifference—united as One in love and harmony.

~

IN APRIL 2011, I FLEW to Los Angeles to meet with Gurudev and introduce him to Mr. Andrew Rowan, the president of the Humane Society International (HSI), and Dr. Hermanta to discuss my proposal. The HSI was willing and happy to sponsor and manage the animal sanctuary and vet hospital at Gurudev's ashram.

My proposal consisted of an animal clinic and sanctuary where the animals would be ambassadors for love and compassion. The sanctuary would also have an educational and international advocacy outreach. I called it the "Sri, Sri Animal Compassionate Sanctuary," and it would be located in the heart of the Art of Living International Center.

The animal clinic would be the first step. We were thrilled. I felt a great sense of relief and joy after a decade of efforts. I always thought if the most popular and beloved enlightened masters could include and speak for voiceless animals and our planet to their millions of followers around the world, we could raise consciousness much faster and eliminate a lot of misery.

During our meeting, I asked Gurudev if he wanted to be our honored guest along with H. H. the Dalai Lama for a unique event on ahimsa, non-violence, and compassion for animals in Mumbai, presented and sponsored by the Humane Society of the United States (HSUS), HSI, and Pratish Nandhi Communications.

"Yes, yes! For the animals, we'll do it!" exclaimed Gurudev. Unfortunately, his schedule did not permit it.

This special event would be the first of its kind, the official World Day of Compassion (WDC) honoring all creatures, spreading awareness on many crucial animal-exploitation issues, Mother Earth, our health, and problems in developing countries. Together we would try to face some of these challenges.

Thirty-Seven

THE MYSTICAL EMBRACE

LONGING IS THE ULTIMATE CRY of our being, a scream filled with the deepest yearning for truth and liberation. After my cancer journey, all I wanted to do was compose music, write lyrics, and sing these songs for the Divine in all its forms. My longing needed to be expressed in music.

After I completed my first music theory course, I found the courage to call the San Francisco Conservatory of Music for an audition. I wanted to learn how to compose music. The next month, with a few of my compositions in hand and my voice recorder, I went for the audition, not sure what to expect. The director of the adult program interviewed me and read my letters of recommendation from my voice and piano teacher.

I told the director, "I don't want to die with this music inside."

He took my recorder, placed the headphones on his head, and listened until the end. "Wow, it's beautiful, Vivi!" he said.

I asked to study with Elinor Armer, who had been associated with the Conservatory since 1969 as a full-time faculty member. I was accepted, and the following week I started my private lessons with Ms. Armer, a well-known Californian composer. I felt so grateful to have this opportunity.

About that time, a woman at my swim club told me that another swimmer, Camellia, had died. I was shocked. Camellia and I had traveled the cancer journey and part of recovery together. She had been diagnosed one month before me with advanced breast cancer. We went through all the same treatment stages together and even had the same holistic doctor. Though we had only been friends for a short while, we shared a close bond. We often swam together like dolphins and shared everything we could to support our well-being and growth. I never had the opportunity to express how much I appreciated her. While swimming that day, I reminisced about how both of us had often stopped swimming to gaze at the blue sky together and to express our heartfelt gratitude for being alive.

The following day with sorrow in my heart I sat by my keyboard and composed "Fly Away," and wrote the lyrics of a song for Camellia. The melody flowed out of my being just like the air passing through a flute. A sense of gratitude and Divine love engulfed my being for Camellia, and for being alive, for having the great privilege and blessing to be able to compose music and sing.

~

IN THAT SAME APRIL OF 2011, a few shafts of sunlight penetrated the hazy sky of Los Angeles as my dear friend Lotus and I walked to the Art of Living center where we were attending the Kena Upanishad teaching with our beloved Gurudev. Before entering the hall, Lotus shared about another beautiful, self-realized master, Sadhguru Jaggi Vasudev, a profound mystic and yogi.

Lotus sought advice from me. "Vivi, I want to ask you something. I don't know what to do. I'm torn apart about Gurudev and this other master, Sadhguru. Some friends took me to his ashram in South India while I was visiting in my recent journey. Sadhguru was not there, but I don't know why I feel very drawn to him. In the coming week Sadhguru will be in your county, only twenty minutes away from our home to teach a program. I am thinking about going." She sounded confused and conflicted.

"Don't hesitate, Lotus—follow your heart," I told her. "Listen in silence. Guidance will flow. From your tone and energy, I can tell you want to go. You are not disloyal to Gurudev by going. There is no competition in the spiritual path. Maybe that is exactly what you need now."

Though Lotus did not say much about Sadhguru, just the sound of his name reverberated in my heart. I could relate to her exaltation and confusion. Lotus uttered his name, "Sadhguru," as if it were a sacred pass-word to the Divine. A satguru (also spelled sadhguru) is a person of deep inner knowing and experiences not acquired from any scriptures.

"I don't know why, Lotus, but I want to meet Sadhguru." These words flew out of my mouth unexpectedly. It was just an inner knowing. I had already enjoyed the great blessing of being in the presence of four enlight-ened masters. I did not intend to leave my Gurudev, whom I treasured so much. By then I had been on the spiritual path for twelve years and was grateful for having had him in my life for almost nine years, yet this new master seemed to be calling to my being.

～

THAT FOLLOWING FRIDAY, LOTUS AND I met near my home. Over dinner she shared only a few details about Sadhguru's talk. I rel-ished hearing all the subtle and indirect ways in which Sadhguru spoke for the well-being of other living beings. As a vegan, animal lover, and animal advocate, I related to his wise words, especially since I noticed that only a few spiritual masters have the courage to speak directly for animals and other elements of earth's well-being.

"Vivi! You will love that part very much," Lotus exclaimed enthusi-astically. "Sadhguru talks about how meat putrefies in the large intestine for many hours and how it negatively affects our pranic energy and our spiritual growth."

"Oh my God! That is so great, Lotus! Yes, I am so impressed with Sadh-guru. I have not met him, and I already love him so much. Wow! I have never heard a spiritual master talking about this very delicate subject with such a wise approach." I already knew these facts as an animal advocate and as a yogini, but I was so thrilled hearing the subtle ways that Sadhguru approached diets and spirituality.

When we left the restaurant, I said with a bursting heart, "Lotus, if you get a chance, would you give Sadhguru a big hug for me? Tell him thank you so much for speaking up for animals. Tell him how much I love him!"

My life was about to be transformed again. The following night I was asleep when the phone rang near midnight. My intuition urged me to pick it up.

Lotus said with a bubbly voice, "I must tell you Sadhguru is inviting friends and family to come to a gathering tomorrow morning at seven. Come, Vivi!"

"What—7 a.m. on Sunday? Can you ask Sadhguru to do it at 11 instead, please?" I said, half seriously. Lotus knew it was hard for my being to get up early. I'd had severe adrenal fatigue. Most days I would sleep for eleven hours and still feel exhausted during the day. "Okay, sweetheart," I said, "if my celestial friends help me get out of bed by 5:30, I'll go."

~

THE FOLLOWING MORNING MY EYES opened wide at 5:20. I rose with the sun and saluted it. While showering, I chanted my favorite mantra, "Om Namah Shivaya," like I did most mornings. I put on a white summer dress and grabbed a matching shawl. I looked through the window. The sky reflected subtle shades of yellows, oranges, pinks, reds, and fuchsias. Its glow caressed the land with such intensity my heart nearly burst with joy. Dozens of birds sang their blissful songs.

Nathaniel woke and looked at his Vivi in surprise. "You're up? Wow, I'm impressed, darling!"

I smiled and kissed his forehead. I went down to the kitchen, fed our nine rescue cats and two dogs, then reached outside the door to feed the deer and the birds while I drank some green tea.

I noticed one magnificent white cow lily flower, standing tall with stem erect. Still dressed in her morning coat of velvet dew, she exuded a subtle, mystical fragrance. I cut the flower at her root, placed her in a tiny plastic bag with water, and wrapped her with an elastic band. "So sorry, beautiful flower. I don't mean to uproot you from your home. You'll serve a higher purpose today!"

As I drove toward the community center, I had vivid flashbacks of my major health crisis. I saw myself lying in agony on the couch with severe anaphylactic shock, dying from my first chemotherapy and feeling resurrected by Christ's energy. Waves of gratitude exploded in my heart as I neared the center, but I still thought how desperately I needed energy to be able to plunge deeper into union with the Divine. I wanted to feel exuberant and vibrant again.

When I arrived, several hundred participants were gathering near the pond, where dozens of geese and ducks greeted us. I spotted Lotus in her black yoga pants, the sun shimmering on her red hair. She looked radiant.

"Oh, Vivi, I forgot. Sadhguru told us to wear our sloppiest clothes."

Here I was, all dressed up, holding on to Sadhguru's flower, hoping to bathe in his presence during the satsang. My past experiences with satsang in the presence of a satguru has always been that participants dress up for such occasions. I smiled and asked, "Where is Sadhguru?" Lotus pointed out a fifty-something handsome man with long silvery hair and beard. In his orange and camel cloth hat, washed-out jeans, and shirt, he blended in with the crowd. The Isha Foundation volunteers gathered everyone into five rows for a game. "I can't play dressed like this," I told Lotus. "But I want to offer this flower to Sadhguru before I go back home."

Lotus said, "Go, Vivi!"

I left her. "Sadhguru!" He turned his head. I could not see his eyes behind his dark sunglasses. I noticed the silver hoops on his ears, his flawless, unwrinkled skin. Up close, he looked more like a man in his early forties. "Sadhguru, I'm just a visitor. I came to say thank you so much from the bottom of my heart for speaking up for animals."

"What! Don't you like human beings?" he asked with an infectious laugh.

"I love all sentient beings, Sadhguru."

His smile stretched from earth to infinity. "Here is a flower for you from my garden of love," I said as I put my other hand on my heart offering the lily to him as if it was my life. He took the flower, and all at once Sadhguru grabbed me in his arms and hugged me tightly for what seemed an eternity. I was so surprised; I stood as silent and motionless as a Shiva statue. I even forgot to introduce myself. Sadhguru saw through my being, and I felt his divinity.

"My friend forgot to tell me to dress casually, and my sandals are too slippery. I'm sorry, I can't play."

"Stay with us. Just play barefoot," he exclaimed with a gleaming smile.

"I'll see what I can do," I said, smiling and waving goodbye. I walked back to see Lotus. In the intensity of the moment, I had forgotten to tell Sadhguru I was afraid of re-injuring my knee if I played with the group. *How ironic*, I thought. I had given a message to Lotus to communicate to him, and here I was manifesting it in the most beautiful way. I sensed intuitively that my world was about to turn upside down again. I tried to run barefoot in the grass, but it felt too slippery. Not long after, I left the playground—still feeling uplifted by his hug.

⁓

A FEW DAYS LATER I discovered these words spoken by Sadhguru: "In a loving embrace there is Divine grace."* Over the following months, I could not stop thinking about him. I signed up for his online Isha Inner Engineering program. All I wanted was to see Sadghuru's glowing face and be with him again. I was attracted to Sadhguru like the roots of a tree are drawn to water after a drought. The feelings didn't seem to make sense, yet I could not resist. I felt strongly devotional toward him, yet I had no guilt or feelings of disloyalty toward my Gurudev. I was at peace. I still loved and revered Gurudev as much as I had on the first day we met. These new feelings and intuitions felt like a natural progression for my evolution and spiritual path.

One day Lotus surprised me with a gift, a framed photo of Sadhguru caressing a white bull with a colorful flower garland around its horns. Sadhguru's words were imprinted on the photo: "All creatures of the world are an expression of the Creator. If you are willing, every Creature is a doorway to the Creator."*

I thought, *Yes, Sadhguru, this has been my doorway since I was a little child.*

⁓

THE FOLLOWING JUNE NATHANIEL TOOK me to Italy for three weeks to celebrate our fifteenth wedding anniversary. On our fifth day in

* © Sadhguru

Rome, I was so exhausted that I decided to spend the day in the garden of the villa, resting and sipping herbal tea and completing my last two classes with Sadhguru online. By the end of his program, I felt so grateful; my body temple filled up with ecstasy. It did not matter that he was not next to my being; his presence was reverberating in my heart.

When Nathaniel and I returned home, my integrative doctor ordered a saliva test. The lab confirmed my cortisol level was way below normal. Without an adequate amount of cortisol secretion from the adrenal glands, it is extremely difficult to function. Life becomes miserable. I knew my adrenal fatigue had gotten worse, so my doctor put me on a more intense regimen. He told me it could take as long as three years before I could fully recover. "No way!" I said to myself. "I can't live like a wilted flower anymore."

Three and half months later, in October 2011, Nathaniel and I flew to Los Angeles for an initiation of the second part of the Isha Inner Engineering program. When we arrived at the airport, I wanted to buy flowers for Sadhguru. I asked our taxi driver if he knew a place on our way to the hotel where I could buy some.

"We don't have time to stop to buy flowers," Nathaniel said, resisting as he usually did. "Besides, you don't need them."

"I want to offer flowers to Sadhguru. We have time, darling. It is not like we are rushing. Please, driver, would you stop somewhere so I can buy flowers?"

"It is not convenient to start looking for a place and stop. You can buy flowers at the hotel," Nathaniel said annoyed.

"They won't have flowers. Come on, baby—it will only take an extra ten minutes. There must be a place on the way to the hotel." The taxi driver was not sure where to go.

Over the previous decade, Nathaniel had resisted change and growth and had never embraced a master as his satguru. He had already disappointed me with Gurunath and Gurudev for not taking them as his spiritual masters and for not being committed on the spiritual path with me. This issue had been a source of significant challenges in our relationship. I thought, *Here's one more wall to break down: having Sadhguru in our lives.* Nathaniel kept saying with an irritated tone of voice that I would find flowers at our hotel. It was not the flower issue, but his resistance and attitude, that drained my energies.

I did not want to argue with Nathaniel. We never stopped along the way. I closed my eyes and remained silent. I focused on the breath going up and down along my spine while chanting mentally, "Aum Namah Shivaya Aum." A part of my being was feeling sad, frustrated, and caged. I knew clearly that unless Nathaniel embarked on the spiritual path and worked on himself as I did, we could not grow together as a loving couple.

This was such a devastating revelation, because I knew I could not spend the rest of my life lingering in a stagnant relationship. It became as clear as the full moon reflecting on a tranquil pond that I needed and wanted a Divine, sacred love relationship—spending the rest of my life with someone and walking the spiritual path together. I did not want a domesticated loving relationship anymore. Unless Nathaniel made a commitment to transform and blossom, there was nothing I could do. I had tried everything a woman can do to save her love, her intimate relationship—I had even tried *not* trying and letting go. I secretly hoped perhaps with Sadhguru there would be a shift and Nathaniel would embrace him.

When we arrived at the hotel, I walked straight to the gift shop. I hoped I was wrong and I could find at least one fresh rose to offer to my beloved Sadhguru, but they didn't have any flowers, not even a rose.

We left and reached the hall right on time, taking our seats up front. The stage was beautifully decorated in natural earth tones. I closed my eyes and meditated.

When Sadhguru walked onstage, a flash of powerful energy traversed my anahata chakra in the heart region, penetrating my abdomen and chest like a beam of laser light. My whole body moved in rhythmic undulations. My eyes were still closed, yet I knew he was among us. While I gasped for air, a fireball of Divine love permeated every cell in my body temple. My tears overflowed. I realized that my new satguru had appeared.

I opened my eyes. Sadhguru stood on the platform with his eyes closed in *namaskaram* hand position ("namaskaram" is the formal salutation of the East. It has the same meaning as namaste: "I bow to the highest in you."). An iridescent taupe orange shawl with a red and brown motif was meticulously draped over his kurta, wrapping his majestic figure. He wore a white turban on his head, not as a religious symbol but as an exuberant expression. He bowed to us. I closed my eyes again. Laughter overwhelmed my being as I sensed an intuitive past-life connection. Or was I just being receptive to his blissful ecstatic state?

I later discovered Sadhguru's words—"Don't go searching for a Guru. When the pain of ignorance within you becomes a scream, a Guru will come in search of you"*—and remembered this moment.

Sadhguru asked if a few of us would like to introduce ourselves, and tell how we came to the Isha Foundation, his international nonprofit organization dedicated to cultivating individual potential and transformation. I took the microphone. As I related my story in front of hundreds of participants and volunteers, he closed his eyes, smiled blissfully as his head moved in a gentle dance while he rubbed his thumbs with his ring fingers to better feel my being. I told him about the tears of gratitude I experienced as he walked in. I reminded Sadhguru of the flower I had offered him last April. At the end I said simply, "Here I am, Sadhguru. I am your flower."

The energy reverberated to a high level of vibration within the hall. During the program, participants questioned Sadhguru on a variety of subjects. With microphone in hand I asked him, "Do you think these Isha yogic practices can work for a person with kundalini blockage?"

Over the decades, there has been much talk about blockages of energy preventing shakti from rising in the proper channel in the sushumna nadi. Since it is so vital, I thought I might have such a blockage.

Sadhguru looked at my being and said, "You don't have any problem. The problem is you!" He closed his eyes, carefully scanning my body while rubbing his thumbs with his ring fingers again. "It'll help. No, it'll definitely work!" Even though his answer was positive and personal, I did not set any expectations in my mind and even forgot about it right away as if we had never spoken about it.

At one point during the program while Sadhguru spoke, I entered into a non-mind state. I felt as if I was out of my body, completely mesmerized in a trancelike state. I saw Sadhguru's physical body dematerialize

★ © Sadhguru

into sparkles of light as faces of others passed through his visage. For several minutes, I was frozen into an eternal moment. Since I had experienced these sorts of mystical experiences many times with Yogiraj Gurunath Siddhanath, my first beloved master, I was not spooked by it. These kinds of experiences only prove we are One.

~

THE FOLLOWING MORNING, SADHGURU ASKED if we were happy. "Checking in with you." Along with most of the crowd, I yelled out enthusiastically, "Yes, Sadhguru!"

Nathaniel and I sat in the first row that morning. Thus far, he had stayed mostly aloof and withdrawn, sitting with his arms crossed and a pouting face. Sadhguru looked at me as if to say, "What is going on with him?" I responded with a questioning look. Sadhguru gazed briefly at Nathaniel and gave me a little smile of reassurance. He seemed to have read my heart.

When Sadhguru initiated us into the *Shambhavi Mahamudra*, a simple yet powerful yogic practice, I felt an explosion of shaktipat traverse my being. I spontaneously quivered as body movements occurred of their own accord. A woman in the far back chanted the name of Shiva out loud.

During the final moments, Sadhguru, his eyes closed, his demeanor humble, said, "For those of you who are willing, I will be available to you in more ways than you understand. This is the start of a lifelong love affair." Then he walked down the platform, stood in front of us on the ground floor with his hands in namaskaram, while tears of joy rolled from his eyes.

We also stood in namaskaram, the humble hand gesture of reverence. Many participants' cheeks were washed in tears of gratitude. My own face and neck were drenched in complete ecstatic rapture. The energy was intense with Divine love. The grand ballroom remained silent except for the band called Sounds of Isha playing in the background. I could not hold it back. I whispered, "Don't go, Sadhguru. Please don't go. We love you so much." Feeling intensely devotional, I walked slowly toward him. As I moved a few steps, two other people followed my being. I touched his feet. When I got back up, I folded Sadhguru in my arms and leaned against his chest in a grand embrace, while the other two women cuddled under his arms. The four of us entwined in a loving hug like swans interlacing. In this precious moment, I lost myself in him.

Then I said to Nathaniel, "This is your opportunity, sweetheart, go now."

He hesitated, but after five minutes he walked to Sadhguru, put his head on his shoulder, and said, "Thank you, Sadhguru." It touched my heart to see such a vulnerable and humble gesture from my husband.

⌒

AFTER THE PROGRAM, NATHANIEL AND I went out for dinner and walked on the avenue. On the way back to our hotel, I asked him hesitantly, "How do you feel about Sadhguru now?"

"I really like the guy a lot. He's very logical."

"Does it mean you can embrace him as your guru, baby?"

The answer was an enthusiastic, "Yes. Oh, yes!"

We hugged right on the curbside. I was exploding with happiness and joy. At last, there was the hope to save our marriage.

Thirty-Eight

MYSTICAL OCCURRENCES OF THE BEYOND

ONE MONTH AFTER OUR INITIATION, an intuition rose within my being to go to the Isha Institute of Inner Sciences (III) in Tennessee to attend one of their more advanced programs—Shoonya Intensive Meditation. It was as if Sadhguru had spoken to my being. It seemed early to participate and rather rushed, but I signed up anyway.

A few days prior my departure, I considered canceling. I could not catch the Institute's late afternoon shuttle at the Nashville airport. The yoga center is approximately two hours from the airport, and taxi fare would cost about $200. I called the center and talked with a lovely volunteer resident. "If I can't find someone to share a taxi with, I don't think I will come." The real reason was I knew we would be getting up around 4:00 a.m. every day. I did not think I could do it.

"Vivi, don't let a single doubt cross your mind," she told me over the phone.

On a deep level, I knew she was right.

A few days before the program, I received an email from Suryakanti, a sweet twenty-something South Indian who also needed a ride and was on the same flight.

When I reached the Nashville airport, we took a taxi together. We arrived at the Institute by 10:00 p.m. and missed the first session. It had been a long day, and I was beyond exhausted.

~

TUCKED IN THE LUSH FOREST of the rolling green Cumberland Mountains, the III is a rare jewel, offering exceptional opportunities to cultivate human potential. Based on the ancient yogic tradition and the guidance of such an enlightened master as Sadhguru, different powerful yoga programs are offered in their full depth and dimension.

If one is willing and receptive, the individual is elevated to transcend his or her limitations to reach and expand into a higher state of consciousness.

The following morning I dragged myself up at 5:00 a.m. to attend the Guru Pooja, as I had many years ago when I was with Gurudev. I was aware of its intense vibrations and ready to experience it again.

I walked fast to make it to the Mahima meditation hall, an ethereal 39,000-square-foot space consecrated by Sadhguru in 2008. It is the largest of its kind in the Western hemisphere. I arrived one minute late and stayed in the back entrance with a few others, chanting. I was too groggy to feel the sweet feminine energy permeating the hall. I had slept only five and a half hours instead of my usual eleven.

After the Guru Pooja, our group of sixty participants sat up front on the floor, facing the platform where a large sepia photo was displayed of Sadhguru seated in a chair. Our teacher led us into intense sadhana to prepare us for initiation into the shakti *chalana* kriya (action)—a series of powerful breathing techniques designed by Sadhguru to purify the main nadis and encourage the flow of shakti into the sushumna. Together we practiced our preparatory asanas followed by the Shambhavi Mahamudra. After a delicious vegetarian breakfast, we returned to the Mahima hall for one hour of preparatory yogic breathing pranayama kriya.

On the night before, I had pulled some muscles in my right shoulder dragging my luggage. Handicapped, I found it almost impossible to practice this specific kriya. I had to stop many times. From time to time, I would open my eyes to peek at the clock and wonder when we would stop the kriya. My mind counted the seconds. My shoulder, wrist, and fingers were cramping and getting numb.

I refused to give up or let my body and mind dictate my actions. When

I opened my eyes, I saw in a few rows ahead of me a tall brunette named Blossom swirling her body in rhythmic circles. I wondered why the teacher or one of the assistant volunteers did not correct her for being disturbing. For a moment Blossom's motion distracted me, but I knew better than to let my mind run the show. I let it go resolving to focus inward and connect with her later.

During lunchtime, as Divine synchronicity intended, the only seat available in the dining room was opposite Blossom. She and I bonded. I joked, "Hey, Blossom, you can't possibly be sore or in pain by the way you're swirling your way to the Divine, like a spinning top." We laughed.

Blossom said humbly with a smile, "I can't control these spontaneous movements."

"When did this phenomenon start for you, Blossom?"

"Not long ago, when Sadhguru entered my life."

"We are so incredibly blessed to have Sadhguru in our lives! Ah, the energy in the Mahima hall and the yogic practices is phenomenal. I can feel Sadhguru's presence as if he is inside of my being, breathing new life energy into my being. Now my heart has become his shrine," I said exuberantly.

Blossom nodded her head smiling. "I feel so grateful too, Vivi!"

We paused for a moment with tears of joy in our eyes, then continued eating in silence for a while.

～

IN THE AFTERNOON, WE RETURNED to the meditation hall for more intense preparatory sadhana. I walked over to Blossom and Suryakanti who sat on the floor. I said, "Guess what we're going to do now?" Both looked puzzled. I whispered, "Another hour of this preparatory yogic breathing kriya!" Their expressions made me laugh.

A minute later the teacher announced, "What are we going to do now? More of this yogic breathing kriya!"

I burst out laughing. Blossom and Suryakanti giggled. Both gave me a look that said, "How did you know?"

By now, my resistance had long evaporated in mirth. I decided to go for it, trusting Sadhguru and the yogic process. By his grace, I transcended the pain. After another hour of this preparatory kriya, we practiced another Shambhavi Mahamudra together.

~

AT 5:00 THE NEXT MORNING, after a sleep of only six hours, I sprang out of bed. As I walked to the Mahima hall, I noticed how light I felt. After the Guru Pooja, our regular sadhana, and breakfast, most of us hiked in the forest under a warming sun that rose after several days of heavy rain. As Blossom and I walked together, I admired the thawing frozen grass. The light sparkled on it the way Divine love shone in my heart. It reminded my being that when we abandon ourselves to our Creator, our mind and personality melt away and our ultimate nature glitters. A blissful, buoyant, and exuberant feeling engulfed my being. Every cell of my body temple was rested, alive, and dancing with joy.

We reached the border of a cliff. A dozen of us stood there admiring the scenery and talking. Our guide said, "This is where Sadhguru learned how to fly a helicopter. You should have seen him hovering it on top of the cliff at three in the morning—after twenty hours of intense work."

I exclaimed, "Oh, I want Sadhguru's energy!"

As we walked back, for a moment I imagined all the things I could do if I did not have this exhausting and debilitating fatigue and needed only four hours of sleep or less like Sadhguru. I admired him for wanting to learn how to fly a helicopter at his age. Why limit oneself? On our path, I saw a swing attached to a tree and jumped on. Blossom pushed me, and as my body swayed in the air and a sense of freedom swept through my being, I exclaimed, "I can't remember the last time I felt so alive and rested! Yippee!" Then it was her turn. She looked like a diamond in the sunlight.

~

THAT GLORIOUS DAY, DECEMBER 17, 2011, marked another miracle in my life. Overnight, the exhausting adrenal fatigue that had plagued my being for the past four years disappeared. I did not even recognize the gift of my renewed power until days later when I returned home.

Our physical body has certain demands necessary for its survival and well-being. However, we hold other beliefs consciously or unconsciously that often act as barriers to these innate needs. Because of our lack of awareness, we rarely challenge these assumptions, yet they often bring us misery and damage different aspects of our lives.

Before my journey with breast cancer, I had believed that my body needed eight hours of sleep to function properly. Unless an individual is recuperating from a major illness, infectious disease, or injury, this isn't really needed. Breaking from that belief freed my being in many ways. Another limiting mindset is refusing to change one's eating habits. Many people think animal flesh is their most important source of protein, or they think being a vegetarian or vegan requires a certain body type. In my experience of removing animal products from my diet, what mattered most was releasing the identification with the physical body and mind.

When we free ourselves from one limitation or barrier, over time we can free ourselves from all of them, opening the secret gate to our boundless power and allowing our divinity to emerge. I find this process both extremely empowering and liberating.

～

BACK AT THE MAHIMA HALL, time had arrived for our initiation into shakti chalana kriya. Everybody was so relieved, happy, and ready! From the start a colossal wave of shakti traveled up my spine. My abdomen began to move rhythmically. I moaned and cried. I was touched by the Divine in the most profound way. Kundalini ascended just as Sadhguru said it would. Though Sadhguru was not with us physically, I could feel his shakti *diksha*, a yogic initiation in which the satguru transmits shaktipat to the seekers.

Energetic transmission of shakti can be initiated in many ways—by thought, gaze, chanting mantras, drumming, or other sounds. In this awakening process, the aspirant's dormant kundalini awakens or ascends along the spine by piercing through different chakras depending on the individual's receptivity, karma, guru's grace, or other factors. This mystical transmission from the satguru can leave you intoxicated with bliss for days. Depending on your receptivity, and your love and trust for your guru, simply touching his or her feet, clothes, chair, or even a hug is enough to receive shaktipat. Just think of being plugged into a powerhouse. You get electrified by the Divine loving current.

We have 114 chakras in our body, but Sadhguru says only 108 are significant to our journey of self-realization. Though chakras and nadis are invisible to the naked eye, they have tremendous influence over the physical body. As of now, no scientific instruments can detect the subtle body and the mystical process of kundalini awakening.

Sadhguru explains the first three chakras. "If your energies are dominant in muladhara, then food and sleep will be the most dominant factors in your life."[*1]

"The second chakra is swadhisthana. If your energies are dominant in swadhisthana, pleasures will be most dominant in your life—you seek pleasures, you enjoy the physical reality in so many ways. If your energies are dominant in manipuraka, you are a doer; you can do many things in the world. If your energies are dominant in anahata, you are a very creative person."[*2]

These three chakras deal mainly with survival and existence. The anahata chakra marks a transition between the lower energy wheels, or survival instincts, and the higher ones, which are natural impulses for God-realization and liberation. Sadhguru says,

> *"The Anahata literally means the 'un-struck.' If you want to make any sound, you have to strike two objects together. The un-struck sound is called 'Anahata.' Anahata is located in the heart area and is like a transition between your lower chakras and your higher chakras, between survival instincts and the longing to liberate yourself. The lower three chakras are mainly concerned with your physical existence. Anahata is a combination; it is a meeting place for both the survival and the enlightenment chakras."[*3]*

★ © Sadhguru

"The next chakra is the 'Vishuddhi,' which literally means 'filter.' Vishuddhi is located in the area of your throat. If your energies move into Vishuddhi, you become a very powerful human being, but this power is not just political or administrative. A person can be powerful in many ways. A person can become so powerful that if he just sits in one place, things will happen for him. He can manifest life beyond the limitations of time and space."[4]

When kundalini reaches the Ajna located in between the eyebrows, Sadhguru says, "If your energies move into the 'Agna' chakra, located between your eyebrows, you are intellectually enlightened. You have attained to a new balance and peace within you. The outside no longer disturbs you, but you are still experientially not liberated."[5]

These six chakras produce many different qualities in our lives. This ascension of the serpent Goddess piercing through these six chakras along the sushumna in the spine are more like benchmarks. They indicate where we have reached in our path. The seventh and highest one from these most well-known chakras is the *Sahasrara* (one-thousand-petal lotus), located above our head. It is only when shakti reaches her final ascension to Shiva into the Sahasrara that we burst with ecstasy, in samadhi.

~

THE FOLLOWING DAY WE RETURNED to the Mahima hall for our second initiations, this time for the *shoonya* meditation. Several of us trembled and experienced uncontrollable and unusual yogic breathing patterns of different intensities. I could feel Sadhguru's presence inside my being. I held tight to my seat. Shakti almost knocked me off my chair several times. My body temple entered into intense spasms. I could not stop or control the involuntarily vibrating, shaking, jolting, quivering, and twitching as if I was plugged into a mega-powerhouse of Divine light. I moaned and wailed at the top of my lungs. Every cell in my body experienced the splendor of our Creator. In less than thirty seconds, the entire hall exploded in high vibrations and echoed sounds of crying, wailing, and moaning.

* © Sadhguru

The ancient ascended masters and modern satgurus called these natural phenomena "spontaneous kriyas." Here the action is transforming and mastering this primordial cosmic energy into a union with the Divine Source. Just as a coconut contains the potential for a palm tree to grow under the right conditions, ascending kundalini contains all forms of yoga best suited for each one of us, depending on our evolution, karmic structure, and grace. These yogic kriyas always take place spontaneously, involuntarily, and naturally.

Swami Muktananda, a world-renowned Siddha master who shed his physical body on October 2, 1982, said, "After shaktipat, one may experience involuntary body movements, such as the shaking and movements of the arms and legs. The head may even begin to rotate violently. One automatically performs various yogic asanas, mudras, bandhas, and different kinds of pranayama. All these physical movements, called kriyas, are spontaneous movement of the kundalini through the body in order to bring about purification. Kundalini is all knowing. She knows what is suited to us."[6]

One may perceive inner sounds, divine smells and tastes, or have visions of different lights, saints, other beings of light, and other dimensions. One may even spontaneously speak in a foreign or ancient tongue, recite mantras, or hiss like a snake, chirp like a bird, or make other unusual sounds. Strong feelings of devotion may arise, or one may reach the capacity to detach from activities.

One of the objectives of awakening kundalini is to attain samadhi, yet still remain in the world and function in daily activities. Many talents may also be discovered. One seeker may feel compelled to compose music, write poetry, or chant the name of the Divine. Other individuals may achieve a state of pure knowingness. Past karma and impressions may also emerge and be released when shakti is awakened. It is one of the main reasons why some individuals experience negative feelings, turbulent grieving and mourning, or even laugh hysterically for no reason. When all life accumulations are peeled away, our ultimate true nature is revealed.

Sadhguru says, "To move from Muladhara to Agna, from the lowest of these seven chakras to the second highest, there are many procedures, methods and processes through which one can raise one's energies. But from Agna to Sahasrar, the sixth chakra to the highest chakra, there is no path. You can only leap."*7

To take this last leap, seekers need to trust their satguru completely and surrender to the Divine. True surrender is the abandonment of oneself, of one's personality, of likes and dislikes to our Creator. Surrender is not submission. It is the grand empowerment of our own inner master by dropping the mind and the ego with all its resistances and accumulations.

When you awake as a buddha (awakened one), you experience and see the whole world like a newborn. Kundalini ascension is the ultimate and greatest treasure of life!

---

* © Sadhguru

Thirty-Nine

MIRACLE OR NOT?

WITH SESSIONS COMPLETED, I LANDED back at San Francisco's new eco-friendly green terminal, which even provides a yoga room. Nathaniel was running late from a business meeting. While waiting for him, I had a deep-tissue neck and shoulder massage at the Express Spa. I could feel the big knots releasing one by one while I contemplated my blessings with Sadhguru and my wondrous journey at the Isha Institute of Inner Sciences. These were some of the most precious days of my life.

Back at home the following morning I woke up at 5:30, full of energy. Nathaniel was stunned. "How could this happen, baby? I'm so impressed!" After a moment he said, "It won't last."

"It is such a great blessing and grace from Sadhguru. I really don't understand it either, my love. It is so hard to believe, I know." I paused for a few moments of reflection. My heart burst with Divine love and gratitude.

"Baby, I love so much getting up and doing my sadhana at dawn when all the kitties are still asleep. It is so tranquil. What a gift!" I felt overwhelmed with tears of gratitude for my beloved Sadhguru. I thought, *Ah! A mindset that always doubts can end up causing trouble, pain, and suffering.*

Several days later it hit me—some kind of miracle must have occurred. The adrenal fatigue was gone. I threw away the hydrocortisone pills. What caused the transformation? The grace of the Divine, the Adiyogi Shiva, Sadhguru, myself? The yogic breathing exercises? Sadhguru's shaktipat? Kundalini ascension? All of the above? Sadhguru says these are only beneficial side effects. The real thing is incomprehensible and unimaginably beautiful. I realized that miracles are daily occurrences, especially when we transcend the limitations of the physical and touch the world of spirit. After all, that is what we are—a spirit in a fleshy garment having a human journey. Just breathing is a miracle!

By deepening and sharpening our sense of perception, we can go beyond the boundaries of the physical into the subtle realm, being one with all of existence. That is yoga. In my experience, the third eye is the gateway to the world of spirit, and of the beyond.

Sadhguru says the idea of pursuing Shiva, which is associated with the third eye, the formless, and the limitless, is to touch the dimension beyond the physical. Unfortunately, most people limit themselves to the five senses to determine the nature of their perceptions. We have a choice. We can live with an ever-expanding consciousness or as a slave to our physical senses and conditioning. Based on what I was experiencing, I knew I had made that profound interconnection with Shiva, "that which that is not."

~

THE DIVINE POWER OF KUNDALINI awakening and rising is a phenomenal and rare spiritual and mystical happening, an immense blessing. It cannot be controlled or coerced. Besides practicing the right ancient yogic techniques, kundalini awakening and ascension are dependent on many other transpersonal factors, such as karma, the grace of the Divine and one's satguru, and our own self-effort to persevere with daily intense sadhana. This Divine energy and grace are always accessible to those who are willing, open, and receptive.

In Dr. Lee Sannella's book *The Kundalini Experience,* he explains how kundalini awakening is a cross-cultural phenomenon. He says, "There is a whole range of phenomena in the process of psycho-spiritual transformation that are constant and universal, transcending personal and cultural differences."[1]

Swami Vivekananda said, "The rousing of the kundalini is the one and only way to the attaining of divine wisdom, super-conscious perception, and realization of the Spirit."[2]

~

IN JANUARY 2012, LESS THAN one month after my program at III, Nathaniel and I attended the monthly satsang in our local area where we practiced with a group of Isha meditators. During a meditation process led by Sadhguru from a video, I entered into an explosive and very powerful trance of spontaneous kriya. Suddenly, I saw Sadhguru in my third eye, then Shiva melted into the vision. I called, "Shiva! Shiva! Shiva!" I felt lifted up as my hands, legs, and head shook involuntarily, even violently, while chanting. My eyes rolled toward heaven, and I could not keep them open.

From moment to moment, I wailed and moaned and fell to the ground with involuntary movements. At other times, unusual pranayamas and *bhandas* locked and tensed some of my key muscle areas. My jaw clapped. Toward the end of these blessed spontaneous kriyas, my body swirled in big circles until I collapsed on the floor shaking and trembling.

It felt as if I was entering into some kind of intense samadhi when an Isha volunteer asked me to open my eyes and helped me get up. I slowly sat up, but even with my eyes open I still trembled and vibrated, feeling peaceful and very light. Tons had been lifted from my karmic structure. Tears of gratitude washed over my cheeks. My dear friend Lotus, who witnessed this mystical episode, told us over brunch that I radiated like the sun. Sadhguru says, "Yoga is the science of getting the plug properly in so that there is an uninterrupted source of power. Once you are connected to this uninterrupted source of power, naturally you will proceed towards the goal of what life is longing for."*[3]

Many years prior, I had painted *Yoga Blossom*, a large canvas richly textured with over five hundred "AUM" signs within a goddess's figure. It took me more than one month to complete. This image symbolizes exactly the powerful spiritual and metaphysical process I was going though at this point in my life, the ascension of kundalini toward the one-thousand-petal lotus by the grace of Maha Shakti. Another one of my artworks, *Divine Blossom,* expresses the divine union in samadhi. No words can ever express to the Adiyogi/Adiguru and Sadhguru my infinite gratitude and love. I bow down.

* © Sadhguru

~

SPELLBOUND AND HUMBLED BY THE unfolding events in my life with Sadhguru, blessed beyond words, I wanted to give back. The following April, the opportunity to volunteer rose for a long weekend in Milpitas, California, for a Shambhavi Mahamudra initiation led by one of the Isha teachers.

On that Saturday night, a large migraine struck my being and lasted until the end of the program. I could not understand why. These mysterious migraines persisted on and off through the entire month, with some lasting over forty-eight hours. This situation did not stop me from practicing my daily sadhana. I refused to let them dominate my life.

Sadhguru was scheduled to be in Houston to teach the entire Inner Engineering program with the Shambhavi Mahamudra initiation in May. I insisted that Nathaniel and I take it again even though we had done the program online and had been initiated by Sadhguru the previous October. So much had happened over the six months since we saw him, and my longing had intensified to a raging flame. I sensed I would explode again just being in his presence.

The morning of our departure I told Nathaniel over breakfast, "Watch. My migraines will go away as soon as we sit with Sadhguru."

Despite knowing better than to hold any expectations, I felt this intuitively.

This time Nathaniel and I arranged to bring a few dear friends with us: Nino, Leilani, and my dear friend Lily, who was afraid of getting caught up in an "ism." I was not surprised. From the first day I had met Lily in a yoga class, I could see her frustration and her painful longing for the Divine.

~

AT THE GRAND HALL AT the Houston Convention Center we participants sat cross-legged with our eyes closed listening to the sound of Isha's music when Sadhguru walked in uttering a sound almost like calling Shiva. Shakti rose up in my spine. I went into spontaneous kriya, trembling and shaking. I knew I could never lose this precious and most significant connection with this magnificent being of light. It was infinite and eternal. My longing intensified to a throbbing blaze as if I had waited hundreds of lifetimes for his coming. New dimensions had opened that I never imagined possible.

My natural spontaneous response only reaffirmed my devotion to Sadhguru. He walked onstage, closed his eyes, and bowed to us in namaskaram for a few minutes. One thousand participants stood in reverence. He sat on his chair and closed his eyes. My whole body temple quivered as I chanted, "Shiva, Shiva, Shiva" while engaging in various spontaneous and involuntary pranayama kriya. I was wonderstruck again by his majestic presence.

In those days, Nathaniel could not understand the mystical power of the Divine feminine energy of Shakti, the grace of Sadhguru, and the phenomenon of spontaneous kriya occurring within an individual when kundalini is awakened and ascending. It is very difficult for people to comprehend these mystical occurrences until they learn more about the yogic tradition, or experience them themselves.

Nathaniel pulled at my being and tried to shut me down by saying with a low voice, "Shhhh! Quiet down! Stop! You will intimidate and scare newcomers who do not know what is happening."

I understood but could not control the spontaneous kriya phenomena. I knew some individuals may hold judgments, false conclusions, or views against such existential phenomena and my being.

"I can't help it. Leave me alone," I whispered with my eyes closed.

I could not help being open to Sadhguru's energy. When shakti explodes within, purifying what needs to be purified, no one can stop it. That is the will and grace of God.

Nathaniel kept saying, "Vivi, open your eyes!"

I did, but not much changed. Every cell in my body detonated with shakti.

I whispered back, "Shhhh! Let it be. Go sit somewhere else, please."

~

DURING OUR FIRST BREAK, I asked Nathaniel, "Baby, please focus on what is happening inside of yourself instead of what is happening with my being. This is the perfect opportunity for you and others to learn how to focus your attention and awareness inward. You may be able to observe your mind reacting judgmentally, perhaps even reaching wrong conclusions about what is happening in the hall." He looked at me in silence, listening.

"Sweetheart if I am disturbing anyone, Sadhguru will have one of the volunteers ask me to leave," I said. "Any moment he may make some wise comments on the subject. Please sit far away for the next session. It will be best for both of us!"

Later during a break, one of the new participants who sat near us told me how moved he was to witness these spiritual phenomena happening to my being. He exclaimed with amazement, "You responded to Sadhguru in such a profound way. How very beautiful!" This gentleman said at first he'd felt envious, but he turned it around and became very happy for me.

Because this gentleman's sharing touched my being, I asked him to speak with Nathaniel. He did. After their conversation, Nathaniel started to see the situation with a different perspective and sat on the opposite side of the hall during the initiation. When Nathaniel returned to sit next to me during other sessions, he did not disturb my being. Thereafter this sweet man always sat behind or beside me, hoping to connect in the same way with Sadhguru. I told him he would definitely get it someday.

When Sadhguru left the stage, he lingered by the front aisle, bowing to us in namaskaram. Many of us gathered closer. A few had the rare opportunity to touch his feet. I greeted him, and then I also touched his feet. Sadhguru looked at my being exclaiming, "You, too!" I smiled, seized his hands, and kissed them with intense devotion.

～

THE FOLLOWING DAY WAS BUDDHA Poornima, the auspicious day of the celebration of the Gautama the Buddha's enlightenment. The biggest moon of the year had been forecast. Sadhguru would initiate us right after the morning games.

After the games Nino, Leilani, and I returned from breakfast and stopped by the Isha tables to browse DVDs. The air conditioning was blasting, and

I was chilled. I selected a few of Sadhguru's DVDs and began to fill out the forms when I told Leilani I wanted to change my clothes before the initiation and would return. I felt I had to go right away.

Leilani told me, "No worry, honey, I'll take care of it for you!"

I jogged off, knowing the program would start within the next twenty minutes. As I reached an intersection in the hallways, Sadhguru walked by in silence with only one attendant behind him. We almost collided face to face. No Hollywood film director could have planned this scene better. I kept silent and bowed to him, slowed my pace, and in reverence walked a few steps behind him.

When we reached the hall door, Sadhguru stepped aside. I walked through to pick up my bag of clothing. On my way back, Sadhguru was still standing there talking to a passerby. I marveled on how the Divine had synchronized this very rare opportunity. I stood there frozen, lost in Divine love and devotion.

I summoned my courage, walked right in front of him, and said, in a faint trembling voice as tears rolled down my checks, "Sadhguru, I want to share with you how extremely grateful I feel."

He stood there, a compassionate warrior in the battlefield of consciousness, formidable and fierce, his aura emanating an intoxicating fragrance of Divine love and bliss. When our gaze met, I could feel myself melt into him. Just a glimpse straight into Sadhguru's fiery eyes was an ecstatic union with the beyond and the truth. I could feel the whole cosmos spin within my being. I was awestruck.

Sadhguru radiated a mighty light; his smile dissolved my being. I tried to speak further, but my voice froze. I felt so lost in Sadhguru's presence, I could barely express myself. His expression and aura glowed. I longed so much to merge in it completely. I seized Sadhguru's left hand and placed it gently on my cheek.

While I held on to his hand like my life, I told him about the many trials of my cancer journey and its debilitating aftermath. I told him about my kundalini ascending, and the miracle that happened to my being by his grace.

He seemed pleased to hear, almost as if he already knew.

I said, "Sadhguru, it's huge!"

He nodded his head yes.

I gently placed my hand on his heart. "I was with H. H. Sri Sri Ravi Shankar, Gurudev, for nine years. Then you came, Sadhguru."

He burst into laughter while nodding yes again. The whole world seemed to be on pause.

"I wrote a beautiful article about my story with you and on the power of yoga. I have also been writing a book, Sadhguru."

He smiled infectiously while asking, "Are you going to talk about all that you shared?" Sadhguru asked this almost in a way that seemed he was suggesting that I should. I nodded my head yes.

He stood there seemingly captivated by the interplay of our spirits. We must have been talking for fifteen minutes. Approximately five feet behind us several of his attendants had gathered and halted dozens of participants from entering the hallway. Alas, the time arrived for him to resume the program. I let go of his hand hesitantly. He gestured for me to enter the hallway. Sadhguru followed behind and asked me jokingly, "Are you going to nail me?"

He took me by surprise. I stopped and turned toward him. "What do you mean by that, Sadhguru?"

He stayed silent, looking at my being with a loving smile. He was being playful. He could have meant: Are you going to capture and reveal my true essence, my divinity?

"I would never do that to you. You have me 100 percent, all the way master!"

What I meant to say was: "Sadhguru, I fell so madly in love with you, my beloved guru, that I can't even think straight, talk intelligently, or hear your jokes when I'm near you. I feel like I have no brain. When I gaze into your eyes, I am lost in your grace. All I see everywhere is your sublime face. My heart is exploding with Divine love. I can't take my longing anymore. When I go to sleep at night and close my eyes, I see your blissful face and chant your name . . . Shiva, Shiva, Shiva. I'm merging with you."

I walked into the grand hall trembling and shaking. I left him behind, but in my heart, I captured this everlasting moment, our hands interlacing, our hearts melted as one forever. I went back to my seat and lay down in savasana with my eyes closed. My whole body temple kept twitching, shaking, quivering from his energy. A wave of bliss engulfed my being.

~

AFTER A CERTAIN SPIRITUAL PROCESS that we did with Sadhguru, we took a twenty-minute silent break. Sadhguru mentioned it was very important to maintain silence, not even make eye contact with anyone until after the initiation. I went to the ladies' room to change clothes and returned to the hall.

On my way back, I saw Sadhguru pacing behind the stage while rubbing his fingers, murmuring audible breathy and whistling sounds like "Shiv . . . Shiv." He seemed to be in another realm of reality. In that moment the grand hall was still almost emptied, already reverberating with powerful shakti. As I passed near him, another wave of shakti swept over my being. I could feel it even more intensively. Every cell in my body vibrated with an ethereal sensation.

I could not hold back. I had to lie down with my eyes closed. I started shaking, quivering again while chanting, hissing the name of "Shiva." Sadhguru had not even officially started to initiate us by transmitting shaktipat, the transmission of Divine consciousness. I was already experiencing spontaneous kriya purifying my subtle body and every particle of my being.

When the time arrived for the Shambhavi Mahamudra initiation, I sensed this time I would explode again in a fury as I had at that very first satsang. When I heard Sadhguru utter a few words into the microphone, I slowly sat up.

"You're sitting only with me. It's only you and me." All the other participants had already sat up, gazing at him silently. "If you hear any sounds, just pretend it's the air conditioner!"

Sadhguru taught us how to do the last part of the Shambhavi Mahamudra yogic technique. We breathed while he clapped with his hands transmitting shaktipat. Within seconds many participants burst into tears and made other sounds. From his first clap, I entered into a trancelike state, shaking violently while remaining transfixed in all kinds of spontaneous pranayamas and kriyas. My body started to swirl clockwise in small circles as I began to speak in tongues. It sounded like an ancient language. I could not stop jabbering.

My circles became bigger and bigger as I uttered several complex phrases completed with the word "Shiva," as if I was given a discourse for Shiva, or on the principle of Shiva (pure consciousness), or speaking to Shiva, the Adiyogi himself. Was I reenacting one of my past lifetimes, or channeling Shiva? Talking to Shiva directly? Was I reciting some Shiva *stotram*? I don't know.

Stotra or stotram in Sanskrit is a hymn that can take the form of a prayer, invocation, description, or even a conversation with the Divine. These hymns praise many aspects of the Divine. What I know for sure is that I became fully aware of this profound state interconnecting my being as one with Sadhguru, the Adiyogi/Adiguru, and our Creator and the whole of creation.

The drums began to beat louder and louder. My body temple kept swirling clockwise until I collapsed to the ground, shaking. After a while, Sadhguru said softly, "Take your own time." I must have stayed on the floor for another ten minutes shaking while everyone else stood and bowed to Sadhguru.

I had never felt any attachment or placed much importance on these kinds of spiritual experiences. By then, I knew it was the normal course of purification of kundalini rising up the spine and that eventually it would die out and be replaced with bliss, ecstasy, and oneness, our ultimate nature. An outpouring of gratitude and love overflowed from my being for Sadhguru, the Adiyogi, all the volunteers, and everyone else who helped manifest these cherished moments together. The Sounds of Isha band started to play an upbeat song. Sadhguru stood onstage bowing to us. He glowed like the full moon, radiating his grace upon all of us.

I slowly pulled myself off the ground and sat up. Still shaken and touched by the Divine Mother, my heart burst in Divine love. For a moment, Sadhguru glanced at my being making sure I was fine. I bowed down and prostrated myself on the floor while weeping. Then I lay back down in savasana while most participants and volunteers danced. Euphoria erupted in the grand hall.

Suddenly, I sprang up, looked around at the celebration, and joyously trotted to where several of our friends were dancing. I hugged many as we jumped up and down dancing and laughing. Toward the end of the song, I grabbed Lily's hands, and we whirled around. At the end, we embraced.

~

ON OUR FLIGHT BACK TO California, it hit me. "My migraines are gone!" I was bathing in Sadhguru's grace, overwhelmed with tears of gratitude and love for having such a rare, precious, beloved master. I gazed out through the tiny window at the vast, blue sky marveling at how every moment of our lives is a priceless gift. Synchronicity of the invisible hand is always orchestrated for each one of us when we are in tune, open, receptive, and aware.

Forty

OF THE BEYOND

TWO WEEKS LATER, NATHANIEL AND I flew back to the Isha Institute of Inner Sciences for the Isha Bhava Spandana program (BSP). I had heard many poignant testimonials in the praise of the BSP held by Sadhguru, but not in my wildest imagination could I have foreseen the grandeur, intensity, and beauty of this program. I felt intuitively it would be an extremely challenging and life-transforming experience.

While flying to Tennessee, I reflected on how hard my teacher-training program had been at the Art of Living Foundation at Gurudev's yoga center in India. I knew all my previous years with Gurunath and Gurudev had prepared my being to experience such an intense BSP in its full depth and dimension. I told myself whatever was going to happen, let it happen. I had left home with no expectations, just a burning longing to merge, an emptied mind, and an open and receptive heart. That is all it takes to merge with the Divine.

The opportunity to experience levels of consciousness beyond the limitations of the body and mind is accessible to everyone. When we reached the grounds of the Isha yoga center, I felt as if I had been an acrobat most of my life, walking far too long on the rim of that mystical wall. I was experiencing life while dipping my little toe into another dimension, then pulling it out quickly. I yearned to establish my being in that infinite consciousness. I knew it on the experiential level. I had tasted the Divine union many times but was never able to sustain it. I deeply longed for Shakti to merge with Shiva within. This revelation was quite clear to my being. The pain of longing became unbearable.

Scientists have speculated awhile that time and space is a relative experience. Sadhguru said, "If you can break the limitations of the illusion that you are separate, and begin to experience the oneness of the existence, that is yoga."*[1]

I had not yet been able to establish it permanently. Yet I knew with the trust, reverence, and love I held for Sadhguru, it was just a matter of time.

This was going to be the biggest BSP ever offered in America. Over 550 participants arrived from different parts of the world. Over 250 volunteers who already had taken the program gathered to make this extraordinary event a success for everyone over the course of three very long, intense days. Everything seemed to be blossoming: the sky, the flowers, the trees, the grass, the birds, the butterflies, the people, and myself.

At our first session in the Mahima meditation hall, one could feel the ecstatic aura in the air. We sat in the second row facing Sadhguru. He looked sublime sitting on his chair, his eyes ablaze with great intensity like an owl perched in the night. His long silvery undulating beard and hair adorned his beatific face.

Each time he gazed at my being, my heart exploded with intense waves of pure bliss and Divine love, and I melted and disappeared. Yet there was no fear and no thought of losing myself, because I was experiencing what some may call sajah samadhi in the yogic tradition. "Sajah" means "effortless or natural." It is an exalted state of extremely deep bliss, non-dualistic, pure, and unconditioned in nature. Many yogis and rishis believe sajah samadhi to be the highest and most complete exalted state because it is our true and ultimate Divine nature.

Lose yourself in the magnificence of your true being . . . the invisible hand of Divine love will melt away all your fabricated barriers and leave you intoxicated in boundless ecstasy. When one is touched so profoundly by even one drop of this Divine love nectar, just one whiff of its fragrance leaves you madly intoxicated. That Divine love is like a white jasmine flower blooming for eternity, transcending its own essence.

I had fallen into a meditative state of nothingness as I listened, gazing at Sadhguru. His face dissolved in front of my eyes into visages of what

* © Sadhguru

appeared to be other celestial saints, ascended masters, or avatars. I knew I was not hallucinating, because not only was I in a heightened and exalted state of awareness, but also I had already experienced that mystical state with him in Los Angeles, and at various times with my first beloved guru, Gurunath.

~

DURING OUR FIRST DAY, SADHGURU led us through a few spiritual processes about how to become more sensitive and aware of our sensations. Such a heightened level of awareness is necessary before we can melt into the Divine and go beyond the boundaries of physicality. Within these first few days, we would explore different methods of how to become and stay in a heightened state of awareness and sensitivity.

In our first spiritual process, we partnered with another Isha meditator, someone we did not know. When Sadhguru transmitted shaktipat, some of us uttered roaring sounds, while shaking and trembling. These gargantuan waves of energy put my being into a profound trance. I screamed, cried, and wailed. I was not afraid. I spoke in tongues and called for Shiva. My body shook and contorted, my head swirled back and forth violently. All these involuntary phenomena and mystical occurrences were beyond my control. To protect their integrity, I am not divulging any specifics of these spiritual processes. This way, too, I free you from forming assumptions, judgments, or coming to false conclusions or even expectations about them.

Purification happens at many different levels. In that experience, there is a sense of liberation from within. Such indescribable sensations of being blessed by our Creator are beyond words, time, and space. Being blessed is to realize that we have wings to fly from the jail we have created, if we just take the leap.

These universal principles and laws affect us all. Everyone experiences the Source of existence according to his or her own openness, karmic structure, evolution, satguru, and by the grace of the Divine. If we make ourselves vulnerable to the Source with authentic ancient yoga, then the experiential journey of our being allows us to merge into samadhi, an ecstatic state of oneness.

Yoga is not based on any blind belief system, doctrine, or dogma. It is not a religion. Yoga is the science of experiencing the whole of existence as One. It is the science of inner well-being, of self-realization. Any genuine and persistent seeker can experience the Source from within and know its ultimate nature of bliss. We may not have the same abilities and capabilities on the physical level, but we have the same possibility on the energetic level to experience it.

~

AT THE END OF OUR first night session, I greeted Sadhguru by the dais. I bowed down to him, took his hand, and kissed it as I wept an ocean of tears. I wanted to hold him in my arms, but I held back. He blinked his eyes several times gazing at mine, acknowledging my expression of devotion and love. In that moment, I did not exist anymore. I was dissolved in nothingness, oneness, where boundaries and separation don't exist.

There was not one instant without a deep sense of interconnection among all of us participants, volunteers, and Sadhguru. Five hundred and fifty of us participants breathed, ate, slept, played, danced, cried, screamed, mourned, wailed, grieved, shared, laughed, and meditated together as One being. Each participant had been assigned a number for a cot, and a linen bag, to sleep on the floor in the Mahima hall for the entire stay. Men were going to sleep on the right side, and women on the left. I had brought my ear plugs knowing the cacophony of the night would keep me awake.

Lily attended the program with us. When the time came to retreat to my cot, all lights in the hall were already turned off. I searched for my bed with a tiny flashlight. Lily and I ran into each other in our nightgowns. Among all the seven hundred numbered beds lying on the ground in the grand Mahima, ours were placed next to each other. We felt blessed by the synchronicity.

For the rest of our time there, Lily and I always seemed to be the last ones to go to bed. We chatted for a few minutes and burst into laughter. We were always exhausted, yet exhilarated. Everyone seemed to be snoring by the time I placed my head on my pillow.

That first night, Lily fell asleep first. I stared at the roof of our "spacecraft," as we called it. Sadhguru's energy and that of the Mahima kept my being in a meditative trance for quite some time; my whole body tingled, and I could not stop whispering, "Shiva, Shiva, Shiva."

~

EVERY MORNING AROUND FIVE O'CLOCK, the gongs woke us as the sun began to peek through the tall windows. Most of the participants sprang up and got ready for the Guru Pooja. I lingered a bit longer with my eyes closed, listening to the birds sing, lost in their tunes.

When we chanted the Guru Pooja together, vibrations traveled up my spine, giving me goosebumps. As I chanted, I wept in gratitude and love for God, the Adiyogi Shiva, my guru, all mahavatars, and the ascended masters. After the pooja, we practiced our sadhana together. When the Divine descended upon my being, I trembled with humility and awe. A sense of veneration and adoration overwhelmed my being with overflowing love and compassion for all living beings.

It was unusually hot for May, in the high 90s. After our daily sadhana, we played fun games with Sadhguru in the large green field next to the Mahima hall. The humidity weighed on us, and we sweated. Most of us took a second shower after the games. I made it a spiritual practice to deprive myself of a few comforts so as to push beyond my physical limitations. Even though we had hot water, I ran only cold water for all my showers while singing, "Aum Namah Shivaya Aum."

~

THE FOLLOWING MORNING DURING OUR sadhana with the immense group, I entered into another powerful, explosive trancelike state. A flood of high-voltage energy burst within my being, shattering this false sense of ego. Again, I spoke involuntarily in an ancient language while my body shook. I conversed with Shiva, often calling his name.

This time the spontaneous kriya made it difficult to complete my yogic practices. An enormous fury ignited and exploded within my body temple.

By the time I left the Mahima hall, I was as light as a dry leaf swirling in the wind. Sadhguru once said,

> *"The path is actually very simple, but because of your personality it has become extremely complicated. If you allow the Master's Grace, then the path is very simple, as the path is the destination. If you simply sit here now, your whole being will pulsate with the existence. But now your energies are moving only to the extent that is convenient for your ego; a little more energy and the ego will burst. If kundalini begins to rise, everything will be shattered and nothing will be left. You will be just a force merging with everything around you. If kundalini begins to move, it settles everything. It is like a flood; your centuries-old world is wiped away in only a few hours of fury. It wipes away your petty creations and leaves you as the Creator intended you to be."[*2]*

The Divine force unleashed a furious flood of energy within my being. I could not stop it. During this trancelike state, I started to refer to Shiva as "Nana Shiva," although I did not know what it meant.

During our program, Sadhguru said, "What is the big deal about people calling Shiva? They are just saying, 'I'm nothing!' Just focus inward."

In reality, these spontaneous kriyas are not of great importance. They are not the final destination of our spiritual journey, just indicative of some milestones. Spontaneous kriyas purify us at all levels. I knew how imperative it was not to expect them. Expectations can be traps. However, some of these spiritual phenomena do unleash profound, sacred, and mystical pathways to the self-realization that leads to liberation. In these moments, I always feel like an emptied vessel possessed by God, an instrument overflowing with the Divine's love.

[*] © Sadhguru

~

TUCKED IN A HEAVENLY COVE beneath a canopy of tall blossoming trees was a courtyard. It became the entire BSP program group's social
meeting place, and we ate our meals outdoors.

Every day the volunteers placed tiny bouquets of delicate green, pink,
and white flowers on our large rectangular tables. At night, the courtyard
transformed itself into a moonlight garden filled with white garland lights.
At every meal, dozens of volunteers lined up behind the tables and served
us delicious vegetarian dishes. Looking into their eyes, I saw Sadhguru's
eyes. I saw him everywhere, in everyone.

One night, while seated at a table among other participants, I could
not eat. Sadhguru's shakti energy reverberated within my being. A profound silence overwhelmed my being. I was mesmerized by the ephemeral beauty, the sacred and miraculous existence of a little green flower. In
every petal I saw Sadhguru's radiant face. The flower, myself, and Sadhguru had become one.

Over lunch on the following day, I asked a lovely Indian couple if they
knew the meaning of "Nana" in the languages spoken in their country. Perhaps this enigma could reveal a glimpse of my past lifetimes since I had called
out "Nana Shiva." They explained "nana" in Hindi means "maternal grandfa-
ther." It did not divulge anything concrete, but I was intrigued by its mystery.

My new friends asked me to share some of my experiences. So I told
them about my first vision during one of the most powerful, mystical,
and intense processes we'd had with Sadhguru. I had felt as if I was dying
while a gentle and sweet wave of energy embraced my entire being with
intense bliss. Shakti rippled from my toes and trickled to the top of my
head tickling every cell. I drifted into a higher, exalted state of consciousness, into a dimension beyond physical boundaries. Then I merged into a
boundless diffused, faint, and infinite light. The sense of "I-ness" did not
exist anymore, yet I was the light, breathing in every particle of existence,
the cosmos, and the beyond. I was breathing pure light. The illusion of
being trapped in my body dissolved. All physical boundaries vanished. My
consciousness expanded to the beyond. I was pure consciousness.

I became the universe, pulsating. Or perhaps it was the creation throb-bing within my being. Everything was blurry, yet I was everywhere. No thoughts appeared, only a sublime sense of timeless serenity, bliss, and tran-quil ecstasy.

In that moment, I transcended beyond the duality of the physical realm into a non-dualistic state. What we call in the yogic tradition nirvikalpa samadhi—in perfect union with the Divine, realizing that all there is, is God. In the yoga sutras, the great Maharishi Patanjali explained in depth the different states of samadhi in the last limb of the eightfold path of yoga.

Georg Feuerstein says, "The Sanskrit word nirvikalpa can mean either 'formless' or 'beyond conception.' When the movements of the mind are completely pacified in the ecstatic state, the ultimate Reality flashes forth."[3]

In that heightened state, all at once in my third eye I witnessed a sadhu or a satguru sitting in padma asana wearing a white loincloth. He sat there less than a few feet away, gazing straight at my consciousness with great intensity. That vision brought forth an avalanche of wailing while my body trembled. I grieved very loudly for over fifteen minutes. Inner knowing surged to my awareness of Sadhguru or Mahatma Gandhi in one of my previous lifetimes. I could not tell for sure since the vision was blurred. Was Sadhguru my previous master at one point? Or was I related to Mahatma Gandhi somehow? I wondered. I slowly regained my physical sensations from that state of oneness.

I shared with my friends at the table, "What I can say now with clarity is that reincarnation does occur even though I used to have a lot of doubts for decades. But I know based on my own mystical experiences, especially my recent past lifetimes. I know that my previous lifetime happened in India, and I had been, even then, in pursuit of truth and liberation. I have been on this path for a very long time."

I paused and remained silent for a long moment looking at my colorful meal. My friends sat on the edge of their seats eager to hear more. "Go on, Vivi!" they gasped.

I told them my second vision took place at home in our sanctum sev-eral months before our BSP. I had witnessed myself as pure consciousness sitting by the feet of the very beautiful Anandamayi Ma, embracing and worshipping her. Within that instant, a shaktipat pierced through my ana-hata, the heart chakra. An oceanic wave of tickling Divine love and bliss deluged my being as tears rolled down my cheeks.

Anandamayi Ma is very well known as Sri Ma Anandamayi, the twentieth-century great holy saint. Right after that meditation, I hugged Nathaniel. In his arms, I shed a river of tears of gratitude and told him, "I feel on the continuum of time and space that I have been Sri Anandamayi Ma's devotee. She lives in my heart."

At the table with my friends, we all then fell into a profound silence again. It was time to go back to session. We gazed at each other for a while feeling grateful. Then I strolled back to the Mahima hall.

~

LATER THAT AFTERNOON AS WE all sat on the floor in the Mahima hall at the beginning of a half-hour break, the Sounds of Isha started to play an upbeat chant. A fierce, uncontrollable fury got hold of my being. I stood in front of Sadhguru's dais in that wide, emptied space, moving to the rhythm of Creation in front of all the participants. The heady chant induced my being into a deep meditative tantric dance. I entered in rapture into the wildest trance of my life, as if Shiva himself danced through my whole being. I did not exist, lost in a beatifying and exalted daze, as I became possessed by a prodigious force. I faced the audience with my eyes closed and began to dance faster and faster without any shame or inhibition, unleashing an inferno within.

I moved my arms and legs in graceful whirls. They spun faster and faster in circles to the rhythm of the cosmic dance, moving, destroying, and recycling the energy. I remained there, alone, with my eyes closed, lost in madness, inebriated in ecstasy.

I moved into a dance with the expanding cosmos within every particle of creation. I tumbled everywhere around the area like a drunkard, losing
: and collapsing several times. With the fury of an erupting vol-
led my arms and legs faster, expanding in all directions. I became
and the dance became my being.

The fierceness of shakti traversed my spine. Perspiration flew off my hair and face and trickled down from my nostrils. I was drenched with sweat as the sweet nectar of drunken, mad love infused every cell of my being.

To the outside world, I must have looked completely insane as I collapsed further into the realm of the beyond, alternately falling into samadhi, then pulling back to this rhythm of the existential dance. For a few moments, I screamed at the top of my lungs so forcefully that I was knocked backward to the ground as my body shook in convulsions. The shakti purified my subtle and physical body.

My voice teacher had warned me many times to treat my voice like morning dew. I knew too well that this kind of screaming would give me, at the very least, a nasty case of laryngitis, or even damage my voice forever. I never would have screamed on purpose. This was not a compulsion. My entire being had entered into this profound, exalted trancelike state where the shakti energy took over the spiritual process and the mystic experience. I could not control it.

Again, I continued to rise, tumble, and dance, only to collapse on the ground. This time, the music stopped. It was dead quiet in the hall. Slowly I opened my eyes, not sure any more where I was.

All at once I felt Sadhguru's presence.

I turned my head. He was sitting on his chair watching me. We made eye contact. Someone nearby exclaimed, "Wow, Sadhguru! She passed out many times, but she got back up. Amazing! She never gives up."

Almost breathless, I crawled to my original place in the first row. I settled in.

Sadhguru looked at me with an expression that seemed to say, "Okay, Vivi, you're fine, right?" He began to give us instructions on dancing with awareness and madness. He quoted Krishna from the Bhagavad Gita, referring to his words as this Divine madness of dancing, chanting, and loving as a "cleansing of the universe."

Sadhguru does not often quote ancient scriptures from any religious or spiritual traditions. My jaw dropped. I could not believe his words. Everything he shared had occurred within my dance. I wondered if he knew what occurred during the break. He must have known, since I became like an instrument of the Divine in that self-transcendent, tantric dance.

～

THE SCIENCE OF YOGA IS Sadhguru's very breath, as is mine. One could call this the pathless path of yoga. I say the "pathless path" because in yoga, by our very nature, we are already in union with the whole of existence, but most of us don't realize or experience it as such. We don't go anywhere, yet we are everywhere in union with the Source of existence when awakened. That which we seek, the true nature of existence, has always been within us, alive, boundless, and eternal.

The names of the Divine may have many forms: Shiva, Brahman, Vishnu, Allah, Kuan Yin, Krishna, Rama, Jesus Christ, Holy Spirit, the Father, Gautama the Buddha, Mohammed, the Divine Mother, Yahweh, the absolute, the nameless, and more. In some ways, it does not matter what word we use to define the truth. Regardless of the name, the truth derives and manifests from the same supreme absolute Source.

"All names given to God have the same power. You can reach your destination by taking any name you like," said my beloved saint, Sri Anandamayi Ma.[4]

I have great and profound reverence for all the Source's manifestations. In some ways, it is a tragedy that we feel compelled to call the Source by a name, causing separation, suffering, and pain. Our ignorant nature and limited mind can be huge barriers to merging with the beyond, and they have caused humanity great separation and war.

It is time for us to wake up, go beyond physicality, language barriers, our minds, and our five senses before we destroy Mother Earth and ourselves. This is the emergency of our times.

～

THAT DAY, SADHGURU LED US in what many of us experienced as the most powerful meditation of the program, a five-step spiritual process that lasted several hours. With my eyes closed, I remained so inebriated in my dance trance that I could no longer stand up. I kept falling, while dozens of volunteers circled around my being, preventing me from crashing on others, or on the floor.

Despite their attention, I hit the ground a few times. When someone grabbed my hands and pulled me up, I would continue the mystical dance. From the very beginning, there was a Divine presence looking over us. Because of my immense trust, I abandoned myself completely, allowing myself to drop all inhibitions. The self-preservation within me had dissolved long ago.

By the end of the process, I was once again drenched in sweat, vibrating, and shaking hard on the floor. At this point, my voice had nearly vanished, and what was left was hoarse and rough. I lay there for some time until the hall was almost emptied.

I lingered far behind everybody else, strolling along to the cove. Each time I set foot on the soil, the universe walked with my being. I sensed the cost of losing my voice would be epic, yet a part of my being was unconcerned. I sat between Nathaniel and one of the male participants. I looked into the man's eyes and witnessed the same intense longing, tearing him apart.

I whispered as I gazed into his eyes, "I can see and feel your pain, your longing to merge." Silently we gazed into each other's eyes in silence. I felt emptied yet full at the same time. My individual self did not exist, only the whole of existence. By the end of our mystical embrace, right in front of my husband, he gave me a little innocent kiss on my mouth. Both of us were drunk in ecstasy. We remained silent for the rest of our meal, lost in this Divine eternal love, lost in the infinity.

⁓

AFTER LUNCHTIME, ALL PARTICIPANTS AMBLED to the green field near the pond for a group photo with our beloved guru. I stood near him and murmured, "Sadhguru, I feel I just had brain surgery. I didn't know you were a brain surgeon."

"I'm a brain surgeon only for people who have brains. Not for you!"

I made nothing of his comment and sat for the photo, flying high. Many days later I realized Sadhguru must have meant that most people are too stuck in their intellects, their minds, preventing them from experiencing the Source of existence. I remembered how Sadhguru talked about this subject many times, even joked about brain surgery. It is crucial to drop the logical mind if a seeker wants to experience the beyond. The intellect is a precious gift in our practical lives, but not for the spiritual process. So, not having a brain for the spiritual process is extremely vital! I realized, many days later, this must have been the greatest compliment my satguru could have bestowed upon my being.

~

DURING ONE OF OUR LAST sessions of the BSP, Sadhguru remarked that if he just sat in silence with us for a day, or even several hours, most of the participants would be gone, and very few would stay. He was saying that those who could not experience his energetic presence by connecting with him on a different plane would grow frustrated and leave. I could sit there in profound silence and just soak in his presence for days. What Sadhguru talked about was a very precious lesson I had learned the hard way with Gurunath and Gurudev long ago—the ability to connect spiritually. In that instant, his words elated my being. I knew I had dumped my garbage bin and cleaned up my attic! A ton of my karmic load had evaporated. I knew that I could sit there in profound silence and just soak in his presence for days, unburdened, at ease, and feeling free.

Sitting close to the satguru is one of the most sacred blessings. It is far beyond listening or interacting with the satguru. Sadhguru said we can only fully experience him in silence. Having the opportunity to do our sadhana and meditate in his presence is also another priceless gift because of the energy flowing from his presence. When we listen to the master's words, it is a human tendency to mentally chat about likes and dislikes, to ____ ents, and to reach quick but erroneous conclusions. That is ____ an untrained mind—a mind loaded with conditioning and accumulations. There is only a minute difference between compulsion and awareness: the practice of mindfulness.

Throughout many spiritual processes, I have observed that it appears easier for a free-spirited being to be more in touch with the feminine energy principle of shakti. This energy is creative, loving, healing, and nurturing. It can also be very powerful and fierce. Without a doubt, the grace of the master, my devotion, trust, longing, reverence, gratitude, and a state of abandonment opened up the gate for my being in a very phenomenal way. Without these gifts and my own effort, merging would not be possible, and I would not be able to sustain the flow of energy. My body had become their temple, my heart their shrine.

I am always in a state of wonderment at the Divine presence within my being and at the way my existence is unfolding. This ecstatic union called yoga is the science of all sciences. Inner power is within all of us. Abandoning ourself to the boundlessness of existence is to tap into the depth of our ultimate true nature.

Forty-One

THE BLUE PEARL

I EMBRACE ALL RELIGIONS AND spiritual paths. Love, kindness, and compassion for all living beings is my very breath. Love and compassion are the pulsating heart of all spiritual paths and religions. When an individual feels Divine love within, the rest blossoms like a wild garden; compassion, understanding, reverence, harmony, and respect all occur naturally within.

All religions are our heritage. They belong to all of us. We need to teach our children about other cultures, religions, and spiritual traditions. We only fear what we do not know.

With globalization of our multicultural planet, it is imperative that we go beyond tolerance to understanding and appreciating others' ethnic, spiritual, and religious backgrounds. An intoxicating aura of spirituality, unity, love, and truth emanates from the very core of oneness. This essence is shared by all religions and spiritual traditions and proves that our differences are superficial; our similarities interconnect us by the same Source. There is only one truth, one Creator in many forms.

To have hope for survival on our Mother Earth is to rekindle the feminine principle energy within and around us. The great cosmic Divine Mother is this feminine principle energy shakti permeating the cosmos and called by thousands of names. Allowing the Divine feminine energy to flow transcends gender, sexual orientation, and all other forms of false identifications. On earth this Divine feminine energy tends to be more associated with the female gender. However, any gender can deeply connect with the feminine energy principle within us. We have both masculine and feminine aspects. The limited mind may look at it as a feminist point of view, but this feminine aspect of the Source is accessible to all living creatures regardless of gender. Because of our male-dominated societies, many men have suffered from this illusory separation.

The Divine feminine energy principle is beyond all physical boundaries. The masculine and feminine principles governing the physical existence need to be balanced and merged within us to experience our ultimate nature. That is crucial both for us as individuals and for our species.

Devi is the Sanskrit word for Goddess and synonymous with shakti, the female principle of the Divine. In the yogic spiritual tradition, shakti means sacred force, energy power, or serpent Goddess.

Shakti is also a name given to the female consort of the male deity. Shakti as a Devi is also the Hindu personification of the Divine feminine aspect, sometimes referred to as the Divine Mother. Devi is quintessentially the core form of every Hindu goddess—such as Durga, Lakshmi, Saraswati, Parvati, Kali, and many more. For instance, Shiva's shakti is Parvati.

Shiva is the masculine principle counterpart, "that which that is not," pure consciousness. When these two principles manifest, it reminds us of the bipolar nature of all manifest reality, consciousness, and energy. Together Shiva and Shakti weave an intricate tapestry of this relative world of time and space. According to Vedanta, shakti represents the dynamic aspect of the universe as opposed to the masculine principle, which personifies the un-manifest aspect of reality. It is crucial to understand that shakti also represents this dynamic principle of feminine power energy, the primordial creative force.

In the Yoga tradition, Shakti is prominent in tantra yoga where the kundalini energy, when manifested, is regarded as the serpent Goddess. This kundalini energy is the most significant and natural psycho-spiritual force of our subtle body. On a metaphysical level, this intelligent, energetic force is the microcosmic manifestation of the primordial creative energy of the supreme absolute within us that is either dormant, awakening, ascending, or ascended. Our body is the mirror of the play of the expanding cosmos.

We can observe the same feminine energy aspect in all spiritual and religious traditions, even in the ancient pagan tradition. The full blossoming of the creative power is unleashed in the merging of the feminine and masculine principle within us, the supreme lover. These two principles, Shiva/Shakti, can be observed at work everywhere in the universe and on all levels. Their union creates powerful and phenomenal forces. By merging with this true Divine marriage within us, we realize and experience our ultimate nature, Divinity.

Whether we are in a male or a female body, celebrating the Goddess awakens us to this feminine energetic force within us and manifests it on earth. It is not a philosophy, a cult, or religion. We desperately need this creative feminine energy to harmonize and solve the grave challenges we are facing today.

$$\sim$$

AT OUR RETURN TO THE Mahima hall after our photo shoot, I drifted in a meditative state with my eyes wide open while Sadhguru spoke. I became transfixed on him in a non-mind state, one with him in heightened awareness.

As I gazed, I witnessed a sparkling turquoise-blue light emanating iridescent rays like Venus in the night sky. It was an extremely beautiful blue. This shimmering star remained floating above Sadhguru's head.

I became mesmerized by its radiant ethereal beauty. I lost myself in its sublime essence, not excited or craving for more. I had never seen such otherworldly beauty before, but I knew I was not hallucinating. With the grace of my beloved satguru, this boundlessness, this refined sense of perception and abandonment, allowed my being to witness it in bright daylight with my eyes wide open.

Over the decades, I had heard many great masters talk about the significance of seeing such a "blue pearl" in the third eye, as they call it. I had never heard anything about seeing it with wide-open eyes. After my journey with Gurunath, I never again craved these phenomena. I learned to remain dispassionate.

Swami Muktananda talked about this blue pearl in his marvelous book *Kundalini: The Secret of Life*. He says:

In the center of that effulgence lies a tiny and fascinatingly beautiful light, the Blue Pearl, and when your meditation deepens you begin to see it, sparkling and scintillating. Sometimes it comes out of the eyes and stands in front of you. It moves with the speed of lightning, and it is so subtle that when it passes through the eye, the eye doesn't feel its movement.

The vision of the Blue Pearl is the most significant of all the experiences I have described. Everyone should see this Blue Pearl at least once. The scriptures describe this Blue Pearl as the divine light of Consciousness which dwells within everyone. It is the actual form of the Self, our innermost reality, the form of God which lives within us. Within the Blue Pearl are millions of universes. The Blue Pearl contains the entire cosmos. But your meditation is not completed just by seeing the blue light. It has to become steady. If you have intense longing for God, deep love for your guru, deep faith in Kundalini, there will come a time when you will be able to make the blue pearl stand still in front of you. Within it, you will see the deity you love.[1]

After experiencing the blue pearl, I felt blessed and awed beyond words. In the past few years, I had come to realize that true transformation can only be witnessed by how we love, how compassionate we are, how we hold ourselves in rough times, and how blissful, mindful, and serene we are in every moment of our lives. Like a bamboo in a hurricane, we bend with strength, grace, and dignity without breaking. What is the point of all these otherworldly phenomena and mystical experiences if we can't break free from our limitations and expand?

During the following break, alone and silent, I lay down on the grass by the pond and gazed at the infinity of the blue sky. With my eyes open, I drifted into samadhi, where the illusion of self, mind, and boundaries dissolved in the ether. Was I the blue sky, or was the blue sky me? I could not tell.

~

ON THE THIRD DAY, OUR beloved master assigned us another powerful spiritual process. This time we had the freedom to roam, as long as we
followed specific guidelines.

I meandered along the green field in a state of mindfulness. I inhaled
the beauty of nature, feeling the love of Mother Earth in every step. My
eyesight became as sharp as radar and focused several feet away on a single
clover among hundreds below a small, very slender tree. As I walked closer,
there was an inner knowing this was a four-leaf clover. When I arrived and
picked it up, it was!

I held it for a while admiring it. I noticed how the tree looked like Shiva's staff with its three curved branches pointing toward the blue sky. The
Adiyogi Shiva is often depicted with a staff with three prongs representing
the three gunas—Tama, Raja, and Satva—celebrating his triumph in transcending these universal laws. How auspicious!

Then I went back again to the grass near the pond to gaze at the
vastness of the blue horizon. This time I felt the universal sound of AUM
vibrating in unison within my being, as if I was the sound. I experienced
my being as the pure consciousness sound of Divine love.

The more I gazed at the blue horizon, the more my bodily sensations
disappeared, lost in profound bliss and stillness. The Creator became my
being, no longer the creation. The universe spinning, the sky expanding,
the stars sparkling, the sun radiating, the oceans waving, the rain falling,
the moonlight shining, the wind dancing, the animals grazing, the children
running, and the flowers blossoming were all my being. All physical boundaries melted away. I dissolved in nothingness, emptiness, oneness.

After over an hour lost in this exalted state of samadhi, I heard a vague
and distant call. I lingered as I slowly regained my limited body sensations.
I stood and returned to the building at a snail's pace.

Experiencing and realizing the beyond and the truth is not about
what one gains. Wanting and expecting samadhi to result in personal gain
could become a great obstacle on the spiritual path. I never desired or even
dreamed of such phenomenal spiritual experiences; though experiencing

any form of samadhi will elevate and exalt the seeker to the most profound state of serenity, equanimity, bliss, and ecstasy a human being can possibly ever experience. The energetic light emanating from such being is enough to have a positive effect on all in his or her surroundings.

～

MUCH SPLENDOR MANIFESTED DURING OUR Bhava Spandana. Words will always fail to transmit its beauty and mysticism. Our hearts overflowed with tears of gratitude and love. Toward the end of our program, Sadhguru invited us to share some of our experiences. Again, I was very fortunate to hold the microphone. Words stuck in my throat. "Sadhguru, so much has happened in the past few days. So much needs to be shared. Yet I feel silent."

I started to weep. "I must share with all of you one experience that happened to me this morning. I lay on the grass gazing at the vastness of the blue sky. The more I gazed, the more my consciousness expanded. My sense of self melted. The wind, the trees, the animals, people, the oceans, the sky, Mother Earth, and the universe throbbed within my being, or I was throbbing within them. Which one? I can't tell if I have become them, or them me. All sensations of boundaries and separation disappeared. I don't feel the same.

"Sadhguru, I wish every living being could feel this Divine love, even the tiniest insects. After this experience, during our second break, I meditated on you for over one hour. It was so beautiful. I'm so grateful." Then I fell silent.

～

AT THE END OF OUR BSP program, we all stood and bowed to Sadhguru, exploding in exuberance. We pleaded with him to stay. He sat there by the stairs of the dais facing us, asking us to come closer to him. As we gathered as close as we could, he started to sing. "It was you who called me . . . " Most began to sing along. Afterward, a few participants sang a few songs.

It was clear Shiva had destroyed my voice by then. I wondered how long I would suffer from laryngitis this time, and if I would ever recover my singing voice. I wanted to sing "Aura Divine," which I had composed not long after Sadhguru came into my life. But I could not even sing one note without my voice failing. I had lost my three-octave range. I wrote the song in French, and though the English version does not sound nearly as poetic, it goes:

> *It is beautiful love when you look into my eyes.*
> *Your fiery eyes nourish my thirsty soul.*
> *The wind carries my being into your arms.*
> *Enlightened Aura*
>
> *It is beautiful love when we merge.*
> *The sun rises.*
> *The birds fly.*
> *The dead leaves fall.*
> *It is your fragrance intoxicating my being.*
>
> *It is beautiful love when you look into my eyes.*
> *I bow down to you.*

I was sitting right by Sadhguru's feet when these feeble words slipped out of my mouth: "Sadhguru, I would love so much to sing the songs I have composed for you, but I have lost my voice."

"That is a good thing," Sadhguru said.

Sadhguru must have meant that losing our voice showed our abandonment, dropping all our self-preservation mechanism.

In his last moments before departing, Sadhguru stood, his hand in namaskaram, eyes closed. He fell into silence as tears welled up in his eyes. A few of us up front felt his unconditional Divine love traverse our entire being. Many of us wept. I could not stop sobbing. Like an emptied vessel, I raised my hands high, forming a cup toward him, as is customary in the yogic tradition. A few participants also were doing it. I knelt on the floor and touched his feet.

Many minutes must have passed. I longed so much to hug him again. I kept whispering, "Thank you so much, Sadhguru. I'm so grateful. I love you so much." He opened his eyes. I noticed how red they were. He could not hold back any longer; like the Ganges River, tears poured out. All at once he opened his arms wide to hug us all. Sadhguru blinked his eyes several times looking at mine, acknowledging my gratitude and love. Several minutes must have elapsed again in this most intense, elated, and infinite loving, intimate moment.

Suddenly, Sadhguru shook his head and cried, "Yes!" while knocking on his chest. I rushed to him first and hugged him tightly. Within a few seconds, another woman squeezed him from the other side. He kept stretching his arms wider around us, trying to reach out. One after another, participants behind us started to hug us in a domino effect, unraveling a grand feathering gesture, like a swan taking off from a pond. Sadhguru started to lose his balance. The volunteers rushed up to stop the crowd. For many reasons, Sadhguru rarely permitted people to hug him anymore. This was beyond a great gift.

～

THE FOLLOWING DAY, NATHANIEL AND I attended the first Isha Invest consciousness meeting with Sadhguru. When he walked in, dressed in his informal clothing without his turban, we were in small groups talking. "Continue. See, I left my halo!" He was referring to his turban.

We burst out laughing. Many of us strolled to greet him. I was wearing a flowing blue dress that day.

He was standing only a few feet away when I murmured, "Sadhguru, during the BSP I saw a tiny blue light—"

He cut me off abruptly. "So what?" he said harshly. "I see a blue dress!"

It was as if Sadhguru had thrown a cold bucket of water on my head. I wanted to share this spiritual experience with him only because the blue pearl was located near his head, and I saw it with my eyes wide open. But I realized he was teaching me a lesson. He did not want me or anyone else getting attached to these kinds of experiences, or getting an inflated attitude about our spiritual journeys. This could be one of the biggest obstacles, the master of all traps. It would be a huge step backward from self-realization and liberation. Sadhguru wanted to make sure we got it. In many ways, he reminded me of beloved Gurunath. Both of their approaches came from the deepest sense of compassion and unconditional love.

I walked away and took my seat in silence. I did not feel attached to any of my spiritual experiences, only awed and humbled by what was happening. I had learned with Gurunath years before that it is always preferable to keep our spiritual experiences to ourselves, and drop them as they finish. That is also why I don't reveal everything in this book. It is best to explore and experience for ourselves. Tapping into the beyond, into other dimensions of consciousness, is accessible for everyone.

Still, sometimes certain things must be revealed and shared with the world for the highest good. Swami Muktananda and several other great masters have stated this. How else are we going to know about the existence of the Source of creation, universal phenomena, and Divine manifestations unless they are genuinely shared? A few wise ones may arrive there by themselves, but Sadhguru says it is extremely rare.

The world needs to know these phenomena exist. Most importantly, that the Source of creation thrives within all living beings and that yoga allows humans to experience the Source of creation in its full depth and dimension.

At the end of our meeting, a few of us asked Sadhguru to bless our *rudraksha*. A rudraksha is in some ways like a rosary, except it has 108 beads. Rudraksha from Sanskrit means the eyes of Shiva. Rudra is another name for Shiva. The seeds grow from the elaeocarpus tree family, an evergreen tree located around the Himalayas and in a few other countries. According to many ancient legends, these rudraksha seeds are the tears of Shiva and have healing, spiritual, and well-being properties when we wear them daily on our skin.

Sadhguru blessed a few of the participants' rudraksha while I waited. Then I extended mine. He looked at my being, smiled, and said as he extended his arms to my being, "You wear this, right. Come here!"

"I'm already so blessed, Sadhguru." He put his hands over my head, blessed me, and afterward blessed my rudraksha. I bowed to him.

~

ON OUR LAST NIGHT, I helped in the kitchen until it was late. The weather was cooler. For the first time during my stay, I took a hot shower to ease my aching muscles, put on my white gown, and wrapped myself in my warm shawl. No one was in sight. The lights in the Mahima were already turned off. By midnight, the scenery invited me to amble along the path to process my mystical experiences.

A profound stillness and heightened state of awareness overwhelmed my being with serenity, like the silence after a tornado. Everything seemed perfect, in pure harmony. The ground was still wet from the rain that had fallen. The fresh spring air made me feel more alive than ever. In every breath, the Divine Source tickled every cell of my body temple.

I lingered alone in the promenade gazing at the stars. The leaves danced to the rhythm of my heart as the crescent moon scintillated her love through a few clouds of mist that were wheeling in. I knew I was never going to be the same, yet the essence within my being had not changed. The wave receded in the ocean of love. I felt showered by the infinite blessings of the Divine Mother, my beloved master, and the Adiyogi's grace.

When I tiptoed back into the Mahima, everyone was asleep. A snoring melody echoed in the hall. In silence, I walked around gently waving my arms over all my sleeping friends, blessing them. Then I dragged my cot to the bottom of Sadhguru's dais, placed it right in front of his chair, and set up camp there. I slipped underneath my blanket whispering, "Good night, my beloved Sadhguru. I'm at your feet." Ripples of love and bliss engulfed my being. For the first time since my arrival at III, I fell asleep within a few seconds like a baby on God's lap.

Forty-Two

LOSING CALLA

ON OUR WAY BACK HOME, I peeked through the airplane window in silence, gazing at the vastness of the blue sky, and fell into a profound meditation.

When we arrived home, I hugged all twelve of our rescued animal companions and then went upstairs. I checked my email and found a message from the spouse of my friend Calla. The two of us had gone through our breast cancer journeys together. The email said, "Dear Vivi, Calla passed away on the 29th. She was not in much pain. Regards."

I whispered, "Oh God, not Calla!" She was not even fifty years old. Calla had never told me how advanced her cancer had become. She was my second dear friend to pass away from breast cancer in less than two years. I closed my eyes and called upon her spirit. I felt her presence. A wave of sweet love and joyful energy invaded my being. I intuitively sensed Calla left her body enlightened. I sent her love, light, and blessings.

Together we fought that disease, but the truth was I never viewed it as "fighting cancer." This image is one of violence. I did not want to hold such energy. Fighting creates tremendous stress on the physical body. Fighting engenders contraction; surrendering begets expansion. In the state of surrendering, of abandoning oneself, the individual has already won. This inner environment is more conducive for healing.

I had embraced the cancer journey as a blessing. By going deep in surrender, healing energy flowed from the celestial spheres. In some ways, my experience with the disease was like a spiritual ascension. That is how I perceived it. I felt empowered at all levels and still do.

I never mourned Calla like I had my friend Camellia. This time I felt too still, serene, and detached. I remembered the last time I ran into Calla at our local organic health-food store; the light in her eyes radiated such a divine beauty. I was content for her. This was another reminder of how ephemeral our journey on earth is. Over the following weeks, I contemplated what Sadhguru said about stillness: "Stagnation is a certain disease. It is anti-life. Stillness is a tremendous amount of life not manifesting itself in any way. It is just there—potent. That is God. God is stillness, not stagnation."*[1]

As the months unfolded, I moved at a slower pace, but with new awareness and consciousness. My focus became sharper, my mind quieter, and my senses more refined. A big part of "Vivi" had died during BSP. Stillness and serenity reigned as waves of Divine love and bliss surged within my being. I hoped this transformation would last.

I implored the Divine Mother to establish my being within that absolute truth of love and supreme bliss for the well-being of all living beings. Sadhguru had thrown gasoline on my divine flame. I tasted the fire of eternity and wanted it to be permanent, to merge with our Creator forever.

★ © Sadhguru

Forty-Three

AS RADIANT AS THE SUN

ONLY A FEW MONTHS AFTER our BSP program, July came with its heat. Nathaniel and I had planned to visit Lake Tahoe, one of my favorite places on earth. We rented a small chalet near the water for three weeks. I planned to work on this manuscript in the tranquility of nature while Nathaniel enjoyed vacationing.

I had pushed my physical limits greatly during our BSP program. My physical body was drained beyond words, though a sense of equanimity and serenity permeated. I had trouble reintegrating and returning to the physical realm, as if my subtle body and spirit wanted to slip out. The harsh laryngitis kept my being deep in silence. Although I had received a boon from Sadhguru in healing my adrenals in the past year, I sensed I may have burned them out again.

I decided to call the director of III who had been my teacher for the shoonya program. I needed help. I explained what was going on and how difficult it was for my being to reground myself after our BSP. He proposed some specific yogic practices to help rebalance my system along with my regular daily practices, amounting to more than five hours of sadhana spread throughout the day. He also suggested I attend at least one week of sadhana offered in a three-week program at the Institute.

In the end, I signed up for the sadhana and for a classical Isha hatha yoga program, designed by Sadhguru and consisting of a set of ancient yogasanas to help heighten one's consciousness and subtle energy. When one has been initiated, it can be practiced every day prior to sadhana. It was considered a major requirement as part of our preparation for my upcoming silent Samyama program in the following year.

We were told by Sadhguru that Samyama is only for very serious seekers on the path. The requirements and preparations are enormous and very time consuming. One's physical body has to be ready and capable of sustaining high-voltage, powerful primordial energy. The participant's longing must be absolute and heartfelt. Not everyone can take or complete the Samyama program even if one wishes to. It is a great privilege and honor to be accepted into this program. If the seeker manages to get in and does not follow through with the preparation and sadhana, the program can be hell. If the individual is genuinely prepared, it can be pure ecstasy and bliss.

I knew intuitively I had been waiting many lifetimes for this Samyama and for my beloved Sadhguru. I wanted to be ready for this rare opportunity, not waste his energy and time.

~

EVERY DAY IN TAHOE I tried to pull myself out of bed by 7:00 a.m., practice my first sadhana, then join Nathaniel for breakfast by the lake. Within the first few days, Nathaniel left on his kayak for half a day while I sat with my laptop near the turquoise water. I wrote only a dozen pages. My eyes kept rolling, and I often drifted into a meditative state. My body and spirit kept telling me to rest and take more time to commune with nature. After I resisted for a while, I decided to listen to the wisdom within. I declared, "Vacation!"

I soaked my toes in this ancient lake. My body went into shock. I wondered where I would summon the courage to swim in its icy cold water. The surface temperature must have been near 60. I turned back, got my long wetsuit, and tiptoed into the crystal water wanting to scream. I swam along the shallow sandy area, the warmest I could find, for no more than twenty minutes.

I decided to increase my swimming distance every day. On our third day, I jumped in with my bikini on, no wetsuit, and swam for over 35 minutes. I wanted to feel the water and the sun's rays on my body temple. Afterward, I lay on the pier like a baby seal, sunbathing for a few hours to absorb vital pranic energy. The alchemy of the sun on my frozen body rejuvenated my entire being. As I drifted into a meditative state listening to nature or music, I invoked the Divine Mother to heal whatever needed to be healed. I rarely exposed myself to the sun like this. Yet I could not get enough of it. I called it my vitamin D, for "Divine!" The act of soaking oneself in a body of water within the womb of Mother Earth charged with ions has special healing power.

When we returned home, I felt a little more rested, a bit more in my physical body. But I was still feeling extremely satvic; I wanted to spend the rest of the summer meditating and communing with nature in deep silence. I had not accomplished any significant work on my manuscript as I had promised myself I would, but I reminded myself again we must always listen to the wisdom of our body and spirit. To listen deep within is a cry of our own divinity, a haunting song we cannot ignore. This humbling experience was another crucial reminder of an already learned lesson.

～

AFTER OUR RETURN HOME, I flew by myself to the Isha center in Tennessee for the sadhana and hatha yoga programs. I was content to be back at the ashram. Every detail reminded me of the rare moments we spent in the presence of Sadhguru during our BSP program. I woke up at dawn, took a cool shower, and walked to the small shrine, a simple room Sadhguru had consecrated long ago.

One day at dawn while I sat right in front of Sadhguru's classic sepia photo in the shrine, feeling his presence within, I drifted into a profound meditation. When I opened my eyes, I realized that the soul does not exist by itself. The soul does and does not exist, like our shadows. In that moment, as Siddhartha Gautama the Buddha realized one day, I realized that phenomena do not exist on their own and do not exist independently. Truth always seems to be a paradox. The soul is like a wave rising from the ocean. The wave can't exist without the ocean. It is always part of the ocean. Yet each wave has a unique form. The wave may have the illusion it exists as its own separated self. Yet when it rises and falls back into the ocean, it realizes it is more than a wave—it's the whole ocean! It is the same with the soul who merges in God, the Source. In that sense, the soul as a separate entity does not exist. I could see and experience this clearly. The microscopic mirrors the macroscopic. It is one thing to think about this insight intellectually, another to realize and experience it.

Sadhguru says, "If you become full-blown consciousness, everything that can be known will be known to you."*

After brunch, I sat by myself on a bench in the green cove, that area where hundreds of us ate together during our BSP program. I had just finished talking with Nathaniel on my mobile when by accident I brushed off a bee with my hand. She was flying straight into my face and had caught me off guard. She was a very beautiful and extremely large honeybee. I had never seen one like it before and did not mean to hit her at all.

The bee flew out of balance and crashed on the grass. "Oh no! I killed her," I gasped. She must have stayed there for a good five minutes without moving. I felt such pain for her, thinking how careless it had been of me to swat at her, what a lack of mindfulness I had displayed. I sent her healing energy and invoked the Divine Mother to reanimate her.

We create our own karma from our lack of consciousness. If we are not aware and mindful of living in this present moment, more karma is accumulated. Our volition and intention also have a crucial part to play. All that we have accumulated—our thoughts, our words, our actions—binds us to the physical realm. It dawned on me that if I lived my life more mindfully, I would not hurt myself so often. The distinction between ignorance and inner knowing is just a change in our perception—our mindfulness and expansion of consciousness.

That is a very beautiful spiritual practice in itself. It is the core teaching of Zen Buddhism. This gentle honeybee reminded me how my lack of mindfulness at times may have caused suffering to myself, other living beings, and nature.

* © Sadhguru

I was still transfixed on the bee when she turned around and flew off. Ah! I was delighted, feeling blessed for this gift. Everything in nature can be our teacher when we remain humble, open, receptive, and mindful. I also realized that it is almost impossible to be in the present moment fully unless we are mindful of it.

~

AFTER SPENDING FIVE DAYS ENRAPTURED in sadhana for over twelve hours every day, I completed my program. I was the only participant for that week. I was instructed to meet with an Isha teacher for my graduation. We met in the small meditation room where I had been initiated into shoonya. In silence, I sat on the floor in lotus position. She sat on a chair behind me. She played a short DVD of Sadhguru in which he talked about the purpose of sadhana, saying yogic practices and spiritual processes are tools to break free from our limitations of self-preservation and boundaries of our own energy. He also said sadhana helps us expand into boundlessness, and because we have done intense sadhana now, we should not expect immediate mangos in our tree. A young blossoming fruit tree needs to grow, be well cared for, and be protected.

Toward the end of the DVD, Sadhguru led me into a simple yet powerful spiritual process. All at once I burst into an unusual spontaneous kriya I had never experienced. My entire abdomen moved violently from bottom to top in colossal undulations for a few minutes as I cried out loud and sobbed, "Shiva, Shiva, Shiva." A torrent of energetic Divine love inundated my being as if he was in the room transmitting shaktipat. Then the teacher congratulated me and handed me a rose.

~

THE HATHA YOGA PROGRAM TOOK place that weekend in the Mahima hall. Over fifty participants attended. During our last morning break, not long before its completion, hot herbal teas were offered by the resident volunteers outdoors. The sun radiated in its full splendor while hundreds of birds sang praises to the intelligent spirit animating creation. A fellow French resident and friend who served my tea said, "The light in your eyes, Vivi, wow! *Merveilleux!* You look as radiant as the sun!"

With a smile I hugged him and whispered in French, "All by the grace of our beloved Sadhguru and Shiva! I'm sooooo intoxicated." I just wanted to close my eyes and continue dropping into this boundless union. In that moment, I noticed that I was feeling physically rebalanced again. I had only six months left before Samyama. While I drank my tea, I realized the time I spent at the III empowered my being for this great blessing and pilgrimage.

Sadhguru says, "Today, there is substantial medical and scientific evidence to show that the very fundamentals of your brain activity, your chemistry, even your genetic content can be changed by practicing different systems of yoga."[*1]

~

I RETURNED HOME FEELING RENEWED and rejuvenated. That day I received a surprise email from Andrew Rowan's secretary from the Humane Society International inviting Nathaniel and myself for the upcoming World Compassion Day event held in Mumbai. Another email came in from my friend Jennifer Sullivan, consultant to the HSI, inviting me to meet His Holiness the Dalai Lama in a special audience organized for several of us before this unique conference.

This was an even bigger astonishment. I could not believe how effortlessly my intention to meet him had manifested. When I had volunteered on the original plan with her and Dr. Mishra, it had never crossed my mind I would be invited to meet the Dalai Lama.

The same week I was interviewed via Skype by an Isha teacher for the upcoming Samyama, the most advanced silent program offered only at the Indian ashram. During the interview, I could not hold back tears of gratitude, realizing this program conducted by Sadhguru was a rare blessing in one of many hundreds of lifetimes. Nothing would stop me from going.

I remembered once that Sadhguru had warned us not to waste his

* © Sadhguru

energy at the Samyama through lack of preparedness; people had been removed from the program before when they were ill-prepared. I knew the requirements were so high and demanding. I wanted to honor Sadhguru by promising myself I would give no less than 300 percent.

Sadhguru says, "Now, when we say 'Samyama,' it is a state where your awareness has reached a point where you are fully aware that you are not the body, you are not the mind, you are not the world. These are the three things that you are always getting identified with—this is the trap."[*2]

I wondered how I would make it to India by the end of November for the WCD event while maintaining my daily intense sadhana, then return only a few months later by myself in the middle of February for the following month. I wondered if it might be too much.

Nathaniel exclaimed with excitement, "Baby, let's go! We could go visit the Taj Mahal! Ah! We could stay in ancient Indian palaces in Udaipur, in Rajasthan."

"That is right, my love. You have never been to India before. That would be so wonderful to be there together! Oh, I don't know why but I always felt attracted to Rajasthan!" I sighed, dreaming of the great legends of the Maharaja's era.

[*] © Sadhguru

Forty-Four

FROM A PERSON TO A PRESENCE

MOST PEOPLE ARE CREATURES OF habit and compulsion. Until we become fully aware, it is difficult to change that. In the past few years, I had started to deviate from the organic living vegan diet. I was still eating vegan organic meals, but with too many cooked carbohydrates, tofu, and high-glycemic fruits. The healthy and holistic raw way of living was still not instilled within me, more a success of trial and error. I could feel what I ate affected my well-being and health. I committed again to eat more pranic and living vegan food that was rich with super food, enzymes, minerals, vitamins, and proteins.

By this time, I was already practicing sadhana over four and a half hours daily. My doctor insisted I receive many vaccinations prior to our trip. I researched and discussed it with Nathaniel. In the end, we decided to go for the hepatitis A vaccine only. I later regretted even getting this. Even though the doctor was lovely, I left him after a year feeling he had not addressed my core health challenges. For a while, I went through a revolving door of doctors wondering why I was still feeling so drained and why my immune system was so extremely weak. Something was making me sick. The question was, what?

I discovered Dr. Todd Maderis, a young integrative doctor. I could tell he was passionate about discovering the cause of his patients' diseases and helping them get well. At his clinic, he told me, "When I hear these kinds of symptoms, Vivi, the first thing I do is order a urine challenge toxic heavy-metals test."

When the results came in, we were both shocked. Some of the graphs and numbers were very elevated. My body was overloaded with toxic heavy metals such as cadmium, arsenic, bismuth, and mercury. After I read the symptoms of each one of them and heard from Dr. Maderis about how these toxins can affect our health, the mystery seemed to be resolved. I was very grateful to him. I even suspected these toxic heavy metals could have been one of the causes of my breast cancer.

He proposed intravenous chelation treatments with a drug called EDTA to remove these toxins, and I signed up for a series—but when I arrived home that day, it hit me: I was not acting as my best health advocate. I spent hours researching detox on the net and found that these chelation treatments reminded me too much of chemotherapy. Any type of detoxification program can be very harsh on the body, especially the liver and kidneys. I hoped to find a more natural and gentle way.

More than ever people are getting sick because of toxic heavy metals, molds, and chemical pesticides and herbicides. We need to be vigilant and mindful about what we eat, drink, inhale, or absorb through our skin and now even where we walk and sit. Detoxification is not a fad, but a crucial necessity in today's toxic and infectious world.

I decided to meditate, knowing inner guidance would flow in. The smiling face of Dr. Gabriel Cousens appeared to my being, the internationally well-known holistic doctor and founder of the Tree of Life Center US and its foundation. After my meditation, I returned to my online investigation. I had forgotten that Dr. Cousens's center specialized in holistic detox fasting with green juices. Long ago I had read one of his detox articles that talked about the use of liquid zeolite to remove these toxins. Zeolite is a natural volcanic mineral with unique crystalline properties that act as a magnet.

I saw on their site a ten-day green-juice detoxification fast offered at the beginning of November only a few weeks prior to our departure for our pilgrim voyage in India. I became determined to do it.

I told Nathaniel of my plan; since I had never fasted for such a long period, he was concerned. I enticed him to come with me, saying being in the desert would be good for both of us.

~

A FEW WEEKS BEFORE GOING to the Tree of Life Center, I began to prepare physically and emotionally, as their protocol suggested. I began fasting, avoiding food but drinking cleansing juices with zeolite drops in it. On the night before our departure, I violently vomited many times, and I woke up the next morning feeling very sick, weak, and faint, with a monster migraine and nausea—unable to travel.

Nathaniel changed our flight and called the Tree of Life. I suspected detox symptoms from the zeolite liquid, but especially from the four ounces of wheat grass juice I'd drunk the night before. When the body is detoxifying too fast, the liver, kidneys, and the lymph nodes can't manage well, and all kinds of symptoms occur.

I stayed in bed resting. Many of these symptoms reminded me of when I was on chemotherapy. It felt like some of those chemicals were flushing out of my body temple.

The next day, we flew to Phoenix. I was still nauseated and felt half-dead. Still, when we landed, the vast, golden, rolling hills of the desert enchanted my being.

We were surprised by the simplicity and rustic aura of the Tree of Life Center. Their property was spread across many acres of land, including a vast mesa where the tiny house cafe was located. A dozen simple wrought iron chairs and tables surrounded its outdoor patio, offering the most wondrous view.

We checked in, then I met with nurse Dahlia for preliminary testing and instructions. A driver brought us to the garden house, a comfortable trailer home not far from the main building. Our roommate, Carmelita, a lovely, tall, chubby, thirty-something woman from South America, opened the door when we walked up, and our spirits immediately connected. She told us about her twenty-one-day detox fasting program. She had already lost twenty-five pounds and was overcoming a major sugar addiction. Carmelita had done many detox fasts over the years at the Tree of Life Center.

The following morning, I began my official fast.

~

ON MY THIRD DAY, I woke up around 6:00 a.m. feeling extremely drained, dizzy, weak, and nauseated. My whole body was in pain. My head throbbed with another dinosaur migraine. I could not get out of bed, feeling I would faint if I did. Nathaniel was sleeping. I wanted to do my sadhana even more so than usual, since I was preparing for Samyama.

Tears welled up in my eyes as I called on Sadhguru with all my heart. I lay there for several minutes, then stood, wobbling, and opened the window for fresh air. Still in my nightgown, I rolled out my yoga mat, skipped my hatha yoga practice, and went straight for my shakti chalana kriya. Not even halfway through it, a prodigious hard ball of tangible intense energy about the size of an orange rose from my anahata—heart chakra—and pierced through the Vishuddhi, the throat chakra, then exploded in the lower part of my head. I fell into an intense, trancelike state, chanting "Shiva" while shakti flowed through my being. Throughout my practice, tears kept rolling down my face; I was feeling so much gratitude and love for Sadhguru and Shiva.

By the time I completed my sadhana, Nathaniel had left for a run up the hills to grab breakfast. I prepared to meet with Dahlia for our regular daily check-in at the gathering room. As I was walking out the door, Nathaniel returned from his run and handed me a green juice.

"Oh no, baby, . . . I can't drink anything now. I feel so sick and extremely weak." I held his arm; slowly we walked together to the main building while I shared what occurred in my sadhana.

"Wow, you're still so pale, my love. Feel better very soon." He kissed me goodbye and left.

I walked into the gathering room and sat on the sofa still and silent, feeling as if a surge of energy from the Divine Source had flowed through my being—as if Sadhguru had plugged my being into the ultimate powerhouse.

Dahlia walked in and asked how I was doing. When I told her what had transpired, she said it was usual on the third day for detox symptoms to manifest. In fact, this was my fifth day of fasting since I had stopped eating at home. As I was relating my early-morning experience, Dahlia closed her eyes and entered what appeared to be a trancelike meditative state. I closed my eyes and said, "I still feel shakti energy flowing through my being. My beloved master heard my cries." I placed my hand on my heart saying, "He's right in here."

I looked at Dahlia, who leaned forward and placed her elbows on her thighs and held her hands on both sides of her head near her temples. I could feel shakti rushing out of my heart region like a jet of water leaving a power hose. I had never felt such sensations before. Dahlia murmured with her eyes closed, "Oh, yes, I feel the energy, Vivi, so strong, so intense."

A long moment of silence took place. I became even more silent, still, and intense, whispering, "Shiva." Then, all at once, Dahlia vomited violently.

I stayed still, intense, feeling like a conductor of energy. Phenomenal occurrences such as vomiting may occur during spontaneous kriya when kundalini is awakening or arising, especially if the energy is too powerful to hold. Shakti purifies. I kept whispering, "Shiva."

Dahlia kept vomiting.

After about five minutes, I opened my eyes and stood, then moved slowly and gathered a cold towel. Silently, I put the cold compress on Dahlia's forehead and led her to the sofa. I removed her shoes and sat next to her. Her eyes had a radiant light. While I smoothed her hair, we lingered, lost in samadhi and gazing at one another, for what appeared to be an eternity. It felt as if I did not exist, yet I was one with her and every particle of existence, feeling Divine love flowing. At last, I murmured, "I'll let you rest, Dahlia." She lay there on the sofa, quiet, intoxicated in bliss.

I walked back to the house feeling deeply humbled. I choked with tears while I shared with Nathaniel what had happened. Then I went to meditate in the bedroom by myself.

Dahlia later told me that she had a full stomach when our interaction took place. In the yogic path, it is highly recommended to have an empty or light stomach if there will be a transmission of energy, also while doing sadhana, because of the greater likelihood of nausea when the stomach is full.

Sadhguru broke through my shell. Dahlia felt deeply connected and experienced his presence. As he says, "Yoga as a process, method, technology and science is essentially to break the limitations of a certain concretization that happens which we call 'personality.' To evolve from being a person to a presence. If you are a person, that means you have made a shell out of yourself. You formed a shell, within that shell only you can operate. If you break this shell, you will no more be a person but simply a presence—as life is, as God is, just a presence."*[1]

Vairagya means to become transparent, be able to take on any colors, not be stuck in limitations. Developing vairagya also means including everything as oneself. It's not colorless—it is beyond colors. In a state of vairagya, one can see clearly the reality, the truth, and go beyond as the Source intended—boundless.

The more one is awakened, the more one experiences the oneness of this precious existence, the more universal responsibility we will have toward all living beings' wellness and happiness.

~

DURING OUR CHECK-IN THE FOLLOWING morning, I hugged Dahlia.

"How are you feeling today, Dahlia?"

"I feel great, Vivi! How are you doing? I'm the nurse, and you have been taking care of me."

"I feel better but still shaky. Would you mind talking with me about what you experienced yesterday, Dahlia? I heard you stayed on the sofa meditating for hours after I left. You must have had a full stomach to get sick like you did."

"Oh yes . . . I had a big breakfast before coming to the meeting. I still feel very humbled, Vivi," she said. "Well, I felt an incredible amount of Divine love flowing from you. I felt blissful and lost gazing into your eyes."

I knew Dahlia understood about shakti and kundalini.

"It's by the grace of Sadhguru and Shiva," I replied. "My being was just an instrument of grace. It is because you're so open and receptive, Dahlia. You may have vomited because the energy was too strong for you to hold."

That night, over herbal tea, I shared with Carmelita and Nathaniel that I felt guided to become Dr. Cousens's patient. I reflected on how Dr. Cousens

* © Sadhguru

had lived in India for many years as the primary doctor at the ashram of the renowned master Muktananda. He had been on the yogic path for a long time and understood the path of self-realization, kundalini, shakti, and spontaneous kriya. As I was falling asleep, I sent out a strong intention.

⁓

THE OFFICIAL FIFTH DAY OF my green-juice detox fast started with a little kiss goodbye from Nathaniel, who was flying to New York that morning for a business meeting. After my sadhana, I walked along the path to the main building, chanting as I went.

Inside the main building, I weighed myself on the scale. Ten pounds had melted away. I inquired at the front desk. The assistant said even though Dr. Cousens had started taking a few new patients, he was fully booked for the next few months.

"His Whole Body Wellness Program requires at least a two-year commitment to see some results," she said. "Are you willing to make that kind of commitment?"

"Yes," I said, knowing it was true.

⁓

ON DAY SEVEN OF MY official fasting, I leaped out of bed at 5:00 a.m. as if I was five years old, bubbling with energy, blissful, and not even hungry. A few hours later, when I returned to check in for a spa appointment, the assistant caught my eye and grinned.

"A spot just opened up with Dr. Cousens tomorrow morning, Vivi!" she exclaimed. "Can you make it?"

"Yippee!" I cried. "I knew it! Thank you so much, Divine Mother."

That night Carmelita and I sat on the sofa sipping herbal tea. She expressed a desire to know more about awakening. I told her about my cancer journey and about Sadhguru and yoga. Tears welled up in both of our eyes. She reached for my hand and said, "I'm so very happy you're still here among us. My mother passed away from breast cancer. It was so hard."

I took her in my arms and held her like a baby while she sobbed.

The following morning Carmelita opened her bedroom door in her pajamas looking groggy. She held her hands over her abdomen and cried, "One more green juice, Vivi . . . I'm going to puke all over the floor!" She was about to complete her nineteen-day detox and had lost over forty pounds. "Oh Carmelita, I am here for you. Hang in there, we are almost done! Look how far you have gone, sweetie. You can't give up now. It will all be worth the effort."

Both of us were going to break our fast the following morning so we could enjoy the last few days slowly reintroducing food to our stomachs. Fats, the hardest to digest, were only allowed five days later.

I left our trailer just before 7:00 a.m. to meet with Dr. Cousens. When I sat with him, we both closed our eyes, and he chanted a mantra in his soft, gentle voice.

During the live blood cell analysis, Dr. Cousens examined my blood underneath his microscope. "Oh my god, my blood looks so scary even after that long fast!" I said. "I can't believe it! It does not make sense. I don't understand. I cut the sugar and have been taking good care of myself since my cancer journey. What is happening?"

"Vivi, your pancreas appears to be producing its own sugar, resulting in blood overloaded with candida. You won't enjoy this test, but we must do a Glucose Tolerance test on you tomorrow morning. I promise we won't do it again."

I showed up the next morning, as instructed, and Dahlia gave me an enormous glass of water mixed with molasses to drink. Thirty minutes later she pricked my finger to get a drop of blood. My blood sugar was high, almost reaching diabetic levels. I started to feel very faint.

"You're hypoglycemic, Vivi," she said.

"Oh I feel faint, Dahlia. Can I break my fast right away?"

"We don't need to continue this test. I will call for your meal. You did great, Vivi!"

I walked outside by the small pool and sat with a colorful plate of a few finely cut low-glycemic fruits. I was so grateful for this nutritious meal. I put my hands over my food and blessed it, sending infinite blessings of well-being, happiness, and love to all living beings. Then I sat there, serene, and looked up at the blue sky for about an hour, chewing every tiny bite. This was my renewal to a deeper relationship and realization with Mother Earth and her gracious nutrients. Experiencing such a long detox fast changes our taste buds and views forever. I could not help but invoke the Divine again for the starving children and creatures around the world.

After I finished eating, Dr. Cousens and I resumed our meeting. He said the morning's test showed I was pre-diabetic hypoglycemic. It explained many things. After hours of many more holistic tests, he concluded that my whole system and many of its organs, my lungs being the weakest, had not yet recovered from all the harsh medical cancer treatments I'd undergone. He put me on his healing Phase 1 organic vegan live food regimen, the one I had followed five years ago for six months from his book entitled *Rainbow Green Live Cuisine*.

"Oh no!" I exclaimed. "Not again." I knew how tough it was to follow. "Please, Dr. Cousens, let me have at least some blueberries. They are very low-glycemic and filled with antioxidants."

"Okay, Vivi, . . . but not a lot and only once a day!" He smiled.

Almost six hours later I left Dr. Cousens's office holding two pages that listed supplements I should take and a grueling protocol for me to follow. I strolled along the path to my trailer in silence, admiring the outline of the serpentine hills against the blue sky and wondering how I would summon the strength and courage to follow such an extremely demanding protocol. For a brief moment, I choked up in tears, reflecting on all the gargantuan efforts I had made with my health. By the grace of the Divine, I was still alive, not relapsing with cancer while many of my dear friends were dying from it. *Well*, I thought, *if I had not made all these crucial efforts, I would not be here today, so my attempts were not in vain. They were only the baby steps that prepared my being for this grand leap.*

I knew deep down that I could have done better if I had maintained a full commitment to this path all the time. But it seems we humans have a tendency to commit only in installments. This was going to be an endless process. I had to continue to transform learned and conditioned childhood habits into healthy ones.

When we empower ourselves with consciousness by allowing our suffering and pain to be revealed and felt deeply, they become our teachers to assist us in awakening to our ultimate nature. Our pain and suffering can be transformed into compassion and unconditional love toward all living beings who also suffer and feel pain, fear, and many other emotions.

~

ON OUR LAST NIGHT, CARMELITA and I toasted with a Yogi tea for a renewed commitment to a holistic lifestyle and perfect health. She offered to drive me to the airport even though her flight was scheduled much later in the afternoon. As we were packing, I walked into her bedroom and asked, "Do you want to see how I celebrate a victory?"

"Yes, Vivi! Love to. Please!"

I jumped on her bed and bounced for a minute, chanting, "We're going home! Aum Namah Shivaya Aum!"

We both burst out laughing.

The following morning Carmelita helped me carry my big luggage to her car and pack the trunk. She drove us to the mesa to prepare a light breakfast box to go. As we entered the cafe, I said teasing, "What about a little green juice, Carmelita?" We both had a good laugh.

After our farewell to every lovely soul at the Tree of Life, together we departed the tranquility of the desert for the Arizona airport, flying like spiritual sisters would.

Forty-Five

WAVE OF BEAUTY

LESS THAN TWO WEEKS AFTER I returned from the Tree of Life Center, the suitcases for my next trip bulged. I had packed my yoga mat, aromatherapy mosquito spray, organic vegan snacks, concentrated chlorophyll, and other supplements. The upcoming three weeks in India promised to be another humbling journey.

After traveling almost forty hours, Nathaniel and I walked through the entrance of the Indira Gandhi International Airport's brand new Terminal 3. We were welcomed and awed by a gargantuan mural of hand mudras lined up against the wall. It was clear we had landed in the motherland of yoga.

Our guide smiled warmly, his palms in salutation. "Namaste, my dear friends! Welcome to New Delhi. My name is Gopala. At your service!"

Nathaniel had spent time selecting the proper traveling company to guide us through our excursions. Their website advised us not to give money or food to mendicants and begging children and suggested donating to the nonprofit organizations listed on their site instead. I knew the aura of India and my heart; however, I could not promise Nathaniel I would observe that recommendation in the face of suffering.

The sun rose in full glory that morning, embracing this vibrant land with an incandescent glow that pierced my soul. While we drove through India's noisy, overcrowded, and beautiful capital, the aromatic smell of saffron, sandalwood, chai tea, curry, incense, and bonfires tickled our nostrils. We stayed overnight to rest.

The following morning we departed for Agra. On the busy highway, we listened to chants for the Goddess Durga. I asked Gopala, our driver, if he was a devotee of the powerful goddess. He grinned and vigorously nodded yes from side to side and responded, "Okay, okay, okay, okay, Maa!"

I laughed and began to chant aloud with devotion to Maa (Mother) Durga. When we reached the airport, we all hugged.

"Jai, Maa Durga!" I said, offering victory for the Mother Durga. We both laughed, feeling a little drunk in her bliss.

In Agra, a representative drove us to the Oberoi Amarvilas Hotel and showed us to our room. When he opened the gate of our balcony, Nathaniel and I gasped at the view of the Taj Mahal, an iridescent pearled jewel of timeless beauty and love, shimmering in the pink sunlight.

The next morning our new guide drove us into town. While we walked along the avenue, the contrast of the exquisite Taj Mahal against the sordid reality of garbage, tacky stores, emaciated homeless dogs, and poor beggars was shocking. I fed a litter of affectionate puppies while wondering what things would be like if the fortunes spent on buildings such as the Taj Mahal were used to uplift and help the destitute and the animals avoid their misery and empower humans in their spiritual quests. I sensed someone was looking at my being, so I turned my head and noticed a deformed, leprous man crawling on the ground with one hand sticking out, begging. I hesitated but remembered what our tour operator told us and walked on. Later, I regretted not having followed my heart.

Once we entered the grounds and gardens of the Taj Mahal, our guide gave his memorized speech. Disinterested by his monotone and lack of passion, I became captivated by a couple of friendly chipmunks in courtship. They crawled around the trunk of a tree playing peekaboo. Each time they found themselves, the lovers embraced each other anew. I stood there fascinated and took photos while Nathaniel joined me and our guide stood nearby in silence. I reflected, *Genuine lovers always embrace each other anew.*

The site was crowded with international tourists. The principal mausoleum was too dark to reveal all its fine detail. We learned that work on this mausoleum began in 1631 with a team of thousands of architects, artisans, and craft workers and was completed in 1648. The palace is an expression of love by the Emperor Shah Jahan for his wife, Mumtaz Mahal. It was inlaid with dozens of precious stones such as pearl, green jade, jasper, diamonds, crystal, lapis lazuli, turquoise, amethysts, and agates, all reflecting the finesse and elegance of the Mughal architecture combined with Islamic, Persian, Ottoman Turkish, and Indian motifs.

By the time we exited, the sun had already begun to set, reflecting a mystical golden light upon the white marble. We stood on the front terrace and admired the grand, elongated ponds with their flowing fountains and adjoining buildings.

Next, we visited the sixteenth-century red-sandstone Agra Fortress nearby, considered the imperial city of the Mughal rulers. While we walked within its long outer walls, we felt transported into a regal world. This historical citadel consists of many palaces with a view of Agra, and two mosques inlaid with precious stones. There was a guard protecting the mosques, but we were allowed to enter.

It was dark, but when our guide lit his lighter, we were delighted to see walls sparkling with such incandescence that it gave the illusion that they were alive and moving. It reminded me that when we turn the light inward, an endless treasure is awaiting. For the first time, our guide's voice warmed up with delight. We walked out of this imperial citadel to reach the main public avenue. A swarm of peddlers assailed us, loudly promoting their postcards, toys, sweets, junk food, and souvenirs as we dashed into an old taxi.

~

THE FOLLOWING MORNING WHILE NATHANIEL was still snoring, I woke to do my first intense sadhana of the day. I opened the doors of our balcony and walked out to breathe the fresh air. The Taj Mahal rose there like a beloved devotee awaiting the tender caress of her master, the fading moonlight. I felt one with her. The odor of smoking bonfires, the sounds of barking dogs, and the chanting of exotic birds such as the peacocks from the nearby mosque infused my spirit with otherworldly resonance. I felt transported into a celestial sphere. This ethereal communion with the essence and beauty of the Taj Mahal engraved an eternal embrace in my heart.

Later that morning we departed for Mumbai for our World Compassion Day event. On the eve before it began, a small group of guests were invited to feast with the organizers on a variety of Indian vegan delicacies prepared by the hotel, celebrating this grand occasion.

World Compassion Day was the first event of its kind to explore many crucial and international animal welfare issues and seek solutions. The dialogue would embrace ahimsa, compassion, and global responsibility for all living beings with a focus on vegetarianism and veganism. Our featured and honored guest speaker was His Holiness the Dalai Lama. The event was sponsored and organized by the National Media Foundation, a charity founded by Pritish Nandy and Project PNC, a special projects division of Pritish Nandy Communications, Ltd., which partnered and collaborated with HSUS and HSI, and the Foundation for Non-Violent Alternatives (FNVA), an institute for developing peace studies.

On the morning of the event, I woke up at dawn, and after a long sadhana, I swam at the hotel's pool surrounded by luscious tropical plants and swaying palm trees. The sun pierced through the foliage, warming the water and my being. The fragrance of bonfires, exotic flowers, and spices permeated the air, reawakening earlier memories of my beloved India, bringing my being to tears of gratitude. The first official World Compassion Day was about to take place, and I was about to personally meet His Holiness the Dalai Lama. I felt so light and alive, as if I was floating above the earth.

Mindfulness of the present allows us to feel what is, while suppressed feelings, suffering, pain, or fears block what we might otherwise feel. These are knots of negative energies stocked in our cells, eating us like poison. If our mental formations dissolve, our ultimate nature will radiate. People around us will feel these emanations. When we embrace the present moment mindfully, we don't identify ourselves with anything and instead become one with the cosmos. This could explain why many individuals avoid being aware of the present moment; they may feel their pain. Being conscious, aware, or mindful all mean the same thing. Though, consciousness is much deeper—like the root of a lotus in the mud. Often individuals live in the future, carrying a load of worries and anxieties, or in the past, carrying resentment, fear, anger, or even deep hidden hatred. Not being mindful can be an unconscious trap, and no matter where we go, it follows us. It takes great courage and energy to live in awareness of the present moment, to see things as they are, to feel what needs to be felt and processed.

~

ON MY WAY BACK FROM the swimming pool, I ordered a large bouquet of fresh coral roses for His Holiness the Dalai Lama. In the early afternoon, forty-five minutes before the event, a dozen of us gathered in a small private banquet room awaiting, with great anticipation, this intimate audience with His Holiness. Distinguished guest speakers who would be gracing the platform of WCD along with His Holiness also attended this special audience, including organizers and well-renowned public figures like Pritish Nandy and Wayne Pacelle, president and CEO of the Humane Society of the United States, the film actor Anil Kapoor, and Indian author Chetan Bhagat. With no expectations, I stood near the entrance, holding the bouquet.

When His Holiness strode in, followed by several of his attendants and bodyguards, a transcendental wave of peace, joy, and love swept over my being. Everyone was silent. "Your Holiness!" I exploded with joy like a little girl. He came straight to me smiling, extending his hands.

"I want to express my love and gratitude to you!" I exclaimed as I offered him the roses.

He reached for my hand and placed it on his heart while with the other hand he took the roses and passed them to his attendant. Slowly, in silence, His Holiness put his forehead against mine, gazing into my eyes, and led me in a reverential and affectionate dance. Together we bowed down touching each other's foreheads. When we rose up, we gazed at each other again. In a profound union, a second time he put his forehead against mine, slowly we bowed down, lower this time, where our one-thousand-petal lotus chakra embraced. The entire process must have lasted several minutes, yet I felt that eons elapsed. Only emptiness existed, free from time, space, and relativity. I bowed to touch his feet in the tradition of the yogic lineage of the great masters. Then His Holiness walked around the room greeting people briefly, and sat between Wayne Pacelle and Pritish Nandy, facing us.

"Why be tense, nervous, or anxious," His Holiness said. "I'm just a simple human being like you."

With that, the room started to relax and breathe. Someone asked him what role religion played in animal welfare.

He said a large portion of the world's seven billion people don't have much religious belief, and many of those who say they do behave as if they don't. He went on to add that what is most important, if one chooses to embark on a spiritual path, is to do so sincerely. "Now, with regard to animals, they not only have life, but feelings of pleasure and pain too. We should treat their lives with respect, which we Tibetans are accustomed to do."[1]

After our short visit, they took a few photographs of us with His Holiness. Because we were late for the event, we were rushed. When it was my turn, I affectionately put my hand on his arm and again he held my hand. "Your Holiness, years ago I wrote a major article about your life and teachings. I'm working on my first book now."

He gazed at my eyes with a mischievous smile and said, "Good, good!"

I wanted to tell him how much I'd learned from the insights based on his life experiences and wisdom through my cancer journey while I researched, wrote, contemplated, and meditated on him and the Buddha's teachings for my article. That alone was a profound journey and a priceless gift and made my heart overflow with gratitude. But more guests were lined up waiting, so it was inappropriate to take the time. I offered him a personal card expressing my heartfelt gratitude. On our way out, I noticed His Holiness was reading it.

We followed the designated route for the guests. A few of us walked first toward the grand ballroom in the walkway on the main floor. A swirl of hundreds of journalists, TV cameramen, and photographers began to write, snap, click, and record as if they were on the red carpet during Oscar night. Flashes electrified the hall. I felt humble and bowed, smiling to the media. Several famous Bollywood stars and renowned socialites and celebrities had already arrived.

This special event was not open to the general public. Armed security guards and police roamed every corner of the hotel. Only about two hundred people attended, a cozy audience for His Holiness. This was the smallest and most intimate event I ever attended with him. His gatherings often attract over tens of thousands of people, filling stadiums. Nathaniel and I were honored to sit up front.

When the program began, Pritish Nandy introduced the guest speakers. Wayne Pacelle started by expressing his gratitude to the Dalai Lama. Wayne Pacelle invited His Holiness to the podium.

The Dalai Lama told the group it doesn't matter whether he is talking to one individual, or to a hundred thousand. "We are the same. I want to live a happy life just as you do." He noted that the moment he begins to identify himself as a Buddhist, Tibetan, or the Dalai Lama, he creates separation between him and our brothers and sisters.

"Today, more than ever before, life must be characterized by a sense of universal responsibility, not only nation to nation and human to human but also human to other forms of life," he said. "Animals deserve our compassion. We must know their pain. We should nurture this compassion through education. Showing concern about animal rights is respecting their life. All of us are born from a mother's womb and nurtured by her love and affection; we human beings share the same origin. This is the basis on which we develop concern for others, because they are just like us. And once we've done that it's easy to extend our concern towards animals and other forms of living beings. The ultimate source of a happy life is warmheartedness. This means extending to others the kind of concern we have for ourselves. On a simple level we find that if we have a compassionate heart we naturally have more friends."[2]

Then the discussion elaborated on farm factories. Wayne Pacelle said, "The closest relationship many individuals have with animals is when they eat them. In India, on average, there is only 3.5 kgs [7.7 lbs] of meat eaten per person per year, whereas in the US and France the average is closer to 100 kgs [200 lbs] of meat per person per year." He emphasized that the need for better treatment of animals in India is already happening, but it needs to be encouraged.[3]

His Holiness added that all media, social networks, authors, and artists have a crucial role and responsibility in bringing out the truth about animal cruelty and exploitation.

I was elated hearing his words. I always felt anyone who is aware of these atrocities must share it with the world and take positive actions, especially influential individuals. The more power an individual has, the more universal responsibility he or she has. Together we can transform our world for the well-being, happiness, and harmony of all living beings. I noticed that many people are afraid to speak up against institutionalized cruelty and exploitation of animals for profit. It may be that people must experience their own suffering before they can feel the animals' cries. Before speaking up about something, as persons of integrity, we need to live what we feel, otherwise a level of discomfort could arise within our core. Having these elements in place helps open a closed heart into a warm and compassionate one. Becoming aware and compassionate toward the pain of other living beings is an extremely important part of our spiritual awakening. This can be a long process for some, but it does not need to be.

After the guest speakers, the panel took several questions from the audience. Toward the end I joined the journalists in front and snapped several photos of His Holiness with them. After the journalists left, the Dalai Lama stood there near the edge of the platform, only a few feet away from me, with his main attendant beside him.

I put a tiny handknit cow finger-puppet in my index finger, and in a baby voice, swinging my finger as if I were the cow, I said, "Your Holiness, we're so grateful and happy you're here today and spoke for us. We love you so much!"

His Holiness gave me his playful smile.

I removed the finger puppet and handed it to him. "That's for you, Kundun. It's a present from the animals."

He took it, looked at it closely, trying to fit it on his index finger, intrigued by the gift. When he succeeded, he gazed at me again, smiling while wiggling his finger with the puppet. We laughed together. He let me take several close-ups of him with his new toy. I will treasure forever that precious moment. I framed my favorite photo along with one of the two of us together. Each time I see His Holiness's photo with his little cow finger puppet next to his mischievous face, I smile or laugh. It reminds me to live every moment of my life with mindfulness, love, joy, compassion, exuberance, and especially laughter!

Forty-Six

SEEKING IN THE
MYSTICAL LAND OF INDIA

AFTER BREAKFAST THE FOLLOWING MORNING, Nathaniel and I hugged our dear friends goodbye. We departed for a place I had dreamed of, Udaipur, a city called the "Venice of the East," located in Western India in the majestic state of Rajasthan.

Udaipur is adorned by the Aravali hills and blessed with five major lakes. This glorious city is the capital of the former kingdom of Mewar. According to history, it is also considered the most respectable of all the Rajput ("son of a king") states in Rajasthan. The rulers of Mewar are still recognized for their courage in protecting their motherland from external invaders.

Nathaniel insisted we stay in an old Indian palace where the moonlight inspired memories of ancient legends and nectar kisses—the Taj Lake Palace. To get there, we had to travel on a small boat. There she was—one of the most romantic hotels in the world—floating in the blue horizon like a serene white swan on Lake Pichola.

~

THE NEXT MORNING, WE ROSE before dawn. I did my sadhana facing the tranquil lake, while Nathaniel attended a rooftop yoga class. Despite our hectic schedule, I remained very disciplined preparing for the Samyama program, doing more than four and a half hours of intense yogic practices every day.

After breakfast we met our new guide, Pradeep, at the pier. A Hindu and devotee of Lord Ganesh, Pradeep was an older man, a true professional. He drove us north to a small town called Eklingji, also named Kailashpuri.

The Eklingji Temple complex is considered the most famous temple in Rajasthan, lost in the midst of the Aravali hills and forests. Pradeep told us this sacred place acquired its name for its renowned compound of 108 ancient temples made of intricately carved sandstone and marble. Eklingnath, also called Sri Eklingji, a form of Shiva, is perhaps the biggest and most majestic temple dedicated to Lord Shiva. Along the way, Pradeep told us this ancient temple complex was built by Bappa Rawal, founder of the Mewar dynasty, in AD 734. Eklingji is the family deity of the Maharana, kings of Mewar.

On each side leading toward this impressive complex, dozens of peasants sat in a row, crossed-legged, making ravishing flower garlands to sell to pilgrims for daily pooja at the temple. We walked barefoot within its tall, fortified walls. We could see all the smaller baby temples shining like a mirage in the near distance. The iconography engraved within the walls and structures of these temples are elaborate, depicting Hindu legends and yogic lore.

Before arriving there, Nathaniel and I were not aware that the Eklingji Temple contained a multifaceted black-marble energy form within its shrine. Sadhguru says,

> *"The word linga means 'the form.' We are calling it 'the form' because when the un-manifest began to manifest itself, or in other words when creation began to happen, the first form that it took was that of an ellipsoid. A perfect ellipsoid is what we call a linga. Creation always started as an ellipsoid or a linga, and then became many things. And we know from our experience that if you go into deep states of meditativeness, before a point of absolute dissolution comes, once again the energy takes the form of an ellipsoid or a linga. So, the first form is linga and the final form is linga. The in-between space is creation and what is beyond is Shiva. The word 'Shiva' literally means 'that which is not.' That means nothing. Nothing is a very negative word. You would understand it better if you put a hyphen in between: NO-THING. That which is, is physical manifestation. 'That which is not' is that which is beyond the physical."*[*][1]

* © Sadhguru

This beautiful energy form had four faces depicting four different forms of Shiva. Facing east is considered Surya, the west is Brahma, the north is Vishnu, and the south face is Rudra, another name for Shiva. It appeared the Shivlinga may have been inserted inside this structure. That was not clear. It was dark and very hard to see.

At the zenith point, the Shivlinga seemed to be garlanded by a silver snake, depicting its mastery over shakti, the primordial energy. The flat top of the Shivlinga seemed to be covered with a mystical drawing yantra, which represented the ultimate reality. Shiva is worshipped there as the ultimate reality and supreme power. Sadhguru says,

> *"A yantra literally means a machine. A machine is a combination of very purposeful forms. For example, a computer is a product of our minds, but still, if we are asked to multiply 1736 with 13,343, we reach for a calculator—a yantra. It is not that the calculation is not possible in the mind, but this purposeful form or yantra allows us to use our body in a much better way. Even though you already have the body—the most sophisticated yantra—with you, it is possible to perform different types of activities better with specific machines for those activities. The process of building temples was fundamentally to create a powerful yantra for everyone."*[*2]

I had been feeling extremely devotional toward Shiva for a long time. I began chanting aloud my favorite Sanskrit verses from the Guru Pooja dedicated to Adiyogi Shiva as we walked up toward the main temple. As in any translation, the poetic and true essence of these words is lost. Approximately, these sacred words mean: "White as camphor, compassion incarnate, the essence of creation, garlanded with Serpent-King, ever dwelling in the lotus of my heart, the creative impulse of cosmic life, to That in the form of Guru, I bow down."

Just prior to entering the temple I stopped singing.

"We arrive just on time for the pooja!" Pradeep said, gesturing to the several musicians in the back sitting cross-legged, playing instruments, and

* © Sadhguru

chanting "Aum Namah Shivaya Aum." The hall was already packed with over fifty pilgrims, mostly Indians.

"Oh, a pooja for Shiva! Let's get some beautiful flowers for him!" I exclaimed.

The three of us walked back out.

"Shiva loves the tiny white flowers," Pradeep said. "These are the jasmine ones! Don't touch them, Vivi. Let the vendors put them in your basket for you. It's not good luck to touch them."

I chose three garlands of dainty jasmine flowers from three different vendors so more of them could earn their living for the day. They were around 50 rupees each, less than one US dollar. I paid with whatever rupees I had left, and Nathaniel chipped in the rest. I was wearing a flowing white dress—like a jasmine flower, I realized. While walking back I said, laughing and pointing to myself, "I'm offering this flower too!"

Then, feeling so exuberant, I continued chanting out loud these sacred verses for my beloved Shiva from the Guru Pooja. We reached the steps of an enormous pillared hall or "mandap" of the Eklingnath and entered in silence. Everyone was sitting with their eyes closed. The pundit had already started the pooja. Nathaniel and I went straight to the shrine with its altar comprised of its multifaceted Shivlinga. As I offered the garlands of flowers to Shiva, my heart filled with devotional love, a mighty pull of energy went through my being. In that instant, as the pundit took the basket from my hands and threw the garlands on the Shivlinga, both of my knees unlocked as if someone had banged hard on them from behind. As I was about to fall to the ground, I quickly grabbed Nathaniel's arm and held him tight to prevent from crashing. I whispered to Nathaniel, "Oh, my God, do you feel the energy here?" Nathaniel seemed clueless.

While I held Nathaniel, we walked in silence and sat in the middle of the crowd on the floor. The musicians kept playing and chanting aloud. I closed my eyes. In a flash, I went into a mystical trancelike state for thirty minutes, while remaining fully aware. I yelled and sobbed, "Shiva, Shiva, Shiva." My being did not exist anymore, only Divinity. My whole body swirled around and around, trembling, shaking violently, overwhelmed by Divine, loving shakti energy. Again, I began to speak in ancient tongues. No one stopped me.

After the pooja, we slowly exited the temple and ambled around outside, admiring the row of shrines. I felt a profound inner knowing that I had been at this ancient temple before. Two Indian children came running from the temple and asked me in broken English where I was from. They seemed to be in a state of wonderment about what had occurred to my being during the pooja. I felt deeply humble and touched by the Divine.

While we walked back, two older Indian peasants came to me, begging. I looked down, sending them love and blessings. I wanted to help them, but I had no more money left. Nathaniel and Pradeep were already picking up their shoes. As we exited the gates of the temple complex, several cows and stray dogs came to see me. I caressed them. I had some leftover food and several pieces of bread in my bag. I often carried food in my bag for the starving animals. It's unfortunately too common to witness starving people, cows, dogs, or other small animals eating out of the garbage in the streets in India and to see women with infants or children begging for food or rupees.

Pradeep went to retrieve the car; Nathaniel and I stayed behind, with me feeding the animals all the while. When I raised my head, five women with one little girl surrounded my being, begging. I asked Nathaniel if he would give me a couple of rupees. He refused, reminding me of what our travel operator had suggested on their website. I said, "I don't care what people say. What about compassion with positive actions right now? What's a few rupees? These people are hungry."

"No! Let's go now!" He got upset. He walked ahead of me, annoyed.

"Please, darling, give me a few rupees," I begged. "I'll pay you back later. I forgot to bring cash." I chased after Nathaniel, and when I did a few of the peasants and the little girl followed me and kept on begging. I felt that if someone brings himself or herself to such a humbling level, I must give them at least something. I was at least able to feed many more bony dogs on my way to the SUV.

When I reached the car, I confronted Nathaniel. "Why won't you just give me a few rupees?" I demanded. "Forget about everything, baby. Please, just do it for me." I was trying to demolish a giant wall of resistance.

By then, only one woman, who appeared to be in her eighties, and the girl child were still nearby, pleading with sign language that they were very hungry. I swore to myself I would never leave without rupees from now on. I gazed at Nathaniel and whispered, "How can I say 'no' to them? The Divine is everywhere."

At the last second, Nathaniel pulled out one rupee and gave it to me. I put it in the old woman's hands, then grabbed two handfuls of nuts and put them into the little girl's hands. I closed the car door.

We departed for the City Palace, once the residence of the rulers of Mewar, but the recent scene continued to haunt my being. I wished I could have done much more for all these living beings. I took a couple of deep mindful breaths, shed a few tears, and drifted into a meditative state until we reached Udaipur.

~

THE CITY PALACE IS SITUATED in the heart of Udaipur near the east bank of Lake Pichola. Pradeep said the Maharana Udai Singh II started the original architecture in 1559, and his successors completed it by the eighteenth century. The City Palace is comprised of eleven exquisite palaces, towers, domes, and arches made of granite and marble, and filled with paintings, antique furniture, glass mirrors, ornamental tiles, murals, wall paintings, silver work, and inlaid mosaics. The palace buildings are enclosed in a resplendent fortress, a work of art on its own.

Along the way there, Pradeep told us, once a year during a festivity such as Mahashivratri, the Maharani gave away a fortune of rupees to all the poor peasants who showed up. My heart melted in hearing that compassionate story.

Upon our return to our hotel's pier, Nathaniel expressed his gratitude and took care of Pradeep. I put my hands over Pradeep's head and blessed him. He looked down with his eyes closed and said softly, "Your blessings are Shiva's blessings." He bowed down, and I did too.

It was dark by the time we returned to our hotel. The main bar courtyard was loaded with international guests. Regional, colorfully costumed dancers performed with big bowls on their heads. We sat in the back admiring their art form. I indulged myself with a chai masala tea while Nathaniel sipped a glass of wine. The following day we rested by the swimming pool, preparing for our next visit to one of the most spiritual and intense cities on earth, Kashi.

~

WHILE WE WERE FLYING TO Kashi, I pondered Sadhguru's words about this "eternal city of light," the oldest inhabited city on our planet. Its primeval name was Benares. Today Kashi is also known as Varanasi. Located in the North Indian State of Uttar Pradesh, this consecrated city is considered the holiest of Hindu cities. Since time immemorial, it has been a powerful religious and spiritual center for Hindus, yogis, yoginis, and seekers. It is also one of the most sacred pilgrimage spots, visited by millions of international tourists and seekers every year. The history, legend, and yogic lore of Kashi are as eternal as the city itself.

Kashi was once considered an important seat of learning in India. This majestic city was designed by the mystics and yogis as a tool for spiritual growth and evolution for humanity, a kind of instrument in the form of a city that united the microcosmic and the macrocosmic. There, the open, receptive seeker can have the potential to unite with the cosmic reality, to experience the ecstasy of becoming one with the Divine in all its forms. At its peak, the city was home to many great enlightened beings and a destination for others who visited for long periods. Kashi is the home to thirty-three million gods and goddesses, all different energetic forms of the same single truth, the same Source of creation—the One Creator of all existential phenomena.

According to yogic lore and Sadhguru, not long after the Adiyogi Shiva and Parvati's marriage, Kashi became their abode. The Adiyogi himself designed a sacred circular mandala of the city by consecrating 108 shrines, each with distinctive qualities. Varanasi was considered by many beings of light as the most quintessential geometrical manifestation of how the macrocosm and the microcosm of the cosmos can be united in harmony. There were seventy-two thousand shrines, the same number of nadis in the subtle body of human beings.

When we landed at Varanasi's small airport, representatives from the tour companies waited outside the gates. One of them seemed to yell our name. He came forward and ushered us to his car, carrying some of our luggage and chatting. Several children ran to us begging. I had an untouched snack box of veggie sandwiches from the flight that I shared between them. They beamed and left, munching on the food.

As we drove toward our destination, the guide lectured me about not feeding the beggars and the animals. "The more we encourage them to beg, the more they will do it," he said with an annoyed tone.

"I understand your point," I said, "but what is the government doing to address these crucial societal challenges? How are they helping?"

"Ah, there are many social services in place for them."

I found that hard to believe.

While conversing, we realized we were going to the wrong hotel. Almost at the same time Nathaniel and I asked him which traveling company he represented. When he told us, we laughed. We'd left with the wrong representative.

By the time we got back to the airport, almost one hour had elapsed. Our representative was still waiting for us in front of the airport's entrance; we switched cars and headed to our hotel.

~

THE FOLLOWING MORNING WHILE NATHANIEL ran through the streets of Varanasi, I did my sadhana for many intense hours. After breakfast, we met our new guide, Pratish, in the lobby. He was a radiant, chubby Indian Brahmin and pundit in ancient scriptures. We sat on the sofa discussing our pilgrimage before departing.

Pratish took us first to an archeological site, the buried sacred Buddhist city called Sarnath. When we arrived in front of the Buddhist museum, tourist buses were already blocking the street. Male Indian teens hung out there chatting, while homeless dogs roamed for a morsel. I took my bag of food out and started to feed the dogs. One of the boys said sweetly, in broken English, "Please feed my friend here, Maa!" referring to the dog he loved most. I did.

We started our tour at a museum that housed an impressive collection of Buddhist art. Then we entered what appeared to be the deer park, Rishipattana, where a symbolic monument of the Dhamek Stupa stood. Many called it the seat of the holy Buddha. According to history, after attaining enlightenment in Bodh Gaya, Siddhartha Gautama the Buddha expounded his first teaching to his first disciples at this sacred location.

We walked within this protected area, which looked like a labyrinth of ruined monasteries and votive stupas—circular burial mounds encircled by stones—surrounded by green. Hundreds of pilgrims, especially Buddhist monks wearing differently colored dress, worshipped around this shrine. Some monks sat chanting mantras with eyes closed or meditating, while others walked around chanting, "Om mani padme hum."

Many of these stupas were built by the great Mauryan King Ashoka (273–232 BC). According to history, being a loyal Buddhist himself, he wanted to preserve and enshrine bones and other relics of the Buddha and his disciples.

While Pratish and Nathaniel had a conversation near the monument, I felt enchanted by the energy of the land. The Dhamek Stupa drew my being in. As I began a silent walking meditation, breathing in and out mindfully, a subtle, bubbly energy took hold of my being. I wondered if it was the same kind of sweet energy the Buddha had exuded while he was still in the body. I stopped, closed my eyes, and stood there like a Buddha statue. Profound reverence and love emanated from my heart for Gautama the Buddha and for all sentient beings. The buzzing from the chanting hypnotized my being into a deeper meditative state.

"Vivi!" I heard. "Time to go!"

I wanted to sit there longer with my eyes closed, but my boys were calling me. Pratish was on a schedule for us. He was so enthusiastic about sharing more about his hometown with us. I had to oblige.

~

LATE THAT AFTERNOON, AS THE sunlight colored the ripples of Mother Ganges River, we took a taxi to the old town, then a cycle rickshaw to cross through the main avenue that leads to the Dashashwamedh Ghat by the banks of the Ganges. We felt squeezed in between a mass of pedestrians, cars, scooters, bicycles, rickshaws, homeless cows and dogs, and garbage invading the road. Pratish said the Dashashwamedh Ghat is considered the most sensational area near the old Vishwanath temple. Hindu mythology tells us that Brahma created it to embrace Shiva in this ancient city of light. Vishwanath is one of twelve Jyotirlinga, holiest of Shiva temples. It is often called the Golden Temple by locals.

Ancient holy scriptures refer to the Ganges River as a Goddess or Mother. Ghats are large and broad steps leading to the blessed water of Mother Ganga (Ganges). There are around one hundred ghats in Varanasi. Pratish said most of them are used for bathing rituals, or pooja ceremonial sites. He added that pilgrims believe bathing in the Ganges River will purify their karma, even perhaps cease the cycle of rebirth. A few other ghats are exclusively for cremation. For thousands of years, at dawn pilgrims have flocked to these waters to offer their invocations for liberation (mukthi), and at night to attend to the light (*aarti*) ritual performed by the priests. Pratish said that according to mythology, Mother Ganga liberates soul from body and delivers it to the Source, the ultimate truth. These ghats are considered the holiest scenes in Kashi. Many of the splendid temples are still standing on the banks and are very active in rituals, busy with seekers and pilgrims.

When we reached old town, the last part of the main road was blocked by a hectic bazaar. We had to walk through it to reach the Dashashwamedh Ghat. It was getting chilly. A few mendicants with leprosy lingered around. This time I reached for some rupees in my purse, and placed several rupees in their bowls. Nathaniel did not say one word. We crossed through the market; it was overflowing in a potpourri of colorful lights, saris, shawls, kurtas, and glittering jewelry. Shiva, Ganesh, Krishna, and Durga and many other statues of goddesses perched left and right along the path within mini shrines. The rhythm of the music, spices, and incense seduced us.

I had started to cough and sneeze and developed a fever before we left Agra. Now the infection was invading my lungs. A fever was developing; my head and throat were heavy and stuffy. I wrapped myself in my thick shawl. It was time for that delicious chai masala tea! We stopped by a tiny stand and sat on a wooden bench to enjoy the sights. I had run out of food again. No cats were in sight. I wondered how they survived with so many stray dogs around.

By now Pratish knew us well enough to say, "There are many dozens of mendicants by the ghats. You may want to change some money into coins beforehand, Vivi."

While Nathaniel exchanged money nearby, an Indian teenager came up and tried to entice me to buy postcards and bindis. We chatted for a while. He had such a contagious smile that I promised I would buy some if we saw him by the ghat the following day.

When we reached the top of the small hill, a few hundred beggars stood or sat in a row shaking their steel bowls along both sides of the long stairs leading toward the Dashashwamedh Ghat. Many were blind, deformed, or handicapped from leprosy, or just plain worn-out, homeless elders. Nathaniel and I took one side as we went down the steps and dropped the same amount in each of their bowls. Silently I blessed them and showered them with love and grace.

We reached the bottom, a broad platform leading to the banks of the river. We were welcomed by two towering pink columns on the other side of where the aarti would take place. One of the columns had a colossal painting in bright colors of Shiva triumphing over a demon, while the other pictured the Goddess Ganga on her pet crocodile. A few big cows lay there, while homeless dogs roamed and licked the ground for a bit of nourishment. Once again I wished I had brought more food. Many sadhus sat or stood there dressed in their orange robes, their hair in long dreadlocks, with smeared faces from their pooja. These sadhus, sages, and ascetics dedicate their whole existence to spiritual attainment, and often do not eat for weeks or even months. I put some rupees in their bowls.

I wondered why most of the homeless cows we encountered in the city streets had such big abdomens. It made no sense, since there was not much grass around, and no one seemed to feed them. They were starving, eating from the plastic bags lying everywhere. Much later I discovered from the Karuna Animal Welfare Association of Karnataka, one of the nonprofit animal welfare organizations that Nathaniel and I support in India, that the cows ingest huge amounts of plastic.

The association performed intensive research and created a heartfelt documentary, *The Plastic Cow*. The film reveals the shocking truth about the challenge India faces regarding plastic's destructive impact on the local environment and the animals, especially the stray cows.

It was around seven o'clock when the sun began to embrace Mother Ganga, adorning her with infinite hues of pink, orange, red, and violet. The entire ghat was bathed with a rainbow of light. Large intricate yellow, white, and orange lamps shaped like umbrellas hung from above the stage of the main platform where the Sapta Rishi Aarti was about to be performed. Hundreds of pilgrims sat outdoors ready to absorb the energy. I stopped and inhaled a few deep breaths in the midst of this hectic and otherworldly scene. Sadhguru says,

> *"One aspect you must witness if you have the opportunity—in the evening around 7:30 there is one particular ritual which is called Sapta Rishi Aarti. After Shiva had transmitted yoga to the Sapta Rishis and they all had become fully enlightened, he sent them to different parts of the world to spread this knowledge. Before they left, they expressed their anguish, 'Now if we go away, probably we will never get to set our eyes upon you again, physically. How can we have you with us when we want you?' Shiva taught them a simple process, which lives on to this day as Sapta Rishi Aarti, conducted by these priests who may not know the science behind it, but stick to the process. I witnessed how they built stacks and stacks of energy, just like that."*[*3]

Rowboats loaded dozens of curious international tourists ready to watch the Sapta Rishi Aarti. Pratish introduced us to our navigator and led us inside our private boat. We embarked and floated around while the Sapta Rishi Aarti ceremony started. Half a dozen priests swirled lit oil lamps in the air while chanting ancient mantras and invocations in Sanskrit. The scene burst with energy, giving birth to a golden dome of light. Most

---

* © Sadhguru

boats floated around the river while people witnessed the ceremony. Others drifted toward the adjacent cremation ghat.

As we moved toward the cremation ghat, Pratish shared some of the spiritual and ritualistic aspects of the Hindu funeral rites. We witnessed many family members carry the corpses of their beloved ones, wrapped in rich colorful or white fabric, and place them on the pyre. These funeral ceremonials and rites are elaborate. We remained silent listening, absorbing the energy from this sanctum. I could feel dozens of disembodied beings hovering over us. Infinite peace and serenity captured my spirit while watching these burning bodies, conscious this will also happen to my body temple one day. I could see that Nathaniel was also moved.

Pratish told us, "Hindus bathe or take a dip at dawn in the Ganga to purify their sins. Having your body burned and its ashes cast into the river are considered auspicious, but dying by the Ganges River is even more auspicious!" We sat there in silence listening.

I remembered that depending on the karmic merits of the individual, Ganga will help with the attainment of liberation, what is referred to as mukthi, moksha, and nirvana. The ultimate goal is the end of the cycle of reincarnation in the physical realm.

Pratish recited invocations in Sanskrit for our liberation while our rowboat turned back toward the light ceremony. We closed our eyes for a while, then scooped water from the Mother River with our hands and sprinkled it on top of our heads and between our eyebrows. I remarked that I wished I could swim in Ganga at dawn, though I knew it was not wise, especially when sick with a fever and sore throat. Pratish said, "Just a few drops from the river is sufficient, Vivi, no need to dip in it."

I know it is the devotional and loving aspect of the individual who can transcend the physical boundaries, and worship the Divine in all its forms, that liberates by the grace of God. There is only one ultimate Source, one Creator, no matter what our background, age, gender, and skin color. My heart floated in Divine love and serenity as physical boundaries melted away.

In silence while we absorbed the energy, I realized a few of the elements that make the Ganges River holy. It is ancient and filled with positive reverberations. For thousands of years, poojas, aarti, invocations, rituals, chantings, offerings, and all kinds of devotional worship have taken place on its banks, many conducted by powerful, enlightened beings. Water has memory and absorbs energy. It would be fascinating to see what would be captured in frozen crystal photographs from the water of Mother Ganga. This water is filled with shakti energy. It is not just the water but the land and atmosphere too. If one has become an open and receptive vessel, one will feel and experience it.

It is not a matter of belief, faith, dogma, or doctrine. Everything in life can be transcended when one knows how to put aside the limited mind with its many false views, identifications, and learned belief systems. The phenomena of Mother Ganga and the essence of Kashi are also about experiencing life in its fullness, permeating every particle of this creation.

I realized long ago that our beliefs do not necessarily encompass universal truth. It is naive to accept that all the accumulated beliefs we hold dear are truth and reality. It may give us some temporary comfort and security, but one day the bubble might burst. For some people, it may happen when they die. Mine burst in my major depression when I realized there was a big difference between being a believer and being a seeker. The believer thinks he or she knows for sure without experiencing the universal truth, while the seeker does not assume to know. Of course, there are some exceptions. To believe in anything without experiencing it is a sure way to stay ignorant about the truth. It is like confining oneself into the tiniest box. The seeker wants to experience and live the truth. For that to happen, we must break free from all our boundaries, especially from our shell.

After Pratish completed his invocations for us, Nathaniel and I let go of two garlands of flowers and offered them in the Mother's womb. We watched them float together on top of the water. Toward the end of the light ceremony, we set free two tiny clay oil lamps nestled in marigold and rose petals as an offering to the Divine Mother in all her forms. Others did the same from their boats. Then we all returned to the shore.

~

AT DAWN, WE MET PRATISH again in the lobby and returned to the Dashashwamedh Ghat for a long ride on the Ganges during the sunrise. It was cold, and I was not feeling well, but I forced myself to go. Again, we walked through the main blocked road. This time there were no bazaars or beggars on the horizon, only committed seekers and the devout making their way through the silent road to their pilgrimage. As we approached the ghat, out of nowhere my charming Indian prince who had tried to sell me bindis the previous night while I was drinking my chai tea appeared with his infectious smile.

"Namaste, Miss Vivi. Here I'm for you. How many postcard and bindis do you need?"

We laughed. "Wow, sweetie," I said, beaming, "I admire your perseverance, enthusiasm, and patience. You'll succeed in life." I bought several packages of postcards. He followed us for a while, enjoying our company. We did not mind at all.

By the time we reached the shore, hundreds of pilgrims and ascetics were already engaged in invocations and pooja, offering incense, flowers, or their hair. We were told the sunrise is sacred for Hindus and that the ghats were always crowded with "Benaris," as the locals and Pratish called them. As the sun rose, capturing the western bank of the Ganges, a magnificent panorama of colorful temple spires revealed themselves. Many women bathed in their gorgeous saris while men wore dhotis, a kind of loincloth, around their hips. Several of these pilgrims were having their hair shaved off in a mundun ceremony. It reminded me of when I had my own head shaved during my cancer journey.

Nathaniel and I were hypnotized by the scenery. Before we embarked in our rowboat, I took a photo of my young Indian prince with his gleaming smile. Then we said goodbye and departed. Our helmsman navigated along the river upstream, downstream, then upstream again. Nathaniel became intrigued by our large rowboat. At his request, the captain allowed him to row the boat. Exalted by the morning's glory, I drifted into a meditative silence with my eyes only slightly open.

At the end of our excursion, Pratish led us to a different part of downtown. We walked through tiny winding alleys until Pratish stopped to receive blessings from one of the oldest priests and sages in Kashi. He was Pratish's favorite holy man and must have been over a hundred years old. The Baba was perched high outside on a small cement platform next to a minuscule shrine. He was wrapped in a red cloth, layered with a red, white, and gray sweater and purple-gray shawl and wore a white turban around his head. Pratish bowed and received his blessings. In silence, I approached the platform and leaned forward bowing, wanting to pay homage to him. He anointed my forehead between my eyebrows on my third eye with sacred ashes called *vibhuti* and a red turmeric paste called *kumkum* while softly reciting invocations in Sanskrit.

We stopped to warm up in a tiny store with the best chai masala tea in town. Then we walked toward the main avenue. Along our path, we noticed many homeless, starving dogs. One of them sat in front of an Indian fellow who was eating breakfast in the street. The dog stared at him from a few feet away, wagging his tail and begging for a morsel. I had no food to feed him. I asked the young man, "Why don't you share with him? Ah, look at him! He's hungry, like you." He gave me a glance of hesitation, perhaps wondering what kind of crazy foreigner would dare to speak out for such a creature. After a few moments, he tore out a big piece of his sandwich and threw it to the dog who, taking no chances, gobbled it up quickly. It was time for us to go. I wore a happy grin when the three of us jumped into the taxi.

Pratish said, "Vivi, you remind me of the beloved saint of Shirdi, Shri Sai Baba. When the holy master was alive long ago, he fed homeless dogs all the time, all kinds of creatures and mendicants. He said he could not eat unless he fed his friends first. He fed dozens of dogs and the poor first, then ate. Watching you in the past few days . . . well, you're inspiring me to do something here for the homeless dogs. I'll look into it for sure."

"That would be so beautiful, Pratish," I said. "You express your devotional love and compassion for the Divine Mother in this way. Many people in India need help. At least many international nonprofit organizations and other single individuals help. The good news is there is a huge humanitarian movement around the world. Together, one day we will end poverty and misery. Though when it comes to the sufferings and pain of the animals, the mentality in India is very different, as it is in many other developing countries. Fewer people help suffering animals, or are sensitive toward their pain. Many people look on them as pests and are nasty and abusive toward them. I have witnessed it too many times. Together we need to help raise consciousness on our planet. Profound transformation needs to happen within each one of us. When we are awakening to our ultimate nature, genuine transformation happens. I was greatly blessed to discover the ancient yogic and tantric paths are extremely effective at that. I'm so grateful to my beloved Sadhguru, beyond words and tears."

A wave of bliss erupted within my being as tears welled up in my eyes.

"Yes, Vivi, you're right," he said. "I see that too. Now I'm determined to do something. Next time you come visit, you'll see."

By then we had reached the lobby of our hotel. We hugged and said goodbye.

That night my fever returned with a vengeance. By nine o'clock, I was in bed, covered by a heavy blanket, and sweating.

I woke up at dawn the next morning and realized that another extraordinary year with our beloved Sadhguru had flown by. The time had come to visit him at the Isha Yoga International Center for the first time. It was located a few hours away from Coimbatore in Tamil Nadu, South India. Although I was still coughing hard and running a fever, I continued to get up at dawn to do my sadhana, preparing for a rare opportunity to attend the Samyama program coming up the following February. I could not wait to be by his lotus feet.

Forty-Seven

THE ANCIENT MYSTICAL SCIENCE OF
CONSECRATION AND TRANSCENDENCE

AS NATHANIEL AND I ENTERED the gates of the Isha Yoga International Center, a volunteer-run nonprofit organization dedicated to raising human consciousness and developing full human potential, its subtle energy enraptured my being. Tucked in the green foothills of the Velliangiri Mountains in the southern Indian state of Tamil Nadu, the yoga center is adorned with tall palm trees and a reserve forest with wildlife on 150 acres—a rare jewel that emanated intoxicating energy. I knew that my beloved master's yoga center was distinctive in its spiritual offerings.

We checked in at the Nalanda Conference Center. We dropped our luggage and had only a few minutes left to catch dinner. We marched to the dining hall, removed our sandals, and entered. Everyone sat silently on the floor, lined up facing each other, finishing their meals. A large photo of Sadhguru hung on the wall. A few volunteers showed up at our feet carrying big buckets and served us delicious vegetarian Indian food. After dinner, we washed our dishes and explored this mystical land.

All I desired was to meditate in the Dhyanalinga. It was past 8:00 p.m., and many volunteers were inside cleaning the yogic temple. I had a day off before starting the Sunethra, a small and intimate program for the well-being of our eyesight.

In the dark, not knowing where to go, Nathaniel and I walked to the Adiyogi Alayam hall where I would be taking my upcoming Samyama program the following February. Along the way, we discussed this extraordinary ancient yogic science of consecration, reflecting on what our beloved master Sadhguru has said: "If you transform mud into food, we call this agriculture. If you make food into flesh and bone, we call this digestion. If you make flesh into mud, we call this cremation. If you can make this flesh or even a stone or an empty space into a divine possibility, that is called consecration."*[1]

The following morning, Nathaniel rose early to run around the ashram while I lingered in bed trying to feel better. I had not stopped coughing all night and had a burning fever. A few hours later I did my sadhana in the bedroom. When my fever had diminished, I decided to tour this magnificent center. I changed into a long white cotton skirt and a kurta and put on my sandals. I strolled through the long pathway that led to the Goshala, the cow sanctuary, and chatted with the cows and their calves for a while. I loved watching these gentle creatures with their long hanging ears. Memories of my profound experience with Krishna's presence and the cows at the Art of Living's Goshala came to my being.

I reached the front of the outer *parikrama*, a walkway to the yogic temple where I saw the prodigious Nandi statue—a thirteen-foot-tall black iron bull, filled with sacred ashes, herbs, and earth. Nandi symbolizes eternal waiting. Sadhguru says that waiting in the yogic tradition is the greatest virtue, and that Nandi represents the symbol of meditativeness.

As I strolled around, people greeted me with the humble hand gestures saying, "Namaskaram." I did the same, smiling, feeling like I was floating. The sunlight cast golden tones everywhere. The tropical heat on my aching body and the ashram's effervescent energy soothed my spirit. Before entering the Dhyanalinga's inner walkway, I removed my sandals and left them at the coat check. I knew the Dhyanalinga temple does not ascribe to any religious faith or specific belief system, nor does it require any worshipping, prayer, or ritual to enter. It is as universal as the sky is boundless, opening its door and welcoming everyone who seeks to experience their ultimate nature.

I walked several steps into a large courtyard where I discovered the Theerthakund—a subterranean copper pool built of granite blocks. It is known in the yogic tradition that bathing in water enhances one's receptivity, especially getting one's hair wet. I always shower and wash my hair

* © Sadhguru

before I do my sadhana. Since I was feeling better, I decided to take a dip in the Theerthakund before entering the Dhyanalinga. The Theerthakund holds an energy form consecrated by Sadhguru based on ancient yogic science; its water is even more conducive to balancing pranic energy that leads to well-being and spiritual unfoldment—a preparatory step for delving deeper into other dimensions of reality beyond the physicality of this realm. This *rasalinga* is designed to help reactivate the dormant kundalini life-force energy within our system.

At the Theerthakund, I took a shower and changed into a long maroon garment. Drenched, I stepped down onto the steep and broad steps leading deep into the earth. I plunged my big toe into its vibrant water. A small linga was immersed at the center. The water was very cold. Chills and goosebumps traveled through my aching body. I submerged my head and played like this for a while until I held the linga in my arms and placed my forehead upon it, sending out invocations for realization, well-being, and happiness for all. The sunlight filtered through its open window frame, creating an ethereal aura. A wave of gratitude overwhelmed my heart, pulverizing it into infinite particles of Divine love. Tears kept rolling down my cheeks. After fifteen minutes of immersion in its blessed water, I rinsed and dressed and walked back to the inner parikrama of the Dhyanalinga, still dripping.

~

Dhyana MEANS "MEDITATION" AND LINGA "form" in Sanskrit. Upon entering the Dhyanalinga's gateway or *thorana*, I bowed in reverence, touching the first high stone step, remembering that Sadhguru says a linga is the first and the final form before dissolution. This perfect ellipsoid becomes an everlasting powerhouse of energy when energized. The science of creating and consecrating this temple is based on ancient yogic knowledge. Sadhguru consecrated the Dhyanalinga using the process called prana *prathistha* that pushes Divine energies and life forces to their highest level, and then locks them. In the beginning, he did it with the help of many meditators, and then for the latest and final stage of its completion with only a few other meditators. As Sadhguru explained it, the linga allows energy to be intensified to the highest level at which it can still retain a form. Beyond that point, the form dissolves.

Sadhguru says that ancient temples were not built as places of worship, but as energized spaces to recharge and transform ourselves within our innermost core. They were built with this knowledge and understanding of inner spiritual evolution.

This Dhyanalinga is the first of its kind to be successfully accomplished in over two thousand years. Its inner parikrama is opened as a central inner pathway embracing the blue sky. On both sides, its covered aisles are adorned with six prodigious granite bas-relief sculptures and two shrines. Each one of the panels depicts a wondrous moment in the lives of six South Indian Rishis who attained enlightenment.

Every fifty minutes throughout the day, the Dhyanalinga's volunteer attendants allow a new group of seekers in. At the sound of a bell, individuals who are already inside may exit at that precise moment. Then a new group of meditators are permitted. One may come in and out or stay as long as desired. While waiting for the bell to ring, I sat in its central pathway with my eyes closed, head slightly turned toward the blue sky while the sunlight and hot breeze stroked my wet hair. I could feel already a sublime and subtle intoxicating energy infiltrate my being. Effortlessly, I drifted into a meditative state. All at once I heard the bell. It was time to enter this splendid elliptical orange temple that sheltered its priceless Dhyanalinga.

Since it was early morning, the yogic temple was not too busy. I walked in with only a few others, smeared sacred ashes on my third eye, neck, and heart areas, and bowed. I followed the flow and sat on the other side of this energy form, facing its opened gates. I closed my eyes and fell into a profound silence. When I heard the bell again, I could not believe fifty minutes had elapsed. I'd only just closed my eyes a few seconds ago! I welled up with tears of gratitude for Sadhguru's master, my beloved Sadhguru, and the other meditators who contributed to the temple's consecration. My heart exploded with Divine love.

I remained there lost in stillness with my eyes rolled up to infinity for close to three hours. I lost track of time. I could not feel my limbs, yet my consciousness permeated the entire cosmos. When I tried to stand up, my legs had frozen. I rubbed them hard to bring back circulation. After a while, I stood, walked to the front, and prostrated with great reverence for the Dhyanalinga and its creators.

～

AFTER LEAVING THE DHYANALINGA, I visited the Linga Bhairavi Devi temple. It was already packed with meditators chanting mantras and making offerings by the Devi's altar. Upon entering, I became enraptured by the Divine feminine energetic field. I noticed the Shiva's trident, signifying triumph over the three gunas, the principles governing the cosmos. The left wall near the shrine was lit with dozens of tiny lamps, creating a translucent golden glow. Shafts of sunlight sifted through the intricate opened ceiling while aromatic incense from the pooja infused the temple with a mystical haze. The aura of this Devi temple intoxicated my being with its otherworldly powerful and fierce energy.

Sadhguru says, "In India, people use deities in very powerful ways. Any number of Devi worshippers are there, when they sit in front of the Devi, they have a tremendous insight into various aspects of life, but once they step out, they will be innocent of what they uttered just a little while ago."*²

Once I entered, there Bhairavi Devi was. Her piercing, haunting eyes gazed at us from her whimsical form. This black, eight-foot-tall Bhairavi Devi linga symbolizes an all-encompassing and compassionate deity and the nurturing and creative aspects of the cosmos. Devi, a manifestation of the Divine Mother's presence, was born on the physical realm in this ellipse form. As Sadhguru explained once at *darshan*, Devi is like a tool, a technology for meditators to express our Bhakti yoga, our love and devotion for the Divine feminine principle aspect of creation.

I held in my hands a small basket of offerings called *samarpanam* consisting of white jasmine flowers, mango leaves, kumkum, a coconut, and a leaflet with Bhairavi Devi mantras. I followed the line leading in front of the Devi linga, where a Bhairagini Maa performed rituals. As I approached, my

---

* © Sadhguru

mind remained emptied and still, while my heart overflowed with love and devotion for the Divine Mother. Deep down I knew the Divine Mother's aspect of creation, this feminine principle energy, has always been within my being. This feminine essence permeates the whole of existence. She manifests in billions of different ways.

Each individual approached the altar with reverence, made their offerings, and sat to experience her energy. When I reached the shrine, I offered my samarpanam. The Bhairagini Maa took the coconut from my hand, broke it in half, and gave me back a few of these items as prasad, the deity's blessings. Then I sat there right in front of the Devi linga with my eyes closed. All at once an intense wave of ebullient energy transported my being. My whole body shook from her shakti.

I did not pray or invoke; I just remained there for over one hour, vibrating with the Devi's compassionate energy in a meditative state with a still, serene mind and bursting, blissful, loving heart. Her presence was so powerful and palpable that my cells vibrated with her Divine energy and grace. These mystical experiences are beyond the physical and can never be comprehended with the logical mind. Worshipping this form or that one does not make a difference to my being. Ultimately, I know that I worship the Divine Source, that creative intelligence which permeates the core of all sentient beings, what many of us may call "God." I already knew, fully realized, and recognized long ago that Devi is not the ultimate Source, Supreme God. The Bhairavi Devi linga itself is not an object of worship viewed as God, rather a vehicle, a portal to the ultimate Source, to experience Divine grace. Linga Bhairavi Devi is another doorway to the Divine for individuals who want to revere the feminine energy in the creation.

Sadhguru says Linga Bhairavi Devi strengthens the three foundational chakras by helping to stabilize the body, mind, and energy in the body. Whether we seek to transcend the physical realm, enjoy life with well-being and bliss, or acquire materials, Devi assists in whatever longing our heart may hold. Before leaving the temple, I prostrated on the stone ground in the "Devi Dandam" with my left arm extended in abandon and reverence toward Bhairavi Devi while tears of gratitude rained down. This prostration is considered the preferred position for becoming more receptive to her grace. Electrified by her grace, all at once my left arm spontaneously bounced back and forth very fast over the ground as my body shook forcefully from her shakti. Over the years, I have discovered from experiencing her energy and grace that Bhairavi Devi has a very distinctive, compassionate, and amusing presence. She often makes me laugh hysterically in ecstatic trances.

~

IN HIS CELEBRATED AND INSIGHTFUL book *Tantra: The Path of Ecstasy*, internationally known yoga scholar and researcher Georg Feuerstein says,

> *"Terms like primitive polytheism that have been applied to Tantra and Hinduism in general are ready-made labels that fail to do justice to the actual situation. The masculine and feminine deities worshipped in the Tantric rituals are personifications of specific intelligent energies present in the subtle dimension. Beyond this, the Tantric practitioners also understand that the gods and goddesses are ciphers, symbols that point beyond their immediate forms of manifestation to the absolute Godhead, the singular Being. The Tantrikas are well aware that a deity is a limited being and not the ultimate Reality itself. Gods and goddesses can, however, become portals to that Reality. Such personifications of the Divine are in the service of devotion (Bhatki yoga) which Tantric practitioners cultivate to varying degrees."[3]*

Our precious blue and green planet is in grave need of a renaissance of celebrating the feminine principle of energy. The great cosmic Divine Mother is that feminine principle energy. This Divine feminine energy has been suppressed and oppressed throughout the centuries by manifestations of many patriarchal religions and societies. For instance, history tells of the Dark Ages where thousands of women, high priestesses who were extremely evolved spiritually, who worshipped the Divine feminine aspect and had many extraordinary siddhis (spiritual powers and paranormal abilities ascribed to the Tantric adepts and masters), were burned alive in public places as witches. They were wrongly perceived as a major threat because of their spiritual powers. For over four thousand years, the masculine mindset has been destroying, oppressing, and exploiting Mother Earth, its animals, and many women and elders.

The feminine energy principle is characterized with many attributes—such as nurturing, nourishing, compassionate, loving, giving, healing, creative, intuitive, and benevolent—and can be very powerful and fierce in a host of positive ways. Many of these qualities have been lacking to some degree on our planet for thousands of years. During the Paleolithic and Neolithic times, many tribes venerated the feminine principle energy manifested in the physical form as a goddess or deity. Over the centuries, matriarchal societies (with a feminine principle mindset) flourished in peace, harmony, and reverence for Mother Earth and all living creatures.

Within the fields of archeology, anthropology, and art history, we can discover many examples where our ancestors worshipped and honored goddess energy around our planet. I remember from my days when I studied art history that the Venus of Willendorf sculpture, which dates back to circa 25,000 BC, and the Goddess Laussel statue struck a chord within my being because they venerated this feminine energy. This Divine feminine energy aspect of the creative Source is accessible to all regardless of gender and is especially beneficial to males who have suffered from the disconnection caused by patriarchal societies or homophobic views.

There is an extremely urgent need to rebalance these male and female principles within ourselves. As I spoke about in earlier chapters, Shakti is the primordial energy of the Source of creation. In the Yoga tradition, Shakti is regarded as the Goddess Mother, especially prominent in Tantra Yoga when kundalini is awakening and arising. This dormant kundalini energy within is the most significant psycho-spiritual force of the subtle body. I discovered that this Divine feminine energy tends to be more associated with the female gender in general. Perhaps our nature is more receptive and open to it. The fact that we women are giving birth to life could make us more open to it, though any gender can deeply connect with this feminine energy principle. We all have within our beings the masculine and the feminine energy aspects.

The merging of Shiva/Shakti, the masculine and feminine principles within us, is the ultimate harmonious and necessary union within our being to experience our full human and Divine potential. Their union creates phenomenal forces allowing us to realize and experience divinity from within. When they merge as One in the one-thousand-petal lotus chakra on top of our head, they are in perfect harmonic marriage. My former beloved master, Gurudev, once said the most precious gift we could offer him on his birthday was to realize how very beautiful we are. He said only then can Divinity dawn within us.

Besides reviving the feminine aspect of the Source, there is also another extremely urgent need to collectively expand the consciousness on our planet by breaking down our limited perceptions and false views, especially the rigid egocentric and logical mindset that causes the illusion of separation. By dissolving this divisive perception into a harmonious one beyond our dualistic mindset, we can experience oneness. If we are going to survive as a species, each one of us has to wake up, realize, and experience that we are all interconnected and interdependent through the same Source, the same truth—an ever-expanding web of life. Devotion is to be devoid of oneself by opening up this grand gate to this highest intelligence of the Source.

~

WHILE AT THE ASHRAM, I reflected on the rich and beautiful path of Tantric yoga, and how terribly misunderstood it is by most Western nations. Most have reduced and degraded it to an acrobatic sexual endeavor. Georg Feuerstein says in *Tantra: The Path of Ecstasy,*

> *"The paucity of research and publications on the Tantric heritage of Hinduism has in recent years made room for a whole crop of ill-informed popular books on what I have called 'Neo-Tantrism.' Their reductionism is so extreme that a true initiate would barely*

recognized the Tantric heritage in these writings. The most common distortion is to present Tantra yoga as a mere discipline of ritualized or sacred sex. In the popular mind, Tantra has become equivalent to sex. Nothing could be farther from the truth!"[4]

Sadhguru says, "Unlike sexuality, which tends to find release at the lower level of the energy system, tantra is about building our energies to the fountain-head of the uppermost dimension of the energy system, so that one's energies spill from the top."*[5]

～

THE FOLLOWING MORNING, THE SUNETHRA eye program began. My heart longed to sit by Sadhguru's lotus feet and lose myself in meditation inside the Dhyanalinga and the Bhairavi Devi temple again.

However, during the night a high fever had consumed my being. I developed an endless cough and a painful sore throat. Over the following few days while I trained in the program, I kept falling asleep; I was burning in fever at night. I feared I was contagious and decided to visit the doctor at the ashram.

She checked my blood pressure, looked in my throat, and put a thermometer in my mouth. She exclaimed in her sweet Indian accent, "Oh! Vivi, your fever is over 103 degrees! You have bad bronchitis. You need to be in bed; get plenty of rest!"

The doctor prescribed some antibiotic, cough syrup, and other medicine. There was no cost for the visit and the medicine. I said I would offer a generous donation in return to help with Isha's social programs. I went to our room, swallowed the medication, wrapped myself up in a big blanket, and slept for over fifteen hours. I woke up a few times aching and drenched with sweat.

The following late afternoon I met with the Siddha doctor who was one of the wonderful Maa who cared for us at the Sunethra program. She took my pulse with her fingers and said, "Vivi, sleep is the best medicine. Go back to bed now! Don't worry about the program."

★ © Sadhguru

During one of those nights, a vivid dream manifested. In noble silence, Sadhguru stood in front of my being extending his arms, holding a blossoming white lotus flower. A subtle ethereal light emanated from the lotus. Sadhguru placed it in my hands and disappeared. I had never dreamed of Sadhguru before, at least that I could remember.

The following morning, when the gong sounded around 4:30 a.m., Nathaniel and our group had left for an extended hike in the mountains where they would swim in the cascade in the forest. I had wished to go, but I was too weak to awaken. When I got up later, I did my sadhana in the bedroom on the floor again. Right after I returned to the Dhyanalinga, I sat there at the same spot on the cold ground of the temple and drifted into what appeared to be a deep, long meditation. Only my consciousness pervaded, expanding over the boundless cosmos like I was falling into eternity. When I emerged from this state three hours later, my fever, harsh cough, and sore throat had disappeared from my body.

∼

AT THE LAST MINUTE THAT afternoon, a satsang was announced for that evening. Sadhguru had arrived at the ashram earlier than expected from his travels—the following early morning Nathaniel and I were returning home! How auspicious! I felt beyond blessed. Exuberant laughter permeated the center's atmosphere. Everyone walked toward the outer parikrama in front of the Theerthakund's entrance, where the satsang was to take place. The sun adorned the rim of these tropical mountains with varying degrees of pink, orange, and violet. Over a thousand of us, residents, meditators, volunteers, *brahmacharis* (monks), and *sannyasis* sat on the grass smiling at Sadhguru's presence while the Sounds of Isha played haunting chants.

Out of respect for the South of India's tradition, women sat on Sadhguru's left while men sat on the right. I sat there like a Shiva statue with my spine erect, feeling deeply meditative and serene in the warm breeze. Sadhguru spoke a little and asked if we had any questions. I raised my hand. A volunteer brought a microphone to me. I stood, saying in a faint and hoarse voice, "Namaskaram Sadhguru," in perfect synchronicity with a gentleman on the other side who also stood to say the same words. A volunteer had run to him on the other side at the same time, and neither volunteer knew what the other had done. Sadhguru and the crowd burst into laughter. I smiled and remained silent waiting for our master. The male participant started to ask his question. Sadhguru gestured for him to sit down, saying, "The lady first!" Tears welled up in my eyes.

"Beloved Sadhguru, it is our first time here at your ashram. Words fail to express my gratitude and joy. It's so beautiful!" I choked up. A knot formed in my throat. I closed my eyes and remained silent while tears rolled on my cheeks. Sadhguru closed his eyes too. Then after a long moment, I said softly, "Sadhguru, how can I express my gratitude? Dhyanalinga, wow! What you and the other meditators have created! I have been very sick since we arrived and could not join our group today for a long hike. Instead I have been going in the afternoon to meditate in the Dhyanalinga. I just close my eyes and drift so deep in meditation that I don't feel my body anymore. All my symptoms go away. It is like I'm everywhere in the universe."

I noticed Sadhguru kept his eyes closed while listening and rubbing his ring fingers with his thumbs. I took a few deep breaths. "Sadhguru you spoke in your book *Mystic's Musing* about karma being like the game of snakes and ladders. Is there a point on the spiritual path where it is safe, where there is no more chance of sliding backward anymore?"

Sadhguru remained silent with his eyes closed for a while. Then he opened his eyes, looked at me, and addressed the crowd with wise words. He repeated very similar words from his book. Here are a few quotes to simplify. "This life is like a snake and ladder game, you know? You go up one ladder, then the next snake catches you, and you come down. Now, yoga is to get out of this game. Enough is enough—how many times to go up, how many times to go down? Now, you want to just strip off all the snakes from the board and just walk straight towards your goal. That is when you become spiritual."*[6] He was referring here in this last line to all the various initiations into sadhana at Isha Foundation.

As he spoke, Sadhguru was looking around. "In indiscrimina' responsibility, there are no more snakes on your board. You c

* © Sadhguru

any more karma; it is over. The moment you focus the whole attention on yourself, you will see you are the source of everything that is happening here. The moment this awareness comes into you, you cannot build any more karma; it's finished. Now only what is stored up, you have to handle. It's very simple. Once some awareness seeps into you, working out the past, working your way through the past becomes simple."*7

Then Sadhguru looked in my direction saying something like: when the day comes for you, you will know for sure. That day has not come yet. I won't miss it. So no matter if you are a little sick, you must continue to put your foot on the pedal and go on full speed. I felt he was speaking to me directly. His wise words resonated deep within my being. I overflowed with profound gratitude and love for Sadhguru. He closed his eyes again and started chanting a Sanskrit mantra about liberation in his rich baritone voice. We all closed our eyes and joined as the moonlight settled in, reflecting a refreshing cool blue light.

At dawn we left the ashram with our driver for Coimbatore's airport. I still had leftover food that I fed to many emaciated homeless dogs on the way. Even though I was still feeling sick, I felt profoundly serene. I could not hold back my tears of gratitude as I contemplated the precious moments we'd had with our beloved Sadhguru so far. I could not wait to return to this mystical land and be at his lotus feet again.

Forty-Eight

BEYOND THE BLUE SKY

NATHANIEL WAS CONCERNED MY BRONCHITIS would turn into pneumonia again. He insisted I see my general physician, and my doctor put me on a much stronger antibiotic. I had only a few months left to prepare for the Indian ashram for the Samyama program. I returned to the complete holistic detox program Dr. Cousens had put me on and returned to waking up around 6:00 a.m. to perform intense sadhana for four hours each day.

One late night after meditation, I stumbled on a step in our sanctum. I lost my balance and almost fell down, my spine absorbing the shock. I righted myself, but the damage was done. The next morning I had painful throbbing spasms where I had herniated my L3 and L4 discs long ago. I wondered how I was going to complete the Samyama—could I meditate for approximately fourteen hours a day for eight straight days in silence and sleep on the floor with almost one thousand other meditators with an injured lower back? I tried everything to nurse my spine, and I continued with my yoga practices but modifying my asanas. I knew while healing my lower back that it would be preferable to stop the postures, but I did not entirely stop them.

One evening Nathaniel was curious about the program I was preparing for.

I told him, "Baby, I don't know much about Samyama. I have not taken the program yet. But I know this much: Because Samyama opens the gateway into a different dimension of reality beyond the physical, most people have a hard time relating to it or understanding it."

"Really!" Nathaniel exclaimed.

"I heard Samyama is about freeing oneself from the bondage of karma, about attainting a heightened level of consciousness. In a state of Samyama, one can experience the most profound state of meditativeness—a doorway into the beyond. I am sure it is a phenomenal program, knowing Sadhguru!"

Not long before my departure, an MRI confirmed I had reinjured my L3 and L4 discs and they were bulging. But I did not want to cancel my trip. My intuition kept telling me, "Go! No matter what, Vivi. Go!" My foot kept pressing at full speed on the pedal as Sadhguru had recommended at the satsang. I was going.

The night prior to my departure for India, I lingered in bed in wonderment. I shared with Nathaniel, "What a synchronicity, baby! Remember over seven years ago I named our white Turkish cat 'Shiva'? I have been calling his name since then. Now Shiva has finally come into my life, my heart, his shrine! Do you remember that following year after rescuing our Shiva, I named our rescued three-legged orange cat 'Isha' without knowing the existence of Isha Foundation and Sadhguru? Isn't that auspicious?"

Nathaniel smiled. "Goodnight darling; it is late! You better go to sleep, otherwise you won't get up tomorrow." He gave me a kiss. I laughed.

~

A BRILLIANT SUN SHONE IN the endless blue sky upon my arrival at the Isha Yoga International Center. A hot breeze played with the folds of my long, flowing white skirt. Everything appeared to be more alive than ever. Again the mystical aura of the ashram swept over my being with its intoxicating energy as I walked toward my liberation. All I wanted to do was disappear and dissolve in the Dhyanalinga and transcend the vastness of that eternal Divine embrace.

I stayed at the Nalanda Center & Suite again, spending my first week adjusting to the time change and the ashram life in a program called Ayur Rasayana Intensive at the Rejuvenation Center. Atika, a loving middle-aged Indian woman, greeted me at the entrance of this center. We had never met before. She had discovered my artwork, in a documentary on yoga in a presentation in London, and had purchased one of my original paintings many years ago.

"Vivianne, at last, I am very happy to meet you! I recognized your name on our list of participants. I am Atika. I bought *Prana* from you! We spoke many times over the phone when I used to live in London. It must have been over six years ago when you were undergoing chemotherapy."

Atika had been living at the ashram for the past few years and had become a full-time Isha volunteer. We hugged for a long time.

It seemed like a dream: Both of us were there at Sadhguru's magnificent and mystical ashram in South India. Our dear friend Lily, who had done the BSP with us, was already sitting for the Ayur Rasayana, almost ready to begin. After talking with Atika for a while, I joined Lily and the group.

Over the following days, Atika and I shared many treasured moments about being on the path with Sadhguru. I could not hold back my tears, feeling overwhelmed by the opportunity of taking Samyama in his presence. In the tropical hut where we took our fresh, raw vegetarian meal every day, Atika inquired about my cancer journey. She remained silent with glistening eyes as I shared.

"I don't know what to call this, Atika. To be here alive today experiencing Sadhguru's grace is beyond the impossible. I feel like I have waited hundreds of lifetimes for this opportunity with him," I said at the end of my tale.

Atika told me about a trip she had taken to the Himalayas at Mount Kailash and Lake Manasarovar with Sadhguru. I was awed by her story and became determined to one day trek to these mystical places with Sadhguru, despite my bad knee and chronic back pain.

A few days prior to entering the Samyama program, participants were asked to keep silence. That night I had dinner with Lily and other meditators at the Rejuvenation Center. Both of us lingered around laughing until everyone left. As we ambled toward the door, I exclaimed, "Okay, Lily, when we walk out that door, we are officially in silence for the next ten days!"

She lingered by the edge. "No, Vivi, I am not coming out!" I tried to pull her out by the hand several times. She kept pulling me in a tug of war. We laughed so loud! All at once in silence I pushed her out the door, bowed in namaskaram, and walked away. It was around 10:00 p.m., and the lights at the ashram had just turned off.

~

ON THE MORNING SAMYAMA BEGAN, I felt invigorated and ready to embrace the plunge into a higher plane of reality. Over nine hundred of us international Isha meditators headed toward the consecrated Adiyogi Alayam, parading to our mystical nest. Each of us pulled large suitcases into the hall. We then packed what we needed for the program into a smaller bag. The rest was stored in a larger room in the back of the hall. Every participant dropped their wallets, jewelry, and phones at counters where volunteers packed and stored them. We picked up our sheets, pillows, and those who had been given permission received a Back Jack meditation chair. All the cots were arranged in perfect rows across the gigantic floor. Around twenty-five female meditators lined up ahead of me.

Upon authorization, participants sprinted in, trying to get a spot as near as possible to Sadhguru's dais. Wherever we landed was going to be our designated living quarter for the next eight days. I found myself right behind Lily's bedding area on the fourth row, facing Sadhguru's dais. The synchronicity reminded me of our BSP.

My bed chosen, I climbed to the second floor with my small suitcase, where several storage rooms, public toilets, sinks, and showers were assigned. I was with all the other female participants; the setup was the same for the male participants on the other side of the building.

Under this single roof we would eat, laugh, cry, sleep, and meditate together in complete silence without any eye contact whatsoever, within the confines of the courtyard of the Adiyogi Alayam. The intention was to be deprived of any outward sensory stimulus, so as to focus inward during the entire eight days. If any of us broke the rules, that person would be disqualified and removed from the hall.

As soon as the Samyama was in process, I lost track of time, space, and sound. We must have been getting up around 4:00 a.m. and going to bed around 11:00 p.m. Each day seemed like a lifetime.

It was 100 degrees almost every day, while at dawn it was freezing. When I did my sadhana, I often covered my head in the small white blanket I had brought from home. By 11:00 a.m., the heat and humidity were stifling. My white kurta often became soaking wet. I took brief cold showers three times a day, and I chanted mantras in Sanskrit in the stall. Then I would change clothing all over again. In the late night, the cold shower rejuvenated my body after an intense fourteen hours of meditation, yoga, and spiritual processes. Even though silence was the golden rule, somehow my chanting was not interrupted by anyone. I never heard anyone else chanting or complaining. With no mirrors in the bathrooms, makeup and hairdos were nonexistent.

Many of the participants began to get the flu. Hard coughing and sneezing were everywhere. A line of buckets lay outside near the entrance for several participants who needed to run out of the hall to vomit. Over the course of the program, several seekers were pulled out from the Samyama.

~

ALL THROUGH THE PROGRAM I did not feel my back at all; it was as if it was numbed. The pain from my tumble at home and my herniated discs dissipated into the ether all by the grace of Sadhguru. He knew my heart—how much I wanted to complete this program. One day at dawn during sadhana I developed a fever and sore throat. I began coughing and sneezing, as another infection attacked my lungs. Feeling faint, I lay down in savasana invoking Sadhguru with a pure heart. Tears welled up in my eyes as I murmured, "Sadhguru, I need your help. How am I going to make it through this program?"

After our practices, it was time for a break. I walked out of the hall, drank a mixture of dried green powder made of various greens and super foods, and mixed it in water which, prior to the program, I had been given permission to take.

Fifteen minutes later, I lay down on my cot. All at once, my fever, sore throat, and coughing disappeared just like that. My energy bounced back as if nothing had ever happened. I kept whispering, "Thank you so much, Sadhguru. I'm so grateful!" as I shed tears. Uplifted by his grace and energy, I knew in that moment that I would make it through the Samyama.

~

ONE DAY DURING AN INTENSE spiritual process with Sadhguru, I became exalted in ecstasy, laughing hysterically and rolling around on the floor with my blanket over my head. Half an hour must have gone by like that. I dropped my blanket, still laughing hysterically with my eyes closed, lost in a sea of ecstatic bliss. Then, I sat with my legs crossed in lotus position. My body temple spontaneously began to rock. It kept rolling into some kind of peculiar headstand of its own accord. Like a dry leaf swirling in the wind, my entire torso and crossed legs became perpendicular to the floor, elevated up in the air for over one minute or more at the time while my hands remained on both sides of my head. This process kept repeating itself spontaneously as shakti blew my body up into this unbelievable acrobatic yoga asana which I had never performed or seen.

Finally, I settled for good on the floor and became very quiet and still. My hands found themselves on top of my head where the one-thousand-petal lotus, Sahasrara chakra, is situated. My wrists touched each other with my opened palms facing toward the sky. My fingers began to spread wide in some kind of geometric rhythmic form and then bloomed into a padma mudra—a blossoming lotus on top of my head.

I must have remained in this hand mudra gesture with my eyes closed for some time. I could feel a strong pull of energy forcing my fingers so hard it was as if someone was bending them as far as possible. A deep stillness and intensity permeated my being, as if my body had dissolved into ether. I have not been able to repeat this kind of acrobatic headstand or this intricate hand mudra since that time and will never be able to. It was only late that night when I went to my cot that I wondered how in the world my body could possibly do such asanas with two bulged discs—and not feel any back pain at all. Only by the grace of Sadhguru and Maha Shakti can such phenomena become manifest.

~

TOWARD THE END OF EACH day's final session, a few dozen of us strolled by the dais and prostrated on the ground in front of Sadhguru. He remained there seated in deep meditation, radiating energy like the sun emanating light to all buds and blossoming flowers. I often lay there sobbing, feeling overwhelmed by his presence and grateful for this extremely rare blessing. As the program progressed, we heard all kinds of sounds from participants experiencing intense spontaneous kriya. One female participant in the far back of the hall kept chirping loudly like a bird almost all day long, on and off. Several times I sent out the intention for her to get out of her cage and fly away free. I often wore my earplugs at night while hundreds of professional snorers made their music; I even wore them during the long meditation sessions because of the noise level from many participants experiencing intense spontaneous kriyas. The irony was—we were all silent!

In one session, Sadhguru asked us to stand up and relax our bodies. When Sadhguru began transmitting shaktipat, my body became like a rag doll. I collapsed face down into Lily's bedding. I almost fell on her. It took me a minute to get up, but I was not hurt. Following this process, we proceeded to a profound meditation. My legs and torso became caramel pudding. In a trancelike state, my body swirled in large circles until it lay itself on the ground. A mystical samadhi transcendence with the mad nectar of our Creator intoxicated my being. I could not get up or walk.

When I heard Sadhguru chanting my favorite verse from the Guru Pooja, the one sacred verse I sang entering the Eklingji temple near Udaipur, I chanted along with him. The Sanskrit words flew out of my being with great love and devotion. In one of the last spiritual processes as Sadhguru transmitted shaktipat, my body became completely rigid. All my muscles tensed, especially my core, as I took on higher voltages of shakti energy. My head began to move violently back and forth while an intense flood of energy pierced my being. I began to speak in tongues as a massive ball of energy moved up from my throat area toward my head, exploding in the area of my third eye. Even though my eyes were closed, I perceived several volunteers surrounding my being in a circle, trying to protect myself and others. This was one of the most important moments of the kundalini ascension.

During our final spiritual processes with Sadhguru, I inhaled his energy as I witnessed what appeared to be his subtle body or presence entering into my left nostril. I felt it penetrating inside my entire being.

~

SAMYAMA VANISHED TOO FAST, LIKE a rainbow after a major storm. On the last day, many of us fell in prostration in front of Sadhguru's dais. We all sobbed like infants, even the men. I remain very humbled by the extraordinary gifts showered upon us. To maintain the sanctity of the Samyama and my experiences of the phenomena beyond the physical, I keep these memories to myself, in a revered silence.

After the ending ceremony, the American participant group sat on the floor of a back room facing each other in rows for a festive celebration. Large banana leaves had been placed on the floor before us. We were encouraged to keep silent until the following afternoon where we would break silence in our final meeting. Volunteers served us a feast of vegetarian delicacies. We had eaten a minimum amount of food—quite bland—during the previous eight days to support our long meditation practices, so every bit tickled my stomach with delight.

I saw Lily sitting against the wall. I joined her, blessed my meal and all living beings, and began to eat. "Wow! This is so delicious, Vivi!" she exclaimed.

I turned my head, gesturing, "Shhh" with my finger on my lips. It was the first time Lily and I had made eye contact during the program.

She gave me a kiss on my cheek. "I am breaking my silence now! I'm done. Oh, come on, Vivi, talk to me! Please, sweetie . . . say something."

I cracked up laughing. She caught on laughing too, but I did not say a word. For once, I did not want to open my mouth. I felt I could remain in silence and stillness for another six months, a year, longer.

~

LATER THAT EVENING I HAD almost reached the Nalanda Center & Suites, when Atika walked by. She called me. We gazed at each other for a while in silence, tears in our eyes. She took me in her arms. We remained speechless for several minutes and cried. She knew.

Atika helped me carry my luggage to the front desk. The area was hectic, overflowing with new guests for the upcoming grand Mahashivratri celebration. The volunteers were busy. So I just sat there with a little smile on my lips by the front desk, lost in stillness in the midst of chaos. My eyes closed, and I followed the sweetness of my breath going in and out with full awareness for the following ten minutes. During my meditation, I tasted the effervescent blissful madness of the Divine nectar in an ecstatic samadhi. When I opened my eyes, I walked around like a drunkard. Divinity reverberated within every particle of my being.

There is no hierarchy in spirituality. There is only devotion, surrender, and oneness. A fragrant and beautiful flower is always born from filth . . . just as genuine and true success is born out of tremendous adversity. Spirituality is not something to teach. We all have it. In many ways, everyone can be a teacher. We can only awake to our divinity. Sadhguru says,

> *"In yoga, we always use the symbol of a lotus flower. A lotus grows best wherever the slush is thick—the filthier it is, the better. It is the same filth which blossoms into a beautiful and fragrant flower. Have you seen these symbolic images of yogis sitting in lotus posture, sitting upon lotuses, or with lotus flowers blossoming out of their heads? This is to show you, a lot of filth was thrown at them and they made flowers out of it. Do not carry a load of filth on your head. Life has thrown enough filth at you—it is time you learn to cure it into manure. Do not carry the experience of life as a wound. Let it become wisdom. This is a choice you have. Out of every experience of life, you can make a wound—or you can make wisdom out of it. The harder life has been upon you, the sooner you should become wise."*[1]

Vulnerability is essential to experience a dimension of reality beyond the physical realm. One must break free from logic to experience the light. When a sincere seeker is profoundly bonded with the beyond, he or she can move from compulsion to the phenomenal magic of existence and rediscover his or her true ultimate nature. Inner power is not about conquest and domination. Genuine power is a divine quality that awakens our ultimate and true nature by including and embracing all as oneself. There is only a minute

★ © Sadhguru

difference between compulsion and awareness. That is the practice of mindfulness. Happiness and bliss happen in that infinite moment.

Without knowing the path to our Creator, the Source, the great blessing of yoga, of Divine union, revealed itself . . . opening the majestic gates of its glorious splendors. My escape in search of myself led my being to lose myself in the boundless beauty of the eternal One. I realized that the tortured suffering and pain of my longing, my wailing of sorrow to be one with the Source, had vanished. An essence of freedom emanated in the heavenly breeze. A baby bird had awakened and flown out of her cage beyond the blue sky.

One month after my return from India in 2013 I flew to III in Tennessee for a four-day darshan with Sadhguru along with almost one thousand other meditators. Darshan means to see, to behold the Divine, and is also often interpreted as a blessing. Through these precious days and many spiritual processes with Sadhguru, a deeper imprint of Divinity implanted within my being, manifesting ultimately in a living process.

Over the course of darshan, I could not help but laugh, often hysterically. My being had become "blissfulness" itself. One night during satsang one of the aspirants in the far back asked Sadhguru a question with a frightened tone. In words similar to these, the aspirant said, "I'm afraid. There are crazy people here. I don't understand, Sadhguru, why many people here yell, cry, mourn, or make all kinds of weird noises and movements in your presence. What is going on with them?"

I burst out laughing. I was so intoxicated and ecstatic and could not control it.

Looking at this person, Sadhguru said, "Don't ask me—ask them! Why be afraid of something that is not yet in your experience? Let's just ask them." Then he looked at all of us. "Is there any one of you?"

I raised my hand, still laughing. The microphone landed in my hand. I stood addressing the crowd, glancing at our master and the other participants. In the fire of the moment, I said, bubbling with ecstasy, "There is no need to be afraid. It's so beautiful and precious to feel this Divine energy! Everyone experiences it differently. I rarely cry or mourn anymore, I just keep laughing! All my garbage is gone! Why be afraid? These divine phenomena can't be explained, only experienced. That is because of Sadhgurudev!"

Sadhguru interrupted me, saying jokingly, "Don't include me in this. I have nothing to do with this!"

Everybody laughed.

As I continued speaking, I noticed Sadhguru was sitting in a very casual and jovial demeanor. His right arm lay against his seat, his head twisted toward infinity, and his smiling, inebriated eyes remained half open in an ecstatic state of blissfulness. He was looking in my direction.

After that satsang, Sadhguru asked all of us to go outside in front of the Mahima hall to meditate on the full moon. It was 50 degrees, very cold for late April, and raining. It must have been around 11:00 p.m. then. I forgot I wasn't in India anymore. I had brought only light cotton summer clothing, one shawl, and sandals.

The rain began to fall a little harder. Not long after, one by one meditators disappeared. My dear friend Lily was one of the last individuals to leave. Later, she told me that when she left, Lily saw my being sitting very still, cross-legged like a goddess statue, mesmerized by the seduction of the blue moon.

I had fallen deeper into an extremely intense and exalted state of inclusive consciousness. My eyes could not remain opened even with all my will; they kept rolling back upward toward my third eye. I had fallen into a samadhi. Many hours must have elapsed into the night as if those hours had been only one breath. By then, my body temple had become soaking wet and frozen—though I did not feel it. The effulgent blue pearl reappeared. The most fierce and intense energy possessed every particle of my being. The blue pearl intensified and turned into an overwhelmingly powerful bright-white beam of light. It grew bigger and drew closer toward my being in an ethereal blue-white light, brighter than the sun and the full moon.

This supreme almighty light cannot be described. It kept expanding further into a dissolution, getting closer and closer and was about to engulf my entire being when suddenly my body temple could not contain this high-peak voltage of shakti energy.

My being snapped out of my physical form and floated into the light.

EPILOGUE

ON THE THIRD WEEK OF September, Nathaniel, Jasmine, and I departed for the Isha Institute of Inner Sciences (III) in Tennessee. The monumental consecration of the Adiyogi, the Abode of Yoga—the first of its kind in the Western hemisphere—would be taking place from September 23 to 25 in 2015. I had long awaited it with great anticipation, joy, and gratitude. This magnificent Abode of Yoga would be beyond the appearance of just a 30,000-square-foot meditation hall. It was to serve humanity as a powerful instrument for inner well-being, individual growth, and help to raise human consciousness so that we could transcend our limitations. This cocoon of transcendence is dedicated to the pursuit and practice of meditation—including all branches of yoga.

Every form in existence has its own reverberation, and a linga is such a form. This ellipsoid would be energized in a specific way to bring about the desired result. The science of consecration is so ancient, profound, and mystical. Even though I knew I was not ready physically to attend such a long, incredible, and very rare, intense spiritual process because of my health challenges and recovery, I would not have missed it for the world—even if I had to crawl to get there. To my being, this was the opportunity of a lifetime to consecrate my own body temple into a linga, as Sadhguru and all of us participants would consecrate the space and the copper linga through the powerful yogic process of prana pratishtha, using our life energies.

Consecration is a live process. As a tribute to the Adiyogi, the first yogi/guru named Shiva who offered this ancient yogic science of self-realization, inner well-being, and consecration approximately fifteen thousand years ago, this phenomenal Abode of Yoga is now available for all sincere and

willing seekers—regardless of age, gender, religious, ethnic, or socioeconomic background.

When we landed at the airport, I listened to a message from one of the
full-time Isha volunteers; we were invited to attend the official procession
at 9:00 p.m. that evening, during which the linga would be brought to the
Abode of Yoga by Sadhguru, followed by an intimate gathering and meditation with him. I was beyond grateful.

I looked at my watch; it was already 9:30 p.m.! And it would take us
approximately two hours, depending on the traffic, to reach III. Silently
I sent a strong intention to Sadhguru to be there by his side, then I let
it go. I knew in the depth of my heart these magical moments would be
historical and significant in my life.

~

BY THE TIME WE REACHED the ashram, it was around 11:30 p.m.
I figured the group might still be meditating. As we pulled the car into
the closest driveway, I could hear participants chanting out loud, the same
chant that haunted and grabbed hold of my being in the Nataraj ecstatic
fury dance at my BSP. A black Hummer with an open trailer was leading
the way, only twelve feet away from us. I trotted toward it. Many participants were walking behind it, chanting out loud. Others already stood
and chanted in the majestic stairway of the Abode of Yoga. Nathaniel and
Jasmine remained far behind. By the time I reached the vehicle, Sadhguru
had made a right turn toward the Abode. I walked alone right next to the
Hummer, only a few feet away from Sadhguru's side as he drove. I did not
plan anything. Grace and the invisible hand of the Divine synchronized this
auspicious embrace.

Sadhguru parked and lined up the vehicle by the stairway, where the
linga would be lifted up into the air with the help of pulleys. When he
opened the door of his vehicle, I stood there right in front of him, only a
few feet away. My heart burst with gratitude, stillness, and silence. My eyes
closed on their own, while tears of gratitude welled up in them. As Sadhguru and several volunteers coordinated the lifting process of the linga into

the Abode, all of us kept chanting out loud the same mantra honoring the Adiyogi Shiva. I stood there by the trailer only a few feet away from him, intense and in awe as my tears kept falling.

~

DURING THE CONSECRATION, NATHANIEL AND I had the immense blessing to sit in front. Men sat on Sadhguru's right side, women on his left side. The lovely volunteer who took care of us sat me right in front of the consecration site, only a few feet away from where the linga would be consecrated and partially submerged in water. Being in Sadhguru's presence, I longed only to close my eyes, to go deeper in silence and stillness.

From the very beginning, Sadhguru had shared with us the way to experience such consecration in depth is to be in silence. He said though most people would not do it and maintain it, a few would. He may have said that because of the magnitude of this event and the enormous crowd of close to fifteen hundred participants. His words resonated deep into my being. I decided to honor my satguru and observe silence for the following five days.

Sadhguru talked about many different kinds of relationships, though none may be compared to the Adiyogi Shiva, since it is a phenomenal energetic connection and an infinite possibility . . . bonding with the beyond. He shared that this consecration opportunity can become a boundless possibility. That is why Shiva is referred to as "shi-va"—"that which is not," that which is boundless. When a sincere seeker is profoundly touched, and bonds with the beyond, he or she can move from compulsion to the phenomenal magic of existence and rediscover his or her true ultimate nature.

Earlier on during the consecration process volunteers unveiled the gargantuan statue of Adiyogi Shiva, a pivotal point for most participants. It is not only the magnitude and impressive tenure of the Adiyogi Shiva statue that grabbed my being the most. It was his presence. An extraordinary and mighty energy engulfed every particle of my being in bliss, ecstasy, and exuberance. During the various and extremely intense mystical yogic processes, a Divine energetic force I could not comprehend and did not bother to understand just grabbed hold of my being. A tremendous phenomenon took over my entire being, transcending boundaries as the Source and creation became one and merged in deeper dimensions. By his grace, my third eye became activated again throughout these processes.

During most breaks, the crowd exploded in great joy, chanting, and dancing to the Sounds of Isha. The energy was so palpable that you could almost hold it. On several occasions, I trotted to the grand entrance mezzanine of the Abode and danced wildly in ecstatic fury. At one point as Sadhguru exited the hall, he signaled with a graceful gesture to a few of us who longed to chant the shivastotram to join the musicians. I flew up from my seat again to that spectacular mezzanine where most of the euphoric actions took place and dozens of musicians played. I sat on the ground with two Indian women. Suddenly, a microphone appeared in front of me. We chanted for another half hour with intensity, profound reverence, love, and gratitude for Adiyogi Shiva.

Sadhguru envisions the creation of many such consecrated Abodes of Yoga all over the world to help raise consciousness, to bring inner well-being to billions, to recognize the Adiyogi for his phenomenal contribution to human consciousness, and to express his profound reverence and gratitude. I joined Sadhguru long ago on his beautiful vision, also envisioning many more powerful, consecrated Abodes of Yoga and sanctums of grace celebrating and venerating the Divine feminine energy that is so needed on our beloved Mother Earth for the sake of all living beings. Just imagine if many more billions of individuals on our planet could experience such powerful transcendence and grace, bliss, and ecstasy! We would live in a transformed world.

Visitors from all around the globe can connect with the powerful energies of the Adiyogi Abode of Yoga at III just by sitting, doing spiritual processes, yogic practices, or simple offerings of water. Because the linga is submerged in water, visitors also have the opportunity to touch it, even pour water over their hands as an offering and connect with the energy that reverberates.

～

ON OUR LAST NIGHT, SADHGURU offered a dozen of the small Adiyogi artworks to several participants in recognition for their major contribution toward the creation of this consecrated Abode of Yoga. Nathaniel and I were beyond honored and humbled to receive a statue directly from his hands. One by one, as each couple and a few individuals approached the dais in silence, Sadhguru applied ashes on the third eye of each of the Adiyogi's statues, never laying one eye upon any of the recipients. He remained there intense and focused in this process as he smeared ashes on each of the statues.

Upon our arrival, we prostrated. When we raised from the ground in silence, I signaled to Nathaniel to bring the statue with him to his seat. He did and departed. I stood there still, silent and emptied as a vessel . . . in great reverence, gratitude, and deep love, making a namaskaram hand gesture, as I gazed at my beloved Sadhguru. Suddenly, he raised his head and gazed back at my being with such intensity while he signaled his head up and down slowly in a "Yes." After a moment, enraptured in each other's gazes, I turned back to my seat. His "yes" did not come across as a recognition for contribution to the Adiyogi Abode . . . just inner knowing. It was beyond that—a strikingly different kind of yes.

OUR ENTIRE WEEK FLEW BY like an ephemeral morning dew. On our last night, Sadhguru was going to impart darshan. At the last minute, he had to fly to California for an urgent meeting. The event still took place at the Mahima hall. When I went to sleep that night, I fell into the deepest meditation ever, in a samadhi state as my third eye exploded into all kinds of intricate, mighty, intense light forms. I kept falling in a bottomless pit into a mighty light, boundless to the beyond. By their own accord, my hands shook violently while my whole body temple became super intense with shakti energy. That was Shiva's darshan!

Words could never express these mystical experiences. The reality is, these dimensions of time and space do not exist for genuine yogi and yogini. When this phenomenal energetic connection is realized, it does not matter where one is on the planet or even disembodied. It is bonding with the beyond. Shiva's presence permeated every particle of my being. I never slept that night, only dissolved into the boundless nature of existence beyond the physical, touched by a formless dimension that is not physical in nature. I united with that which is boundless. These priceless moments during our week at III were the most glorious ones of my life so far.

On the morning of our departure, around 5:00 a.m., I rose from my samadhi and departed for the Abode of Yoga. As I walked into the space, I could clearly feel the intense powerful energy. That hall was no longer the same. It had been transformed into a mystical cocoon of transcendence.

~

IN THE SUMMER OF 2014, the magic of synchronicity and intuition created a rare opportunity for my being to walk and sit with the beloved Nobel Peace Prize nominee and Zen master Thich Nhat Hanh (known to his students as Thay, which means "teacher") at Plum Village in the South of France. It was a silent mindful retreat—the last one he ever conducted before suffering from a brain hemorrhage in November 2014.

During one walking meditation, Thay had us all stop in the countryside to have a picnic on the grass. I was blessed to sit diagonally from him. I had brought the only avocado I could find at a tiny market in the nearby village. We sat there all in silence and began to eat. I put my hands over my salad, blessing my meal and all living beings with happiness and well-being, then held the avocado and cut it in half. Without a word I offered one half to Thay; very mindfully, he scooped a tiny bit and offered it to the kids sitting around him. It was beautiful to witness. On my side, I did the same with a few adults.

Later that day, after a lecture on Gautama the Buddha's teachings, Thay was on his way back, walking in silence with only two of his attendants far behind him. No one else approached this Zen master throughout our entire retreat. But I went to him with my hands in a bowing gesture and offered him a small bag of the most delicious and delicate tea, which I'd brought in my luggage. I expressed in French my deep love and gratitude for being able to have this precious opportunity to practice with him. I told Thay I had a special little gift for him, my favorite jasmine-pearl green tea.

"The package is worn out from the journey, Thay," I told him. "It is what is inside that matters."

His face lit up like a beaming shaft of the sun, his smile from heaven to earth. He said bowing, "*Merci beaucoup, très gentil!*" He held the package up in the air in slow motion, looked at it from all sides, twinkling.

After a silent loving moment in communion, I bowed and departed feeling showered again by another rare blessing.

⌒

IN THE PAST THREE YEARS of my life, I have discovered I have Lyme disease and several life-threatening tick-borne co-infections, which have debilitated my entire being for so many years. This is an important subject, and I plan to discuss it in depth as a separate download on my website. Going through another major health crisis has deeply tested the very core of my being at every level. I realized that we can go through only so many major challenges without completely abandoning ourselves—having faith and a graceful and grateful attitude. Never take "no" for an answer and never give up, even in the face of the greatest adversities. Courage, spiritual strength, perseverance, and determination are always within the core of our being—even though at times we may feel extremely depleted, discouraged, and drained. Let's remember that our thoughts and attitude can be our worst enemies. Eternal bliss is our very essence.

⌒

BECAUSE OF YOGA'S UNIVERSAL ATTRACTION and the wealth of benefits it generates for individuals and our beloved planet, the United Nations proclaimed the first International Day of Yoga on June 21 as a way to foster its awareness, accessibility, and opportunity for all humans. It is also Sadhguru's vision as well as mine that the infinite possibilities and offering of the various yoga branches be celebrated around the globe—and that each and every individual is given this blessed opportunity to explore the depth of their own wealth within their being; to experience meditativeness, bliss, happiness, joy, serenity, inner well-being, and exuberance of life; and to expand their perception from exclusiveness to inclusiveness, from being a separate, independent individual to being a universal, embracing, compassionate being.

Today we are seven billion people on our precious planet. This number is predicted to increase to ten billion by 2050. Given the current rate of ravage, exploitation, abuse, cruelty, and neglect that we are inflicting on ourselves and our planet, our home is in great peril. It may not survive to reach 2050.

There is only ONE tribe. Consciously or unconsciously, the same shared, ultimate interest of all living beings is to experience happiness and inner well-being. Every living being seeks to be happy—even the bees and the ants. It is all the same energy. I belong to ONE tribe. Do you?

A worldwide, collective awakening must blossom now on our planet. Mother Earth needs millions of walking Buddhas (awakened beings) to survive and strive. Yoga is the way "in." And the way "in" is the boundlessness of our existential true nature.

Don't seek "out," delve "in"! When we go deep inside our own cave, there can never be any conflict, war, or in disharmony . . . only serenity, bliss, love, and beauty. We don't need to go into the Himalayan caves to meditate. That sacred cave is right within all of us. May we walk together, hand-in-hand, into a world of harmony, love, serenity, and joy beyond our present limited boundaries and see our children, their children, and their grandchildren walk forever with new hope upon beloved Mother Earth.

～

ONE NIGHT, JUST A FEW weeks after the Adiyogi consecration, while I was still physically struggling to regain my full strength and vitality despite my diseases, I experienced another intense moment where I needed to reach out to Sadhguru. I don't often call him in that way, but my heart, my energy, and entire being reached out crying for him, without any expectations.

That night, his energetic presence came during my sleep. Thousands of people silently surrounded him in the namaskaram hand gesture, as Sadh-guru walked toward my being. Suddenly, he extended his arm to reach for my hand while everyone else disappeared. In that instant, infinite thou-sands of rose petals manifested everywhere. Hand-in-hand, Sadhguru led my being to sit right next to him. No words were spoken; only intoxicating *Amrita* nectar emanated in the heavens.

ENDNOTES

CHAPTER *Nine*

1. "Paramahansa Yogananda The Secret of Life (1)," http://yogananda.com.au/gurus/yogananda_quotes_secret_of_life_45.html.

CHAPTER *Fourteen*

1. "Enlightenment Is Like a Joke," The Art of Living Foundation, Isha School of Yoga and Health, https://yoga-sa.com/enlightenment-is-like-a-joke.

CHAPTER *Fifteen*

1. Siddhanath Yoga Sangh, "Who Is Babaji?," http://siddhanath.org/about/who-is-babaji.

CHAPTER *Seventeen*

1. Georg Feuerstein, *Tantra: The Path of Ecstasy* (Boston, MA: Shambhala, 1998).

2. Swami Vivekananda, *Raja Yoga* (New York: Ramakrishna-Vivekananda Center, 1982).

CHAPTER *Eighteen*

1. Jaggi Vasudev, *Mystic's Musings* (New Delhi: Wisdom Tree Press, 2003), 326.

CHAPTER *Twenty*

1. Georg Feuerstein, *The Yoga Tradition: Its History, Literature, Philosophy and Practice* (Chino Valley, AZ: Hohm Press, 1998).

2. Ibid.

3. Ravi Shankar, *God Loves Fun* (Bangalore, India: Sri Sri Publications Trust, 2008).

CHAPTER *Twenty-One*

1. Ravi Shankar, *Celebrating Silence* (London: Arktos Media Ltd., 2014), 175.

2. Ibid., 160.

3. Ibid.

4. Ravi Shankar, Narada Bhakti Sutra: *The Aphorisms of Love* (Bangalore, India: Art of Living, 2005).

5. "Love: Human and Divine," Self-Realization Fellowship, http://www.yogananda-srf.org/HowtoLive/Love__Human_and_Divine.aspx#.WfxzvIZrzaY.

6. Jalāl ad-Dīn Muḥammad Rūmī, *The Illuminated Rumi* (New York: Broadway Books, 1997).

7. Shankar, *Celebrating Silence*, 133.

8. "Longing Itself Is Divine," The Art of Living, https://www.artofliving.org/jo-ar/wisdom/knowledge-sheets/longing-itself-divine.

9. Ibid.

CHAPTER *Twenty-Two*

1. Ravi Shankar, *Celebrating Silence* (London: Arktos Media Ltd., 2014).

2. Ibid., 161. See also: "Stretching the Emptiness," The Art of Living, https://www.artofliving.org/triveni-ashram/wisdom/knowledge-sheets/stretching-emptiness.

CHAPTER *Twenty-Four*

1. Tenzin Gyatso (Dalai Lama), Facebook post, April 6, 2015, https://www.facebook.com/DalaiLama/posts/10152789277292616.

2. Pope Francis, Twitter post, June 18, 2015, https://twitter.com/Pontifex/status/611684848130879488.

CHAPTER *Twenty-Five*

1. His Holiness the Dalai Lama. AZQuotes.com, *Wind and Fly* LTD, 2017. See: http://www.azquotes.com/quote/864900.

2. Bodhipaksa, "Wildmind Buddhist Meditation," May 16, 2007, https://www.wildmind.org/blogs/quote-of-the-month/dalai-lama-compassion-quote.

CHAPTER *Twenty-Six*

1. Ravi Shankar, "Victory to the Big Mind," Wisdom by Sri Sri Ravi Shankar, http://www.wisdom.srisriravishankar.org/jaigurudev/.

CHAPTER *Twenty-Nine*

1. Mahatma Gandhi, *Basic Education* (1951), 89.

CHAPTER *Thirty-One*

1. Masaru Emoto, *The Miracle of Water* (New York: Atria Books, 2007).

2. Tenzin Gyatso (Dalai Lama), Facebook post, September 21, 2015, https://www.facebook.com/DalaiLama/posts/10153166736257616.

CHAPTER *Thirty-Two*

1. Thich Nhat Hanh, *The Art of Communicating* (New York, NY: HarperCollins, 2013).

CHAPTER *Thirty-Three*

1. Robert O. Young, *The pH Miracle* (New York: Hachette, 2010).

2. James L. Wilson, *Adrenal Fatigue* (Petaluma, CA: Smart Publications, 2007).

3. Mahatma Gandhi, "The Doctrine of the Sword," Young India, August 11, 1920, http://www.mkgandhi.org/nonviolence/D_sword.htm.

CHAPTER *Thirty-Eight*

1. Sadhguru Jaggi Vasudev, "The 7 Chakras and Their Significance to Your Life," The Huffington Post, April 15, 2011, https://www.ishafoundation.org/news/columns/ Huffingtonpost.com/2011/HP-15Apr2011.pdf.

2. Ibid.

3. Ibid.

4. Ibid.

5. Ibid.

6. Swami Muktananda, *Kundalini: The Secret of Life* (South Fallsburg, NY: SYDA Foundation, 1994)

7. Sadhguru, "The 7 Chakras and Their Significance to Your Life."

CHAPTER *Thirty-Nine*

1. Lee Sannella, *The Kundalini Experience* (Lower Lake, CA: Integral Publishing, 1987).

2. Swami Vivekananda, *Raja Yoga*, (New York: Ramakrishna-Vivekananda Center, 1982).

3. Sadhguru Jaggi Vasudev, "How Do You Plug into Kundalini?," Isha, April 16, 2015, http://isha.sadhguru.org/blog/yoga-meditation/demystifying-yoga/kundalini -awakening/.

CHAPTER *Forty*

1. Sadhguru Jaggi Vasudev, "The Science of Hatha Yoga," Isha, http://isha.sadhguru. org/yoga/yoga_articles_hatha_yoga_asanas/the_science_of_hatha_yoga/.

2. Sadhguru Jaggi Vasudev, "Yoga for Flexibility of Body, and Mind" Isha, July 26, 2015, http://www.ishafoundation.org/us/blog/yoga-for-flexibility-of-body-and-mind/.

3. Georg Feuerstein, *The Deeper Dimension of Yoga: Theory & Practice* (Boston, MA: Shambhala, 2003), 8.

4. http://www.anandamayi.org/pb/p36a.html. Chapter 41.

CHAPTER *Forty-One*

1. Swami Muktananda, *Kundalini: The Secret of Life* (South Fallsburg, NY: SYDA Foundation, 1994)

CHAPTER *Forty-Two*

1. Sadhguru Jaggi Vasudev, "From Stagnation to Stillness," Kavita Chhibber, October 2007, https://www.ishafoundation.org/news/columns/kc/KC_Oct2007.pdf.

CHAPTER *Forty-Three*

1. Sadhguru Jaggi Vasudev, "From a Person to a Presence," Isha, October 31, 2012, http://isha.sadhguru.org/blog/sadhguru/spot/from-a-person-to-a-presence.

2. Sadhguru Jaggi Vasudev, http://www.ishafoundation.org/Sadhguru?option=com _content&do_pdf=1&id=178.

CHAPTER *Forty-Four*

1. Sadhguru Jaggi Vasudev, "From a Person to a Presence," Isha, October 31, 2012, http://isha.sadhguru.org/blog/sadhguru/spot/from-a-person-to-a-presence.

CHAPTER *Forty-Five*

1. "His Holiness the Dalai Lama Participates in World Compassion Day in Mumbai to Promote Animal Welfare," November 29, 2012, https://www.dalailama.com/news/2012/his-holiness-the-dalai-lama-participates-in-world-compassion-day-in-mumbai-to-promote-animal-welfare.

2. For the Dalai Lama on animal welfare, see: https://www.brainyquote.com/quotes/dalai_lama_139179; and http://tibet.net/2012/11/his-holiness-participates-in-world-compassion-day-in-mumbai-to-promote-animal-welfare; and https://www.dalailama.com/news/2012/his-holiness-the-dalai-lama-participates-in-world-compassion-day-in-mumbai-to-promote-animal-welfare.

3. Wayne Pacelle, *The Bond: Our Kinship with Animals, Our Call to Defend Them* (New York: William Morrow, 2012).

CHAPTER *Forty-Six*

1. Sadhguru Jaggi Vasudev, "Linga—A Doorway to No-thing," Isha, July 18, 2013, http://isha.sadhguru.org/blog/yoga-meditation/demystifying-yoga/linga-a-doorway-to-no-thing.

2. Sadhguru Jaggi Vasudev, "What Are Yantras and How Can They Benefit Me?," Isha, August 9, 2014, http://isha.sadhguru.org/blog/yoga-meditation/science-of-yoga/yantras-benefit.

3. Sadhguru Jaggi Vasudev, "Kashi—The City of Light," Isha, October 9, 2014, http://isha.sadhguru.org/blog/yoga-meditation/history-of-yoga/kashi.

CHAPTER *Forty-Seven*

1. Sadhguru Jaggi Vasudev, "What Is Consecration?," Isha, September 14, 2012, http://isha.sadhguru.org/blog/yoga-meditation/science-of-temples/what-is-consecration.

2. Sadhguru Jaggi Vasudev, "Doorway to the Beyond," Isha, April 10, 2013, http://isha.sadhguru.org/blog/sadhguru/spot/doorway-to-the-beyond/.

3. Georg Feuerstein, *Tantra: The Path of Ecstasy* (Boston, MA: Shambhala, 1998).

4. Ibid.

5. Sadhguru Jaggi Vasudev, "What Is Tantra Yoga? Definitely Orgasmic, But Not Sexual," Isha, May 27, 2013, http://isha.sadhguru.org/blog/yoga-meditation/demystifying-yoga/the-truth-about-tantra.

6. Jaggi Vasudev, *Mystic's Musings* (New Delhi: Wisdom Tree Press, 2003).

7. Ibid.

CHAPTER *Forty-Eight*

1. Sadhguru Jaggi Vasudev, "No Disasters, Just Situations," Isha, April 18, 2017, https://www.innerengineering.com/online/blog/no-disasters-just-situations.

AUTHOR Q & A

1. What advice would you give people looking to start their journey? What challenges can they expect? How can they overcome them?

Everyone encounters tribulations and trials, even more so on the spiritual path. It is part of the physical world that mirrors duality. My story demonstrates the most common challenges. Even though I don't give advice, I can provide a few suggestions. A huge part of the process of awakening is about breaking free from our self-imposed limitations, preconceived ideas, identifications, and boundaries. To overcome any challenges we must be persistent, patient, humble, determined, and in a state of surrender with a deep faith in the process. It is crucial on the spiritual path to never give up and be committed 100 percent. Do not judge or compare yourself to others. That is poison. Our inner voice is a haunting song we must never ignore. Learn to listen. I suggest you read this book again and again. Many answers are in here. Each time you will read it, it will resonate differently within you and you may gain new insight, revelation, even epiphany.

2. What was the biggest challenge in your journey?

Heartbreak from Ian and major depression.

3. Hardest thing to change or give up?

Cheese. . . Ha! Ha!

4. As you continued in your journey did changes come easier?

Yes, it becomes easier as you evolve and awake.

5. You have had challenging experiences with a major depression, a violent upbringing, and a turbulent medical history. Did these experiences challenge your faith or strengthen it? How and why?

I was born with faith in our Creator, in myself, and in the goodness of humankind because the Divine permeates our being and all of creation. I am not referring here to faith in terms of religion. I am not religious at all. I don't believe in God because I am experiencing God within every particle of my being.

Spirituality is not about believing something; it is about experiencing and realizing the light within. Intense and prolonged suffering definitely can make seekers wonder about existential questions. Pain and sufferings can become a magical doorway to the Divine if one is open, receptive, and in a state of surrender. A broken heart brings us to our knees with humility, vulnerability, and surrender. It was the case for my being. Suffering and pain make us vulnerable. Vulnerability can also become a majestic portal to the Divine. In the state of abandoning oneself, we have already won the victory because a fragrance of equanimity will exude from us. Surrendering begets expansion of consciousness. Vulnerability is essential to experience a dimension of reality beyond the physical realm. One must break free from resistance and logic to experience the light. Sensitivity is not a weakness. It is one of the most precious qualities of the heart. It reflects our openness and receptivity to all life forms. All my experiences, mystical or mundane, as well as my realizations and insights expanded my consciousness.

6. You have referred to a higher being most often as Divine Mother. This is an unorthodox name, especially for those who have not heard it before or were raised as Catholic as you were. Why Divine Mother?

I refer to the Divine Mother as what many may call God. I feel this reference comes from my previous lifetimes in India. The yogis and rishis (sages) often call the supreme intelligent energy (Maha Shakti) as the Divine Mother, as I explain in this book. Though there is also an aspect where the Divine feminine energy can be manifesting in a specific form in the tantric yogic tradition—in a certain Divine entity or deity.

7. You say at one point, "The less resistance we have toward the events in our lives, the more we can accept the situations and process them—and the better we can detach and surrender to what is." Many people have a hard time surrendering the control they think they have. How were you able to accomplish this, and what advice would you offer others?

Since you asked, I may make a few suggestions. Control is just an illusion. Any moment we may exhale our last breath. Can you control that? Actually for a perfect self-realized siddha yogi, this is possible. That is called Maha Samadhi. But for the great majority of people, that is impossible. However it is easier for a humble, open, receptive, and sensitive person to be in a state of surrendering and to detach. This kind of openness takes vulnerability, but most people put themselves in cages in order to attempt to protect themselves. Transcending the logic and mindset patterns is crucial. Don't believe everything your mind is trying to make you swallow. It is society's garbage container. The way of the heart is the magic for surrender. Also looking at the situation with a different perspective can be extremely beneficial. I looked at my cancer journey as a spiritual ascension—and it turned out to be one! To expand your horizons, let love overwhelm you and overflow from you by embracing all living beings, and also make sure you meditate regularly. It is important to remain humble and flexible in your approach, and to say a big yes to new opportunities even if they may appear minuscule. The fastest way to self-realize is to embrace all living beings as yourself and see God in you and in them. With time, deep meditation, and sadhana you will realize we all are interconnected by the same Source.

In a state of "I don't know" you are keeping yourself open and receptive to experience, to grow by seeing things as they are with clarity. Jumping to conclusions, assumptions, and judgments are detrimental for your being and for others. Being in a state of wonderment is to allow yourself to blossom. Be willing to set yourself free from your patterns, self-imposed limitations, and start looking at life with different perspectives. See things as they are. But, that takes awareness and mindfulness. That is much harder, but if you render yourself sensitive, open, receptive, humble, and at ease, you will ride the wave.

8. You mention that "our own spirit attracts certain individuals into our lives for specific purpose. We even attract these people unconsciously to help us heal, grow, and evolve." Who in your life has helped you grow and evolve the most?

All my satgurus have contributed in their own ways. Though Sadhguru has had the most phenomenal impact upon my being because I was incredibly ready, open, and receptive to him and his grace. I humbly bow down to them and to the lineage of all ascended masters. On a different level, Ian and Nathaniel have impacted my growth. A loving, intimate relationship can become a great teacher and healer. Romantic love is one of the most intimate relationships we may have. They provide us with a great opportunity to evolve, heal our wounds, expand our consciousness, and awake to our true nature. The intimacy and vulnerability can allow us to blossom into our ultimate nature in unimaginable ways, freeing us from the prison of our past, especially if the intimate relationship is or becomes a sacred Divine love relationship.

9. You are very honest about past struggles. What was it like for you to revisit these painful memories?

I felt detached. The karmic structure of these memories has lost their power. Though through this process of writing I shed many tears of gratitude for being so blessed with grace.

10. What inspired or compelled you to share your journey with us?

It was just an inner knowing that one day I will write this book. At the time my own suffering propelled me to want to help allevi-ate the pain people and animals endure. When I went through my own darkness, a book like this one could have helped in guiding me, maybe even giving me hope, inspiration, and guidance. I feel profoundly humbled and grateful to have had this opportunity to share with you a gateway that may be potentially beneficial to so many willing seekers.

11. If you could meet your younger selves—what would you say to them? Do you think they would listen?

The way I would approach the message would be different accord-ing to the age level of maturity, evolution, and understanding, but the essence would be the same: Delve deep within and you shall uncover your beatific nature. The Divine is right inside of us, breath-ing. There was always that subtle inner voice I would hear. I listened the best I could at these stages, but listening is not enough. One must follow through by taking proper actions. That is the most chal-lenging part, because often we must rely on the kindness and loving compassion of others to help us out of darkness.

12. A lot of memoir writers believe that they need to portray themselves in a positive way, yet your memoir is very honest. Was it hard for you to write about your flaws so publicly?

No, not at all. Do you know someone who is perfect? And yet we each are a perfect, divine being in the here and now. From ancient times it has been considered in the yogic tradition that when kundalini shakti has ascended and merged with Shiva in the Sahasrara in the one-thousand-petal lotus chakra at the crowd of the head, the individual has become a perfected being, a siddha. There was no other way to write this book except with an intimate and authentic voice. I would not have written it otherwise. How would you have witnessed my growth, my evolution, and my spiritual awakening over the many decades?

My book is much more than a spiritual memoir. This physical life is filled with duality, thus a memoir has to reflect that too. No story can ever be all good and positive. That would be boring and misleading. My book would have never been insightful, inspiring, uplifting, and able to guide and help. I had to become the light so to speak. If one is self-realized, humble with integrity, kindness, and loving compassion, these qualities permeate within all their projects and presence. The truth is—it is not about "becoming the light." This is only the title of this book in reference to the context of my unfolding story within the narrative. We don't become the light, per se. We realize that we are already the light when we realize our true divine nature and tap into the beyond. We move out of the way, and the Divine takes over! We are all spiritual beings dreaming a human dream. Only within the depth of our inner shrine can we experience the light. The almighty presence is there. If you are tuned in, in frequency, anyone could feel a Divine presence emanating from this kind of self-realized being. That is the light. We write because we want to give something back, and in the process we may offer a part of our true nature. This book is my embracing you, my boundless gift to you. I hope through your reading you have allowed yourself to go deep within, and could feel my being. In that process you may have felt the universal spirit that animates all particles of this creation.

13. As you revisited past memories, did anything surprise you? Were there any connections you hadn't made before or seeing new elements of your life in a new light?

It is obvious that I have been on the spiritual path in many past lifetimes, especially in India. I am convinced of reincarnation, which I used to have so many doubts about. I can see even more clearly my past lifetimes' connections, and my connection with the ascended masters.

14. What was the most rewarding experience through your spiritual journey? What has been the most important or beneficial lesson you have learned?

My most blessed experiences always have been in being in the presence of the ascended masters and my satguru. Lessons belong more to the social realm in many ways. Awakening is about insights, realizations, experiencing an energetic flow, and realizing our divinity. Spiritual awakening belongs to the realm of the beyond. Having insights, realizations, and mystical experiences can be far more beneficial in the long run. It all depends on many circumstances.

15. Now that you have completed this book, how do you feel?

My heart is overflowing with so much gratitude for having the great blessing of being on this spiritual path and being an instrument of grace and light. I feel deeply humbled to still be alive in order to share, to help others and the animals. May you discover the boundless treasures of your true blissful nature, and give back abundantly to others and the animals in dire need. Sending you a garden filled with divine love, light, grace, and blessings.

READING GUIDE QUESTIONS

1. Vivianne points out that many individuals develop a system of beliefs based on what our parents, siblings, peers, school, government, and religious authorities and the media have fed us during our childhood and adolescence. Do you agree? How has this been present in your life?

2. Vivianne mentions "part of self-realization, or enlightenment, is to free oneself from all limiting conditioning, brainwashing, and boundaries—especially norms or false views such as objectification that prevent the individual from blossoming to their true nature." What examples of limitations and boundaries are present in your life or have you noticed? What are some ways to overcome or change these?

3. Dreams play a significant role. Discuss the role dreams play throughout and give examples of why they are important.

4. Discuss family dynamics presented throughout. How did this shape Vivianne's journey?

5. What is the importance of love and belonging in her book? Why? How are they similar? How are they different? What do these mean to Vivianne?

6. The search for truth and Divine love is a big theme that is mentioned throughout. Discuss the role it plays and its development.

7. What is the role power and inner power play in her book? What kind of power do you exert in your life? What kind of power do people exert around you? How do they affect you? How do you affect them? Is there a change that needs to be made?

8. Was this book successful as a spiritual memoir and as a book of wisdom

and spiritual knowledge? Would her story have been more or less impactful if it was written as fiction?

9. Was there any lesson, insight, or realizations that could be taken away from Vivianne's life? What was it and why is it important?

10. Did Vivianne's experiences, longing, and seeking for the truth and Divine love affect you after reading her story? If so, how? Explain.

11. After reading Vivianne's book, do you feel guided, uplifted, inspired to start your own spiritual journey? Or if you are already on the path do you feel empowered to continue and go to the next step? Do you feel "changed" or guided, uplifted, or inspired in any way? Did it expand your perceptions, horizons, range of experience, or challenge your assumptions and conclusions (for example, did it take you to a place you haven't been before or help you see a place you know in a different light)? Did reading it help and guide you to understand a person better, or even yourself?

12. Some memoir authors feel like they have to portray themselves in a positive way, but Vivianne shares her experiences, good and bad. Do you think this helped the story? Did it change how you viewed her? Were you able to connect and relate to her more and deeper?

13. The memoir starts off with Vivianne in the hospital after a suicide attempt, and one of her darkest moments in her life. How does this frame the rest of her journey?

14. Overall how has Vivianne's book made an impact on your life? Did it expand your horizons and perspectives? Do you feel touched by *Becoming the Light*?

ABOUT THE AUTHOR

 Vivianne Nantel, who is often called Devi, is a yogini, spiritual guide, visionary, mystic, vocalist, humanitarian, speaker and author of *Becoming The Light: Realize Your True Enlightened Nature.*

Vivianne graduated *magna cum laude* with a Bachelor of Fine Arts from San Francisco State University. As a published writer and poet, Ms. Nantel's work has appeared in *Yoga Magazine, Poet's Paper,* the *National Literary Journal,* and *Animal Wellness Magazine,* among others. In addition, Vivianne is a visionary artist and prolific painter whose artwork has been exhibited in museums, fine art galleries and private and corporate collections. However, she stopped working as a fine art artist after going through her cancer journey in 2007-08.

Articles about Vivianne Nantel's work have been published in *The San Francisco Chronicle,* the *Independent Florida Sun,* and *Alaska's World* magazine. In addition, Vivianne has been interviewed on various television talk shows including *Earth Advocate* and *Bridging Heaven and Earth* and appeared in the documentary film *Harp Seals* by the Sea Shepherd Conservation Society. Vivianne has also volunteered for many animal welfare initiatives. She has spoken at the National Animal Rights Conference, in Washington, DC, and collaborated on special projects with the Humane Society of the United States (HSUS) & Humane Society International (HSI).

As part of her passion, Vivianne spent more than two years studying music composition with Elinor Armer at the San Francisco Conservatory of Music. During this time she wrote more than twenty instrumental music pieces. She has also been studying voice with Deborah Benedict Jackson. A soprano, Vivianne has had two recitals in the San Francisco Bay Area. Devi is committed and dedicated to helping others spiritually and will continue to raise consciousness and be an instrument of grace. She hopes to offer multimedia recordings of her guided meditation, books, and chants soon. She hopes many more projects and plans will materialize soon.

FOR MORE INFO PLEASE VISIT:
Website: www.VivianneNantel.com
Facebook: www.facebook.com/Viviannenantel
Instagram: www.instagram.com/viviannenantel/
Vivianne is also on YouTube.